LOCKE'S TRAVELS IN FRANCE
1675–1679

JOHN LOCKE, *ca.* 1675

From a portrait by John Greenhill, in the possession of
W. Sanford Esq., of Chipley Park, Som.

LOCKE'S
TRAVELS IN FRANCE
1675-1679

*As related in his Journals, Correspondence
and other papers*

EDITED
WITH AN INTRODUCTION AND NOTES
BY
JOHN LOUGH

*Professor of French in the Durham Colleges,
University of Durham*

CAMBRIDGE
AT THE UNIVERSITY PRESS
1953

PUBLISHED BY
THE SYNDICS OF THE CAMBRIDGE UNIVERSITY PRESS
London Office: Bentley House, N.W. 1
American Branch: New York
Agents for Canada, India, and Pakistan: Macmillan

Printed in Great Britain at the University Press, Cambridge
(Brooke Crutchley, University Printer)

CONTENTS

ILLUSTRATIONS

ACKNOWLEDGEMENTS

I am indebted to the Delegates of the Clarendon Press for permission to publish the following selections from the Journal for
1675–8 and from the correspondence and other papers relating to
Locke's stay in France which were recently acquired by the Bodleian
Library, and to the Trustees of the British Museum for permission
to publish the relevant parts of the Journal for 1679. I am also
grateful to the Curators of the Bodleian Library for depositing the
first three volumes of the Journal in the Cambridge University
Library for a total period of twelve months; without this assistance
I should certainly have been unable to carry out the laborious task
of transcribing these manuscripts. The portrait of Locke by John
Greenhill is reproduced by kind permission of Mr William Sanford,
of Chipley Park, Somerset.

I am also indebted to Professor F. C. Green for his interest in
my work on Locke and for his assistance in the matter of publication.

I have received valuable guidance from Dr W. von Leyden, of the
University of Durham, who introduced me to the Locke papers in
the Bodleian and has always been ready to put his unrivalled knowledge of the collection at my disposal. I have also greatly profited
from discussion of common problems with Professor Gabriel Bonno,
of the University of California, who is working on Locke's contacts with French intellectual circles, and with Mr Peter Laslett of
St John's College who is studying Locke's political ideas.

In solving many of the difficulties raised by the annotation of
a text of this kind I have derived invaluable assistance from specialists
in a great variety of fields. Professor John Read, of the University
of St Andrews, has elucidated the problems concerning the history
of chemistry, and Professor J. M. Stratton those concerning the
history of astronomy. Professor Ernest Weekley has contributed
some valuable suggestions concerning linguistic points in the text,
while Dr E. K. Borthwick, of Christ's College, has checked the

Latin quotations. Dr N. J. G. Pounds made some useful suggestions about points of geography and history, and Mr T. S. Wyatt, in addition to offering comments on the Introduction, has given many helpful pieces of advice.

My work at the Bodleian has been greatly facilitated by the assistance given me by Dr R. W. Hunt, Keeper of Western MSS., and Mr P. Long, Assistant in the same department. As the greater part of the work on this edition has been carried out in the Cambridge University Library, I owe a great deal to the help given me at all moments, convenient to them or otherwise, by a large number of members of the Library staff. I also increased my debt, incurred since undergraduate days, to Mr C. C. Scott, senior assistant librarian at St John's College.

In the task of editing the Journal I have received a great deal of assistance from persons and institutions in France. Both the Bibliothèque Nationale and the Archives Nationales have provided much helpful information. The Librarian of the Société de l'Histoire du Protestantisme Français, M. le Doyen de Félice, kindly allowed me to use the library during the vacation period, while I also received help from M. Louis Irissou, Secretary of the Société de l'Histoire de la Pharmacie, in the matter of Locke's acquaintances among the apothecaries of Montpellier.

Thanks to a generous grant from the Ernest Cassel Educational Trust I was able in 1949 to carry my researches south of Paris and visit most of the places to which Locke travelled. Mlle Violette Méjan, Librarian of the Bibliothèque Municipale of Arles, continued, after my brief visit there, to clear up for me obscure points in Locke's account of his travels in Provence. At a later stage in my tour I also received valuable assistance from the Bibliothèque Municipale of Bordeaux. In Montpellier where Locke spent some fifteen months, I was able to achieve a great deal in a short time, thanks, in the first instance, to Professor Pierre Jourda who put me in touch with all those people likely to be able to help me in my inquiries. To Professor Hervé Harant and Mlle Y. Vidal, Librarian of the Faculté de Médecine, I am indebted for information about the doctors whom Locke knew in Montpellier, and I was also put on to much valuable material about seventeenth-century Montpellier by the staff of the Bibliothèque Municipale. My chief debt, however, is to M. Oudot de Dainville, Archiviste de l'Hérault, who not only helped me to find my way among the collection of the Departmental and Town Archives, but also spent many hours of his valuable time answering my inquiries.

To elucidate problems in the text I had recourse to the good offices of other Departmental Archivists, and am greatly indebted for information on a variety of questions to MM. B. Faucher (Haute-Garonne), J. de Font-Réaulx (Isère), Marcel Gouron (Gard), R. Lacour (Rhône), Jacques Levron (Maine-et-Loire) and J. Salvini (Vienne). I am also grateful to Mlle M. Bonnet, of Lyons, for useful information on points arising out of Locke's visits there.

Finally, my greatest debt of all, especially in the establishment of the text published here, is to my wife. Without her patience and ingenuity it would certainly not have been possible for me to decipher the passages of shorthand in the MS. In addition, she has helped me with the arduous task of checking the transcript of the MS. and in the copying of all manner of documents in a great variety of libraries between Oxford and Montpellier.

J. L.

Cambridge
October 1951

LIST OF ABBREVIATED TITLES USED IN THE INTRODUCTION AND NOTES

Aaron & Gibb	R. I. Aaron & J. Gibb, *An Early Draft of Locke's Essay on the Human Understanding together with Excerpts from his Journals*. Oxford, 1936.
D'Aigrefeuille	Charles d'Aigrefeuille, *Histoire de la Ville de Montpellier depuis son origine jusqu'à notre temps.* 2 vols. Montpellier, 1737–9.
Basville	Lamoignon de Basville, *Mémoires pour servir à l'histoire de Languedoc.* Amsterdam, 1734.
Benoist	Élie Benoist, *Histoire de l'Édit de Nantes.* 5 vols. Delft, 1693–5.
Boissonnade	P. Boissonnade, *Colbert: le Triomphe de l'Étatisme.* Paris, 1932.
B.S.H.P.F.	*Bulletin de la Société de l'Histoire du Protestantisme Français.* Paris, 1852– .
Christie	W. D. Christie, *A Life of Anthony Ashley Cooper, 1st Earl of Shaftesbury.* 2 vols. London, 1871.
Clamageran	J. J. Clamageran, *Histoire de l'Impôt en France.* 3 vols. Paris, 1875.
Clément	*Lettres, instructions et mémoires de Colbert* (ed. P. Clément). 10 vols. Paris, 1861–82.
Delort	André Delort, *Mémoires inédits sur la ville de Montpellier au XVIIᵉ siècle.* 2 vols. Montpellier, 1876–8.
Depping	*Correspondance administrative sous le règne de Louis XIV* (ed. G. B. Depping). 4 vols. Paris, 1850–5.
D.N.B.	*Dictionary of National Biography.* London, 1885–1900.
Mme Du Noyer	Anne Marguerite Du Noyer, *Lettres historiques et galantes de deux dames de condition.* 5 vols. Amsterdam, 1738.

LIST OF ABBREVIATED TITLES

Firth & Lomas	C. H. Firth & S. C. Lomas, *Notes on the Diplomatic Relations of England and France, 1603–1688.* Oxford, 1906.
Forbonnais	F. V. de Forbonnais, *Recherches et Considérations sur les finances de France.* 2 vols. Basle, 1758.
Fox Bourne	H. R. Fox Bourne, *The Life of John Locke.* 2 vols. London, 1876.
Furetière	A. Furetière, *Dictionnaire Universel.* 3 vols. The Hague, 1690.
Gachon	P. Gachon, *Quelques préliminaires de la Révocation de l'Édit de Nantes en Languedoc, 1661–1685.* Toulouse, 1899.
Haag	E. & E. Haag, *La France Protestante.* 10 vols. Paris, 1847–58. 2nd ed. (incomplete). 6 vols. Paris, 1877–88.
Jouvin	Albert Jouvin, *Le Voyageur d'Europe.* 6 vols. Paris, 1672.
King	Lord King, *The Life of John Locke with Extracts from his Correspondence, Journals and Common-Place Books.* London, 1829.
Le Conte	*List of Men of War, 1650–1700. Part II. French Ships, 1648–1700,* compiled by Pierre Le Conte (Society for Nautical Research, Occasional Publications, No. 5). London, 1935.
Leibnitz	Leibnitz, *Sämtliche Schriften und Briefe,* ser. I, vol. II. Darmstadt, 1927.
The Library	An article to appear in *The Library,* entitled 'Locke's Reading during his Stay in France' (1675–1679).
MS. Locke	Lovelace Collection, Bodleian Library.
Monspeliensia	*Monspeliensia, recueil de pièces rares inédites des XVIIe et XVIIIe siècles, publié par la Société des Bibliophiles de Montpellier.* Montpellier, 1899.
First Note-book	MS. Locke, f. 15 (30 June 1677–30 June 1678).
Second Note-book	MS. Locke, f. 28 (1 July 1678–).
Observations	Locke, *Observations upon the Growth and Culture of Vines and Olives, the Production of Silk, and the Preservation of Fruits.* London, 1766.
O.E.D.	*Oxford English Dictionary.*

Ollion	*Lettres inédites de John Locke à ses amis, Nicolas Thoynard, Philippe van Limborch et Edward Clarke* (ed. H. Ollion). The Hague, 1912.
Piganiol de La Force	J. A. Piganiol de La Force, *Nouvelle Description de la France.* 6 vols. Amsterdam, 1719.
Pilatte	*Édits, déclarations et arrêts du Conseil rendus au sujet de la R.P.R.* (ed. Léon Pilatte). Paris, 1875.
Roschach	Devic & Vaissette, *Histoire générale du Languedoc,* Nouvelle édition. (Vols. XIII and XIV are by E. Roschach.) Toulouse, 1876.
Skippon	Philip Skippon, *An Account of a Journey through part of the Low Countries, Germany, Italy and France*...in *A Collection of Voyages and Travels,* Vol. VI (pp. 359–736). London, 1732.
Smollett	Tobias Smollett, *Travels through France and Italy* (ed. T. Seccombe; *World's Classics* edition). London, 1935.

INTRODUCTION

Of the two visits which Locke paid to France, the first, in the autumn of 1672, took him as far as Paris, but was very short (it appears to have lasted only two or three weeks) and very little is known about it. His second visit was to last altogether nearly three and a half years and to take him twice, by somewhat different routes, from Paris to the Mediterranean by way of Lyons and Bordeaux.

He left London on 12 November 1675 (o.s.) and, sailing from Gravesend, landed at Calais two days later (24 November, N.S.). From there, as far as Abbeville, he travelled in the suite of Lord John Berkeley, Ambassador Extraordinary to the French Court, and then, accompanied by his Oxford friend, George Walls, made his way to Paris. After a short stay of ten days in the capital they resumed their journey southwards to Montpellier. They travelled first by the *diligence* to Châlons, and then took the boat down the Saône to Lyons. After less than a week there, they rode on horseback down the Rhône valley as far as Avignon, where they turned south-west to Nîmes and Montpellier.

For the next fifteen months this last town, famous for its Medical Faculty and a favourite resort of the English, especially of those who, like Locke, were consumptive, was to be his headquarters. During the hottest part of the summer (from the end of June to the middle of September) he retired to the neighbouring village of Celleneuve, and in the spring of both 1676 and 1677 he undertook more or less lengthy excursions in the neighbourhood. In March 1676 he made two short expeditions to explore the Mediterranean coast between Sète and Aigues-Mortes, and in the following month he made an extensive tour of Provence, visiting such places as Arles, Marseilles, Toulon, Hyères and Aix, and travelling as far north again as Avignon. In February 1677, just before he left the South, he set out on another journey, this time through a considerable part of the province of

Languedoc, taking in towns like Castres, Castelnaudary and Carcassonne, and inspecting some of the completed parts of the *Canal du Midi* which was then in course of construction.

His original intention appears to have been to make a relatively short stay in France. As early as February 1676 Shaftesbury's secretary, Stringer, wrote to him, as if expecting him soon to return home: 'Be sure to remember sending word when you will be back at Paris, that Sir William Cooper, Mr Hoskins and myself may have an opportunity of meeting you there.'[1] At first his stay at Montpellier does not seem to have brought about any improvement in his health. 'I am very sorry', wrote Stringer in April, 'to hear that your cough doth increase upon you. Sir Paul Neile is still of an opinion that to come to England and marry a young woman is the best remedy.'[2] However, the summer seems to have brought a change for the better, for in June the same correspondent expressed his pleasure at learning that Locke was 'soe well recovered',[3] and in the following month his cousin, Mrs Anna Grigg, wrote to say that she was sorry to learn that he was coming home, since another winter in the South of France 'would perfect and settle your recovery'.[4]

Locke certainly stayed another winter in the South, but what his plans were at this stage we have no means of telling. However, in March 1677, just after he had returned to Montpellier from his tour of Languedoc, he received a pressing request from Sir John Banks,[5] a wealthy London merchant, to return to Paris and take charge of his son, Caleb,[6] whom he was proposing to send over to spend five

---

[1] Christie, II, 220. [2] Ibid. II, 221.
[3] MS. Locke, c. 19, ff. 123–4. [4] Ibid. c. 10, f. 118.
[5] Sir John Banks (*c.* 1627–99) was the son of a woollen draper (Evelyn's *Diary*, 25 Aug. 1676). He was made a baronet in 1661 and was an M.P. in several Parliaments. His London address was Lincolns Inn Fields, and he had an estate at Aylesford in Kent. The Lovelace Collection contains, besides the draft of three of Locke's letters to him, 37 of his letters to Locke.
[6] Caleb Banks was admitted to Gray's Inn on 2 Feb. 1675. He was elected an M.P. in 1685 and sat in various Parliaments down to the time of his death. He died, three years before his father, at the age of thirty-seven.
The Lovelace Collection does not contain a single letter of his to Locke. Since it belongs to the period of his stay in France, it would be a pity not to print here the following undated and unsigned letter, a masterpiece of seventeenth century feminine orthography, endorsed by Locke: 'To C.B. 78' (MS. Locke, c. 23, f. 201): Sᵣ.
I did not think you had ben so ill bred as to denid a Lady so small a favor sa that was I desier of you bout sin you ar so uncind I am resalf to wat of you as soun as my clos is

or six months in France. Locke acceded to this request, which was backed by his patron, Shaftesbury, in a letter of 23 March, and left Montpellier for Paris two days later.[1] This time he decided to travel north by way of Toulouse, Bordeaux and Poitiers. After riding on horseback to Castelnaudary, he travelled by boat along the new Canal as far as Toulouse and, after that, down the Garonne to Bordeaux. Here his journey north was interrupted for six weeks: at Agen, just short of Bordeaux, he was hit over the head by a pole in the boat, got chilled and found himself laid low by a severe attack of ague. It was not therefore until 2 June that he reached Paris, after a hot and somewhat troublesome journey. Even then he was still feeling the after-effects of his illness.

Despite the fact that his pupil was originally intended to spend only a few months in France, Locke's stay in the capital lasted over a year. During this period he never moved far afield, limiting himself to excursions to such neighbouring *châteaux* as Fontainebleau and Chantilly and, of course, Versailles, which he never tired of exploring. A good deal of his time seems to have been spent in showing his pupil the sights of Paris; occasionally they went to the theatre or the opera. He also had a certain number of contacts in learned and scientific circles. During these months he occasionally practised as a physician, numbering among his few patients such illustrious personages as Thomas Herbert, 8th Earl of Pembroke, whom he had already encountered at Montpellier, and to whom he was later to dedicate his *Essay on the Human Understanding*, and the Countess of Northumberland, now the wife of the English Ambassador, Ralph Montagu.

In July 1678 Locke set out with his pupil on a second tour of France. As Caleb Banks appears to have been a rather delicate youth, his parents, especially his mother, were loath to allow him

mad wich will not be long forst I am suer you ar the worst naterd man in the world suer your corig is not so litell as to be dantd by a woman I hop the sit of me would not a fritid you mouch bout rather then a disableg you I would a pot on a mask I hat my self when I think that ever I should have the lest of pasion for won that hats me now far well the worst of men.'

[1] He must have turned down a request, made to him in July of the previous year in a letter from a certain Samuel Eyre, that he should take charge of the son of his neighbour, Mrs Pierpoynt, who was heir to the Earl of Kingston and was 'designed for an Academy in France for two or three years & afterwards to travell' (MS. Locke, c. 8, f. 92).

to travel far from Paris, particularly in the hot weather; but Locke's views on the desirability of visiting other parts of the country eventually prevailed, and they set out in a leisurely fashion to explore the Loire valley. Their first stop, at Orleans, was prolonged by a fever which overcame his pupil there. After spending nearly three weeks in this town, they travelled by boat down the Loire to Blois, Tours, Saumur and Angers, spending from four to ten days in each of these places. They then proceeded, by way of Richelieu, to La Rochelle and on to Colbert's new naval port at Rochefort. Bordeaux and Toulouse were visited in turn, and from there they passed to Montpellier. This time Locke made only a short stay (just over a fortnight) and from there they made their way by rapid stages to Lyons.

The reason for this last journey is indicated in Locke's correspondence. On 30 September (O.S.) Sir John Banks wrote to him to give his consent to his son's undertaking, in his company, a journey into Italy.[1] 'Wee shall grant his request', wrote Sir John, 'upon your assurance that he come home in the Springe'.[2] Unfortunately their plans for this journey came to nothing. The reasons for this disappointment are given in a letter which Locke wrote to his friend, Mapletoft, from Lyons on 8 November:

If all the world should goe to Rome, I think I should never, haveing been twice firmely bent upon it, the time set, the company agreed, and as many times defeated. I came hither in all hast from Montpellier (from whence I writ you) with the same designe; but old father Winter, armed with all his snow and iseicles, keeps guard on Montsenny and will not let me passe.... Were I not accustomed to have fortune to dispose of me contrary to my designe and expectation, I should be very angry to be thus turnd out of my way when I imagined myself almost at the suburbs of Rome, and made sure in a few days to mount the Capitol, and trace the footsteps of the Scipios and Ceesars; but I am made to know 'tis a bold thing to be projecting of things for to-morrow, and that it is fit such a slight buble as I am should let itself be carried at the phancy of winde and tide without pretending to direct its own motion.[3]

---

[1] His approval of his son's project had apparently only been sought in a letter of Locke's of 24 Sept. (N.S.).

[2] MS. Locke, c. 3, ff. 114–15.

[3] *European Magazine*, vol. xv, p. 353. A draft of a letter to Sir John Banks (MS. Locke, c. 24, f. 23), written a few weeks later, contains the statement that, had it not been for the responsibility of taking his pupil with him, 'I doubt not but that I should

A week later Locke set his face northwards again towards Paris, but this time he varied his route by cutting across the mountains to join the Loire at Roanne, and followed its banks as far as Orleans. After spending two days there, he set out again for Paris which he reached on 28 November. Through the failure of his plans for a journey to Italy, he had another five months to spend in Paris before returning to England with his pupil. His stay there ended on 2 May when, accompanied by Caleb Banks and by the Danish astronomer, Römer, who was to spend a few weeks in England, he travelled (this time by Amiens) to Calais. From there he sailed direct to the Thames, landing at the Temple on 10 May 1679 (30 April, o.s.).

I

The main source for our knowledge of Locke's movements during the years he spent in France is the four volumes of the Journal which he began to keep from the time he left London in November 1675. This is not a completely unpublished document. In 1936 Professor R. I. Aaron and Mr Jocelyn Gibb edited copious extracts on philosophical questions from these and later volumes of the Journal, and over a century earlier, in 1829, Lord King devoted quite a number of pages of his *Life of Locke* to a selection of passages from it, both philosophical essays and a considerable number of the entries in which Locke described his impressions of life in France. Shortly afterwards a translation of some of the latter extracts, from the pen of Philarète Chasles, appeared in the *Revue de Paris*.[1]

A comparison of the text of the Journal as presented in the following pages with that given by Lord King will soon convince the reader that, since the Lovelace Collection of Locke's papers in the Bodleian Library has been made available to scholars,[2] there is ample room for a new, more complete and accurate edition. Given the frame-

have ventured a step farther over the hills, for though the first falling of the snow had made the passage mighty inconvenient and pretty dangerous, yet I found afterwards that the faire weather had much mended it, and that people went and came without any great difficulty.'

[1] Vol. XIV (1830), pp. 5–18, 73–9. The articles are unsigned, but the table of contents gives 'M. Ph. Chasles'.

[2] The fourth volume of the Journal (that for 1679) is in the British Museum (Add. MS. 15642).

work in which his extracts from the Journal appeared, no one can blame Lord King for only offering fragments of the manuscript, the more so as, in its complete form, it contains for these three and a half years over 1,400 pages. But his choice of passages and his transcription of them can scarcely be commended. Inevitably he chose some at least of the more interesting entries for his book, even though he often failed to transcribe them fully and accurately. Since, however, he did not take the trouble to master Locke's shorthand, he missed much that is of the highest interest, while his choice, even among the longhand passages, is very arbitrary. For instance, he wastes space in reproducing in full Locke's notes from a well-known book like Bouhours's *Entretiens d'Ariste et d'Eugène*, and yet cuts out the whole of Locke's account of his journey from Paris to Lyons in 1675. He gives one of Locke's conversations with the Oriental traveller and Epicurean philosopher, François Bernier, but not the second. Locke's visit to Arles in 1676 is recounted in the laconic phrase: 'To Arles', while the vivid sentences in which he summed up his impressions of Provence[1] are left out altogether.

Lord King's transcription is often erratic. In his version Locke is made to write on 8 February 1676: 'Mr. Herbert's man enticed into a shop, and there fallen upon by three or four', whereas the MS. has: 'Mr. Harvy's man inticed into a shop & there fallen upon by 3 or 4 & beaten for poysoning their dog'—a somewhat different story. Or again, while the vivid picture of the life led by a poor peasant family in the Graves region[2] is fairly accurately reproduced in Lord King's edition, he seems to have considered it beneath Locke's dignity to converse with a 'poore paisant's *wife*', since he cuts out the word and remodels the passage accordingly. In the same passage the sentence: 'Other times she span hemp, which was for their clothes & yeilded noe mony', is strangely distorted in his edition, where it appears as: 'Other times the spinning, which was for their cloth, yielded more money.'

It would be tedious to list the errors in dates and figures and all the other inaccuracies in Lord King's version of the Journal; yet one more of its defects requires a mention. In his anxiety to reduce his

---

[1] 23 April 1676.   [2] 15 Sept. 1678.

extracts to a reasonable length he often violently abridges them, inevitably with unfortunate results. Not only is the original text often falsified, but passage after passage is stripped of just those details which give it life and vigour. Thus Locke's account of the ceremony at Montpellier at which a doctor of medicine was admitted to his degree[1] is boiled down to about a quarter of its original length. In the process vanish such details as Locke's references to similar occasions at Oxford, the new doctor 'making legs' to the assembled professors, the procession through the streets after the ceremony, and the dinner which he had to stand his seniors. Locke's account of the galleys and the French Navy's shore establishments at Marseilles[2] is cut down even more drastically, while Lord King ruthlessly suppressed the realistic passage which explains the advantages of the Quay at Marseilles over the ordinary streets of the town as a walking place in the evenings. However justifiable for reasons of space, these constant abridgements of even the longer passages given by Lord King in his extracts from the Journal rob it of the life, colour and fun which are so often present in the original.

Of Philarète Chasles' two articles in the *Revue de Paris* it would be unnecessary to speak, were it not that even the most reputable French works of scholarship[3] quote them without any warning as to their complete unreliability. Seeing that he was only producing two short review articles, it would be idle to reproach the translator with giving merely extracts from Lord King's extracts from the Journal. What is deplorable is that his rendering of the passages which he selected is so often a travesty of the English text. It is, to begin with, fantastically inaccurate. Thus *a pretty large town* becomes *une petite ville*; 160 *churches, plus de dix*; 11,000 *men, onze cent mille hommes*; 16 *livres, soixante francs*; and 18,000 *men, dix-huit cents hommes*. Moreover, the translator took other liberties with his text. Finding in the version of the Journal presented by Lord King only 'des indications très laconiques, des descriptions fort sèches, des notes écrites en courant, des *memoranda* dénués de style et souvent inachevés', he did his best to give it a colour of his own: the result

---

[1] 18 March 1676 (the entry of 20 March on the same subject is completely omitted).
[2] 10 April 1676.
[3] Including E. Bourgeois & L. André, *Les Sources de l'Histoire de France (1610–1715)*.

can be imagined. Thus, in Locke's description of a degree ceremony at Montpellier, his reference to the Chancellor's speech 'against innovation' is expanded to 'contre les innovations et la circulation du sang'; while, finding 'A company of fiddlers...played a certain time' rather flat, the 'translator' improved on his text by rendering it as: '*Dix* violons jouant des *airs de Lully*'.

II

The edition of the Journal which follows in these pages cannot claim to offer the complete text of the manuscript for the period of Locke's stay in France. Under present conditions any publisher would take fright at the notion of producing a work of such dimensions. In any case, apart from the not very reliable series of extracts printed by Lord King, the main philosophical passages in longhand have already been published by Professor Aaron and Mr Gibb, while those in shorthand are about to be published by Dr von Leyden. All the philosophical passages in the Journal during these years have therefore been omitted from these pages, though a complete list of them, indicating whether and where they have been published, is provided in Appendix C. The following classes of entries have also been systematically omitted:

1. Lists of books and of Locke's notes on his reading: these have been collected together in one long article to be published in *The Library*.

2. A number of entries under the heading of *Atlantis*, i.e. notes for a sort of Utopia. (A list of these passages is also given in Appendix C.)

3. Weather observations, which are specially detailed for the period from May 1676 to February 1677 and frequently include temperature readings. Only those remarks on the weather which are of general interest have been retained.

4. A great mass of notes on the Old and New Testaments, especially on the subject of Gospel Concordance. These appear to have been derived (*a*) from Locke's own study of the Bible, (*b*) from the works of John Lightfoot, and (*c*) from conversations with Nicolas Thoynard during his stay in Paris.

5. Medical notes. These are numerous enough to form quite a considerable volume in themselves. However, the names of Locke's informants, whether physicians, apothecaries or laymen, are carefully indicated in the footnotes at the points at which they occur.

6. Long lists of coins, weights and measures of a great variety of countries. Those for France (their chaotic state before the Revolution and the introduction of the metric system is notorious) have been preserved as they are often essential to an understanding of the text.

7. Repetitions. These are not frequent, and passages left out for this reason are carefully indicated in footnotes.

The aim of this book is to offer an edition of the Journal which retains, with the above exceptions, everything which Locke wrote down in its pages about what he did, observed or heard in conversation during the three and a half years which he spent in France. It would have been more satisfactory for the editor if the text had been of the type and dimensions which permitted it to be reproduced *in extenso*; and his task would have been even easier if he had simply set out to extract from the four volumes of the manuscript the most interesting, lively and amusing passages, and had ignored all the rest. The general reader might have been better pleased with a book produced according to this second method, but such a version would have been almost useless to scholars. In the form in which it is presented here the Journal is, within the limits indicated, complete. No entry which comes within the programme set out above has been left out, since no editor is qualified to decide where to draw the line. For instance, Locke's references to his conversations with François Bernier may not be particularly exciting; but they are of interest because they show, first, that the latter was in Paris in the years 1677 and 1678 (a fact on which doubt has recently been cast);[1] and (less certainly) that Locke's relations with him were with the Oriental traveller rather than with the disciple of Gassendi. Again, Locke's unpublished notes on the portrait of Nostradamus in the Cordeliers' chapel at Salon and the inscription under it have permitted a scholar[2] to whom they were shown by chance to identify

---

[1] See the note on this question in P. Clarac, *La Fontaine, l'homme et l'œuvre* (Paris, 1947), p. 186.

[2] M. Raoul Busquet, in his *Nostradamus, sa famille et son secret* (Paris, 1950), pp. 186-7.

this portrait as the one now in the Musée Calvet at Avignon. No doubt various apparently insignificant remarks and observations scattered through the pages of our text will provide interesting finds for scholars working in a great variety of fields.

It would be absurd to claim that the entries in the Journal are of a consistently high interest. It must be admitted, for instance, that Locke's account of the time he spent in Paris is on the whole disappointing. How well an editor could have dispensed with the entries which contain his carefully paced out measurements of the Invalides or the gardens of the Tuileries! How gladly he would exchange the tedious pages in which Locke minutely describes the fountains of Versailles for a detailed account of his impressions of the Court of the *Roi Soleil*! Such laconic entries as 'Plays £3-0-0' infuriate the historian of seventeenth-century French drama who seeks in vain for a line of comment on the plays, the actors or the audience, or even a bare mention of the titles of the works which Locke saw performed. When we see what a lively and interesting account he could give of the sights he saw on his travels, we cannot help feeling that only too often he failed to see his plain duty to posterity. The Journal is not a carefully composed book on the France which he knew, nor even complete notes for such a book.

We have to content ourselves with such jottings as he saw fit to set down in its pages, without, apparently, a thought of publication. With all their gaps and reticences they offer something which is by no means negligible: first-hand impressions of life in France at the high point of the reign of Louis XIV from the pen of a man who spent altogether three and a half years there, came gradually to know the language and the people, and travelled twice round the country from Paris to the Mediterranean and back. Unlike most other accounts of seventeenth-century France left behind by English travellers, our text is not the work of a mediocrity or nonentity: it is the Journal of Locke.

There is indeed little to compare with it in the way of English travellers' accounts of seventeenth-century France. Dallington's *Method for Travel* (1604?) deals with the state of the country at the close of the previous century, on the morrow of the Wars of Religion. Lord Herbert of Cherbury's autobiography offers an account of a visit to France in 1608, and later describes his impressions of the country in the years between the murder of Concini and the coming to power of Richelieu, for most of which period he was ambassador to the French Court. Coryate's *Crudities* (1611) is concerned only briefly with his stay in France, and is in any case not a very profound work. Peter Heylin's *A Full Relation of Two Journeys*... (1656) which recounts visits paid some thirty years earlier, is a meatier book, despite its padding, exaggeration and strained wit. For the middle of the century we have the parts of Evelyn's *Diary* which describe his travels in France, and also his essay on the state of the country in 1652. At the end of the period there is the *Voyage to Paris in the Year 1698* of Dr Martin Lister which is packed with interesting detail on manners and on the intellectual life of the capital; and, for the previous decade, those parts of Veryard's *Account of Divers Choice Remarks*... (1701) which concern his journey through France.

Unfortunately the most brilliant years of the reign of Louis XIV, the period from 1661 to about 1685, are not well covered. Sir John Lauder's account of his stay in Poitiers, Orleans and Paris in 1665 and 1666, though recently honoured with a French translation,[1] is on the whole a rather puerile affair, while John Ray's *Observations* (1673) which contains chapters on a journey into France about the same time, is mainly botanical in interest. It is true that there is more substance in the pages of his companion, Philip Skippon, whose account of travels in Languedoc, Provence, and up the Rhône valley to Paris and Calais furnishes some interesting parallels with Locke's Journal. Yet Skippon's stay was a short one, and though there is some valuable material in his chapters on France, they are slight compared with our text. The same can be said of John Clenche's *Tour in France and Italy* (1676) which is much more concerned with the latter country than the former. Even if Locke's Journal cannot be put on the same level as the writings of Arthur Young or Smollett in the next century, it occupies none the less a unique place among English travellers' accounts of seventeenth-century France.

It is not, however, a complete record of his activities in these years. What he chose to note down in its pages was to a considerable

---

[1] By the late Professor Jean Plattard (Paris, 1935).

degree arbitrary. Even such details as the names of his companions on his different journeys are frequently omitted, while there is not a word in the Journal about his disappointment at not being able to cross the Alps into Italy in the autumn of 1678. In order to supplement the text of the Journal as presented in these pages, every effort has been made to extract what was relevant from the other papers of Locke, published and unpublished. Such rare letters of his for this period as have already been printed have been carefully studied in order to elucidate points in our text; and a thorough examination has been made of the new material made available in the Lovelace Collection. The latter, however, contains very few letters of Locke: for the period of his stay in France there are altogether five drafts of letters, only one of which—a long fragment of a letter to an unknown friend, written during the early part of his stay in Montpellier— deserves to be reproduced in full.[1] On the other hand a great deal of information about his movements in France has been gleaned from the letters which he received in these years from a variety of correspondents; and useful material has also been found among the miscellaneous papers of the Collection. All this has enriched the commentary on the text of the Journal and has helped to clear up points which are left vague there.

III

The first interest of the Journal, especially of the unpublished parts of it, lies in the contribution which it makes to the biography of Locke. Fragmentary as it is, it nevertheless provides us with a detailed account of his travels and occupations in France. If in our version there is relatively little to show the importance of these years for the development of his ideas on a variety of subjects from metaphysics, ethics, politics and education to religion and the allied problem of toleration, not only do the pages which follow tell us where and how Locke travelled in France; we also learn a great deal about the man.

The Journal for these years reveals, first, the breadth and range of

---

[1] See Appendix A, p. 276 (Lord King reproduced parts of this document in place of the opening entries of the Journal).

his interests. On his journeyings he showed a sensitive appreciation
of the new sights brought before his eyes. The valleys of the Saône
and Rhône and the parts of Provence which he explored made
a specially strong impression on him. The sight of the little town
of Villefranche-sur-Saône aroused his enthusiasm:

A league from Belville we came to Vil Franche where, what with the
town situate on a gentle rise at the bottom of the mountain, & the country
houses all about for a league or 2 downe the river, & the side of the
mountain divided into woods & vineards, & the sun there shining on them,
I scarce ever saw a finer prospect.[1]

One of the most striking sights which met him as he travelled through
Provence, was that of the orange and lemon groves on a hillside
below Hyères:

Below the towne the side of the hill is coverd with orange gardens, in
one of which we gatherd & eat very good, ripe china oranges which were
there in incredible plenty & grew sometimes 9 or ten in a bunch....The
colour of the fruit, leaves & flowers mingled enterteind the eyes very
pleasantly as well as their smel & tast did the other senses, & it was one
of the most delightfull woods I had ever seen.[2]

Even here, however, Locke's interest in Nature is utilitarian rather
than purely aesthetic. If his Journal cannot compare, for wealth
of technical detail, with Arthur Young's *Travels in France*, his
interest in agriculture made him observe with a keen eye the sights
which he encountered as he travelled through the countryside. In
one of the very first entries in the Journal he describes how, on the
road between Calais and Paris, he saw peasants '*digging their vineyards*'.[3] In the Rhône valley he observed men digging and others
'a ploughing with a very litle, light plow with one handle, drawne
by a pair of cows, steers or asses...' and turning up the soil 'not
above 2 or 3 inches deepe'.[4] In Languedoc, especially during his
stay at Montpellier, he made copious notes on the cultivation of
corn, vines and olives, interrogating the peasants he came across in
the fields as to the reasons for the different operations which he saw
them carrying out. During his later travels he seldom failed to note

[1] 20 Dec. 1675.   [2] 14 April 1676.
[3] 4 Dec. 1675. (Words in italics quoted from the Journal are in shorthand in the
MS. See p. lxiv.)
[4] 30 December 1675.

down in the Journal the character of the country he traversed, its crops and its prosperity or poverty.

Ancient monuments and famous buildings interested him too, though sometimes not quite in the same way as they would a more modern traveller. The Roman antiquities of the South of France made a strong impression on him: the Pont du Gard, like the Amphitheatre at Nîmes, he describes as 'an admirable structure'. Towards medieval architecture he is, after the manner of his age, less sympathetic: the famous west front of the Abbey of St Gilles, for instance, is dismissed somewhat scornfully.[1] Old buildings interested him less on the whole than those of his own century. 'The magnificent house of Richelieu', which he took care to visit twice, seems to have impressed him more than Chambord. Chantilly and even Fontainebleau made no great appeal to him, but half a dozen visits to Versailles did not exhaust his interest in the Château, its gardens and especially its 'water works'. The Louvre, the Invalides and the Observatoire among buildings in Paris were all to him fit subjects for laborious pacing out.

A Studentship at Christ Church had not made him one of what Gibbon was to call 'the monks of Oxford'. He was a man of the world, interested in people and their ways as well as in books and ideas. Picturesque details of contemporary French manners are far from absent in the pages of the Journal. Indeed, the very vividness of Locke's powers of observation makes one regret that he did not note down his impressions more frequently. One encounters such lively pictures as that of women at one of the gates of Montpellier 'carrying earth...in litle baskets on their heads, & singing & danceing in their sabots as they returned for new burthens'.[2] He saw the *Hôtel de Ville* there, as at Avignon, 'adornd with false weights, ballances & measures naild upon the outside'.[3] He notes the inhabitants' passion for the game of mall: 'All the highway[s] are fild with gamesters at Mall, soe that walkers are in some danger of knocks.'[4] Indeed, a few months later, some such accident did take place, leading to international complications, described in the laconic note: '*For an* accidental *blow with a mall ball a* quarrel *begun*

---

[1] 6 April 1676. [2] 14 Jan. 1676.
[3] 15 Jan. 1676. [4] 9 Jan. 1676.

by the French, and 50 *or* 60 *set on* 9 *or* 10 English *with swords, malls and stones.*[1]

On Easter Monday, as he rode into Provence, he observed people dressed 'in their holyday clothes which were but ordinary, espetially young wenches rideing upon asses & belabouring them with their boots'. A few miles further on, at Saint-Gilles, he watched 'a congregation of men & wenches' who 'danced heartily to the beating of a drum for want of better musick'.[2] Dancing, he and other travellers noted, was a passion with the French. 'Danceing here by moonshine in the streets', he wrote at Avignon in April 1676, and at Montpellier, at the beginning of October: '*After a rainy day dancing along dirty streets in the night to a* hobboy.' On Shrove Tuesday he found 'danceing in the streets in all manner of habits & disguises, to all sorts of musick, brasse kettles & frying pans not excepted'. During his stay at Celleneuve, just outside Montpellier, he attended the Village Sports, at which 'annual Olympiad' youths and maidens, boys and girls competed for a variety of prizes '*tied to the end of a pole*'. The entry concludes: '*and after all, what never fails, dancing to* hoboy *and tabor*'.[3] He notes down a scene in one of the inns of Montpellier: 'The Captain at Petit Paris telling the storys of his amours (camp Laundresses) & rebuking the frier complaining of his businesse & fatigue.'[4] There are frequent references in the Journal to crimes of violence, especially during his stay at Montpellier, where a murder was attempted in the house where he was living.[5] Though it is not described, but merely mentioned in a brief note of expenses, the experience of attending a public execution was not one he would deny himself or his pupil. On 18 February 1678, during his stay in Paris, he made the following entry:

> The danceing master broke on the wheele. Chamber
> room   3 – 0 – 0.

Interesting notices did not escape his keen eye. He carefully copied out a list of official prices for food, wine, hay and oats 'affixed to one of the back gates of the Chasteau' at Fontainebleau,[6] and a placard giving the text of an edict, which was solemnly verified

---

[1] 15 Oct. 1676.   [2] 6 April 1676.
[3] 14 Sept. 1676.   [4] 9 March 1676.
[5] 7 Feb. 1676.   [6] 25 Sept. 1677.

by the Paris *Parlement* in 1677, granting to no less a personage than Louis XIV's Grand Chamberlain, the Duc de Bouillon, a monopoly in the sale of 'a receit to kill lice'.[1]

An interest in mechanical things, in everything relating to technology and industrial processes is revealed very clearly in the pages of the Journal. Locke records unwearyingly the details of such processes as silk-weaving, oil-pressing, the boring of guns, soap-making and other chemical industries; similarly his attention was at once attracted to all manner of devices and gadgets which contributed to what his friend, Henri Justel, called 'les commodités de la vie'. At the sight of a rapid and light *chaise roulante* he notes down in the Journal full details, including its precise measurements. Devices for easing the labour of raising water in a well, a way of providing constant hot water without extra cost, a cover to keep the dust off a coach while it was not in use, a device to put candles out, a heated container for transporting meals from one part of a building to another: notes on all these occur in the pages of the Journal. Locke's interest in guns, in an age which saw rapid advances in artillery, was natural enough; it seems also to have been stimulated during his stay in Paris by his friendship with Nicolas Thoynard.

As one might expect from an early Fellow of the Royal Society, Locke shows in the pages of his Journal a decided taste for scientific questions. Notes on botany and zoology (apart, of course, from copious entries on gardening and agriculture) are to be found there, along with discussions on such problems as fermentation and its causes, innumerable weather observations, details of eclipses of the sun and moon, mentions of a revised version of the Cartesian system of *Tourbillons* and of all manner of inventions in scientific instruments. Though Locke's interest in these matters was somewhat intermittent and at times superficial, the pages of his Journal reflect in no uncertain fashion the scientific revolution which was taking place in the Europe of his day.

This breadth of interests reveals itself in the variety of the notes in his Journal: entries on metaphysics, science or medicine are mingled with a mass of detailed observations on the most diverse

---

[1] 11 April 1679.

themes—the King's behaviour at his *lever* or the operations of the peasant working in the fields, a new type of latch on the bedroom-door of an inn or cookery recipes, the spectacle of 'a lusty, tall fellow riding pillion' behind a woman or notes on the diet of the elephant at Versailles, 'a vast mountain of an animall'. With these goes a lively sense of humour, more prominent in the Journal than in the *Essay on the Human Understanding* or the *Two Treatises of Government*. His fondness for picturesque anecdotes (even when they are perhaps of somewhat dubious authenticity) appears in the stories which he so carefully noted down of the tricks played on the friars by the worthy Bishop Camus,[1] or of the origins of the Rosicruceans.[2]

In the Journal, as in much of his correspondence with his friends, there is frequently a noticeable striving after wit. Lady Masham in whose house he spent the last years of his life, once compared his letters with those of the seventeenth-century *bel esprit*, Vincent Voiture.[3] Those written in this period (unfortunately those which have come down to us are only too rare) confirm at times this judgement: witness the fragment of a draft of a letter which he wrote from Montpellier in March 1676.[4] He speaks there of the contrast between the high-sounding terms of French *cuisine* and the sad reality of a bad meal in a sordid village-inn:

> We had the ceremony of first & 2d course, besides a disert in the close, for were your whole bill of fare noe thing but some cabbage & a frog that was caught in it & some haws of the last season, you would have a treat in all its formalitys, & would not faile of three courses.

Even though the loss of most of these letters prevents us from being certain of the point, it is reasonably clear that some of the longer and more elaborately written passages in the Journal were destined for his correspondents.[5] While he never descends to the level of Mascarille or Trissotin, his *badinage* occasionally becomes so involved as to be almost incomprehensible, as in the following

---

[1] 24 March 1679.   [2] Appendix B (p. 282), 1 April 1679.
[3] Fox Bourne, I, 53 n.   [4] See Appendix A.
[5] In a letter of 1677, in answer to a letter of Locke dated 25 June, James Tyrrell thanks him for his account of Versailles which, as we see from the Journal, Locke had just visited (MS. Locke, c. 22, ff. 36–7).

maze-like sentence describing the way in which, after showing them over the Minims' monastery at Arles, a friar took leave of him and his fellow-travellers:

The Frier shewd us these & other things very courteously, & as civily at parting desired something to say Masse for our good journey, which a Swisse that was then there understood to be mony to drink our healths, & said it was the first Frier he had ever observed to aske mony to that purpose, & some thought his mistake not soe far out of the way, saying, soberly thinking of it, it was to aske mony to drink.[1]

Yet such examples of a somewhat precious obscurity are rare. There are many other passages in which Locke's love of fun comes out more pleasingly. The sight of certain paintings, attributed (very dubiously) to King René of Anjou, in an old, barn-like building at Angers, gives rise to the delightful observation: 'but soe litle reverence was now paid to this royal workmanship that it served only to enterteine a cow that was lodged at that end, the rest being full of wood & straw'.[2] Speaking of the notoriously dirty habits of the people who frequented the Court, and particularly of what he observed at the Château of Fontainebleau, he wraps up the crude reality in delicate euphemism:

The gardens are everywhere full of nosegays, espetially all along under the long gallery windows, & there was *one laid on* Monsieur's *back stairs to mark, I suppose, the good housekeeping rather than the* cleanlynesse *of the place, and at all the stairs one is sure to meet with a parfume which yet hath nothing of* Vespatian's *good savour*.[3]

Airy nothings are apt to crop up in the most odd places, as, for instance, this unexpected sentence at the end of his severely technical description of blanching wax: 'They...set it abroad again in the sun upon coarse clothes to kisse away the remainder of its blushes, if there be any left'.[4] Again, contrasting the snow in the Cévennes in January with the mild weather and rain at Montpellier, he comments:

Winter makes but little excursions into the vale of this country, but keeps his court in the mountains, & if I were to draw his picture, he should not be crowned with turneps & carrots, but with violets & Jasmin studded with olives.[5]

---

[1] 7 April 1676.   [2] 23 Aug. 1678.
[3] 25 Sept. 1677.   [4] 1 May 1676.
[5] 24 Jan. 1676.

Occasionally sights seen on his travels arouse his sarcasm. Balaruc-les-Bains, for instance, made a most unfavourable impression on him.

It hath [he wrote] the shortest, narrowest, crookedest streets that I ever saw any where, & I beleive never were soe few pitifull & ill placed houses girt with a wall any where else. Round about the room where the Bath rises, are rooms for beds, bad enough & fiter for an hospitall then receit of strangers that come here for health or diversion.[1]

Apothecaries' assistants, he noted at Montpellier, administered clysters to men and women alike. 'Only the meaner sort of women about Montpellier', he adds, 'are with difficulty brought to take them after this manner'.[2]

Finally a host of minor details about his private life are scattered through the Journal and other papers relating to his travels in France preserved in the Lovelace Collection. In these entries which were certainly never intended for prying eyes, Locke shows himself *en déshabillé*. Besides occasional references to the state of his health (they are rare), we learn from the Journal and various notes on expenses something of his mode of living and dress during these years.

To Locke, as to any traveller, inns were a subject of the highest importance. He was no Smollett who could recklessly pen the sweeping generalization: 'All the inns in this country are execrable.'[3] It is true that his first impressions were not very favourable. At Lucy-le-Bois, on the way from Auxerre to Châlons-sur-Saône, he had 'miserable lodging', but, he adds philosophically, '*that must be borne with in* France'.[4] Poix, a village on the route from Calais to Paris, had by his account most unpleasant accommodation to offer the seventeenth-century traveller, as he had already discovered on his first trip to France in 1672. This 'memorable lodging' furnished every conceivable discomfort, not excluding '6 legd creatures':[5] Locke can only speak of the 'Feinds of Poy'. Yet the very next night,

---

[1] 5 March 1676.   [2] 17 March 1676.
[3] *Travels in France and Italy*, p. 93.   [4] 16 Dec. 1675.
[5] The prevalence of noxious insects in French inns at this period perhaps accounts for the following entry (16 July 1678): 'Take the leaves of kidny beans (phaseolorum) & put them under your pillow or some convenient place about your bed. They will draw all the puneses to them & keepe you from being bit.'

at Tillart, he found at the inn at which they lay, 'a good supper...,
clean sheets of the country & a pretty girle to lay them on'.[1] His
later impressions of French inns (it must be remembered that he did
not always keep to the main roads, but also travelled in out-of-the-
way places) were, no doubt like the reality, equally varied. In the
Journal names of inns and prices for accommodation and meals
are followed by 'moderate treatment' or 'mediocrement' as well as
by 'ill treated' or 'excellently well treated'. If the *Chapeau rouge*
at Cadillac, near Bordeaux, is blacklisted as '*the most cut-throat
house I ever was in*',[2] the *Hôtel de Malte* in which he stayed at
Marseilles is described as 'the fairest inn I ever saw'.[3] Here,
as so often, we may admire the fairness and objectivity of his
judgements.

On his travels he enjoyed sampling the local wine. In 1678, on
his journey up the Rhône valley, he stopped to drink 'excellent
Hermitage wine'.[4] When satisfied, he noted the point in his Journal.
'At St. Chinian de la Corne', he writes, '*we drank the best wine I have
met with on this side* Paris, *which yet they sell for* 2 sols the pot'.[5] At
Amboise he enjoyed the wine more than the bill: 'A la Corne
excellent coole wine, but make your bargain before hand or expect
an extraordinary reconing.'[6] From the entries in the Journal we can
follow the different modes of travel—horse, boat, the *diligence*, even
a litter in the heat—which he made use of, and what each cost him.
We learn, too, that he did not like being overcharged or cheated. In
describing his trip in a boat up the Garonne from Blaye to Bordeaux
he pens the warning: 'When you make a bargain with them for soe
many rowers, you must have a care they put not boys instead of
men.'[7] Elsewhere, speaking of the ride from Ponts-de-Cé to Angers,
he writes: 'We paid 15 s. a peice for our horses for this league; the
usual price is but 10 s. at most, but they made use of our necessity.'[8]
Yet he had other, happier experiences on his travels. Of the people
of the inn he stayed at in a little town between Moulins and Nevers

---

[1] See Appendix A (p. 280). Characteristically Philarète Chasles omits the second
of these two passages which counterbalances, to some extent at least, the effect of the
first. [2] 4 April 1677.
[3] 12 April 1676. [4] 3 Nov. 1678.
[5] 1 March 1677. [6] 27 May 1677.
[7] 13 Sept. 1678. [8] 19 Aug. 1678.

on his way back to Paris in 1678, he wrote: 'The reasonablest people that I met with in France, for they would not take mony for 3 picotins of oats we had extraordinary.'[1]

From the Journal we learn, too, what he bought in the way of clothes during his stay in France. We see him buying shoes, or holland for shirts, *serge d'Uzès* and green ribbons for a suit, a pair of silk stockings and 'a morning goune'—all these at Montpellier. His return to Paris in June 1677 led to a heavy drain on his purse, though his pupil's father seems to have helped to fit him out for the capital. From all accounts he was fastidious in matters of dress, and since what was good enough for the provinces, was not smart enough for Paris, we find him, immediately on his arrival, investing in 3 *aunes* of cloth for a new suit, a beaver hat and one of the now fashionable periwigs. His expenditure on laundry during his stay in Paris is quite prominent in the pages of the Journal, but reference to his note-books for this period shows how carefully he kept a check on every item entrusted to his laundress. A gift of money from Sir John Banks in November 1677 for his 'winter conveniencys' led to the purchase of velvet and satin for a smart new outfit. Lists of clothes left behind in Paris or taken with him on his tour of France in 1678 provide some interesting glimpses into the state of his wardrobe as into the customs of the age. He packed away in a trunk, to be left in Paris, his 'shamway drawers' and two 'flanen shirts', and laid beside them his black velvet cap, purple cloak and velvet coat along with his muff. The list of linen which he took with him on his tour included the significant item: 'Handkerchiefs 4.'[2] A month later the weather in the Tours region was so cold, though it was early August, that he wrote: 'I found it convenient to get on my flanen shirt, & should not have been troubled with a wastcoat.' Yet before the month was out, he found himself and his pupil, 'feareing the heat', travelling from Angers to Saumur in a litter.[3]

All these little details, relatively insignificant though often entertaining, help to build up a more vivid picture of the man.

---

[1] 19 Nov. 1678.   [2] 2 and 8 July 1678.
[3] 10 and 29 Aug. 1678.

IV

As an English gentleman of modest extraction, Locke never moved in the highest circles in France. At Montpellier and Paris he was in contact with one or two members of the English aristocracy—if not perhaps with the Ambassador himself, at least with his wife, the Countess of Northumberland, and with the future Earl of Pembroke —as well as with various members of the gentry whose names crop up from time to time in the Journal. So far as the upper classes of French society were concerned, his contacts were negligible: he may have dined with the local *Intendant* at Rochefort and have been presented to the young Prince de Conti, but he never moved in the more or less aristocratic world of the *salons* then so flourishing in Paris.

His contacts with French people, when they were not simply with innkeepers and servants, shopkeepers and peasants, or his different landlords in Paris and Montpellier,[1] were mainly in intellectual circles. Yet one must remember that although, when he landed in France in 1675, he had already reached the age of forty-three, he was quite unknown in the world of letters. It was not until 1689 that he published his first work, the *Letter on Toleration*. If he had come to Paris after 1690, when he had already published his *Essay on the Human Understanding* and his *Two Treatises of Government*, he might not have equalled the success of David Hume in the *salons* and intellectual circles of eighteenth-century Paris, but at least his presence would not have passed almost unnoticed.[2]

During his long stay in Languedoc he met, however, a number of interesting people. When, in the spring of 1677, he inspected the *Canal du Midi* and the new port in course of construction at Sète, he met Pierre Paul Riquet, the tax-farmer turned civil engineer who was responsible for their creation, and discussed his plans and problems with him. At Montpellier he records several conversations

---

[1] It is noticeable that at Montpellier and even in Paris he lived and took his meals for a good part of the time in the houses of apothecaries—Puech, Verchand and Charas.

[2] There is a complete absence of references to Locke in official documents, both at Montpellier and Paris, a fact which is accounted for by the blameless existence which he led in France. He was not, for instance, imprisoned in the Bastille like his friend, Charleton.

with Pierre Régis who was shortly afterwards to return to Paris and add to the reputation which he had acquired in the South of France as a popularizer of Cartesianism, which was then, despite the official ban on its teaching, in process of becoming the fashionable philosophy.

At such a famous centre of medical studies, Locke inevitably made the acquaintance of some of his fellow doctors. It is perhaps significant that he nowhere mentions any personal contact with the professors of the Faculty of Medicine. His only allusions to this august body can scarcely be called flattering, whether he is describing a degree ceremony or the disputations which he attended at the 'Physick Schoole'. His first impressions of one of those disputations which at that time formed a considerable part of the French medical student's training, to the exclusion of more important matters, were highly unfavourable. Not long after his arrival at Montpellier he noted in his Journal:

Disputation at the Physick Schoole. *Much* French, *hard* Latin, *little* Logic *and little* Reason. Vitulo tu dignus et hic.[1]

A few days later a second visit produced equally unflattering comment:

At the Physick Schoole a Scholler answering the first time, a Professor moderating. 6 other professors oppose with great violence of Latin & French, Grimasse & hand.[2]

His description of the installation of a new Doctor of Medicine[3] is almost certainly one of those carefully written passages which he intended to insert in his letters for the edification of his friends. He has, as usual, a keen eye for the comic side of the proceedings, as in his reference to the doctor's cap 'that had marchd in on the Bedle's staff'. More significant is his poor opinion of the orations offered to the assembled company by the presiding professor and the new doctor. In the latter's speech Locke 'found litle for edification' since, so far as he could make out, it mainly consisted in compliments to the assembled members of the professoriate, while the Chancellor's oratory was directed 'against innovation', a favourite theme in the

[1] 26 Feb. 1676.   [2] 3 March 1676.
[3] 18 and 20 March 1676.

LLJ   xxxvii   c

very conservative Faculties of Medicine in seventeenth-century France.

Locke's main contacts seem to have been with three Protestant doctors: Jolly who, from the entries in the Journal in which his name is mentioned, appears to have had a strong interest in astronomy, and two men who, despite their eminence in their profession, were excluded because of their religion from the chairs of the Faculty—the distinguished physician, admired by both Locke and Sydenham, Charles Barbeyrac, and the famous botanist, Pierre Magnol.[1]

In Paris he does not appear to have moved in literary circles in the narrow sense of the term, though we know from his Journal and other papers that he showed some interest in contemporary French literature. Among the books he acquired in France were the plays of Molière and the brothers Corneille, though he appears to have left the masterpieces of Racine to his pupil. Of contemporary poets Boileau is the one most frequently named in his various papers. Among the books which he acquired during his stay in the South of France was a copy of 'Boiloes Satyrs', and in a list made the following year a set of his *Œuvres* is mentioned. In the note-book which he kept in Paris between 30 June 1677 and 30 June 1678 we find the following entry on 'Boyloe', communicated by a 'Mr Duncom':

Les Satyrs.
Epistres.
Art poetique d'Horace.
Lutrin.
Sublime de Longine.

2 Additional Chants of his Lutrin,[2] his satyr of mariage[3] and 2 or 3 other new ones are now in the presse.[4]

Yet, if a study of his reading and purchases of books, combined with his mention of occasional visits to the theatre and the trouble he took to copy into his Journal for 1679 an epigram directed against Pradon's latest play, reveals a certain interest in contemporary French poetry and drama, there is not a shred of evidence to show

---

[1] Some years after his conversion in 1685 he was appointed to a chair.
[2] The last two cantos appeared in 1683, nine years after the publication of the first four.
[3] His 'Satire x', directed against women, appeared only in 1694.
[4] P. 8.

that he had any personal contacts with French playwrights or poets, illustrious or otherwise.

It was rather in learned and scientific circles that he moved in Paris. On his arrival in the capital in June 1677 he at once wrote to Robert Boyle. After apologizing for the silence which he had kept since his departure and offering to execute any commissions which he might have for him, he went on:

> I would beg the favour of two or three lines from your hand to recommend me to the acquaintance of any one of the *virtuosi* you shall think fit here. I know your bare name will open doors, and gain admittance for me, where otherwise one like me without port and name, that have little tongue, and less knowledge, shall hardly get entrance....[1]

Whether through Boyle's intervention or not, he gradually began to make contacts. In October, four months after his arrival, he records a conversation with Henri Justel, a Protestant soon to be a refugee in England, at whose house met a group of learned men. At a slightly earlier period Leibnitz had been one of the foreigners visiting Paris who attended these gatherings. Though, despite his interest in his writings and the controversy which they aroused, there is no evidence to show that Locke ever made the acquaintance of the greatest living French philosopher, Malebranche, he met, round about the same time, another well-known figure of the period, François Bernier. The interest in travel books which he showed during his stay in France would lead one to expect references in the Journal to other famous French travellers. The silence of the Journal, apart from two references to Bernier, shows how incomplete a record it is of these years, for his correspondence and other papers show that he knew personally Melchisédec Thévenot, and possibly also the two famous Oriental travellers, Chardin and Tavernier.[2]

It is not until April 1678 that he records his first encounter with Nicolas Thoynard with whom he was to carry on a voluminous

---

[1] Boyle, *Works* (London, 1744), 5 vols., v, 569.

[2] Thévenot is frequently mentioned in his letters to Thoynard after his return to England (see Ollion, pp. 53 f.). His Second Note-book contains (p. 177) the following entry: 'Chardin. Chez Mr. de Montauban dans la rüe Tibaudè proche la monoye.' The same note-book (p. 154) has an entry, 'Tavarnier [sic], 1679', headed 'Recueil. Maps & Cuts', which contains a list of engravings of Oriental scenes, beginning with '2 cuts of him self'.

correspondence[1] for some twenty years and whose name constantly recurs in the Journal from this point onwards. Thoynard is best known to-day for his *Evangeliorum harmonia graeco-latina* which appeared posthumously in 1707, but after the less specialized fashion of his age he was also interested in problems of science and technology, especially in artillery, as we see from the copious notes on his inventions which Locke faithfully copied into his Journal. It was apparently through him that Locke was presented to the Prince de Conti.

During his stay in Paris Locke took care to seek out such famous inventors and instrument-makers as Michael Butterfield, an Englishman who had settled in France, and Father Chérubin, just as during his visits to Orleans in 1678 he made the acquaintance of the prolific inventor, Jean Hautefeuille. It was, however, among the astronomers of the period that he made his most eminent acquaintances. Soon after he arrived in Paris, he visited the recently erected Observatoire, and there in due course he got to know three of the most distinguished astronomers of the age: the Frenchman, Picard, and two foreigners whom Colbert had attracted to Paris, the Italian, Cassini, and the Dane, Römer. With the last Locke seems to have become specially intimate, though it is only towards the very end of his stay that the first mention of him occurs in the pages of the Journal; it was he who brought Römer over to England for a short stay in 1679. During his time in Paris Locke also seems to have been on intimate terms with the mathematician and astronomer, Adrien Auzout.

Thus, though the Journal contains no sensational revelations concerning what is now regarded as one of the most fertile periods in the intellectual life of France, it does offer scattered pieces of information about the occupations of learned men and scientists in the 1670's. If some great names are missing from its pages, the publication of this text will no doubt contribute something to our knowledge of the activities of learned circles in France at this time.[2]

---

[1] Locke's letters have been published by Ollion, Thoynard's are in the Lovelace Collection.

[2] This aspect of Locke's stay in France, along with his later correspondence with Justel, Thoynard, Du Bos and his translator, Pierre Coste, is being studied in detail by Professor Gabriel Bonno, of Berkeley University, California.

V

The main interest of our edition of the Journal lies, when all is said and done, in the light which it throws on the state of France[1] at the moment when, both at home and abroad, the prestige of Louis XIV was at its height. The *Roi Soleil* appears in person in its pages on more than one occasion. Locke saw him devoutly praying at his bedside at his *lever* at Saint Germain; attending a performance of an opera of Lully and presiding over a ball at Fontainebleau; reviewing, on two different occasions, the troops of the Royal Household; crossing Paris in February 1678 on his way to the siege of Ghent, accompanied by the Queen and Madame de Montespan in the same carriage; and walking and driving with his mistress in the gardens of Versailles and (here Locke made judicious use of his shorthand) inspecting the fountains and other 'water works':

The King *seemed to be* mightily *well pleased with his water works and* severall *changes were made then to which he himself gave sign with his cane, and he may well be made merry with this water since it has cost him dearer than so much wine, for they say it costs him* 3s. *every pint* (i.e. 2 lbs.) *that run there.*[2]

The France that Locke knew was a country at war, absorbed in a struggle which, beginning with Louis's attack on Holland in 1672, was gradually to bring in Spain, the Emperor and various German states, and was to last until the Treaty of Nimeguen in 1678. Indeed, despite the lavish bribes which Louis doled out to Charles II, England nearly joined in the war, too, in its concluding stages. Of the war itself Locke saw nothing but the bonfires which were lit to celebrate French victories. He took some interest, however, in the organization of the French army, in the pay of officers and men, and in their recently introduced uniforms, and he several times comments, generally somewhat disparagingly, on the appearance of the troops whom he encountered on his travels. He also describes a minor riot caused at Montpellier by the fraudulent methods

---

[1] It will be seen that his curiosity also extended to the French colony of Canada. This in its turn is part of his wider interest, reflected very clearly in his conversations as well as his reading for these years, in distant countries and the ways of their inhabitants.

[2] 23 June 1677.

employed by recruiting sergeants to get men to join the army.[1] What interested him especially was the efforts of Colbert to strengthen the French navy, to build large numbers of new ships and to set up the necessary shore-establishments. At Marseilles and Toulon and later at the newly created port of Rochefort he goes into considerable detail to describe the warships and galleys which he visited, and the shipyards and stores on shore.

Though he is mentioned only seldom by name, Colbert and his multifarious activities figure prominently in the pages of the Journal. Besides his work for the French navy and his conduct of the French finances during the war years, a subject to which Locke devoted much space, we see reflected here his attempt to bring about a great development of French trade and industry. At Carcassonne, for instance, Locke noted the successful use of skilled labour, imported from Holland, to build up the local cloth industry:

They have got into this way of making fine cloth by means of 80 Hollanders *which, about* 5 *or* 6 *years since,* Mr. Colbert *got hither. They are all now gone but about* 12, *but have left their art behind them.*[2]

In the same region of France the progress which he witnessed in the construction of the *Canal du Midi* was yet another example of the energy of the *Contrôleur-Général* when it was a question of carrying through a project such as this which held out great hopes for the expansion of trade in the surrounding provinces. In Paris he admired Colbert's encouragement of the arts in the recently reorganized *Académie de Peinture et de Sculpture*, and the tapestries which, under his stimulus, the Gobelins were busily turning out. The Observatoire, an offshoot of the newly founded *Académie des Sciences*, Locke inspected along with the Bibliothèque du Roi. These were all part of Colbert's plans to secure the intellectual as well as the economic pre-eminence of France.

The Absolutism which Louis XIV and his ministers imposed on France, was first studied by Locke from the remote province of Languedoc. He gives in the Journal a detailed and often vivid description of the two sessions of the Provincial Estates which took place during his stay at Montpellier. It is perhaps strange that

---

[1] 1 Feb. 1676.   [2] 6 March 1677.

while in the pages which he devotes to an account of the government of Languedoc, he describes in some detail the functions of the Governor, the old and gouty Duc de Verneuil, who was a mere figurehead, he should have said not a word of the important role played in the province by the *Intendant*, the new agent of the central government. Yet this lapse is corrected, almost to the point of exaggeration, when, after his return to Paris, he wrote (again prudently in shorthand) the following lines which show that he clearly appreciated the importance of the role of the *Intendants* and the effacement of the once-powerful Governors of provinces:

In France there are Governors *of* provinces *as* formerly, *but they have no power at all.* Leiutenants *of* provinces *are watch and guard upon them, and on the least* occasion *can seize them, and the King's* man[1] *is spy and guard on them both. Besides, the* Intendant *gives* constant intelligence *of all things to the Court.*[2]

He clearly discerned that, despite the measure of autonomy which Languedoc enjoyed through the part played by its Estates in the assessment and collection of taxes, they were in fact impotent in face of a monarch who was determined to wield absolute power. Earlier in the century, down to the civil wars of the Fronde, the Estates had frequently flouted the authority of the distant central government. During his visit to Carcassonne Locke recorded the following conversation:

One of the States told me that he was at an Assembly 20 *years agon when, the King asking* 7 *or* 800,000 livres Tournois, *they thought it too much and gave nothing at all.*[3]

Even after the beginning of the personal reign of Louis XIV, there had followed a period in which the assent of the deputies to increases in taxation had been secured only by the secret distribution of substantial bribes. However, by the time that Locke arrived in the province at the beginning of 1676, the Estates could do nothing but offer prompt compliance with the ever-growing demands of the Crown, which were swollen by the need to meet the heavy cost of the war. Hence his summing up on the functions of the Estates:

They...have all the solemnity & outward appearance of a Parliament. The King proposes & they debate & resolve about it. Here is all the

---

[1] The *Intendant.*   [2] 12 July 1677.   [3] 7 March 1677.

difference, that they never doe, & some say dare not, refuse whatever the King demands.[1]

It is significant that the informant who had told him of the Estates' refusal, some twenty years earlier, to vote the *Don gratuit* demanded by the Crown, had added that 'they dare not do so now'.

Locke also picked up, during his stay at Montpellier, a certain amount of information about other aspects of local government in Languedoc. He notes the decline in the power of the municipal authorities in Montpellier where the *Consuls* 'are litle more then servants to the Governor of the towne'.[2] The name of Cardinal Bonzi, a distinguished diplomat rather than a model of piety and sober living, appears frequently in these pages. He was then at the height of his power: since he was President of the Estates, he had an important part to play as intermediary between the province and the central government, and he contributed much to its final subjection to the power of the King. Yet the scandal of his private life and the corruption of his entourage were in the long run to undermine his position in the province. Under the heading, 'Cardinal's Mistress', Locke wrote in his Journal: '50 pistols *the way to have a* captain's *place in the new* regiment *of dragoons*.[3] . . . *This made men of worth and good* soldiers *miss places*'.[4] He adds resignedly, no doubt with thoughts of Restoration England and the court of Charles II in his mind: 'Mistresses *get money all the world over*.' The shady methods of raising money employed by the Cardinal's sister, the Marquise de Castries, widow of the late Governor of Montpellier and mother of his youthful successor, are set forth in a vivid shorthand entry:

500 escus *made a year by Mme* de Castres *for a* dispensation *to* tipling houses *for breaking the rules of the town, which are that no* townsman *eat or drink in* cabarets *which are for* strangers, *and if anyone be drunk or found in these houses on holy days in time of* divine service, *to pay so much*. . . . *She also makes a* profit *of the* stores *of the* Cittadell *and allowing bakers to sell light bread; and besides ploughing up the* Splanade, *which* formerly *belonged to the* officers *of the* garison, *she also sells the mud of the town ditches*.[5]

We have here a detailed picture of the depredations which members of the privileged orders, in positions of authority in the province,

---

[1] 8 Feb. 1676. [2] 24 Feb. 1676.
[3] Recently raised by the Estates, at the command of Louis XIV.
[4] 13 March 1677. [5] 10 Feb. 1677.

were still able to carry out, despite the vigilance of the central government and the *Intendant*.

The many pages of the Journal given up to notes on the finances and taxation system of France bear witness to the care with which Locke sought to inform himself on such questions. It was, of course, impossible in this period of French history that even educated opinion could be well informed about the financial state of the country, since such matters were the concern of the government, not of the governed. Moreover, even students of the history of French finances, from the eighteenth century down to our own time, have not altogether succeeded in unravelling the tangled skein of the government's expenditure and revenue in this period. The standard works of reference on the subject sometimes give startlingly different figures for both sides of the national accounts. It cannot therefore be expected that Locke should have formed an altogether accurate picture of the financial state of France under Louis XIV; so that, though some of his figures tally exactly with those generally accepted, others do so only approximately, and the rest not at all.

What is more valuable is his account of the workings of the taxation system and the echoes which we find in the pages of the Journal of popular discontent with the high level of taxes. There is no doubt occasional exaggeration in the entries of the latter type, for instance, in the statement: 'Merchands & handicrafts men pay above ½ their gain.'[1] Then, as in more recent times, the majority of Frenchmen had a rooted aversion to the operations of the tax-collector. However, Locke is not content with such vague generalizations as he picked up in conversation; he obviously strove his hardest, wherever he went in France, to get precise figures as to the burden of taxation and the inequalities which were part and parcel of the system. Thus he carefully noted down the different prices of salt in the various parts of the country which he visited. In Languedoc, despite the increase in the *Gabelle* which took place during his stay in Montpellier, the price still remained relatively moderate compared with that paid in Paris or other provinces in which the tax was highest, while at La Rochelle, in a region exempt from the *Gabelle*, salt was

---

[1] 1 May 1676.

in comparison dirt cheap. Hence the precautions to prevent salt being smuggled from such areas into those provinces where the tax sent up its price to a great height. Locke describes the *gabeleurs'* searching of goods brought into the town of Angers:

They have also in their hands iron bodkins about 2 foot long which have a litle hollow in them near the point, which they thrust into any packs where they suspect there may be salt concealed, & if there be any, by that means discover it....I saw a Gabeller at the gate serch a litle girle at her entrance, who seemd only to have gon out to see a funerall that was prepareing without the gate, which had drawn thither a great number of people.

Attempts to evade the tax were savagely punished:

The penalty for any one that brings in any salt that is not a Gabeller, pays 100 ecus or goes to the gallys. It is also as dangerous to buy any salt but of them.[1]

It was, however, in the levying of the *taille*, the principal direct tax, that the greatest inequalities lay. A province like Languedoc which had its own Estates to assess and levy the tax, came off on the whole relatively lightly. Yet even here, though the tax was based on ownership of land (*taille réelle*) and not, as in most other parts of France, on estimated income (*taille personnelle*), there was, as we see from the following passage, grossly unequal treatment for land owned by members of the privileged orders, the nobility and clergy, and land owned by *roturiers*:

To these 2,700,000£ *which this* province *is to pay this year*, land *of* 100 escus per annum *will pay about* 130l. *The* terre noble *which is about* 1/20th, *pays nothing. What was not* anciently noble, *but en*nobled *by grant, pays* 1 *year's* value *every* 20 *or* 30 *years, but the* ancient *doth not, and* [if] a Roturier *or* Commoner *buys it, it pays this year's* value. *Monks, when they get land by gift or* purchase, *if the* Estates *do not spare them, they* usually *get the* King *to en*noble *them, and so the* burthen *still increases on the rest.*[2]

In the system followed in most of the rest of France in the so-called *Pays d'élection* (i.e. those provinces without Estates) Locke observed shocking inequalities. There was, first, the tendency among the upper classes of society (including the *bourgeois* as well as the privileged orders) to throw the main burden of the *taille* on the peasantry. Again, he points out, the tax was levied very unfairly in

[1] 22 Aug. 1678.   [2] 27 March 1677.

the parishes where favouritism and 'influence' caused one man's tax to be reduced at the expense of his neighbours. The somewhat repetitive fashion in which Locke gradually built up in his mind, over the years of his stay, a picture of the workings of the system, and the occasional errors of detail in his notes which he gradually corrected, should not blind us to the insight which he brought to his examination of this question. Thus, while still at Montpellier, he noted among the details which he had assembled on the collection of the *taille* in other parts of France:

A Gent. *pays nothing*, i.e. *he may keep in his hand as much land as he can* manage *with* 2 *ploughs. If he has any more, he must pay for it, but as well as they can, the* burthen *is shifted off on to the* paisants, *out of whose labour they wring as much as they can, and rot lights on the land.*[1]

In a later passage he contrasts the *taille réelle* of Languedoc with the arbitrary *taille personnelle* of other provinces:

The tax to be paid being laid upon the parish, the Collectors for that year assease every one of the inhabitants or house keepers of the parish, according to his proportion as they judg him worth, but consider not the land in the parish that belongs to any one liveing out of it.... This is that which soe grinds the paisant in France. The collectors make their rates usually with great inequality.[2]

Three days later he picked up more grumbles about the burden of the *taille*: for instance, that 'in Normandie they often pay more for the taile then their land is worth to be lett', but, he adds, 'this lights heaviest on the poor & lower sort of people, the richer sort befreinding & easeing one an other'.[3]

At Orleans, during his second tour of the country in 1678,[4] he returns once more to the question, and points out some of the worst features of the whole system. First, there is the principle that the whole parish is responsible for the payment of each individual inhabitant's payment of the tax: 'If any one be found non solvendo, his taxe is laid upon the rest of the parish.' Then there is the pressure brought on the collector (not a civil servant, but a private individual elected by the inhabitants to carry out this unpleasant duty) to collect all the tax by a fixed date: 'If the Collector pays not in the

---

[1] 29 Sept. 1676. [2] 26 May 1677.
[3] 29 May 1677. [4] 21 July 1678.

mony to a farthing by the day, he goes to prison.' Finally, there is
the glaring contrast not only between the peasants and the privileged
orders, but also between the countrymen and the inhabitants of the
larger towns who have gained exemption from the *taille*:

> The inhabitants of free towns, as Paris, Orleans, etc., whereof there are
> many in France, are not taliable, & sometimes the Land adjacent, as the
> land a league about Orleans, is free.

It is true, as Locke points out, that this freedom from the *taille* was
not quite as valuable as the townsman fondly imagined:

> The inhabitants of free towns that have land in the country perswade
> them selves that they nor their land pay not, because 'tis the pore tenant
> that pays, but yet according to the increase of their taxes their rents
> decrease.

Even so, the contrast with the peasant's burden was still sufficiently
striking. Moreover, as Locke points out, the peasant was tied to the
land and to the fiscal burdens which were his lot, since it took him
ten years to secure exemption from them, even if he took refuge in
a free town:

> A paisant that has land of his owne or otherwise, if he leaves his land
> & lets it to an other & goes & lives in a free towne, he shall be obleiged to
> pay every year as much taile as he did for the last year of his living in
> a tailiable place & this for 10 years togeather, his tenant paying neverthe-
> lesse as much taile also as he is assessed or judged able, but after ten years
> liveing in a free towne, a paisant becomes free of Taile unlesse he returne
> to his husbandry again. This makes all these people, as much as they can,
> send their children to live in free towns to make their persons free from
> taile.

Taken together, these scattered entries show that Locke had laid
his finger on most of the weaknesses and inequalities of the system.

There are also references in the Journal to the new burdens which
the war had imposed on the people of France. In addition to increases
in the *taille* and the *gabelle*, there were new taxes such as the State
monopoly of tobacco introduced by Colbert in 1674. Of this Locke
writes:

> For tobaco here they pay a livre a pound excise, for the Farmers who
> rent it of the King, sell now all the tobaco, & sell it for 33 s. per lb. what
> they formerly bought for 13 or 15 s. per lb.[1]

---

[1] 24 Feb. 1676.

In addition to imposing heavier excise duties on wines, the government was driven by necessity of war to employ all sorts of expedients to raise money. The billeting of troops on the inhabitants of towns was hated and feared, as Locke notes in his Journal with his usual gift for understatement: '33 Companys quarterd at Moulin upon free quarter, which the people like not.'[1] The government was thus in a good position to wring large money payments from the towns in exchange for exemption from this burden. At Tours in 1677 Locke wrote:

They gave the King this year 45,000£ to be excused from winter quarter, which came to 1/10 on the rent of their houses.[2]

And at Orleans in the following year:

The town of Orleans, though a free towne & by particular priviledges exempted from quartering any soldiers, yet the last winter, to be exempt from winter quarters, though noe soldiers were neare, were [sic] fain to compound at the rate of 52,000£; & Poictiers, a towne of extraordinary merit towards this very King, by whom it had that amongst other priviledges granted it, was fain also the last winter to buy its exemption at a round sum.[3]

Another burden which fell on the towns was the recurrent demand for money which the King would make to the guilds. At Tours Locke also noted:

Besides he sends to the severall companys of trades men for soe much mony as he thinks fit. The officers of each corps de mestier taxes every one according to his worth, which perhaps amounts to about 1 escu or 4£ to a man counted worth 100 escus.[4]

It is true that before he left France in the spring of 1679, the ending of the war had brought some relief in the burden both of direct and indirect taxation; even so, the picture which he gives of the arbitrary and complicated system of taxation, and the grumblings which it produced, is no doubt evidence of its oppressive effects on a great part of the population. On leaving the Pope's territory at Avignon, he observed that the land outside did not seem so well cultivated. 'Moderate taxes & a freedom from quarter', he concluded, 'gives the Pope's subjects, as it seems, more industry'.[5]

What of the economic state of France in these years when Colbert

---

[1] 21 March 1676.   [2] 26 May 1677.   [3] 21 July 1678.
[4] 26 May 1677.   [5] 22 April 1676.

was in full control of internal affairs and the Absolutism of Louis XIV was blossoming forth in the splendours of Versailles? Locke gives due weight, as we have seen, to the beneficent influence of Colbert on the state of French industry during this period. In his visits to industrial towns—large and small—he notes various signs of prosperity. At Castres and Carcassonne in Languedoc the cloth industry was in a flourishing condition; at Cosnes, the arms industry; and the naval ports of Marseilles, Toulon and Rochefort were full of activity. Yet there was another side to the picture. The effects of the war, whether they were the result of increased taxation or the closing of foreign markets, are shown to have been extremely serious.

Moreover, in a country in which the peasants still formed the overwhelming majority of the population, the prosperity of agriculture was of prime importance, since that of trade and industry was largely dependent upon it. It is now an accepted fact that in the years shortly before Locke arrived in France in 1675, there set in a disastrous fall in the prices of agricultural products which was to continue, except in years of great scarcity, for many decades, and to produce a serious decline in land values and in the general prosperity of the towns as well as the country. Twenty years later Vauban and Boisguilbert were to paint in vivid detail the serious consequences of this decline in prices. Locke, too, contributes his quota of evidence on this subject.

He notes on his travels various examples of the decay of trade and industry which had taken place in recent years. In 1676 he declares that at the famous fair of Beaucaire there were '*but 3 barks this year whereas there used to be 2 or 300*'.[1] At Tours in 1678 he found the silk industry in an alarming state of decline:

Where as there were lately 6,000 silke weavers here in Tours, there are now but 1,200, & those that could gain 50s. an aulne for weaving of figurd silkes have now but 30 or 35s. There have broke here since Easter last for above 6,000,000 £.

When he inspected a workshop, he noted:

The worke men complain of want of worke, decay of trade & abatement of wages. In the house we saw it, were lately 12 looms & there are now but two.[2]

---

[1] 4 Aug. 1676.   [2] 10–11 Aug. 1678.

When he went from Angers to visit some nearby slate-quarries, he observed:

> They employ about 100 men in diging, spliting & cuting these stones. Formerly there were 200, but the war as on other parts hath had an influence on this vent to.[1]

In the Loire valley he notes the low price which the producers get for their wine and the heavy taxes paid to the Treasury on it. At Saumur he writes:

> The white wine here of this towne is very good & wine soe plenty here that they sell it for 18 deniers la pinte at their boushons, i.e. where people in privat houses sell their owne wine by retail, & of these 18 deniers per pinte the King hath 10 deniers for excise & the proprieter 8 d. for his wine.[2]

At Angers 'the wine that was formerly sold here for 4 s. per pinte is now sold for 1 s.';[3] while at Orleans, on his way back to Paris later in the same year, he notes:

> A tun of wine holding two poinsons which contein 400 pints is sold here now, vessell & all, for £7, the vessell itself being worth neare the mony, & this not bad or decayd wine, but that which is very good.[4]

At Bordeaux, on the same journey, he had found similar depression in the wine trade, though here this is directly attributed to the war with Holland and to the ban on the import of French goods which Parliament had proclaimed in a moment of tension with France; the consequence of this was that wine which had formerly sold for between 40 or 50 *écus* a *tonneau* was now fetching only about 25.[5]

These and various other references scattered through the Journal show that, long before the disasters which befell France in the second half of the personal reign of Louis XIV, the general condition of the country, despite all the efforts of Colbert, was far from satisfactory. Perhaps the most pregnant sentence on this subject which is to be found in our text is one which occurs quite early in Locke's account of his stay in France. At Montpellier in May 1676 he noted in his Journal:

> The rents of Lands in France fallen above ½ in these few years by reason of the poverty of the people & want of mony.[6]

---

[1] 26 Aug. 1678. [2] 18 Aug. 1678.
[3] 26 Aug. 1678. [4] 24 Nov. 1678.
[5] 20 Sept. 1678. [6] 1 May 1676.

This generalization may be too sweeping and yet, broadly speaking, it does fit in with the modern historian's picture of the disastrous consequences of the decline in the price of agricultural products which set in during the first part of the personal reign of Louis XIV and continued to have its effects well into the eighteenth century.

Locke did not miss on his travels in France the poverty which during this reign serves as a background to the splendours of the Court at Versailles. Everywhere he went, he jotted down notes on wages and working conditions in the various industries which he had an opportunity to observe. There is a vivid picture of the toil exacted from a girl working in the silk industry at Tours:

> We saw also the twisting & windeing of silke in one of their mills, which is drove about by a maid & turnes at once above 120 spooles & windes the silk off them. The maid works from 5 in the morning till night, only rests twice in the day an hour at a time, & has for her day's work 5s., a small recompence for drawing such a weight 7 leagues, for soe much they say she goes in a day. The wages was formerly greater.[1]

Summing up his impressions at the end of his tour of Provence, he found that 'the people, if one may judg by their clothes & diet, had, like the country, 5 acres of poverty for one of riches', a remark for which he provides a vivid illustration:

> I remember at Aix in a gardiner's house, where we found them eating, their Sunday dinner was noe thing but slices of congeald bloud fried in oile, which an English gent. was with me would needs tast, though to the turning his stomach.[2]

Two years later, as he travelled through Poitou, he found *bourgs* which, 'considering the poornesse & fewnesse of the houses in most of them, would in England but scarce amount to vilages'. Their one-storeyed dwellings were so frequently in ruins that, though Locke found the land well cultivated, he hazards the guess that 'the people of France doe not at present increase, at least in the country'.[3] Perhaps the most memorable passage in the whole Journal is the one in which he describes a conversation with a peasant woman in the wine-growing district of Graves to the west of Bordeaux.[4] We obtain from this page a clear picture of the poverty-stricken existence led

---

[1] 11 Aug. 1678. [2] 23 April 1676.
[3] 31 Aug. 1678. [4] 15 Sept. 1678.

by a peasant whose only land was a tiny vineyard which he rented, and which, after the labour and cost of making the wine had been added up, 'was as bad as noe thing'. The family of five had to exist on the 7 *sous* a day which the man earned when he could get work, and on the occasional earnings of his wife who received only half that miserable wage. For their vineyard and their house 'which, God wot, was a pore one roome & one story open to the tiles, without window' they paid 36 *livres* a year in rent. Their *taille* came to another 4 *livres*, and recently, as they had not had the money ready, 'the collector had taken their frying pan & dishes'.[1] The diet of this family consisted of rye-bread and water; meat 'seldome seasons their pots'. On special occasions, as a great treat, writes Locke, they buy 'the inwards of some beast in the market & then they feast themselves'. Even so, according to what he heard in this corner of France, he had not plumbed the depths of poverty:

And yet they say that in Xantonges & severall other parts of France the paisants are much more miserable then these, for these they count the flourishing paisants which live in Grave.

This last remark cannot, of course, be taken quite literally; but this picture of desperate poverty was no doubt generally true of at least one section of the peasants of seventeenth-century France—those who depended for a living on their casual earnings as agricultural labourers.

On the subject of the relations between the different social classes of seventeenth-century France Locke has relatively little to say. He collected some information about the fines imposed on pushing *roturiers* who, like the poet, La Fontaine, had usurped noble rank.[2] There is also in the Journal a brief, but pregnant shorthand sentence on the gulf between nobleman and *roturier* under the *Ancien Régime*: '*The nobility and gentry have very little trust in the common people.*'[3] Perhaps the most striking entry on this subject is the one in which he describes the treatment meted out by a nobleman to an inhabitant of Aigues-Mortes who had committed some minor poaching offence. The Marquis de Vardes, he tells us, 'not long since clapt a townsman up in a litle hole in Constance's Tower, where he had just roome to

---

[1] Rent and *taille* add up to 40 *livres*, i.e. the wages of 114 working days.
[2] 22 May 1676. [3] 23 June 1676.

stand upright, but could not sit or ly down, & kept him there 3 days'.[1] Such acts of tyranny had to be paid for a hundred years later.

We have left to this point the question of Locke's accuracy as an observer of French life. No doubt there are occasional contradictions and errors in his notes on what he saw or heard in conversation in the course of his travels. To begin with at least, he cannot have been too well equipped linguistically for his investigations. It is true that in the learned circles in which he chiefly moved, conversations could easily be conducted in Latin, the international language of the time: occasionally entries in his Journal have been left in the language in which he had heard the subject discussed, and when he took French lessons at Montpellier, his teacher's and his own notes on French grammar were written in Latin. Yet when he arrived in France, his command of French, especially of the spoken language, must have been very weak. At Lyons, in December 1675, his visit to Mr Servière's museum was not, for a variety of reasons, an unqualified success; he was unable to satisfy his curiosity about several points, the owner 'haveing not Latin nor I French'.[2] As soon as they arrived at Montpellier, he and his companion, George Walls, began to take French lessons for an hour a day, five days a week.[3] However, though he could, of course, have easily conversed in Latin with such acquaintances as pastors, doctors, learned men and the like, his conversation with the ordinary people of the region who spoke *patois* rather than French, must have presented certain difficulties, since he cannot easily have learnt both. Yet we find him, shortly after his arrival, questioning the peasants in the fields about methods of vine-growing. Indeed, only once in the pages of the Journal does he admit to having been beaten by the language difficulty: that was much later in his stay, in May 1677, when, on a visit to the famous vineyards of Haut-Brion, near Bordeaux, he found that his inquiries from the workmen came to nothing 'for want of understanding Gascoin'.[4]

There seems little doubt that in the course of his long stay in France Locke acquired a very adequate practical knowledge of the

---

[1] 24 March 1676. [2] 22 Dec. 1675.
[3] 9 Jan. 1676. [4] 14 May 1677.

language, though his writing of it was always somewhat defective, and though, to the end of his stay, his spelling of French words in the Journal remains very inaccurate and is even more inconsistent than his English spelling. From such evidence as is available we may conclude that his knowledge of French was sufficient to enable him to prosecute his inquiries about conditions in the country.

Where his facts can be checked, they are seldom found to be inaccurate. A minute examination of the Journal makes it clear that he was a conscientious observer, who took great pains to get to the bottom of questions that interested him, and who was endowed with a healthy scepticism (the number of occasions on which reservations like 'as they say' precede or follow statements copied into the Journal is significant). If at times there are infuriating gaps in his figures for such things as rents and prices, these are themselves a tribute to the care with which he collected his information, since he preferred leaving a blank to writing down figures about which he was uncertain.

There are, very understandably, certain lapses in the impartiality and objectivity displayed generally in the Journal, particularly in those entries which refer to his contacts with French Catholicism. Not only does he judge the Catholic Church from the outside and, to some extent at least, through the eyes of his Huguenot informants: he is almost invariably hostile and contemptuous. It is well known that he, the apostle of the Liberal doctrine of religious toleration, would have denied it to Catholics in England. The Journal was written at a time when the aggressive policies of Louis XIV and the complicity of Charles II and especially of the future James II made a restoration of Catholicism to a dominant position in this country more than a remote possibility. Beneath the humour of Locke's account of a conversation which he had with a Carthusian at Villeneuve-lès-Avignon in 1676, there lies something approaching apprehension:

The Carthusian that shewd us the covent seemd not very melancholy. He enquird after their houses & lands in England, & asked whether, when we came to be papists, they should not have them again. I told him yes, without doubt, for there could be noe reconciliation without restitution. He told me I was a very good divine & very much in the right.[1]

---

[1] 22 April 1676.

Only four years after his return from France the bitter struggle over the succession to the English throne which involved, among other things, the question of the victory or defeat of Catholicism in this country, was to drive Locke into long years of exile in Holland. Not until after the arrival of William of Orange in England and the 'Glorious Revolution' was he at last free to return home again. It would therefore be idle to seek in the unexpurgated text of the Journal any impartial assessment of the role of Catholicism in the France of his time.[1]

His notes on the wealth of the higher clergy, whose members were recruited almost exclusively from the ranks of the nobility, are in the main accurate. His occasional references to sexual immorality among members of the Catholic clergy could give offence only to a modern reader entirely ignorant of the realities of life in seventeenth-century France. The *Abbé* whose morals he reflects on unfavourably during his journey down the Saône to Lyons in 1675,[2] could have stepped straight out of the pages of La Bruyère. The scandals inside the Society of Jesus in the 1660's which he records in his Journal[3] are also related by Olivier d'Ormesson, Guy Patin and Condé. His account of Cardinal Bonzi's relations with his mistress, Jeanne de Gévaudan,[4] is amplified by Saint-Simon, and the story is in any case part and parcel of the *chronique scandaleuse* of seventeenth-century Montpellier.

On his travels he collected with elaborate care notes on the abuse of relics, miracle-mongering, the cult of the Virgin, the worship of images, everything most distasteful to an ardent Protestant. These subjects give rise to some of the liveliest and wittiest passages in the whole Journal. The service for the canonization (or rather beatification) of St John of the Cross which he attended at Montpellier in 1676, is described with fairly mild irony:

This being the close of the solemnity, there was a sermon which was the recital of his life, virtues & miracles he did, as preserving baptismall grace & innocence to the end of his life, his driveing out evill spirits out of the possessed, etc.[5]

---

[1] There are occasional passages which are marked by complete objectivity, such as the short, but on the whole accurate account of Jansenism in the entry for 18 March 1679.
[2] 19 Dec. 1675.   [3] 13 Feb. 1679.
[4] 7 Feb. 1676.   [5] 10 Feb. 1676.

His account of his visit to the Minims of the *Alyscamps* at Arles
becomes sharper in tone when he relates how he and his companions
were shown the tombs of 'eminent saints, one whereof, as well as
St. Denys, caried his head in his hands a good way'. He goes on:

> They shewd us also one of these toombs which was always wet on the
> outside & that under it always drie, for they piled them one upon another,
> & had always water in it which increased & decreased with the moon. This
> the Frier that shewd the toombs said was a constant miracle. He dipd in
> his cord at a litle hole to give us demonstracion, & I thought it noe lesse
> then a miracle to beleiv upon such a proof.[1]

His visit to the famous Provençal shrines of Mary Magdalene at
Ste Baume and St Maximin did not particularly edify him. The first
entry on the subject is laconic in the extreme:

> Here we saw the reliques, as at St. Baum we saw the lodging of
> St. Mary Magdalen, both shewn with great devotion. What they are,
> v: the book.[2]

The next day he goes into a little more detail on the subject of
St Maximin, but his chief memory of the place seems to have been
of the unwelcome attentions which he suffered on his arrival from
a host of women who filled his room, 'offering beads & medals to
sell', and who would 'pull you to peices almost with their impor-
tunity to buy them'; and of the guard of 'dores, grates, locks &
bolts' behind which the relics were kept.

At Aix, as several times later at Montpellier, he witnessed processions of religious bodies. His accounts of these are generally
factual and often full of vivid detail; but occasionally his feelings of
hostility come out. Commenting on the Corpus Christi procession
through the streets of Montpellier, he writes:

> *This is the most* solemn procession *of the year, but if one judge either by
> the habits of the tradesmen or the hangings of the streets* which were in *many
> places* blankets & coverlids, *one is apt to think that either their* fortunes *or
> devotions were very scanty.*[3]

Another characteristic passage occurs in his description of the
Carthusian house which he visited at Villeneuve-lès-Avignon. There

[1] 7 April 1676.
[2] 16 April 1676. ('The book' is Jouvin's *Voyageur d'Europe*.)
[3] 4 June 1676.

he was shown the tomb of Pope Innocent VI and, in a small chapel, a 'plain, old chair in which he was infallible'. There follows the dry comment: 'I sat too litle a while in it to get that priviledg.'[1] At Tarascon on the following day he went to the church in which were displayed the relics of St Martha who is alleged to have converted the whole region and to have rid it of a monster called 'la Tarasque'. Here, however, his expectations were, as he explains, disappointed:

All the other Saints we had made visits to, received us very civily & allowd time to our curiosity to survey them, but St. Martha allowd us but a short apparition. For the priest that shewd us these sacred things, first producing the arme in silver guilt, the fingers whereof were loaden with rings with stones of value on them, & holding it out to us & discoursing upon it, but findeing we paid not that reverence was expected, he approachd it very neare the mouth of one of the company, & told him again that the bones that appeard through the cristal were the bones of St. Martha, which not prevailing with the hardened heretick for a kisse, he turned about in fury, put it up in the cubbard, drew the curtain before all the other things, & with the same quicknesse he that had refused to kisse, turnd about, went his way, & the rest followed him.[2]

A year later, at Toulouse on his journey northwards, he made the characteristic entry:

At the Church of St. Sernin *they tell us they have the bodies entire of 6 of the Apostles and the head of a 7th. This is much, considering what need there is of such reliques in other places, but yet notwithstanding they* promise *you 7 of the 12 Apostles.... We saw not these Apostles, but being told by a spiritual guide of the infalible church, we believed, which was enough for us.*[3]

Once he had left Languedoc and Provence behind, his notes on such manifestations of seventeenth-century French Catholicism tend to become less frequent. One of the rare allusions to such matters which he makes during his two stays in Paris is to what he saw in the Franciscans' chapel at St Denis:

I saw upon the west dore of the Church of the Cordiliers, graved on one of the valves, a litle statue in demi relieve & under it St. Hanry, & on the other a woman with her head in her hand & under it St. Denise, which two saints are noe thing but a man & his wife of those names which were benefactors to this covent, & St. Denise has her head in her armes by conformity to St. Denis, her namesake.[4]

---

[1] 22 April 1676.   [2] 23 April 1676.
[3] 30 March 1677.   [4] 24 April 1679.

The life of the religious Orders evidently had its interest for him. At Montpellier he had made careful notes on the ceremony of a nun taking the veil; and on his arrival in Paris he made an entry about a recent dispute in the Jacobins of the Rue St Jacques, who 'fell into civill war one with an other & went to gether by the ears', the battle growing so fierce that 'severall of them sallied out into the street & there cuffd it stoutly'—a scandal which caused Colbert to take administrative action against the culprits.[1] Towards the end of his stay in Paris, through his acquaintance with Father Chérubin, an authority on optics, he gained some insight into the life of the Capuchins, 'the strictest & severest order in France'. Father Chérubin had been able to continue his researches only through being given, by the King's order, a special lock and key to his cell, for the policy of the Order was to prevent a man who had any special skill from using it and to compel him to do quite different work. Indeed, Locke continues:

To mortifie those of their order they often command them seeming unreasonable things which, if not considered as conduceing to mortification, would be very irrationall & ridiculous, as to plant cabbadge plants the roots upwards & then reprehend the planter because they doe not grow.

For the remainder of this entry he made use of shorthand:

Sometimes also they order a brother to enter the refectoir *on all fours with an ass's pad on his back and a bridle in his mouth for* humiliation, *which happening once when a stranger was there, was like to have cost the* Gardian *his life.*[2]

The most outspoken passages in the second half of the Journal are to be found amongst those in which Locke describes his impressions of Angers during his visit there in the summer of 1678. In the now demolished chapel of the Minims he saw brass tablets, complete with portraits of the people who had left money to the Order for masses to be said for their souls after their death. He notes how all the portraits were of women—'for I saw noe men there soe pious'—and concludes:

Soe that if there be any benefit to be had from these things, it is, it seems, only for those who have faith & mony enough to pay for them.[3]

[1] 28 June 1677.　　[2] 19 March 1679.　　[3] 20 Aug. 1678.

This passage is only a prelude to the contemptuous irony with which he speaks of the display of relics which he saw at the Cathedral. These included 'the tooth of one Saint, the bone of another, etc. whose names I have quite forgotten as well as he had, of some of them, that shewd them us, though they were his old acquaintance'. But, he continues,

the things of most veneration were a thorn of the crown of Our Saviour, some wood of his crosse which I beleive was there, though I saw noe thing but the gold & silver that coverd it. There was also some of the haire, a peice of the petticoat & some of the milke of the Virgin, but the milke was out of sight.

Finally, he was shown one of the waterpots in which Christ turned water into wine at the wedding-feast of Cana.

That which made this morcell pretty hard of digestion was that it was porphyre, a sort of furniture a litle to costly in all appearance for the good man of the house where the weding was kept, & which made it yet worse, was a face in demy releive on that side that stood outwards, a way of ornament not much in use amongst the Jews.

Yet, he adds ironically, he would willingly have had the pot because of 'its admirable effects to cure diseases', for once a year it was filled with wine which was consecrated and distributed 'to beleivers who there with cure feavers & other diseases'.[1]

In contrast, the numerous entries in the Journal on the position of the Protestants before the Revocation of the Edict of Nantes are coolly detached and objective. During his three and a half years in France Locke's main contacts were with Huguenots: he lodged with them, at least during most of the time that he was settled in one place; he worshipped with them at Montpellier, at Charenton outside Paris, at Bègles outside Bordeaux; and he must have had endless conversations, both with laymen and pastors, on their gradually worsening position. Nevertheless there is no word of feeling in any of the numerous passages on the subject; and yet the very care with which he accumulated all this material, especially during his stay in the Protestant stronghold of Languedoc, bespeaks deep and genuine sympathy. However, despite the strong feelings which their persecution must have aroused in him, his objectivity

---

[1] 23 Aug. 1678.

was great enough to make him inquire, on separate occasions, both from Dr Barbeyrac and the senior pastor at Montpellier, René Bertheau, whether the lives of their co-religionists were better than those of the Catholics, and record their answers, that 'the Protestants live not better then the Papists',[1] and that '*there was very little* piety *or religion among their* people *and that the lives of the* Reformed *was* [sic] *no better than that of the Papists*'.[2]

As he was keenly interested in statistics, Locke collected a certain number of figures, which are perhaps worth quoting, on the vexed question of the number of Protestants in France before the Revocation. He noted, for instance, that Protestant christenings at Montpellier came to about 300 a year, and funerals to about 260.[3] He was told that the Protestants numbered one-sixteenth of the total population of France (i.e. just over a million if we take the generally accepted estimate of the population at this period), and that there were some 200,000 in Languedoc.[4]

Locke came to France too early to see with his own eyes the terroristic methods which were finally used to create a pretext for the Revocation of the Edict of Nantes in 1685: the fiction that since all the members of the Protestant minority had been converted, they had no further need of protective legislation. He thus did not witness the infamous *Dragonnades*, though there is a kind of foretaste of them in the story which he heard at Niort in the summer of 1678 from the lips of a 'poore bookseller's wife', in whose house two soldiers had been billeted the previous winter, which,

considering that they were to have 3 meales a day of flesh, breakfast, dinner & supper, besides a collation in the afternoon, all which was better to give them, & a 5th meale too if they desired it, rather then displease them, these 2 soldiers, for the $3\frac{1}{2}$ months they were there, cost them at least 40 ecus.[5]

Yet, during the period of his stay, open violence was not yet being used against the Protestant minority. The official policy still consisted in using milder and more subtle forms of pressure, such as making difficult the careers of those Huguenots who remained

---

[1] 5 Feb. 1676.   [2] 20 May 1676.
[3] 28 March 1676.   [4] 1 May 1676.
[5] 1 Sept. 1678.

faithful to their religion. The great nobleman who refused to be converted, found, like the Marquis de Malauze of whom Locke speaks,[1] that promotion in the army was blocked until he abjured his religion. Similar obstacles were put in the way of those Huguenots who belonged to the professional or trading classes. It is true that at Montpellier in 1676 Protestant advocates were still allowed to practise, and there were six Huguenots among the judges of the *Cour des Comptes*.[2] Yet that the trend was all in the other direction, is illustrated by such entries as: '*But ⅓ of any trade in any town suffered to pass masters, i.e. to set up, of those that are of the Religion.*'[3] Again, Protestant schools and academies were hemmed in by all sorts of restrictions which reduced their numbers, and when pastors tried to teach pupils in their own homes, this too was stopped. '*This fortnight*', wrote Locke in August 1676, '*Protestant ministers forbid to teach above 2 scholars at once*'.[4]

In Languedoc the Protestants had been by this time practically squeezed out of municipal offices, and were prevented from sitting in the Estates either as Barons or as deputies from the towns. At Nîmes Locke noted, the Protestants still had, like the Catholics, two *Consuls*, but at Montpellier they had long been excluded from municipal affairs, while at Uzès in January 1676, just as he arrived in the province, a Royal edict was issued ordering the inhabitants 'to choose noe more consuls of the town of the Religion'.[5] The hospitals which the Protestants had founded for their sick were taken out of the control of their community and handed over to the Catholics. At Nîmes, for instance, Locke observed:

The Protestants had built them here too an hospitall for their sick, but that is taken from them. A chamber in it is left for their sick, but never used, because the preists trouble them when there.[6]

The heaviest blow struck at the Protestant minority in the period between 1661 and 1680 was the demolition of their churches whenever the slightest contravention of the Edict of Nantes could be proved or even suggested. Everywhere he went Locke picked up complaints about these destructions. 'At Nismes', he wrote, 'they

---

[1] 20 Oct. 1676. [2] 17 Feb. 1676.
[3] 25 Oct. 1676. [4] 9 Aug. 1676.
[5] 31 Jan. 1676. [6] 3 Jan. 1676.

have now but one Temple (the other by the King's order being pulled down about 4 years since)'. At Montpellier he learned that the Protestants of Uzès were about to lose their church—'the only one they had left there, though ¾ of the town be Protestants'. 'The pretence given', he continued, and here he was well informed, 'is that their Temple being too near the papish church, their singing of psalms disturbed the service'. Shortly after his arrival in France he was told that 'within these 10 years at least 160 churches' had been destroyed.[1] The process continued so that, three years later, just before he left for home, he noted in his Journal: 'The Protestants within these 20 years have had above 300 churches demolishd, & within these 2 months 15 more condemned.'[2]

He occasionally gives us some information about the attitude of the French Protestants in face of this persecution. There was now no question of the Protestant minority offering, as they had done as late as the time of Richelieu, armed resistance to the Crown. From then down to the Revocation their spokesmen always proclaimed their complete loyalty to the Monarchy. In face of this increasing persecution Locke found only a patient resignation. In most places he observed a steadfast adherence to their religion. At Nîmes, for instance, he noted:

Notwithstanding their discouragement, I doe not finde that many of them goe over. One of them told me, when I asked him the question, that the Papists did noe thing but by force or mony.[3]

At Montpellier Dr Barbeyrac told him that 'they & the papist laity live togeather friendly enough' and that 'they sometimes get & sometimes loose proselytes'. His informant added that in recent times their number 'neither increases nor decreases much', and that the Catholic Church made converts only by making fine promises which were generally not fulfilled, or, in the case of poor people, by offering money.[4] A somewhat different picture was given him a few days later by another informant:

They tell me that the number of Protestants within these twenty or thirty last years are manifestly increased, & doe dayly, notwithstanding their losse every day of something, some priviledg or other.[5]

---

[1] 5 Feb. 1676.   [2] 25 April 1679.   [3] 3 Jan. 1676.
[4] 5 Feb. 1676.   [5] 12 Feb. 1676.

Only once, and then paradoxically enough in Provence where the Protestants were relatively weak, does he record a complaint. At Aix in 1676, in speaking of the tiny Protestant colony there (it consisted of four families), he noted that nine of the thirteen churches in the province had been demolished. 'They complain', he adds, 'that those who are garantie of the Edict of Nantes [i.e. the Protestant powers] interpose noe thing in their behalf'.[1]

A comparison of Locke's account of the gradually worsening conditions under which the French Protestants lived before the final persecution and the Revocation of the Edict of Nantes, with the relevant documents and with modern studies of the question, shows, that, as in other matters touched on in the Journal, on nearly every point he was extremely well informed. There is no doubt that he was a careful and shrewd observer, and that he strove to arrive at the truth. Fragmentary as the Journal is, and however tantalizing the gaps, it remains by far the fullest and most reliable account of life in seventeenth-century France left behind by an English traveller. As such it is, for the student of both national and local history, a document of great significance.

VI

Some account is now necessary of the methods used to reproduce here the text of the Journal and especially the shorthand sections of it. The shorthand system which Locke used, or rather adapted for his own purposes, was that first published in 1642 by Jeremiah Rich in his *Semography or Short and Swift Writing*.[2] Words and parts of words which are in shorthand in the MS., are italicized in this edition. It is impossible to discover any general principles underlying Locke's use of shorthand in the Journal for these years, for

---

[1] 19 April 1676.
[2] It is interesting to see what Locke has to say on the subject in *Some Thoughts concerning Education* (§ 161, 1): 'Short-hand, an art, as I have been told, known only in England, may perhaps be thought worth the learning, both for dispatch in what men write for their own memory, and concealment of what they would not have lie open to every eye. For he that has once learned any sort of character, may easily vary it to his own private use or fancy, and with more contraction suit it to the business he would employ it in. Mr. Rich's, the best contrived of any I have seen, may, as I think, by one who knows and considers grammar well, be made much easier and shorter.'

while it is clear that on occasion he used it for purposes of secrecy, the large-scale use of it seems to have been purely a matter of whim. Thus we find that, although the Journal opens in shorthand, long-hand predominates until May 1676. There is then an almost solid block of shorthand which lasts until April 1677 when he arrived in Bordeaux. After that its use is relatively restricted, and it is mostly kept for entries of a rather ticklish nature, though even in this period it is occasionally used for such harmless subjects as notes on the weather.

In transcribing the shorthand passages, it has been necessary to add the definite and indefinite articles which are nearly always omitted in the MS. Words in shorthand must inevitably be transcribed into modern spelling, even though this produces a certain clash with the spelling of the words in longhand which Locke almost invariably interspersed among the shorthand symbols in these passages. In the longhand entries the spelling of both French and English words has been reproduced in all its eccentric variety. On the other hand, there seemed little point in keeping the abbreviations which Locke frequently makes use of in these private notes. Such abbreviations as y^u for *you*, wch for *which*, y^e for *the*, ag^t for *against*, *K* for *King* and B^p for *Bishop* merely hinder rapid comprehension of the text, and since Locke used them to save time, it would be absurd to keep them when they have precisely the opposite effect for the reader. Occasionally letters and words which are missing in the MS. have been added to the text: these are indicated by square brackets.

In the shorthand passages punctuation is practically non-existent, while in the longhand entries it is, of course, based on principles very different from those accepted to-day. Indeed, since the Journal consists mostly of hastily written notes and jottings, the text is, even by seventeenth-century standards, underpunctuated. To present the text in its crude state would once again be to set up an un-necessary obstacle to its comprehension. Punctuation has therefore been modernized throughout, and this in its turn has necessitated some modifications in capitalization, especially at the beginning of sentences. In general, capitals have been added wherever modern usage requires them, though capital letters have been left in the text even when to-day they seem superfluous. The apostrophe, which Locke uses rarely, has been added wherever it is omitted in the MS.

It is hoped that in this form the text will satisfy both the historian of the language and the reader whose chief interest is in the matter of the Journal.

A NOTE ON FRENCH MONEY IN THE 1670's[1]

The basic unit of French money in the seventeenth century was the *livre tournois* or *franc*. This was divided into twenty *sous* and the *sou* into twelve *deniers*. Three *livres* made one *écu*, and eleven *livres* a *pistole* or *louis d'or*. Locke frequently uses the sign £ for *livres*, and adds *sterling* to indicate English pounds. From his frequent notes in the Journal on the rate of exchange we learn that he and his pupil received approximately thirteen *livres* for every pound sterling which they changed into French money.

---

[1] See the entries in the Journal for 1 Feb. 1676 and 11 Aug. 1678.

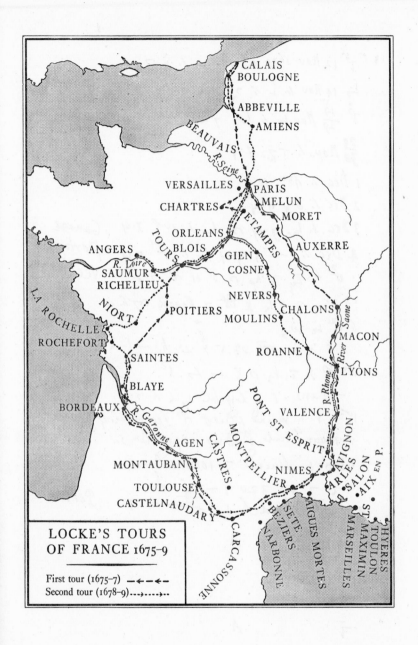

CALAIS
BOULOGNE

ABBEVILLE
AMIENS

BEAUVAIS

R. Seine

VERSAILLES · PARIS
MELUN
CHARTRES
MORET
ETAMPES

ORLEANS
AUXERRE
ANGERS BLOIS
TOURS GIEN
R. Loire COSNE
SAUMUR
RICHELIEU
NEVERS
NIORT POITIERS CHALONS
MOULINS

R. Saone

LA ROCHELLE
MACON
ROCHEFORT
ROANNE
SAINTES LYONS

BLAYE

R. Rhone
BORDEAUX
R. Garonne VALENCE
AGEN
CASTRES
MONTPELLIER
PONT ST ESPRIT
MONTAUBAN
AVIGNON
TOULOUSE NIMES ARLES SALON
CASTELNAUDARY AIX EN P.
SETE
CARCASSONNE BEZIERS AIGUES MORTES MARSEILLES
NARBONNE ST MAXIMIN
HYERES
TOULON

LOCKE'S TOURS
OF FRANCE 1675–9

First tour (1675–7) ← – ← –
Second tour (1678–9) ⋯→⋯→

1

12 Nov 1675 [...]

14 Nov [...] Calais
33

19/29 Nov [...]

28/30 Nov. [...] 7·4

1 Dec /. [...] 10·4

2 Dec /. [...] 9·4

3 Dec /. [...] 9·4 [...] 3·4   ~~Cariage~~
4 Dec /. [...] 8·4   portage
[...]   Vectura
                      7

12 [...] Bagage [...]

6 [...]

[...] Diging

[...]

— Paris [...] hospital [...]

[...] maind soldiers [...] Ley invalidy Invalides
1 magnificent building capeable [...]
les [...] finisd 7 1000 soldiers

[...] 3207 — [...]

* 1 vil Brisack [...]   Pension

1675   A

A

The first page of the Journal
(MS. Locke f. 1)

THE JOURNAL

1675

Friday. 12 NOV. 1675. *In the evening I went to Gravesend.*

Sunday. 14 NOV. *Took water at Dover and that day arrived at Calais.*

Calais

Friday. 19/29 NOV. *Went to Boulogne, 7 leagues.*

20/30 NOV. *To Montreuil, 7 leagues.*[1]

1 DEC. *To Abbeville, 10 leagues.*

2 DEC. *To Poix, 9 leagues.*

3 DEC. *To Beauvais, 9 leagues, and thence to Tillart, 3 leagues.*

4 DEC. *To Beaumont, 5 leagues, thence to Paris, 8 leagues. I paid to the messenger for horse and diet between Calais and Paris* 12 *crowns, and* 3 *sous* per lb. *for* bagage, *except shoes and* 6 lbs. *which were allowed.*

Portage[2] Vectura

I saw on the way peasants digging their vineyards with hoes made something like ours, but much broader and turned more toward the handle.

Diging

In Paris I saw the great hospital which this King of France has built for his maimd soldiers, *called* Les Invalids.[3] *'Tis a* magnificent building capeable, *as they told us,* when finishd, of 1000 soldiers. *Length of front* 320 *of my paces.*

Invalides

At the Vil Brisack[4] *we were in pension for* 20 s. *a day, but paid beside for fire and candle;* but N. lay at Madame Varennes' au bas d'or au Palais[5] for 10 crowns per *month.*

Pension

---

[1] For a fuller account of Locke's journey from Boulogne to Beaumont see the fragment of a draft of a letter written by him to a friend, reproduced in Appendix A (pp. 276 f.).

[2] The word 'Cariage' is crossed out.

[3] Founded by Louis XIV in 1670, the Hôtel des Invalides was begun in 1671 and completed, except for the dome which was added later, in 1676.

[4] The *Ville de Brisach* was a Protestant inn in the Rue de Seine, Faubourg Saint-Germain (see Tallemant des Réaux, *Historiettes*, ed. G. Mongrédien, Paris, 1932–4, 8 vols., v. 304).

[5] Skippon (p. 731) describes Varennes as 'the only Protestant bookseller' in the Palais de Justice.

Cough
Tussis
At Paris *the greatest part of the people had colds as they had in* England *when we left it, so that they called it the* maladie a la mode.

14 DEC. *We took* coach *at* Paris *in the diligence for* Lyons *and, after having dined at* Melun, *got by an hour or 2 in the night to* Moret *where we* lodged. *It is* 16 leagues from Paris.

15 DEC. *Before 4 in the* morning *we were in the* coach. Dind at Pont
Joyny sur Yonne & reached Joyny,[1] 17 Leagues.

16 [DEC.] *We dined* at Auxerre & hitherto kept company with the Yonne for the most part, which is navigable hither & higher & the country plain. Past this towne the country begins to be more hily
Lacie le Bois & very stony & thence more fild with vineards. We lay at Lacie le Bois,[2] 15 Leagues, *where we had* miserable lodging, *but that must be borne with in* France.

Arnan le Duc 17 DEC. *We lay at* Arnan le Duc,[3] 14 Leagues. The country here began to be very unequall & rocky & had more inclosures then the other parts from Paris hither, & some what like England, but noe vineards all this day, but great woods & cornfields & some pastures
Lignum which I had seldom seen in other parts of France. Wood at Arnan le Duc soe cheape that a load as much as 3 horses could draw is bought there ready cut in the woods for 20s. This day we also saw
Oxen carriages drawn with oxen, but the harnesse was fastened to their hornes, & the catle were very little.

Chany 18 DEC. We dind at a litle town cald Chany,[4] 8 Leagues, the country hilly & rocky, much like the country about Bath. Noe milk to be got here or at the 2 last nights' quarters.[5] The sides of the hills had
Challon vineards. 8 horses in our diligence & 2 postilions. Lay at Challon,[6] 3 Leagues, an old, but pretty large towne.

19 DEC. We took boat at Challon on the Saone, a quiet, slow runing river, as broad as the Thames at Hendly. It passes through a pleasant vally, the hills about ½ mile distant on each side, some

[1] Joigny.   [2] Lucy-le-Bois.
[3] Arnay-le-Duc.   [4] Chagny.
[5] Smollett tells us that he had the same experience in this part of France: 'Almost all the ground seems to be ploughed up, so that there is little or nothing lying fallow. There are very few inclosures, scarce any meadow ground, and, so far as I could observe, a great scarcity of cattle. We sometimes found it very difficult to procure half a pint of milk for our tea' (p. 71).   [6] Châlons-sur-Saône.

places more, some lesse, coverd with wood & corne, but most wood.
We passed by Tornus,[1] a litle, olde towne, the buildings ill & old,   Tornus
the walls decayd, in it an Abby belonging to the Cardinall of   Abbatium
Bouillon, worth 20,000 crowns per annum.[2] The day very fair & the
aire as temperate as it uses to be with us about the later end of
September. On this side Paris we felt very litle cold, but hard frost
between Calais & Paris.

In the boat we played for doubles, *at which, I having won* 3 d., *the*
French were willing to avoid paying. M. l'Abbé and a woman lay in
the same chamber, as the first night, and so 2 *or* 3 *nights after.*

    5 Leagues from Tornus we came to Mascon where we lay. This   Mascon
town seemed the most thriving that I had seen on this side Paris.
It is a town about the bignesse of Bath or litle bigger. The roofs
of the houses very flat, covered with pan tiles & the eves extended
6 or 8 or more feet beyond the walls, soe that they in some places
almost coverd the street quite over, & sat on the houses like an
Oxford cap on a scholler's head. In it a Cathedrall & another church,
whose Canons, being 12, were to be noblesse per four discents.[3]

20 [DEC.] We enterd our boat again & at 5 leagues' distance came to
a pretty towne calld Bel-Ville which well deservd that name, being   Belville
situated in a pleasant plain on the west part of the river, having on
the West at a little distance a high mountain which, at a mile or
two distance or some places more, ran along the tract of this river
almost all this day's journey. A league from Belville we came to
Vil Franche where, what with the towne situate on a gentle rise at   Ville Franque
the bottom of the mountain, & the country houses all about for
a league or 2 downe the river, & the side of the mountain divided
into woods & vineards, & the sun there shining on them, I scarce
ever saw a finer prospect. On the side of this mountain we saw
a very fine, large, new house built by a merchant of Lyons.

    Two Leagues farther we came to Trevou[4] on the east side of the   Trevou

---

  [1] Tournus.
  [2] Emmanuel Théodose de la Tour d'Auvergne (1643–1715), a nephew of Turenne,
was made a Cardinal at the age of twenty-six. He later fell into disgrace with the King
and was exiled for a time to his Abbey at Tournus. Later he was allowed to retire to
Rome where he died. Locke appears to have exaggerated his income from this abbey.
  [3] *O.E.D.* 'generations'. MS. has 'p.', presumably standing for *per*.
  [4] Trévoux.

river, just on the Thon,[1] a principality of Mademosile Mompansier.[2]
Here we saw[3] a maypole, a little town on a riseing ground, & a castle
just above it. The tract of mountains on the west side this river were

Baujolais in some places very high (called Montain de Baujolais),[4] which,
they say, accompanys this river to the Rhosne & that to the sea.
From thence to Lyons 3 leagues, all the sides of the river beset with
fine houses, some where of were very large & most belonging to the
merchants & inhabitants of Lyon. They are all very flat roofd,
coverd with pan tiles as those of Mascon. Soe that from Vill
Franch to Lyons we were never out of sight of severall fine houses
& vilages, but the thicker the nearer Lyon, soe that I count this one
of the pleasantest places I have seen.

Vectura   Thus in 7 days we came from Paris to Lyon, 100 leagues, in
Portage a coach cald the diligence for which we paid 25 crowns. The passage
to Challon in it was very troublesom, for we were most commonly
cald up every morning between 2 & 3, staid about an hower at
dinner & then on till an hower or 2 in night, & were some times
inconveniently enough lodgd. To light the coach in the dark
mornings the postilion carried a great bundle of wases[5] before him
which were our Flambeaux, & we carried a candle & contrivd in
the coach to light them again when they went out. The passage
from Challon by water was very easy & convenient & the river very
quiet.

Lyons 21 DEC. We visited Mr. Charleton & Mr. Williams[6] who treated us
extreame civilly. They shewed us upon the top of the hill a church

---

    [1] Dombes.
    [2] Louise d'Orléans, Duchesse de Montpensier (1627–93), daughter of Gaston
d'Orléans and cousin of Louis XIV, known as *La Grande Mademoiselle*.
    [3] The last three words are doubtful, being written on top of others.
    [4] I.e. 'Monts de Beaujolais'.
    [5] *O.E.D.* 'a wisp or bundle of straw or weeds: in early examples with reference to its
use as torch'.
    [6] 'Mr. Williams' is not readily identifiable, but William Charleton (1642–1702) is
a better-known, if enigmatic, figure. His real name was William Courten. He assembled
a large natural history collection which was bought by Sir Hans Sloane and is to-day
part of the British Museum. There are 29 of his letters in the Lovelace Collection which
show that he remained in Montpellier until 1681, when he moved to Paris. In the
following year he spent a fortnight in the Bastille. A voluminous dossier (Archives de
la Bastille, No. 10,384) describes him as 'Etranger et religionnaire de Montpellier
suspect de tenir pour ceux de la R.P.R. et d'intelligence avec les ennemis de l'etat'.

now dedicated to the Virgin Mary which was formerly a Temple of Venus. Neare it dwelt Thomas Becket, when banishd out of England.[1]

22 DEC. We saw the Jesuits' Colledg.[2] At the first entrance there is a pretty large quadrangle, all the sides of which are high buildings, having the walls coverd with various pretty well painted figures, representing some the 4 parts of the world, others other things which, for want of time & a instructer, we could not soe particularly observe. Only there was represented, in one row of them continued quite round the square, in certain squares put at a distance, the most considerable accidents that had happened to this citty. Within we saw noe thing but the library which is the best that ever[3] I saw except Oxford, being one very large, high, oblong square, all set with shelves as high as one can well reach standing upon a stoole, & above a galery round to come at the books. Out of this goes an other round, not soe high nor broad, like a litle short galery. This is the forme: It is yet but moderately furnishd with books, being made, as they told us, not above a year agon. It stands very pleasantly on the banke of the Rhosne, & hath a very excellent prospect, but it being a misty day (which often happens here at this time of the yeare), we could see noe thing.

We saw also Mr. Servir's Closet, *an old, morose, half-mad Gent.*,[4] where were many excellent peices of turning in ivory,

Jesuits' Colledg

Mr. Servir Musaeum

According to this account, Charleton, who had spent five years at Montpellier, 'a eu commerce avec les dits Religionnaires touchant la demolition de leur temple et les memoires qu'ils vouloient présenter au Roy pour avoir la permission d'en faire batir un hors la ville de Montpellier'. He was also suspected of carrying on a correspondence with 'quelques milords d'Angleterre'. In an article in the *Revue de Littérature Comparée* (1933, p. 593 n.) M. René Ternois declares that Charleton was in the pay of Louis XIV. His letters to Locke refer somewhat mysteriously to his secret reasons for being out of England, but otherwise throw little light on his activities in France.

[1] The chapel of Fourvières, built on the site of a temple of Venus. I have been unable to trace any evidence of Becket's stay at Lyons, but an earlier chapel of Fourvières had been founded by one of his friends, Olivier de Chavannes.

[2] Now the Lycée Ampère; only the old chapel remains.   [3] MS. has *every*.

[4] This famous museum, visited by Louis XIV in 1658, is fully described by the owner's grandson, Grollier de Servières, in his *Recueil d'ouvrages curieux de mathématique et de mécanique ou description du cabinet de M. Grollier de Servières* (Lyons, 1719).

better then ever I had seen any where, some of them inclosed in glasses, very hard to conceive how they were got in, espetially one fine, branchd, hangeing candle stick, a ring in wood as at Oxford, but soe that one might perceive the Sodder.[1] Also short peices of wood of one sort put into holds of wood an other[2] & turnd there, both whose ends were bigger then the hole. Many sorts of clocks, espetially some that goe with their own weight rolling upon declind[3] peices of wood, a great many modells of pumps & other engines which, he haveing not Latin nor I French, besides the particular temper of the man, I could not particularly enquire into. 2 things there were of use. A way he had there with 2 threads slideing upon a ruler to draw any plain figure into perspective, the place of view & distance being given. The other was the way of designeing any prospect by a mouving index & a pencill fastend to it mouving on paper, & a sight through which to govern the Index by your eyes. A good microscope. Some magneticall tricks rather then experiments. A dore in a paire of dornes[4] with 2 locks where of, when you lock one, the dore would turn, as it were, on hinges on one side;[5] if you unlockd the other, it turned on hinges on the other side. There were severall other pretty curiositys which would have taken up long time to examin. Also the cubberd that changed scenes only upon locking and unlocking the dore.[6]

St. John's   23 [DEC.] We saw St. John's Church, the Cathedrall of the place, a very plain, ordinary building, & had noe thing in it very observable
Horologium   but the clock, which they say cost 200,000 livres. It hath many motions, but I had not time to observe them all accuratly. There is a minute hand moves round in an hower, & the minutes are marked out in it in equall spaces on an oval, not a circle, & both ends of the hand keepe stil even with the inner line that describes the oval, shortening & lengthening stil as they approach the lesse or greater axis of the oval, & the end of every hower a cock that stands

---

[1] *O.E.D. solder.*   [2] I.e. of another sort?
[3] *O.E.D. sloped.*   [4] *O.E.D. the framework of a doorway.*
[5] MS. has 'one one side'.
[6] See Grollier de Servières, op. cit., p. 19. The scenes which were changed by turning a key in the lock were (1) a château and garden; (2) gold and silver coins; (3) flowers; (4) a collation.

on top of all, claps his wings & crows. Then an angel comes out of
a little door & visits the Virgin. She bows. A dove descends, & the
image of an old man, designed for the Father, shakes his hand. This
is what is most looked at, but of least moment, there being other
things far more considerable in it, as the place of the sun, the
dominical letter, Epact, golden number, moveable feasts, etc., and
other things of an almanac for almost an hundred years yet to come.

24 DEC. I saw a litle castle, cald the Peir encise,[1] upon the river   Peire encise
Sone, at its entrance into the town. It is a place used to keepe
prisoners, & indeed is much fitter to keep criminals in then enemies
out. It is a litle, irregular fortification on a rock, which hath a precipice on all sides, & is extream high towards the river & two other
sides, but is of noe strengthe, being commanded by hils much
higher then it, that hangs [sic] over it on one side from the river.
The way up to it is a litle pair of stairs where two can hardly passe.
Here Fouquet[2] was once prisoner.

Here & some time before it comes hither, the Sone passes (in
a very narrow bottom not much broader then the river) between
very high, steep, rocky hills which continue all a long on the right
hand beyond its joyning with the Rhosne, but a litle within the
towne the hils on the left hand of this river turne short towards
the Rhosne, & soe leave a long, plain neck of land between these
two rivers, on which the greatest part of this citty is built, in narrow,
irregular streets & high stone houses, flat roofd & coverd with pan
tiles & some turrets & the angles of the roofs with latin.[3] A good
part of the town lyes also on the right hand the Sone, & the sides
of the hills on both sides the town are set with houses & other
buildings with gardens, orchards & vineards up to the top, soe that
it is a pleasant place. The Town House[4] here is a stately building.   Maison de
                                                                         ville

25 [DEC.] I saw the town from the hil on the north side where is   Hostel de
a fair prospect of it lying on the promontory south from this   Dieu
                                                                     Nosodochium

---

[1] An old form of Pierre-Scize, derived from the Latin *Petra incisa* (Mme Du Noyer
writes the name 'Perre-Encise'). There is nothing left of the castle to-day.

[2] Nicolas Fouquet (1615–80), Finance Minister of Louis XIV until his arrest and
trial in 1661. He presumably passed through Lyons on his way to Pignerol after being
sentenced to imprisonment for life in December 1664.

[3] *O.E.D. latten*: 'a mixed yellow metal like brass'.

[4] Built between 1646 and 1655.

riseing, the greatest part between the two rivers. I saw also the Hostel Dieu, a fair, large Hospital, containing, as they told me, 500 sick persons. They lye in a room which is a large crosse, & 3 rows of beds in each[1] & in one part 2 in a bed, in the other but one, as I observd. Two of the arms of the crosse have men, the other two women. In the center is an altar.

Procodochium
Charité

We went also to see the Charite, where bastards are receivd & bred.[2] We could get in noe farther then the outer court & the Chappell, where we staid & heard the women there sing Vespers which they did well, both in vocal & in instrumentall musick. They performed a great part of the evening service & were of those that had been bred up in that house.

Prochodo-
chium

26 DEC. I saw the Charitie, consisting of 9 square courts, & there were in it then, as I was told, 1500 maintaind & lodgd there. There they receive bastards, male & female, &, as soon as they are able, are imploid in winding silk, the manner whereof, it being holy day, we could not see. The most considerable thing we saw was their

Granary
Horreum

granary, 100 steps long & 36 broad, windows open all round. It stands on the banks of the Rhosne. There are constantly in it 6,135 asnees of wheat. When we were there,[3] they told us there were more in it. One asnee is an asse load of 6 bushells. They turne all the corne every day, about which 7 men are imployd. When the boys are grown up big enough, they binde them out to trades, & the girles they either marry or put into nunnerys. It is a very noble foundation, and hath a large revenue.

Vienne

After this, we took horse & rode to Vienne, 5 leagues. The way is somewhat hilly towards Vienne. Vienne is an old towne, ancienter then Lyons, but Lyons hath swallowed it, for it looks decaying. They said there were many antiquities, but I saw noe thing but

Passer
solitarius

some old Roman medals, a bird they call passer solitarius, somewhat bigger then a larke, of a black & yellow colour, that sings very well, but the bird is rare. The owner of this asked 3 Luidors[4] for it.

---

[1] Presumably 'arm' understood.
[2] All that remains to-day of this building is the belfry of the chapel. Cf. the fuller description given in the entry for 7 Nov. 1678.
[3] These four words are repeated at the end of the sentence in the MS.
[4] 3 louis d'or, i.e. 33 livres.

27 DEC. We went 7 leagues to St. Valer[1] through a pleasant valey by   St. Valer
the Rhosne, fild with corne feilds & these coverd with walnut trees
& mulberrys, the mulberry trees in many places set in exact
quincunx & at the distance of our apple trees in England.

28 DEC. To Valence 7 leagues, a pretty large town, ill built, the   Valence
Cathedral the plainest I had any where seen. The Schola Juris et
Medicinae here very meane. As we came along, we passed by the
Hermitage, the place soe famous for wine. It is the side of a hill   Hermitage
lying open to the south and a little west, about a mile long,
begining just at Thuin.[2] We saw also the Citadell which we got   Thuin
into with some difficulty, & there was reason for the caution, we
being 4 & there being a garison in it but of one man and one great
gun, which was left behind, when the King lately took away all the
rest for his ships, for a fault very frequent in this country, viz. in
the touch hole.

29 DEC. To Montelimar,[3] 8 leagues. This towne is wald,[4] as Valence   Montlimar
is, the streets broader & the buildings better, but the town not
altogether soe big.

30 DEC. From Montelimar to Pon St. Esprit, 5 leagues. A league   St. Esprit
from Montlimar we came to a little town cald Chasteauneuf, where   Chasteauneuf
had formerly been a citadell which now is demolishd, & the towne
very litle & very poor in appearance.

From Vienne to this place we had passed all along a valey without
any considerable rise at all in soe many days' journey, having all
the way the Rhosne on the right hand & high, barren hill[s] of
Dauphiné on the left. This valley is in some places a league or
2 broad, in some broader and in some very narrow, & in a great
part of the journey the soyle was coverd with great round pebbles,
in some places soe thick that noe earth was to be seen, & yet all   Husbandry
along there was corne sowed, though in many places the mulberry   Agricultura
& almond trees, set in quincunx, coverd the corne as thick as apple
trees in an Orchard in England. In many places walnut trees were
set up & down in the cornfield, & the wheat green under them as

---

[1] Saint-Vallier.   [2] Tain.
[3] Montélimar.   [4] 'walled.'

the other trees quite to the stocks.[1] In this valley we saw severall diging the ground, & other where [sic] some a ploughing with a very litle, light plow with one handle, drawne by a pair of cows, steers or asses which the ploughman drives himself. The soyle is generally light & sandy, & they turne it up with their ploughs not above 2 or 3 inches deepe.

In this valley we crossd many rivers & rivulets; one by ferry, some by bridges & most of the rest by ford, & the channels of some quite drye; but these & all of them appeared to be sometimes great & swift torrents, when either raine or melted snow is powerd down into them from the high hils of Dauphiné, which lay all along on the left hand of our way.

Pilati domus   About half a league from St. Valer we saw an house, a litle out of the way, where they say Pilate lived in Banishment. We met with the owner who seemed to doubt the truth of the story,[2] but told us there was Mosaic work very ancient in one of the floors.

Chasteau Neuf   At Chasteau Neuf sur Rhosne we got up a hill which runs directly to the Rhosne, & the Rhosne through it, as the Avon at the Hot Well.[3] The surface of this hill was most part rocke; much box, a great deale of Lavender, little or noe grasse, but where ever there was earth, the country men improved it to corne or wine. From the top of this hil we had a prospect into a large valey, much broader then any part of that between Vienn & Chasteau Neuf.

Pallu   Three leagues from Chasteau Neuf we came to Pallu,[4] a litle town belonging to the Pope.

Pont St. Esprit   1 league from thence we came to Pont St. Esprit. There is a bridg over the Rhosne, long on the heighth over the great arches, which are 18, 1100 of my steps. The ascent to the top about 120 steps, over 6 lesser arches at the east side. On the west how many arches there be, I know not, but they recon 27 in all, besides a litle one between each of the 18 great ones. The bridg is very narrow, not roome for 2 carriages to meet & pass, well paved with litle, square, blew stones very regularly placed. At the end of it, on the west side, is the town of Pont St. Esprit & a citadell to guarde the bridge & the Rhosne. In it we saw some soldiers &

---

[1] 'trunks.'   [2] His scepticism is shared by modern authorities.
[3] The Hot Wells, at Bristol.   [4] Lapalud.

4 litle brasse guns, but never an one mounted. The bridg is not exactly straight, but about the midle makes an obtuse angle towards the current of the river.

3 Leagues from Pont St. Esprit we came to Orange, a litle towne Orange within a square wall, lesse then Bath within the wals. The half moons at the entrance of the gates are demolishd by the King of France, & the castle which was upon a rocky hill just over it.[1] Here we also saw Marius's triumphant arch, a peice of very handsom building with trophys etc. & Marius's old sybil on it. There remains also a very stately peice of Roman building, very high, & 176 of my steps in front, on 17 arches. They cal it an amphytheater, but the figure of it seems not at all to favour that opinion, it being thus ⌐_____⌐ as it now stands. There is also in the floor of a litle house mosaic worke very perfect, divided into squares something like our inlaid floors. There was but one figure in that which we saw, which was of a cat, the bignesse of the life.

Here I also saw the way of windeing silk by an engine that Bombycina turnes at once 134 bobins. It is too intricate to be described upon Silkwindeing soe short a view, but all these were turned by one woman, & they both twisted & wound off the silk at once.

The Parlement of the towne are 12, ½ Protestants & ½ Papists, & 4 Consuls, 2 Protestants & 2 Papists. There are 2 Protestant churches in the towne. One we were in of a pretty sort of building, one long stone arch, like a bridg, runing the whole length of the church, & supporting the rafters like the main beam of the building, a new, but not incommodious way for such a room.

31 DEC. We came to Avignion,[2] 4 leagues from Orange, part of the Avignon way over a hil & part through a valey, both very stony, covered thick with pebbles, & amongst those pebbles mulberry trees, corne & vineards.

Avignon is placed in a large valey on the banks of the Rhosne, which goes about half round it. The wals are all entire (& noe

---

[1] The town, which belonged to the family of Orange-Nassau, was seized by Louis XIV in 1660; the fortifications and later the castle were demolished, though the territory was not formally incorporated in France until the Treaty of Utrecht (1713).

[2] Avignon and the territory around it, known as *Le Comtat Venaissin*, were acquired by Pope Clement VI in 1348 and remained in papal hands until 1791.

houses near them) with batlements & towers at litle distances, after
the old way of fortification. The compasse of the walls is about

ᵃ Vid. Le
Voyageur
d'Europe¹ 6,000 common paces.ᵃ The streets wider & the town better built
then any between this & Lyons. The Pope's Pallace is a large, old
building with high towers. We saw, besides the hall, 3 or 4 rooms
of a row, 2 hung with damask & beds of the same, but old. In
another part of the Pallace a very large, handsome roome where
formerly the conclave was kept when the Popes kept their residence
here.²

1676

Nostre Dame WEDNESDAY 1 JAN. 1676. The Church of Nostre Dame is placed
upon an high rock above the towne close by the Palace. The quire
St. Peter's of St. Peter's church is very rich in guilding & painting, & soe is
Celestins the altar of the Celestines' Church, & their covent, a very large one,
kept very cleane. Here were roses blown at this time, & by the way
between this & Lyons we had green pease, though but a few. It
was here soe warme that we dind without fire with the windows
open. The Vice Legate went to the Jesuits' Church with a guard of
about 12 Swisse.

Judaei   Here the Jews have a quarter to themselves where they have
Jews a synagoge. The place where they inhabit is the nastiest & most
stinking that ever I was yet in, & they all clad like beggers, though
we were told some of them were rich. They were yellow hats for
distinction, as at Orange, where are about 12 familys of them.

Here are some arches standing of the bridge which was built much
after the fashion of Pont St. Esprit, but some years since it fell,³
& to encourage the rebuilding of it, this last yeare upon the Key
(which is a very handsome one) they have set up the statue of one
Rodanus St. Benedict, a shepheard, who built the former bridg.⁴ The
Rhosne Rhosne is sometimes very unruly, soe that about the middle of

---

¹ By Jouvin de Rochefort, Paris, 1672. Vol. 1 deals with France.
² From 1309 to 1378.
³ After many mishaps the Pont Saint-Bénézet was destroyed in 1670 by the freezing
of the Rhône and never restored.
⁴ Between 1177 and 1185, according to the legend.

November 1674 it overflowed the head of the Statue of a Bishop which stands there on the Key &, I beleive, is at least 15 foot higher then the top of the water as it now is. At the same time it overflowd all the plain about Pon St. Esprit & made it a sea. Some marks of this inundation we saw on the way a good way off the river.

Avignon is governed by a Vice Legate. The present is Carolus Anguisciola de Picansa, a fat, well-looked man. The imployment is worth about five thousand pounds sterling per annum. There is noe taxe laid upon this country which is   ¹ long and   ¹ broad. Here is also an Archbishop, cald at present Jacinto Libelli of Perugia. His revenue is much above that of the Vice Legate's, but the donation of all the spiritualitys is wholly in the Vice Legate.

The greatest part of the trade of this towne is silk manifacture, & the town, as it is bigger then any between this & Lyons, soe the people look more comfortably, & the towne more thriving, & the streets are broader. Here we staid a whole day & paid one liver² per meale for each of us, & one liver per night for our horses, & 10s. for Mr. Charleton's servant per diem.

2 JAN. 1676. TH. We passed the Rhosne partly by the Trill,³ a way of Ferry usuall in these parts, & partly by the remains of the bridge, at the end whereof we paid a toll of 3s. per person & 3s. for our portmanteaus, but were not searchd nor examind what we carried, as we expected, our Voiturine making us passe for Swisse.

Hence we went to Pont du Gard, 4 leagues over barren, rocky   Pont du Gard hils, a good part of the way well stord with time, & pebly vallys. The bridge it self is an admirable structure, vid. the discription of it in Le Voyageur d'Europe, p. 144, 8º, Paris, 1672. In this day's journey we passed by a grove of oaks, & those noe very good ones, the only place that I saw between this & Lyon that had any shew of timber. At Pont du Gard some of the arches of the 2nd row were 30 steps wide.

Memoranda the *house of office*⁴ at the Celestins in Avignion.

---

¹ Left blank in MS.   ² French *livre*.

³ Not in *O.E.D.* Presumably for French *traille*, described by Jouvin (1, 78) in the following passage: 'Nous repassâmes la rivière [the Rhône] dans une barque qui, de son propre mouvement (je veux dire, sans ramer ni travailler), traverse l'eau par le moyen d'une corde, qu'ils appellent la *traille*, laquelle se glisse par le moyen d'une petite poulie le long d'un gros câble qui est élevé d'un bord à l'autre de la rivière'.

⁴ *O.E.D. privy.*

Vineae   Between Orange & this we saw them pruning their vines in
severall places, some vineards being prund, some not, & soe on all
the way to Montpellier.

Nismes   3 JAN. FRID. We went from Pont du Gard to Nismes, 4 leagues.
Amphitheater   Here we saw an amphitheater of very large stones, an admirable
structure, if we consider that it hath stood ever since the Romans'
time & built without any mortar. At the entrance, which is under
an arch, the wall is 17 of my paces thick. Ascending up a paire of
stairs we came to a walke round in which there is, towards the
outside from whence the light comes, 60 Arches in the whole
circumference, the space of each arch being 11 of my paces, so that
in the whole circumference it is 660 of my steps in a circle 2 or
3 yards within the out most bounds of it, for soe thick is the wall in
all those arches. To support the walls over the passage where you
goe round, there is a stone laid, about 20 inches or 2 foot square &
almost 6 times the length of my sword, which was near ab ut
a philosophical yard[1] long, upon which were turnd other arcnes
contrary to those by which the light enterd & were open to the
outside. Most of these stones I observed in my walk round to be
crackd, which I suppose might be the effect of the fire which the
Christians heretofore applied to this Amphitheatre with designe to
Deyron   destroy it, as Deyron tells us in his Antiquites de Nismes, 4°,
Nismes, 1663....[2]

Thus stands almost entire yet this wonderfull structure inspight
of the force of 1500 years & the attempts of the first Christians who
endeavord both by fire & with tools to ruin it. There are a great
many other antiquitys remaining in this towne, which who will,
may see exactly describd by Deyron....

On the east side upon a pillaster of this Amphitheater is a priapus
in memory of Osyris, the father of Nemausus, the founder of
Nismes. On the West another[3] with 2 lesse at the root of it, bridled,

---

[1] I.e. three philosophical feet, a form of linear measurement invented by Locke
(English foot = 0·920 of his philosophical foot); cf. entry for 29 Jan. 1678.
[2] Both this paragraph and the next are followed by extracts and summaries of
passages from this work.
[3] This was removed in 1822, according to Mérimée (*Notes d'un voyage dans le Midi*,
p. 366) because of the intervention of the Bishop of Nîmes.

& a woman holding the reins, both winged. For the use of Nismes   Pont du Gard
& the Theater there the aqueduct of Pont du Gard was built &, as
is supposed, about the same time. Pont du Gard is built over the
river Gardon on 3 rows of Arches, one over an other: 136 canes
longue, 31 canes high above the water of the river, & 3 canes
4 pans broad; the water course 4 pans broad & as high as one's
midle.[1] It caried the water of the Fountain d'Aure to Nismes from
whence it is 3 leagues, but the aqueduct, sometimes carried on
Arches, sometimes cut through rocks, is 9 leagues long. On
Pont du Gard is an other priapus & is all of huge stones.

At Nismes they have now but one Temple (the other by the   Protestantes
King's order being pulled down about 4 years since),[3] its roof   La Religion[2]
supported on an Arch like that at Orange. 2 of their Consuls are
Protestants, two Papists, but are not permitted to receive the
sacrament in their robes as formerly. The Protestants had built
them here too an hospitall for their sick, but that is taken from
them.[4] A chamber in it is left for their sick, but never used,
because the preists trouble them when there, but notwithstanding
their discouragement, I doe not finde that many of them goe over.
One of them told me, when I asked him the question, that the
Papists did noe thing but by force or money.

Their fountain is about the bignesse of an ordinary pond, but,
they say, bottomlesse.

Here I saw also an engine to twist & winde silke.[5] Two winches   Bombicina
going in a wheele turnd 3 engines w[h]ere in were turnd at once
30 dozen of bobbins. It is too curious a thing to be describd at
large, & requires a longer time to observe all the parts of it. The
town is now but small, not soe big, I think, as Reading, but its
girdle is shrunk with its body, haveing walls close about it.[6]

---

[1] For these measures see the entry for 21 Feb. 1676 (8 *pans* = 1 *canne* = 6 ft. 6½ in.).
[2] I.e. 'la religion prétendue réformée', the official name for Protestantism in Catholic
France in the seventeenth century.
[3] Though the Protestants were in a substantial majority in Nîmes, the smaller of their
two churches was demolished by order of the government in 1664.
[4] The hospital was handed over to Catholic control in 1666.
[5] Nîmes was an important centre of the silk industry which was severely hit by the
emigration of Protestants after the Revocation of the Edict of Nantes.
[6] There follow some incomplete notes on the *canne* and *pan*.

Montpellier SAT. 4 JAN. We arrived at Montpellier late in the night, haveing dined at a Protestant Inn at Lunel, 3 leagues from Montpellier, where we were well used. But Mr. Girald's breakfast, who enterteind us at Nismes in the morning, made this day's journey of 8 leagues to keep us on horseback till within night. We lodged at the Pettit Paris[1] & paid there 2 l. per day for meat, drink, lodging, candle & fire. A bottle in ice to coole the drinke was used even at this time of the year.

SUNDAY 5 JAN. Having horses, we rode out to the seaside, which is a league from the town southward. Here is a beach all along that separates the lake from the main of the Mediterranean. In this lake is great plenty of foule.

Vectura MONDAY 6 JAN. We paid our Voiturin 12 crowns apeice for horse
Portage & provision from Lyons hither. We had liberty to goe out of the way or stay any where, but were to pay our selves for our own & the
Dinner horse meat where we stayed, which is usually 15 s. dinner, 25 s.
Lodging supper, for all the company eat togeather, & 15 s. for horsemeat
Horsemeat a night.

TUESDAY 7 JAN. I removed to Mr. Puech's[2] house, being told that that part of the town which lay towards the sea was less healthy, as the Pettit Paris doth, the south & South-east winds being
Pension counted unhealthy, comeing off from the sea. At the Pettit Paris I paid £2 per diem, at Mr. Puech's 10 crowns per *month* for diet only. Lodging, fire & candle I had at an other place.

Olives WEDNES. 8 JAN. I walked abroad & found them gathering of olives, a black fruit, about the bignesse of an acorn, with which the trees were thick hung, & just without the town, especially on the west side, the fields coverd with olive trees in quincunx.

---

[1] The inn has disappeared, but there is still an old street called the 'Rue du Petit Paris'.

[2] Locke's letters were addressed to 'Jacques Puech, Apothicaire à Montpellier'. The tax rolls for 1665 give the name of Jacques Puech, an apothecary, as living in the Rue du puits de fer (Archives Municipales, Compoix 1665, f. 411). His name appears in a list of 'Nouveaux Convertis' drawn up in 1685 (ibid. G.G. Réformés) (his household is then said to have included 'trois pensionnaires Anglois'); but he later took refuge with his family in England.

T. 9 JAN. We saw them throwing of Olives in the fields to separate Olivae
the fruit from the leaves. The way is the seting up 3 sticks & laying
there on a wim sheet¹ much after the fashion of a fire shovel, the
open end towards the labourer, who, at a good distance from, takes
up the olives out of a heape with a wooden shovell & soe throws them
into the sheet. The olives out flie² the leaves which fall by the way.³
All the high way[s] are fild with gamesters at Mall, soe that
walkers are in some danger of knocks.⁴

This day I got me a French Master⁵ who was to teach Mr. Wall⁶
& me one hour per diem 5 days in the weak at 4 crowns per month.

FRI. 10 JAN. I walked out to a fine garden, a litle mile from the Walks
towne. The walks were bays & some other cipresse trees, soe close Hortus
that⁷ they were not to be passed, & of a great heigth. There were
rows of other trees, but without leaves soe that I knew them not,
unless it were some elms. There were also some pine trees. There
is also at the entrance a faire, large, square pond where, 'tis said,
the ladys bath in summer, and if the weather at midsomer answer
the warmth of this day, which was with the 4 or 5 preceeding very
fair, the Ladys will certainly need a cooler.

---

¹ O.E.D. winnowing-sheet.
² I.e. 'fly further than'.
³ Locke later worked up all his material on these subjects into a little essay entitled
*Observations upon the Growth and Culture of Vines and Olives, the Production of Silk and
the Preservation of Fruits*, which he dedicated to the Earl of Shaftesbury from Christ
Church on 1 Feb. 1679/80. It was first published in 1766.
⁴ According to the historian D'Aigrefeuille (I, 646) Montpellier produced the finest
mall players in Europe.
⁵ The Lovelace Collection contains two sheets with exercises in French grammar in
the handwriting of Locke's teacher, M. Pasty, and of Locke himself. Both Pasty's
explanations and Locke's notes are in Latin. The sheets are endorsed by Locke: 'Mr.
Pasty, Grammer Francois. 76.' Locke's method for learning languages is given in
a letter of 1679 to Thoynard (Ollion, p. 36): 'Quand vous aurez la fantaisie d'apprendre
la langue angloise, vous n'avez qu'à suivre ma methode, en lisant tous les jours un
chapitre du nouveau testament et en un mois vous deviendrez maistre.'
⁶ George Walls, Scholar of Westminster and Student of Christ Church. He was
appointed Prebendary of Worcester in 1694 and Rector of Holt in 1695. He died in
1727. In the *Letters of Humphrey Prideaux to John Ellis*, London, 1875, p. 49, there is
a letter, dated 8 Nov. 1675, referring in not very friendly fashion to his accompanying
Locke on his journey to France: 'George Wall goeth to London on Monday in order to
journey into France. What is his business there I know not, unless it be to be John
Locke's chaplain, whom he accompanyeth thither.'
⁷ *That* occurs twice in MS.

Kitchin **SAT. 1/11 JAN.** Rayny all day. A spit before & pipkins behind the
Lignum fire. I paid Mr. Puech for wood & coals £4. 2½, Wood 6s.,
Carbo Charcoal 18s. Kentall,[1] i.e. 100 lbs.

SUN. 12 JAN. In Kitchen at Mr. Wall's some peuter, some brasse &
aboundance of pipkins. All the world at Mall & the Mountebank
at's tricks.

M. 13 JAN. Several asses & mules loden with green brush wood of
evergreen, oake & bays, brought to towne for fuell. Most of their
Mules labour don by mules & Asses. Between Lyons & Vienne we met
people rideing post on Asses, & on the road we met severall
drivers of mules, some where of we were told have 800 lb. weight
upon them, and severall women rideing a stride, some with caps &
feathers. We met more people travelling between Lyons & Montpellier by much then between Paris & Lyons, where were very few.
Blanching   This day I also saw a garden where they blanch wax. They begin
Wax in March & then I intend to see it.[2] Here were Jasmin flowers blown
& ready to open.

Side Sadle **TUES. 14 JAN.** A woman rideing on a pretty sort of saddle made like
a pad, pretty high before & behind, & on the far side a thing
comeing up on the back of the woman, something like the back of
a chair, & made of cloth stuffed with helme[3] or some such like
thing, & fastend to the fore & hinder part of the sadle or pad. The
women carrying earth at the gate in litle baskets on their heads, &
singing & danceing in their sabots as they returned for new
Stipendia burthens. The Wages per day for men 12s., for women 5s. at this
Wages time of the yeare; in summer, espetially about harvest, 18s. for
men & 7 for women.

WEDNES. 15 JAN. Mr. Puech bying glasse bottles by weight & she
apples. The Towne House adornd with false weights, ballances
& measures naild upon the outside. The same at Avignion.

T. 16 JAN. Fair. N.E. Cold.

FRI. 17 JAN. Fair. Frost. N.E. Ice quarter of an inch thick.
Women barelegd washing in the litle streame on the north west

---

[1] *O.E.D.*: old form of *quintal*.   [2] See entry for 1 May 1676.
[3] *O.E.D. straw.*

side.[1] The picture *of God the Father over the altar* in   [2] Imago
Church.   God the
                                                                  Father

SAT. 18 JAN. About 9 in the morning I went to the Towne House Ordines
where the States of Languedock, which were then assembled in   States
this towne, used to sit every day. The room they sit in is a pretty
fair roome. At the upper end, in the midle, is a seat higher some
what then the rest, where the Duke of Vernule,[3] governor of this
Province, sits when he comes to the Assembly, which is but seldome
& only upon occasion of proposing some thing to them. At other
times Cardinal Bonzi,[4] who is Archbishop of Narbone, takes that
seat which is under a canapey. On the right hand sit the Bishops of
this province who are 22 besides Archbishops; on the left hand the
Barons, about 25. This seat is high, soe that the floor of it is about
a yard higher then the other where the Deputies of the towns sit,
who are about 44, & of these consists this assembly. About ten
they began to drop into the room, where the Bishops put on their
habits, i.e. putting of their long, black cloaks, they put on upon
their cassocks a short surplice, richly laced commonly at the bottom
with straight sleeves, & over this a black hood & a square cap. Only
one I saw in purple, & the cardinal was all scarlet except surplice.
It is soe orderd that, when the Duke comes, he never is there, soe
that he never sits out of the chair. The bell tolls till he comes &
then it ceases. When he & the Bishops are habited, away they go to
Nostre Dame[5] to masse, a church just by, & soe about 11 they
returne & begin to sit, & rise again at 12, seldom siting in the

---

[1] The stream is known as Le Verdanson or, more accurately, Le Merdanson.

[2] Left blank in MS.

[3] Henri de Bourbon, Duc de Verneuil (1601–82), natural son of Henry IV and the
Duchesse de Verneuil. Appointed Bishop of Metz in 1608, he was created a duke in
1663 and married five years later Charlotte Séguier, daughter of the Chancellor. In
1666 he was appointed Governor of Languedoc on the death of the Prince de Conti. He
played quite an insignificant part in the affairs of the province, and his period of office
saw the final establishment in Languedoc of the power of the central government.

[4] Pierre de Bonzi (1631–1703). An Italian by birth, he fulfilled many diplomatic
missions and, after being made Bishop of Béziers in 1659, he was appointed to the
Archbishopric of Toulouse in 1669. In 1672 he was made a cardinal and in the following
year he was appointed to the Archbishopric of Narbonne which carried with it the post
of president of the Estates. Until the appointment of Basville as *Intendant* of Languedoc
in 1685, he was the most powerful man in the province, though his influence rapidly
declined from this time onwards (see entry of 7 Feb. 1676).

[5] This church, like the old *Hôtel de ville* where the Estates met, has disappeared.

afternoon, & that but upon extraordinary occasions. I beleive them
men of businesse & dispatche, for in this manner they sit & are
assembled constantly 4 months in the yeare, beginning in October
& ending in February.

King's Garden SUND. 19 JAN. The Physick Garden[1] well contrived for plants of all
Hortus regius sorts, even to shady & boggy, set most in high beds, as it were, in
long stone troughs, with walks between, & numbers in order
graved in the stone, to direct the student to the plant. I gatherd
blew violets there, full blown & very sweet. Father & son *that
walked there who would pistol any one in any place for small* occasion.[2]

TUES. 21 JAN. Good husbandry in every thing. Their coaches
coverd with oyléd cloth when they travell & in wett days in towns.
None of them guilded.

Shoes THUR. 23 JAN. Paid for a pair of new Spanish leather shoes 45 s.

Olivae FR. 24 JAN. People gathering of Olives. The hils of about 10 or
Snow 12 leagues to the N.W. distance[3] coverd with snow, though we had
here 4 days continuall hard rain. Soe that winter makes but little
excursions into the vale of this country, but keeps his court in the
mountains, & if I were to draw his picture, he should not be
crowned with turneps & carrots, but with violets & Jasmin studded
Fuell with olives. Time, rosemary, bays & Lavender for fuell. In their
Wells gardens they generally raise water by a wheele & earthen pots
Puteus drawn by an asse, the wheele about 12 or 14 foot diameter.

Doctrins SAT. 25 JAN. Discourse of Port de Set[4] with P. & Mr.   [5] at
Petit Paris, & the teaching biding to cheat the Hugenots: Nulla
fides servanda cum Hereticis, nisi satis validi sunt ad se defen-
Stipendia dendos. Our servant at Mr. Fisquet's[6] had 6 crowns per annum
Wages

---

[1] Founded by Henry IV in 1593 as part of the Faculty of Medicine, the *Jardin des
Plantes* of Montpellier is the oldest in France.
[2] *O.E.D. pretext, excuse.*   [3] The Cévennes.
[4] Cette or (since 1927) Sète. The construction of this new port was begun in 1666 and
taken over in 1669 by Riquet, the creator of the Canal du Languedoc. Locke twice
visited the port (see entries for 4 March 1676 and 11 March 1677).
[5] Left blank in MS.
[6] Fesquet was Locke's landlord for the first half of his stay in Montpellier. The name
is a common one and references to it in the documents of the time are too numerous for
one to identify Locke's landlord with any certainty.

wages at Geneva, the under servant had $\frac{1}{2}$ crown & the upper
1 crown per annum, & a hinde 3 crowns per annum, who told
Mr. Diggs[1] unless he had $3\frac{1}{2}$ crowns next year, he would leave his
service.

SUN. 26 JAN. At church[2] in the afternoon the bride & bride groome   Marriage
standing under the pulpit & the minister in the pulpit joyned them   Nuptiae
according to their liturgie, just before the psalme that precedes his
extempory prayer.

M. 17/27 JAN. 1675/6. Gathering of olives.   Olives

T. 28 JAN. Pruning of vines. Fashion[3] of the hooke. In prueing   Vines
they leave of the shoot that comes streight out of the top of the
stock about an inch. All the rest they cut of cleane to the old stock.
If a vine be decaid or gon in any place, they dig a trench about $\frac{3}{4}$ or
a foot deepe to the next stock which hath most flourishing branches,
& there they dig down till they soe loosen his roots that they can
lay him, & then cuting off all but the 2 bigest shoots of the last
yeare, one of them they bend gently about & bring up to the top of
him just in the place where the old stock stood. The other they lay
all along in the trench & bring up the tip of him in the place where
the other was wanting, & soe cover all the rest with earth. These
look like litle plants & they cut them off at about 8 or 9 inches high,
& stick a good strong peice of a branch by, a litle longer then the
plant, close by it to defend it. I asked of some fellows that were
doing this whether the cutings would not grow. They answered
yes. I asked them why they took soe much pains for a plant. They
told me this would have grapes the next vintage, but a cuting not
in 3 or 4 years, where with I was satisfied. These single plants,
I guesse, they cut next year close by the ground, for soe the
divisions & branchings of the old stocks would make one thinke.

---

[1] In a letter to Thoynard of 29 Oct. 1679, published by Ollion, Locke speaks of a recent
visit to 'M. Digge [sic], une personne de qualité proche Canterbury', apparently a
member of the Digges family of Barham, Kent. There are several references to a person
of the same name in the letters of Charleton to Locke from 1678 onwards.
[2] The only remaining Protestant *temple* in Montpellier was demolished in 1682.
[3] *O.E.D.* 'shape'.

They are planted by line in rows about 4½ or 5 pans distance & some at 6 pans distance, & stand in perfect quincunx.

Weights   At Montpellier 1 Cental[1] continet lb. 100.
Pondera   1 lb.   .... 16 ozs.
                         1 oz.   ....   8 drachms.
                         1 drachm ....   3 scruples.
                         1 scruple .... 20 grains.

A pan is 9¾ & almost $\frac{1}{16}$[2] English measure.

This is the common weight, but in all medecinal praescriptions they allow but 12 of these ounces to the pound, soe that pondus medicinale is but ¾ of the civilis; and in weighing gold, silver, ambergris, musk & civet the scruple hath 24 grains, & soe the ounce 72, & consequently the drachm & other weights are all ⅙ bigger.[3]

WED. 29 JAN. The Citadell[4] on the N.E. side the town of 4 large bastions faced with stone.

THUR. 30 JAN. A hard shower with thunder & lightening.

Olives   Mrs. Fisket eating for breakfast black olives & brown bread. Olives not well tasted, for when they are black, they are as bitter as gaule. To cure this, they who pickle them to eat, gash them in 2 or 3 places & soe soak them 14 or 15 days in water, changeing it every day, & then boyle them in salt & water & soe keep them pickled. They retain some thing of their oyly tast & are much worse then if pickled green, but I suppose will goe much farther & there-

Pomam fore commonly used. Apples 4s. per lib. They are brought from
Apples   Grenoble & are admirable good pepins.

Protestants FRID. 31 JAN. Uzes, a towne in this province, not far from Nismes, was wont to send every year a Protestant deputy to the assembly of the States here at Montpellier, the greatest part being Protestants, but they were forbid to doe it this year.[5] And this week the Protestants there have an order from the King to choose noe more

---

[1] *Quintal*. A less complete list of Montpellier weights is given in the MS. on 20 Jan.
[2] *Inches* understood.
[3] To make sense, the words *ounce* and *drachm* should be transposed.
[4] Built by Louis XIII after he had put down the revolt of the Protestants in 1622.
[5] There seems to be some confusion here, since Protestant deputies had long since been excluded from the Estates (Gachon, p. 20).

consuls of the town of the Religion,[1] and their Temple is orderd
to be puld down,[2] the only one they had left there, though ¾ of the
town be Protestants. The pretence given is that their Temple being
too near the papish church, their singing of psalms disturbed the
service.

SAT. 1 FEB. Today I saw anemonys & white stock jully flowers[3] **Flowers**
blown & Jasmin open. I also saw oyle pressed. Here was in the
street a bustle to day, the cause this. Some that were listing soldiers **Milites**
slid mony into a country man's pocket, & then would force him to **Soldiers**
goe with them, haveing, as they said, receivd the King's money. He
refusd to goe & the women, by crowding & force, redeemed him.
These artifices are necessary in a country where presseing is not
allowed & where volunteers come not forwardly[4] to the beat of the
drum, & 'tis a usuall trick, if any one drink the King's health, to
give him presse money & force him to goe a soldier, pretending that
haveing drank his health, he is bound to fight for him.

Interest by law here is 6¼ per cent.,[5] but those who have good **Interest**
credit may borrow at 5 per cent. **Usura**

This King hath made an edict[6] that those who merchandise, but **Trade**
do not use the yard, shall not loose their gentility. **Mercatura**

Their pot at Montpellier is, I thinke, a pretty deale bigger then **Measures**
our Quart, for half a pot of common water weighd 1 lb. 6 ozs.

They count their mony in France by livers, sols & deniers, i.e. **Mony**
ll. s. d., but there is noe money now in France of this coin, for that **Moneta**
which was coind for a sol, is now marked with a little flower de Luys
& soe goes for ¼ more then a sol or sou, & all of that coyn, whether
marked or noe, goe for soe much & are all calld sou marqués. I see
noe thing coind for either livers or Deniers, but that coin which was

---

[1] Royal edict of 3 Jan. 1676.
[2] The *Petit temple* of Uzès had been demolished about twelve years earlier on the
pretext of 'la proximité de la paroisse' (Gachon, p. xxiii).
[3] *O.E.D. gillyflowers.*
[4] *O.E.D. readily, eagerly* (an example is to be found in the *Essay on the Human
Understanding*).
[5] A decree of Colbert, issued in 1665, had reduced the rate to 5%.
[6] This edict (13 Aug. 1669) reminded noblemen that it was only retail trade which
involved loss of noble rank, and declared that they could take part in 'le commerce de
mer' without losing caste.

called double & hath still that name on it, is cald & passes now for a denier. Their coyn then is thus:

1 pistol or Luis d'or		11 Livers.
1 Escu	3 Livers.	
1 Liver	20 sous.	
1 Sou	4 Liards.	
1 Sou	6 Doubles.	
1 Sou	12 Deniers.	
1 Escu d'or	£ 5 – 14 – o.	

Flowers SUND. 2 FEB. Anemonys, double blew, & striped stock jully flowers & double violets blown.

Soldiers MUND. 3 FEB. Drums beat for soldier, & 5 Luis d'or offerd to any
Miles one that would list himself.

Verdegrise Verdegrise is made thus. The plates being well coverd with verdigrise, they take them out, & the stalkes with the supporters.
Aes viride When all these are out, take an handfull of fresh, drye stalks & with them rouse about the wine that is in the bottom of the pot, & wash it well there with. Power out this wine as uselesse & wipe the pot very cleane. Put the handfull of fresh stalks where with you roused about the old wine into a basin of fresh wine which stands by for that purpose. When they have laine there a litle while to soake whilst you are wipeing the pot with a cloth, take out the handfull of fresh stalks out of the basin of fresh wine & sprinkle with the fresh wine the old stalks that came out of the pot before, & mingle these fresh stalks with them, & then in a broad basket made of sticks, like an half ovall or a litle flater, mould the stalkes altogeather in a bundle, rubing them at every turne strongly against the bottom of the basket, where by some part of them breaks off & falls through. This they doe, they say, to cleanse them, but I rather thinke to worke them close togeather to promote the fermentacion.

The stalks being thus made up in a lump, put them together agen into the same pot from whence they & the plates coverd with verdigrise were just before taken, & power on them two pots of fresh wine, & puting the stalks a litle on one side, with the hand stir the wine soundly in the pot till it froths. Put the cover on the pot & so leave it 24 howers. The stalks haveing lain thus in the wine 24 hours, take them out, & puting the supporters in their places, put in the lump of stalks upon the supporters & the cover upon the pot, & soe let them stand till they are ready.

The first marke of their approach to being ready is a very strong scent, as of a thing in fermentacion, which you will smell sufficiently if you take off the cover of the pot; & at that time the cover will be very wett & the sides of the pots also. After this the scent decreases, the cover grows pretty drie & the sides of the pot in the inside quite drye, & the wine in the bottom will have a white cream on it, & this is the time when the plates are to be put in, & the stalks are said to be ready. This is soe short a season in the summer time that 24 howers quite looses it. Another signe of the time is that which they call the rose,[1] which is a moisture from top to bottom, espetially the bottom of the lump of stalks, whilst the sides of it are drye; but for the more surety they put in a plate with the pott and, leaving it there 6 or 8 howers, by the turning of that blew guesse at the fitness of the time.

The pots of stalks being now in a readinesse, they again take the lump of stalks out of the pot &, puling it all on sunder that the moist & drye may be all equally mingled, they again mould them as before, throwing away at their first takeing out any part that hath fallen through the supporters & lain soakeing in the wine; & haveing with their hands gatherd & thrown out the white skim of the wine, they again, with a fresh handfull of stalkes which serves for the same use to all the pots, they reinse the wine in the bottom all about the sides of the pott & then, wipeing the supporters very cleane, they put them in their places & upon them a laying of plates, taken immediately out of the stove, as hot as one can well handle, close by one an other & a laying of stalkes so thin that one may see the plates through, & so S.S.S.[2] till the pot be full, & soe puting on the covers, let them stand till the plates are well coverd with verdigris.

When the plates are coverd well with verdigris which now was don in a weeke, they take them out, dip their edges in a litle fresh wine, wrap them up in a cleane, linnin cloth & soe lay them upon

---

[1] I.e. *rosée* (dew)?
[2] An abbreviation for *stratum super stratum* ('layer upon layer').

the floor of the seller in an heape, & a great stone upon them, & soe leave them 15 days or more, the longer the better, not exceeding 6 weeks. This is to make the verdigrise come off from the plates the easier. They then scrape of the verdigris with knives, & cleanse the plates very well, & soe lay them by to use again.

N.B.

1.   That the pots are about the bignesse of large be hives & much of that fashion, but only brought in a little narrower at the mouths & wider at the bottom to stand on.

2.   That the stalks are the stalkes of bunches of grapes.

3.   The supporters are 2 peices of pland wood about 1½ or 2 inches broad a peice & ½ inch thick, & of such a length as, leaneing against the sides of these taper potts, the plates that lye upon them may be about 3 inches above the top of the wine.

4.   The covers are of helme, made flat with a lip to hang over the sides of the pot, each one fit to his pot, of the same workmanship & matter that be hives are.

5.   The plates are thin plates of copper about the bredth & length of one's hand & as thick as latin.

6.   If the plates be not put in hot, you will not have half soe much verdigris.

7.   The wine is the courser sort or that which is turnd, but it must not be acid. Not but that good wine will doe, for it must have spirits, but cheapnesse findes more profit in the bad. White wine alone will not make good verdigrise but a whiteish, uselesse concoction; but white wine mingled with red in a small quantity, will doe as ⅛, and the stronger the better, as Fronticiack.[1]

8.   The stove is like a chest with grates in the midle to put a pan of coales under, & in the upper part the plates are put edgling & rest on a grate; the cover as of a chest, & the place to put in the coales is below at a Clyse.[2]

---

[1]   Frontignan?
[2]   Wright's *English Dialect Dictionary* gives for *clize* 'the valve or swinging door in a drain, dike, etc.'.

9. The Stalks were ready & the wine had its cream now in 18 days from puting in the wine & leaveing them to ferment to-geather. It was now pretty warme weather. In the coldest winter weather it is some times a month in preparing, & in the heat of sommer 4 days' time is enough to bring it to perfection & make it ready for the plates. If you put in the plates to soon, whilst the fermentation is high, instead of verdigris there will be a black corrosion. If you stay too long, you will have litle or no verdigris.

10. In the whole worke you must have a great care to keepe everything very cleane. On[e] drop of oyle or grease in a pot spoyles the work of that pot.

11. Their 2 pots of wine is about 5 pints or 2 quarts of ours, for half a pot of their ordinary water weighs 1 lb. 6 ozs. of their weight, they haveing 16 ozs. to the pound, & 100 lb. of Montpellier make 91⅓ lb. of London weight.

12. That the plates that were put in this 3d of Feb. were designed to be taken out 10 or 11, but in colder weather they stay 10 or 12 days. In hotter 6 are enough. If you let them stay too long, you spoile the verdigrease which will turne white.

13. It does best in a vault or cellar, but may be made in other places.

14. A drop of oyle in the pot makes the verdigrease white & the plates as if they were coverd with grease.

WED. 5 FEB. Fair & soe warme that the sun beams were rather trouble some then not. A litle out of Montpellier westward a bed of oyster shells in an hollow way, in some places 2 yards under the ground, appeared all along for a good way. We could see some of the shells perfectly fit one to an other, & dirt in the place where the oyster lay. The shells are now very rotten & the place where they lye much higher then the present levell of the sea. Q. — Have not these been left there by the sea, since retreated?   **Sea** *Mare*

The Protestants have here common justice generally, unlesse it be against a new convert, whom they will favour. They pay noe more taxes then their neighbours, are only incapable of publique charges & offices. They have had within these 10 years at least   **Protestants**

160 churches pulled down.[1] They & the papist laity live togeather friendly enough in these parts. They sometimes get & sometimes loose proselytes. There is noe thing don against those that come over to the reformed religion, unless they be such as have before turned papists & relaps: these sometimes they prosecute.[2] The number of Protestants in these latter years neither increases nor decreases much.[3] Those that go over to the Church of Rome are usually drawn away by fair promises that most commonly faile them, or else mony if they be pore. The Protestants live not better then the Papists. Dr. *Barbeyrac*.[4]

Vines
Uva

FRID. 7 FEB. I sent this day away into England[5] a box of vines of the following sorts:

    1. Muscat.
    2. Spiran, both black & green.
    3. Picardan.
    4. Corinth.
    5. Marokin.
    6. St. John's.
    7. Crispata.
    8. Claret.

Grapes

The Muscat every one knows. Of the Spiran there are 2 sorts, the black & the green, both very good for eating & wine too, but the black the better, which are thought so wholesome that they eat them here in great quantities, & that by the advice of the physitians. The green also are a very good sort of grapes & keepe well till winter.

---

[1] The chief period, prior to Locke's arrival in France, in which Protestant *temples* were demolished was 1663-5, for which Haag (X. 378-80) gives the figure of over two hundred. The next ten years saw a relative lull, though demolitions still continued.

[2] An edict of 20 June 1665 laid it down that relapsed Catholics and priests and monks who were converted to Protestantism should be liable to banishment.

[3] Gachon (p. 123) quotes a document (now missing from the Archives Départementales) which gives seventy to eighty abjurations at Montpellier for the period 1661-80.

[4] Charles Barbeyrac (1629-99), one of the best known doctors of Montpellier in this period, though his Protestantism prevented him from holding a chair in the Faculty of Medicine. Both Locke and Sydenham were on friendly terms with him. The Journal contains several notes on medical questions which bear his name.

[5] These were for Shaftesbury: cf. the letter of Stringer of 6 April (O.S.) acknowledging their receipt (Christie, II. 221).

The Picardan is a white grape & makes a very good sort of wine. It is large & longish, very sweet. Of the Corinth grapes we have already in England.

Spiran is midle sized, round, black, very sweet & very wholsome. The green Spiran ripens later, seldom used in wine, but keeps till winter.

Marokin very black, fleshy, round, very large, good to eat, but seldom used in wine.

The St. John's is a grape which they had at the Physick Garden here from India. The grapes are very good & ripen here at Midsomer two months before any of the other sorts. Black.

Crispata is also a very good sort of grapes. They call it soe from the jagged leaf, & I guess it is the parsly grape we know in England. White.

Claret. White, longish, midle sized, sweet & good to eat & good for wine, alone or mingled, as is the Picardan.

Mrs. Fisket tells me they seldom make red wine without the mixture of some sort of white grapes, else it will be too thick & deepe coloured, & they most commonly grow mingled severall sorts in one vineard. *Vinum*

In seting the vines, they dig the ground sometimes all over, sometimes only in trenches where they set them. They set the cutings about 18 or 20 inches into the ground & leave only 2 knots above ground. The next yeare at pruning they cut them soe that, if conveniently there can, there may be 4 shoots the next year neare the ground, at least 3 spreading severall ways, that in the succeeding years may be, as it were, the old stock out of which the shoots are to sprout. They set them exactly in quincunx, & the rows are in some places 4, in some 5 pans distant, I suppose according to the difference of the ground or grape. *Vines* *Vinea*

The States every morning goe to Notre Dame to prayers, where mass is sung. All the while the priest who says Masse is at the altar saying the office, you cannot hear him a word, & indeed the musick is the pleasanter of the two. The Cardinall & Bishops are all on the right hand the quire, i.e. standing at the altar & looking down to the west end of the church, & all the lay barrons on the left or south side. The Cardinall sat uppermost, nearest the altar, *States* *Ordines* *Devotion*

& had a velvet quishon,[1] richly laced with broad silver & gold lace; the bishops had none at all. *He also had his book and* repeated *his office apart very* genteelly with an unconcearned look, talking ever[y] now & then, & laughing with the bishops next him. *He keeps a very fine mistress*[2] *in the town, which some of the very papists complain of, and hath some very fine boys in his train.*

Oyle
Oleum

The best oyle in France is the oyle of Aramont, a town in Provence, not far from Avignion.

Assassin

One ran his sister into the head a litle above the temple in the house where I lay.[3] The father was lately dead & he had but a small legacy.

Wood
Lignum

Bend a bord with 2 holdfasts & then apply fire to it with helme & soe let it stand till cold. This way you may bring it to any shape.

States
Ordines

SAT. 8 FEB. This day the Assembly of the States was dissolved, who meet & sit here every winter about 4 months, breaking up usually in the begining of February. The States of this province of Languedock consist of 22 Bishops, 24 or 25 Barons & about 30 or 35[4] Deputys of towns. They sit as Jan. 18, & have all the solemnity & outward appearance of a Parliament. The King proposes & they debate & resolve about it. Here is all the difference, that they never doe, and some say dare not, refuse whatever the King demands.[5] They gave to the King this year 2,100,000 livers,[6]

Tributum

---

[1] *O.E.D. cushion.*

[2] Presumably the notorious Jeanne de Gévaudan, whom the Cardinal married off in due course to a local nobleman, the Comte de Ganges. The scandal caused by this long *liaison* contributed to the complete undermining of the Cardinal's influence in the province after 1685, as the now devout and strait-laced King was unfavourably impressed by the affair. (For further details see the memoirs of Saint-Simon and especially Mme Du Noyer, in particular Letters IX, XI and XIII.) The Comtesse de Ganges died in 1719, but the date of her birth appears to be unknown. However, it is almost certain that the affair goes back to 1676, since a traveller who visited Montpellier in 1669 puts her among the beauties of the town (see *Monspeliensia*, p. 11).

[3] If one could discover the documents connected with the trial of this personage, we should know with certainty the house in which Locke lodged during the first part of his stay in Montpellier. Unfortunately the collection of papers concerning the relevant local court (*le Présidial*) has a gap for the year 1676.

[4] Added above in the MS.: 'rather 44'.

[5] This had not always been the case, as Locke himself points out in the entry for 7 March 1677.

[6] Reference to the *Procès-Verbaux* of the Estates in the Archives de l'Hérault shows that this figure is correct.

& for their liberality are promisd noe soldiers shall quarter in this Quarters country, which yet never the lesse sometimes happens. When soldiers are sent to quarter in Montpellier, as some Switz did here that were going towards Catalonia, the Magistrates of the town give them billets & take care according to the billets that their Landlords be paid 8 s. per diem for each foot soldier, which is paid by the town, not by the soldiers.

Besides these 2,100,000 given the King for this yeare, they give him also for the canal 300,000 l.;[1] and besides all this they maintein 11,000 men in Catalonia, raisd & paid by this province.[2] These taxes & all publique charges come sometimes to 8, sometimes to 12 per cent. of the yearly value of Estates.

The States being resolved to break up today, the ceremony was this. Te Deum was sung in the State house &, that being don, the States Cardinall with a very good grace gave the benediction, first puting on his cap, & at the later end of the benediction he puld of his cap & made a crosse, first towards the Bishops, then towards the nobility, & then strait forwards towards the people who were, all the while the benediction was giveing, on their knees.

Mr. Harvy's man[3] inticed into a shop & there fallen upon by Assassin 3 or 4 & beaten for poysoning their dog. A man shot dead by an other in the street some time before, & an other at Lyons when I was there. N. Very fair & warme.

MUND. 10 FEB. The manner of makeing oyle is this. Oyle
Oleum

They take 4 Septies[4] of olives a litle heaped & put them into a mill which is drawn by a mule, where they grinde them as tanners grinde barke, to a fine pulpe, one standing by as the mill goes round & shoveing in a litle of the olives or pulp towards the

---

[1] The Estates had been compelled to contribute, very grudgingly, to the cost of the construction of the Canal du Languedoc. On this occasion, according to the *Procès-Verbal*, the Estates finally agreed to pay 1,600,000 l., in four annual instalments of 400,000 l. (see entry for 12 Feb.).

[2] This point is less clear. Twelve months later the Estates had to agree to furnish a regiment of dragoons in place of the province's militia which had been used in the war; but no precise figures about the size or cost of the militia seem to be available.

[3] King read this name as 'Herbert' (see entry for 2 Oct. 1676), but there is no doubt that it should read 'Harvy'.

[4] *Sétiers* (or *septiers*).

center, & clearing the part of the stone at the bottom where he stands with the shovell. This he does soe by degrees & in succession that, I beleive, the mule goes round near 100 times for his once. They being sufficiently ground, they put them into a stone trough, two whereof stand between the mill & the presse. Out of these troughs they take the pulp & put it into frailes[1] & spread it in them equally, that they may lay them plain, one upon an other. Of these frailes there was, when I saw them presse to day, 24 upon each pedistall, viz. in all 48, in which were co[n]teind ten Septies of Olives. Some times they presse twelve Septies of Olives at once, & then they use more frails proportionably.

Oyle

The frailes being fild with pulpe & placed evenly & upright upon the two pedistals in equall number, they set the presse on workeing, first lifting up the scrue end that soe the end of the beam, sinkeing upon the hinder pile of frails & presseing them, may make way for the puting in the wedges into the great Mortis & discharge the wedge in the litle mortice which, whilst they were placeing the frails upon the pedistall, supported the beame, which being taken out, they worke the scrue the other way, & soe bringing down the scrue end of the beame, presse both on the fore & hinder pile of frailes; a man attending in the meane time at each pile of frailes with a leaver in his hand which, resting in the gutter where the oyle runs, he thrusts & keepes in the pile of frailes, if it happen to swell or bend outwards any way when they are in presseing, espetially at the beginning, by this meanes keepeing the piles streight & upright; the other in the meane time not ceaseing to turne the scrue till the great stone at the end of it be clear of the ground.

Oyle

When the oyle ceases to run or but in small quantity, they lift up the scrue end of the presse, & then, puting a wedg in the litle mortisse, get up the other end also & soe bring the beame to a levell dischargeing it cleare from the frailes. Then they take off all the frailes except the 8 or 10 lowermost &, stiring the pulp, put it upon those that lye still on the pedistall, & then one pours into it a bucket of scalding water, after which he stirs the pulp again & lays it flat

---

[1] *O.E.D.* 'rush basket for packing figs, raisins, etc.'

& equall as at first, & then stirs & puts on an other as before, with a bucket of hot water powerd on it, & soe they serve them all, & then they set the presse a workeing again as at first, as long as any quantity will run, & then, lifting up the beame again, take off the frailes, stir the pulpe & power on fresh hot water upon every fraile, a litle bucket full as at first, & then presse as long as any thing will run, leting the stone hang cleare a great while, puting the end of the leaver in a hole in the wall to hinder the scrue from turneing & soe leting downe the stone.

When the presseing is all don, one with a broad, but very shallow skiming dish of brasse skims of the oyle from the water, puts it into a brasse vessell like a tumbler, but holding, I guesse, about a pot & half, & with that pouring it into the vessels of the owners by a brasse tunnell.[1]

When the oyle is well skimd off from the water, they pull out a stopple in the bottom of the cisterne, & soe let goe the water which runs into a great place they call hell, which is a great large cisterne in a place locked up, where, the water comeing in & goeing out at the bottom, soe that it leaves the cisterne still full, the water only runs away & leaves the oyle & saves that which scaped the skiming dish, but that, I suppose, belongs to the master of the presse; for every body's water runs in here to the former oyle & water.

Oyle

N.B.

1. That the mill which grindes the olives is after the same maner with that which our tanners use to grinde barke, only with some difference, as 1° that in the center of this there stands up a round stone, very smooth & true wrought, about 2½ pans in diameter & about the same heigth, which the inside of the great grindeing stone touches in its turning round, soe that noe olives scape the great stone towards the center, nor get besides it that way. 2° that the floor of the mill, upon which the great stone bares in its turning round, is also of hard stone & smooth & a litle shelveing,[2] the declivitie being towards the center, to answer which the edg of the

Oyle presse

---

[1] *O.E.D.* 'Obs. funnel'.
[2] *O.E.D.* 'that shelves or slopes'.

Oyle presse   broad stone which is to grinde the olives, that it may beare in its
whole bredth upon the stones in the floore, is not cut with a derect
perpendicular to the sides of the stone, but the line of the inside
of the said grindeing stone & that of the edg or thicknesse make an
angle something lesse then a right one, & on the outside there is
left noe angle at all, but it is cut of with a round. By which meanes
I suppose the great grindeing stone slides constantly towards, & is
kept close to, the round stone that stands fixd in the midle before
mentioned, upon which the perpendicular turning beam stands.
3° soe much of the floor or inside of the mill as the grindeing stone
does not touch or is a litle without his breadth, is coverd with bords
lieing more shelveing then the stone floore where at first the olives
are laid, which are not thrown all at once under the grinding stone,
but by small parcells shoveld downe under the grinding stone by
the man that attends the mill, every passeing round of the stone
a few; & here lyes also the pulp which the stone workes out in its
grindeing, which is also shoveld in in its turne, for the floore of the
mill where the grindeing stone bears on it, has always very litle
upon it, its great weigh[t] workeing it still out towards the circumference, for the stone in the midle hinders it from goeing inwards.
4° the grinding stone is about 7 pans high & about $1\frac{1}{8}$ pan thick,
& on the edg & inside is wrought very smooth & stands upright,
without leaning that I could perceive, though the edg be not square
to the sides, which is recompensed in the sinkeing of the floore
towards the center. The stone seems to be very hard, & it need be
hard & heavy to break the stones of olives to pouder.

2. The shovels that they use to shovel in the pulp under the
grinder &, when it is fine enough, to take it out & put it in the stone
troughs, & then into the frailes, are more like bakers' peels[1] then
shovels, & there was not any iron upon any of them.

3. To put the pulpe in, there are between the mill & the presse
2 great stone troughs; in the presse 2 pedistalls, & below 2 stone
cisternes into which the oyle runs from the 2 pedistalls by distinct
passages, soe that 2 people's oyle may be pressed at once without
the danger of mingleing a drop.

---

[1] *O.E.D. peel*: 'shovel, esp. baker's for thrusting loaves, etc. into oven'.

4. The presse is made thus. 1. There are two pedestals about Oyle presse
2 litle pans on sunder which lye just under the great beam. That
which I call a pedistall is a round, plain stone about 2⅔ pan
diameter, round about which is cut a grove in the same stone,
about ½ pan broad or a litle lesse, & from thence a passage to the
cisterne. Upon these pedistals the frailes are laid, & into these
grooves or trenches the oyle drops & thence runs into the cisterne.

5. Behinde the hinmost pedistall stand erect in the ground
2 great beames, well fastend in the ground, as far on sunder from
each other as the breadth of the pressing beame, which is to passe
up & downe between them. From the nearest side of the hinmost
pedistall to the midle of these beames horizontally is about 3 pans.
In the midle of these beames, in respect of their thicknesse, is cut
a mortise about 4½ pans long & about 5 or 6 inches broad. The
bottom of this mortise is about 4½ pans higher then the pedistal.

6. This mortice they fill with severall peices of wood reaching
quite a thwart from one mortice to an other, hanging out on both
sides as thick as the breadth of the mortice & some what broader.
These I call wedges. With these, I say, they fill up this mortice
when this end of the presseing beame is sunke below the lowest
part of it & there by pin downe this end of the beame to keepe it
downe upon the frailes when the other end is drawn down by the
scrue.

7. The presseing beame is 38 pans long, 3⅓ broad, & to increase
its weight & strength, another great beame was fastend to it all
along with bands of iron.

8. At the other end is a scrue where of the very scrue is, I guesse
(for standing upright I could not measure it), about 16 pans, the
square for holes for the leaver almost 4 pans; & at the bottom
a great, round stone in which one end is fastend with iron worke
& turnes; which stone, when the scrue is turnd faster then this end
of the beame sinkes, lifts up even this great stone[1] which is   [2]
broad &   [2] thick, as big as an ordinary mill stone.

9. Between the scrue & the 2 erect beames before describd stand

---

[1] Cf. *Observations*, p. 43. 'The screw, when it is turned faster than the end of the
pressing beam sinks, lifts up this great stone from the ground'....
[2] Left blank in MS.

Oyle presse 2 other beames, erect as the former, with a mortis in them long enough to hold one only wedg, the top of which is higher then the levell of the highest fraile when they lay in most. Upon this wedg the beame is to rest when they are laying in or takeing out the frailes. Soe that the leng[t]h of the great beame is thus divided: behinde the pining wedges 3 pans, from the pining to the supporting wedg 20 pans, from the supporting wedg to the scrue 15 pans.

9. [sic] The ground where the great scrue stone lyes is much lower then the levell of the pedestals, which affords also a convenience for the placeing the 2 cisternes which are just under the great beame & a litle distance from the outmost pedistall.

10. A peice of wood fastend on to the great beame crosse it, hanging over on each side, & placed just by the midle erect beames on the side towards the pedestals, to keepe it from slideing towards the scrue.

11. The matter of the frailes & texture the same with the frailes that bring raisons to England, but the figure just the same with that of an hat case, the crown being taken away. They are exactly all of a breadth & scarce discernably narrower then the pedistals; the hole to put in the pulp about ⅓ of the diameter.

12. The oyle that runs at first presseing before the mixture of water they call virgin oyle, which is better then the other, but all say it will not keepe, but spoile in a month or 2, unless you put to it salt or sugar, but salt is the better, & then it will keepe 6 months. As much as you can hold in your 2 hands is enough to put into
Septié a Septie of oyle. A Septie is 32 pots.

13. Therefor they usually let the virgin & the other of the 2d & 3d presseing all mingle togeather in the cisterne which, being
Oyle afterwards put up in jars & kept in coole cellars, will keep good 7 yeare; but the mingleing of some of the hot water with virgin oyle after presseing will not preserve it, soe that it seems to be some thing either in the skins or stones of the olives that comes not out but by the mixture of hot water & hard presseing, that serves to preserve[1] it.

---

[1] MS. has *preserves*.

14. They begin to gather their olives about St. Katherin's Day, Oyle which is 5 days before the winter solstice,[1] though I saw some gatherd here in the later end of January.

15. All confesse that oyle is better which is made of Olives fresh gatherd then of those that have been kept (in heapes as they doe) a month or 2; but some tell me they delay soe long because those that are kept yeild more oyle. Others say the reason why they are not pressed sooner is because every body's grist cannot be ground at once, & they must stay till they can get a turne.

16. 4 Septies of olives usually yeild one septie of oyle, but I observd they were some what heaped.

17. The goodnesse of the oyle depends exceedingly upon the propriety of the soyle. This makes the oyle of Aramont in Provence the best in France.

18. When they are either filling the frailes or new stiring the pulpe in them, there are 2 men at worke at each pedistall, besides a 5th that takes the pulpe out of the trough (that stands by) with a shovell & puts it into the frailes as they bring them, or else lades boyling water out of the furnace (which is also by, & the top levell with the grounde, with a trap dore cover) & powers it on the frailes as they are ready.

19. After they have gatherd the olives, they lay them in heapes in the corner of a cellar or some such other place, with sarments[2] between them & the ground, where after some time black water will run from them. This they call purgeing them. In these heapes they lye till they presse them. None lye lesse then 15 days.

20. All agree that the oyle pressed from olives new gatherd is sweetest, but noe body does before 15 days' lyeing. But the reason why they keep them longer, as 2 months some times, they give differently. Some say, because they cannot have turns at the mills sooner; others say, after keepeing they both yeild more oyle & grinde better, for the new gatherd spirt away from the stone, & though they begin to gather their olives about St. Katherin's Day, they never set their mills on worke till Twelf[th] Day or, at

---

[1] St Catherine's Day being 25 November, it is not easy to see how it could be five days before the winter solstice. This last remark is omitted in *Observations* (p. 47).

[2] *O.E.D.* 'twig, cutting of a tree'. In his *Observations* Locke speaks of 'vine cuttings'.

Oyle   soonest, New Year's Day. The reason whereof is, they say, that the
Master of the mill hires a great many men for the time that oyle is
made, which keepe the mill going day & night, but that those whose
oyle is makeing give these worke men meat & drink; but that, if the
Master should entertein them before Christmas, he must not only
pay them for soe many holydays whilst they stand still, but finde[1]
them too.

21. When the oyle is made, they usually take ¾ of the upper part
(this they call the flower) & put it in earthen pots for eating. The
remainder, being thicker, is kept for lamps & other uses, & the very
thick sediment they put in the sun to get as much oyle out as they
can.

22. The pulp that is left after all the presseing & affusion of
boyling water belongs to the master of the mill who sells it for
4 or 5 s. a millfull to others who presse it again & make a course oyle
for soape & other such uses.

23. The remaining pulpe bakers use to through a little of into
their ovens as they are heating, it makeing a very violent fire.

Bishops   The Bishops of this province are:
Episcopi

Archbishop of Narbon, primas totiae provinciae et semper praeses
senatus.
Archbishop of Tholose.
Bishops of Alby, Montauban, Castres, Carcassonne, Lavaur, Pamies,[2]
Mirepoix, St. Papoul, Aletz, St Pons de Tomieres, Rieux, Beziers,
Agde, Loudeur,[3] Montpellier, Nismes, Uzes, Viviers, Mandé,[4]
Le Puy.

States   The States are always summond by the King's authority, but
Ordines   when they have donn their businesse, they dissolve themselves.

Canonization   At the Carmes' Church this day was an end of their octave of
open house, as one may say, upon the occasion of the canonization
of St. John de Croix,[5] one of their Order lately canonizd at Rome,
dead 80 years agon. During the 8 days of their celebration there
was plenarie Indulgence over the door of their chappell & at the

---

[1] *O.E.D.* 'maintain, provide for'.   [2] Pamiers.
[3] Lodève.   [4] Mende.
[5] St John of the Cross (1542–91), a Spanish Carmelite, beatified in 1675 and canonized
in 1726 (24 Nov.).

doore a pavilion of bays with emblems set round it & his picture in
the midle. This being the close of the solemnity, there was a sermon
which was the recital of his life, virtues & miracles he did, as
preserving baptismall grace & innocence to the end of his life, his
driveing out evill spirits out of the possessed, etc. Besides musick
at their vespers & instead of an organ a bass violl, at the end of all
the Benediction, which is a very considerable matter amongst
them. Here was the Duke of Vernules, Dutchesse[1] & her gard of
musketoons with her.

TUESD. 11 FEB. They sell pigs here alive by weight, 2s. per lb. They
tye the fore leg & hin leg crosse togeather & so hoist them up by
a pully to the ballance.

The usuall rate of good oyle here some years 3, some years 4 livers   Oyle
& some years 4 livers 10s. per quartall, i.e. ¼ Septie or 8 pots.   Quartal

WED. 12 FEB. Very fair & the shade desireable. I visited Mr. Birto.[2]
A generall synod they have not had these 10 or 12 years.[3] A provin-   Protestants
cial synod of Languedock they have, of course, every yeare, but not
without leave from the King, wherein they make ecclesiasticall laws
for this province, but suitable still to the laws made by the Nationall   Synod
Synod. Their synod consists of about 50 pastors & as many Deacons
or Elders.

These have power to reprehend or wholy displace any scandalous
pastor. They also admit people to ordination and to be pastors in
certain churches, noe body being by them put into orders that hath
not a place. The manner is this. When any church wants a pastor,   Ordination
as for example at Montpellier any one of their 4 pastors is dead or
gon, the candidates apply themselves to the Consistory of that
church. Whom they like best, they appoint to preach before the
congregation. If they approve of that, at the next Synod he presents
himself. They appoint 4 pastors to examin him in the tongues,

---

[1] Charlotte Séguier (1623-1704), daughter of the Chancellor, married (a) in 1639 the
Duc de Sully who died in 1661, and (b) in 1668 the Duc de Verneuil.
[2] René Bertheau was one of the four pastors of Montpellier when Locke was there.
He stayed on after the demolition of the *temple* in 1682, but after the Revocation of the
Edict of Nantes took refuge in England where he was given a doctorate at Oxford in
1686 and naturalized in the following year.
[3] The last National Synod met in 1659.

university learning & divinity. Espetially he is to produce the testimonials of the university where he studied, of his life & learning. He preaches before them a French & Latin sermon &, if all these are passable, they appoint 2 pastors to ordein him, but before his ordination he 3 successive Sundays preaches in his congregation. This being donne, the 2 appointed come. The senior makes a sermon teaching the duty of a minister, after which, coming out of the pulpit, he & the other come to him that is to be ordeind, read severall chapters to him in the Epistles wherein the minister's duty is conteind, & then, after a prayer, they lay their hands upon him & make a declaration to this purpose: that, by authority & licence of the provinciall synod, he has power to preach, forgive sins, to bless marriages & to administer the sacraments, & thereupon he is pastor of that place. The allowance that he shall have depends on the consistory. After this upon removall to an other church he is not to be ordaind, but he cannot remove without the leave & approbation of the synod.

Toleration   If any one hold tenets contrary to their articles of faith, the King punishes him, soe that you must be here either of the Romish or their church; for not long since it happend to one here, who was inclineing to and vented some Arrian doctrines, the Governor complained to the King. He sent order he should be tried, & soe was sent to Tholose where upon triall, he denying it utterly, he was permitted to scape out of prison; but had he owned it, he had been burnt as an Heretick.[1]

States   The States here this year have given £400,000 for each of the next succeeding 4 years,[2] having given £300,000 every year for the
Tributa   6 last past, all these 3,400,000 livres being particularly for carrying on the canall, besides their taxes towards the warr, as 2,100,000 l. given for this next year.

Montpellier   Montpellier is in circuit about the bignesse of Oxford or lesse, but they say there are 30,000 people in it, & that there are 8,000 communicants of the Protestant church.[3] The streets are narrow & houses high.

---

[1] I have not had an opportunity of investigating the truth of this story in the archives of the *Parlement* of Toulouse.   [2] See note to entry of 8 Feb.
[3] Gachon (p. xxix) quotes an official (i.e. Catholic) document of this period which gives the figure of 20,000 Catholics and 7,000 Protestants for Montpellier.

They tell me that the number of Protestants within these twenty Protestants
or thirty last years are manifestly increased, & doe dayly, notwithstanding their losse every day of something, some priviledg or other.
Their consistorys had formerly power to examin witnesses upon
oath, which within these ten years hath been taken away from them.

TH. 13 FEB. N. Very fair. Windy, sun very warme. Women siting
in the feilds upon the ground. A pretty sort of cover for women
rideing in the sun, made of straw, something of the fashion of tin Parasols
covers for dishes.[1]

FR. 14 FEB. The States are about 80: 22 Bishops, about 25 or States
Ordines
30 Barons, the rest Deputys.[2] They are all paid by their respective
towns & countrys, but the Bishops & many of the Barons receive
it not. They that have least have 50 ecus per month, & they run
their time from the time they are summond by the King to meet,
though they meet not in almost a month after; & though they depart
the 2nd or 3rd day of the 4th month, they are paid for a whole one.
The first Consul of Montpellier hath 1,000 ecus for every session.
If the States meet & sit at Montpellier, the other 5 Consuls of
Montpellier have the priviledg to sit in the States & then have
50 ecus a peice per month; but when the States sit in any other
towne, the Premier Consul of Montpellier is alone admitted for
that town, & all the Consuls of the town where they sit have their
places in the States. The King appoints the town every yeare
where they shall sit, when he summons.

Of the 22 Bishops 17 have revenues to about 3,000 l. sterling Episcopatus
per annum & upwards, the other 5 much more.[3] The Bishoprick of
Alby is worth 40,000 ecus per annum.[4]

---

[1] *Parasol* was originally used for headgear. *O.E.D.* quotes this example from King.
[2] Of the towns of the province.
[3] £3,000 sterling were worth, roughly, 40,000 l. at the prevailing rate of exchange.
In his memoir on the province, drawn up in 1698, the *Intendant*, Basville, gives figures
for all the dioceses of Languedoc. If we are to believe this list, Locke would appear to
have exaggerated the figures, since on Basville's showing, only two dioceses had an
income of over 40,000 l., and six had less than 20,000 l. On the other hand, bishops and
archbishops augmented their income by holding one or more abbeys: e.g. the Archbishop of Narbonne, in addition to his income of 90,000 l. from his diocese, drew another
29,000 l. from three abbeys. Thus Locke's figures are perhaps not far wide of the mark.
[4] Basville gives for Albi, which had in the meantime become an Archbishopric, the
figure of 80,000 l., i.e. only two-thirds of Locke's figure.

Serge Mr. N. bought a sute of Uzes serge which is a litle broader then tabby. He had for coat & briches 3½ cans at £6 – 5 per can & for

Measures lineing 19 pans of waterd tabby at £11 per can. 8 pans make a can. 3 cans make 5 Auns of Paris.[1]

Orange trees SAT. 15 FEB. Bought of a Genoese, who brought them from Genoa
Aurantia & usually comes hither every year with the like merchandise, Orange & Citron trees as follows:

Hermaphrodite	2		
Pom Adam	2		
Portugall	3	Pom de Paradise	2
Common	2		
Pouketer	1	Spanish Jasmin	20
Spadafora	2	Arabian Jasmin	1
Ryé	1		
Citron	1		
Citron Muscat	2		

The orange & citron trees cost me one Livre a peice, the Arabian Jasmin 15 sous & the Spanish Jasmin 2s. a peice, in all £20 – 15.[2]

Pot SUND. 16 FEB. At Mr. Pueche's we weighed a pot of their water & it weighed of Montpellier's weights 2 lbs. 14 ozs.

Stable A wooden trident used in stables, the teeth set like our prongs by beathing.[3]

Consistory MUNDAY 17 FEB. All the power of church discipline is in the Consistory of every particular church. The consistory of this of Montpellier consists of their 4 Pastors & 24 Diacones which they call Anciens. These, by majority of votes, order all their church affairs as their publique stock, censures, etc. The majority of votes determin the matter, though there be noe one of the Pastors of that side. If there be any disagreement or controversy of law amongst them, they refer it to some of the sober Gentry of the towne &

---

[1] There follows a medical note, derived from 'Mr. Cox', presumably the son o Dr Thomas Coxe (1615–85), who in a letter of 2 June 1678 (o.s.) thanked Locke for his kindness to his son at Montpellier (MS. Locke, c. 7, f. 182; cf. the draft of Locke's reply, *ibid.* c. 24, ff. 33–4).

[2] These were for Lady Shaftesbury: cf. Stringer's letter of 6 April (o.s.), acknowledging their receipt (Christie, II. 221).

[3] *O.E.D.* 'the heating of wood to render it flexible'.

lawyers that are Protestants, for they have here still 6 Councellors[1] of the Religion, & the Advocates may be of what religion they please.[2]

The Consistory manage their Church censures thus. If any one live scandalously, they first reprouv him in private. If he mends not, he is called before the Consistory & admonished there. If that works not, the same is donne in the publique congregation, & if after that he stands incorrigible, he is excluded from the Eucarist. This is the utmost of their power. All things are proved in the Consistory by witnesses which were formerly sworne, but the King hath taken from them the power of giveing oaths.[3]   *Excommunication*

The consistory here at Montpellier are chosen every 6 years, at other places in other circuits of time, as at Nismes every yeare. The present consistory choos the next Anciens & commonly severall of the former are reteind. The names of the new chosen Anciens or Elders are reported to the congregation, & if any one of them be after ward excepted against in the consistory with sufficient reason & proof, he is laid by & an other chosen.

The herbs in the Physick Garden are set in long beds wald in on both sides. The beds are in the cleare 3 large pans broad & the walls on the sides 2 large pans high, coped with hewn stone with numbers on one side & on the other a gutter cut all along to convey water to any part of the bed. These stones are about $\frac{5}{8}$ pan broad.   *King's Garden Hortus*

Mr. Charleton told me that at Pezenas over the dore of the Capouchins' church there is this inscription in an oval: 'Prima Trias Virgo est', and under it an other: 'Sanctissimae Trinitati sacrum in honorem Beatae Mariae Triadis Imagini'.   *Inscription Virgo*

SHROVE TUESDAY, 18 FEB. The heigth & consummation of the Carnival. The town fild with mascarades for this last weeke, danceing in the streets in all manner of habits & disguises, to all sorts of musick, brass kettles & frying pans not excepted.   *Carnival*

Grana kermes[4] grow on a shrub of the kinde of Schene vert   *Kermes*

---

[1] Judges of the *Cour des Comptes et des Aides* (see entry for 24 Feb.).
[2] This state of affairs was not to last much longer.
[3] Locke gives a cross-reference to the entry on this subject on 19 Feb.
[4] Before the advent of cochineal, kermes was extensively employed as a dye in Europe. Its manufacture was a considerable industry in Montpellier and Locke, as will

called ilex coccifera, & are a sort of oake apples with litle animals in them.

Olive trees   Olive trees grow a very long time. Mr. Jacques[1] tels me that there are about Montpellier olive trees that were planted 200 years agoe. The slips[2] grow, but better the ofsets from the roots. As we came along, in severall places we saw 4 or 5 younge ofsets let up about old stocks, in some places the stocks growing, but where the ofsets were grown pretty big, the old stock was generally cut away close to the ground.

Sent away by Mr. Waldo who departs to-morrow the following seeds:

Seeds   Melons of 1672 & 1675.
Semen   Balsamum.
             Cyanus.
             Jacea Cyntheroides.
             Astragallas africana odorifera.
             Marum.
             Lychnis Constantinopolitana.
             Jonkils.
             Acacia.
             Petroselinum Macedonicum.
             Brassica alba.
                     crispata.
                     capitata major.
                     campestris.
                     flore albo.
                     capitata.
                     viridis.
                     Capucinorum.
             Raphani Parisienses.
                     Tholosani rubri.
             Lactuca Valentiana.
                     Romana. Good to blanch.
                     hiberna.

---

be seen, was very interested in all the processes. The *Quercus cocciferus*, which grows abundantly in Southern Europe, has on its leaves a wingless, female insect. Numbers of these were collected, killed by exposure to a vapour of hot vinegar and dried: the resulting reddish-brown grains furnished the dye. Kermes is now quite obsolete as a dyestuff.

[1] Apparently a minor employee as there is no trace of him in the archives of the Faculté de Médecine.

[2] MS. has *slilps*.

Pomea or apple lettuce, best sort.
capitata.
cochleata.
Glandes ilicis semper viriscentis. Galli: schene vert.

ASH WED. 19 FEB. This year the Synod of this province meet here   Synod
at Montpellier. They meet some times at other places. They consist
of about 50 Pastors & as many Elders, each church sending one of
each sort.

Publique admonitions of their consistory happen seldom. The   Excommuni-
last two instances were, one for strikeing a cuff on the eare in the   cation
church on a communion day, for which he was hinderd from
receiving. The other for marrying his daughter to a Papist, for
which he stood excommunicate six months, but their excommunication reaches noe farther then exclusion from the Eucharist, not
from the church & sermons.[1]

They plough the earth here very shallow & usually with one   Ploughing
mule. The plough share is about 1½ pan long & one half pan broad   Aratrum
at the broad end, from whence forwards it grows taper & very
sharpe & slender. From the broad end backwards it hath a shaft
about the length of the share which is put into a mortis in the lower
end of a crooked peice of wood, the upper end whereof is fastend
to the 2 peices of wood which serve for traces. In this mortice the
shaft of the ploughshare & the end of the stiva[2] are both fastend
with a wedg, & under the plough share lies a litle peice of wood of
the bredth or a litle broader then the plough share, & shaped like
it, but shorter, & 3 square the great angle downewards. This is to
make it rise towards the great end & soe turn up the earth. This is
also fastend by two litle sticks, riveted in each side of it, & coming
through the peice of wood of the harness through two holes, on
each side one, above the mortise & these fastend with two litle
wedges. When they leave work, they take their plough in peices
& fasten the severall parts to geather with a cord & soe draw it home.

THURS. 20 FEB. Mr. Pattray knew not the benediction.
A guiny which weighs of our English weight 5 penny weight   Pondera

---

[1] Locke gives a cross-reference to the entry for 23 Feb.
[2] *Plough-handle* (Latin).

45

10 gr., i.e. 130 gr., weighs at Montpellier 2 drachms 15 grains,
where   60 grains make 1 drachm.

8 drachms – – 1 oz.

16 ozs.   – – – 1 lb., their common pound by
which they buy & sell in their markets almost all things, for wood,
apples, lobsters etc. are all bought by weight. Lobsters cost 8 s.
per lb.

This day my orange trees went away.

Canne FRI. 21 [FEB.] A canne is 2 yards 6½ inches of English measure.
A canne conteins 8 pans. ⅓ of a pan which is 3¼ $\frac{1}{24}$ inches English,
added to our English yard, makes a demi canne or half a canne
Montpellier.

⅓ pan is 3¼ $\frac{1}{24}$ inch. ¼ pan is 2½ inches, wanting about $\frac{1}{24}$ inch.

Revenue of the SAT. 22 FEB. Estat du revenu de l'Eglise de France.
Church
            L'Eglise Romaine de France Gallicane est douée pour le present
Archiepiscopi de quinze Archevechez qui sont:

Lyon	Reims	Aix
Sens	Bourdeaux	Vienne
Auches	Toulouze	Rouen
Arles	Bourges	Ambrun
Tours	Narbonne	Paris.

Episcopatus Soubs lesquels Archeveschez sont contenus le nombre de quatre
Bishops
Parishes vingts quinze Eveschez fournis de septs vingts mil cures ou paroisses.
Abbayes   Plus il se trouve treize cens cinquante six Abbaies. Douze mil
Commende- quatre cens prieurez. Douze cens cinquante six commenderies de
ries Malthe. Cent cinquante deux mil chapelles ayant toutes des
Chapelles chapelains sans comprendre les abbayes des Religieuses dont le
Abbayes nombre est de cinq cent cinquante sept.
Cordeliers   Outre ce il se trouve cinq cens couvens de Cordeliers, sans
comprendre les Jacobins, Carmes, Augustins, Chartreux, Celestins,
Jesuits, Minismes, at autres Religieux desquels le nombre se monte
Couvens a quatorze mil soixante dix-sept couvens.

Sont fournis lesd. ecclesiastiques de deux cens cinquante neuf
mil mestairies et dix sept mille arpens de vignes, qui sont par eux
ballées [sic] a ferme, sans comprendre trois mil arpens ou ils
prennent le tiers ou le quart.

Partant il se trouve que lad. eglise a de revenu par an la somme de   Revenu
deux cens soixante seize millions, sans y comprendre les reserves   Reditus
qu'ils font de leurs beaux [sic] a ferme qui se montent à trente six
millions / which is 24 millions sterling.[1]

SUND. 23 FEB. v. p. [   ],[2] but there is now noe feare of excom-   Marriage
munication upon that account, the King haveing made a law that
persons of different religions shall not marry, which often causes
the change of religion, espetially sequioris sexus.[3]

At church today aboundance of coughing.

MUND. 24 FEB. The province of Languedock is thus governd. The   Languedoc
Duke of Vernule, their Governor, commands over the whole
Province, & has a power somewhat like the King's, though he be
most properly Lord Leiutenant, & I doe not heare that he meddles
at all in Judicial causes, either civil or Criminal.[4]

In his absence the province is divided into 3 districts, each having
a deputy Governor[5] with the same power in his respective district.

Every citty also hath its Governor whose power is much like the   Cittys
Governor's of a Garison.

---

[1] This document is reproduced again in the Journal under the date of 29 Sept. 1676
(pp. 450–2), but less accurately as far as the French is concerned, and with part of an
extra paragraph between the third and fourth paragraphs of the text given above. This
begins: 'Lesquelles ecclesiastiques tenent ensemble et possedent 9,000 chasteaux et
maisons, y ayant toutes haute', and then breaks off.

I have been unable to trace the source of this document, but a very similar passage is
to be found in the journal of the Alsatian traveller, Élie Brackenhoffer, with the difference
that the figures given are those of an earlier period (see his *Voyage de Paris en Italie,
1644–1646*, ed. H. Lehr, Paris, 1927, p. 66, and *B.S.H.P.F.* 1903, p. 254).

Skippon (p. 734) summarizes a similar document and adds: 'The said calculation
was made by order of the assembly of the clergy of France, held in the Augustines
convent, at the end of the Pont-Neuf in Paris, the 16th of November 1635'.

Two contemporary estimates of the total income of the Catholic clergy of France
(made in 1639 and 1700) agree on the figure of 270 million *livres*, but they are not very
reliable (cf. P. Sagnac, *La Formation de la Société Française Moderne*, Paris, 1945–6,
2 vols., vol. I, p. 32).

[2] Locke here gives a cross-reference to the second paragraph of the entry for 19 Feb.

[3] 'the inferior sex'.

[4] In this account of the administration of the province of Languedoc, Locke con-
centrates his attention on the position of the governor who now possessed little real
power or influence, and ignores the importance of the new agent of the central government, the *Intendant*: but cf. the entry for 12 July 1677.

[5] There were three *Lieutenants-généraux* of the province. In 1676 these were the
Marquis de Calvisson for Haut Languedoc, the Comte du Roure for Vivarais, Velay
and Uzès, and the Marquis de Montpezat for Bas Languedoc.

Montpellier
Consuls

Montpellier hath 6 Consuls who have the Government of the politie of the towne, order the building or repair of publique places, seeing the bread weight & flesh sold at its due rate, & looking after the weights & measures, & can determin all causes not exceeding five livres. They had formerly a considerable authority, but now they are litle more then servants to the Governor of the towne. They were formerly 3 Protestants & 3 Papists, but the Protestants have been excluded about these [1] years.

Judicature
Premier
President
President
Conseillers

The civil causes of the province are judgd here by a court cald the Court of Aides.[2] The judges are: the Premier President, his place worth about 12,000 livres per annum; 8 presidents, their places worth about 6,000 livres per annum; & 30 Conseilers, their places worth about 2,000 livers per annum. They sit on a high bench in an handsome roome.[3] The Premier President sits next the corner, leaveing it on his right hand, where is a seat elevated a litle higher then the bench, where the King only sits. On both sides this corner sit the other Presidents & next them the Conseilers, who are all judges, & the cause is determind by majority of votes which the Premier President pronounces. If in the pleading there be any papers or other specialtys[4] alleadged on which any part of the cause depends, they then doe not give judgment here, but after the pleading is over, retire all into an other room by them selves & there examin the writings & after that give sentence, & to this Court are brought all the causes of this whole province of Languedoc & Vivares.[5]

Provost
Senescal
Judg
ordinaire

Criminal causes are judged by 3 severall persons. Assassinats, highway men & theives are judgd by the Provost[6] without appeal; Manslaughter etc. by the Senescal;[7] lesse crimes by the Judg ordinaire. There are Provosts & Senescals in every citty, & in every litle country towne a Judge ordinaire, who, seizeing on Criminals, if the offence be above his authority, he remitts them to a superior power. These men's places are not very considerable.

---

[1] Locke wrote '15' and then crossed it out. Haag (x. 368) mentions an *arrêt du conseil* of 28 Aug. 1656 excluding Protestants from these posts.
[2] *La Cour des Aides.*   [3] The building has now disappeared.
[4] *O.E.D.* 'a special contract, obligation or bond, expressed in an instrument under seal'.   [5] Vivarais.
[6] *Prévôt.*   [7] *Sénéchal.*

Besides these, here is another Court cald the Court of Compts,[1] something like our Exchequer, for they examin & pass all accounts of the officers of the King's revenue within this province. With them also all grants from the King are enterd, without which they are not valid.

Court des
Comptes

When any publique tax is given the King, according to an old Survey which they call a Compois, it is first divided & laid upon each diocesse, in the Diocesses respectively distributed upon the severall towns & villages, & in the towns upon the houses & Lands belonging to it, according to their Compoys, which hath not been made new in Montpellier this 100 years,[2] soe that old ruins & new buildings & other circumstances having in soe long time very much alterd the value of their houses, the taxes on them are very disproportionate. Mr. P. pays now but 13 or 14 ecus, but upon a new survey would pay 30 or 33 ecus per annum. His house is worth 500 livers per annum.

Taxes
Tributa

From these taxes are exempted all Noble land which is to pay a year's value to the King every 20 years, but as they order the matter, they pay not above ¾ year's value. All ancient priviledged land of the Church is also exempt, but any that is given to the Church that hath been used to pay taxes, pays it after the donation.

Besides this, excise is paid on severall commoditys. For tobaco here they pay a livre a pound excise, for the Farmers who rent it of the King, sell now all the tobacco, & sell it for 33 s. per lb. what they formerly bought for 13 or 15 s. per lb. These farmers give the King 600,000 l. per annum for the farme of the Tobaco of All France, & it costs them as much more in officers.

Peuter also pays 1 s. per lb. for all that is made.[3]

Wine also, sold in Cabarets, pays about 3 livres per Tunnau, which is worth about 27 or 28 livres, for the tax follows the price.

This day Mr. Fisket prund his vineard. He did it thus late because, it being apt to shoot early in the spring, if cold weather nip the young shoots, it makes the vintage less.

Vineard

---

[1] United with the *Cour des Aides* in 1629.
[2] The tax-rolls were revised in 1600 and 1665, but the assessments were not altered.
[3] The monopoly of tobacco and the tax on pewter were introduced by Colbert in 1674 to help to finance the war. According to Clamageran (II. 655) the two taxes were farmed out at a total of 500,000 l.

This day Mrs. Fisket's father, an old, experienced planter, planted a vineard, & some others, they chooseing, as they call it, the last quarter of the new moon. The moon will be at full on Saturday next, 29th this month.

W. 26 FEB. Disputation at the Physick Schoole.[1] *Much* French, *hard* Latin, *little* Logic *and little* Reason. Vitulo tu dignus et hic.

THURD. 27 FEB.

A Paris ce 8me may 1674.

Revenue   Ce mot n'est que pour vous apprendre d'abord les nouveautes
Reditus   sur le chapitre des Fermes, sur lequel je vous diray qu'enfin c'est tout de bon que l'on travaille a les adjuger separement,[2] et moi que [sic] vous escris je me suis rendu aujourdhuy adjudicataire des Gabells de France sans huictaine[3] moyennant 15,500,000 li.

Les aids et entrees ont este adiugées aussi sans huictaine a 15,600,000 pendant la Guerre, et 15,700,000 a compter trois mois apres la publication de la Paix, et pour les cinque grosses Fermes, convoy de Bourdeaux, marque du Papier et Parchemain, elles ont esté adjugées pareillement a la somme de 10,400,000, le tout sans huictaine. Je croi que tout cela finira Samedy prochain. Enfin Je vous en donnerai des nouvelles et Je vous nommeray ses marques plustost et plus surement que personne.[4]

All others besides the English, even the French themselves, pay in their pensions & lodgings before hand in this town. Our credit is better then soe[5] here. *Pasty.*

Spiritus vini FRID. 28 FEB. They make good brandy here, & one may buy for 8s. per lb. that which will burne ¾ away, & for 32s. per lb. that which will burne quite away, & they may yeild it soe, for the wine

---

[1] The Faculty of Pharmacy is to-day housed in this building.

[2] Instead of making one *bail* for the lot, as had been done in 1668.

[3] This presumably is a mistake for 'sauf huictaine'. Furetière gives, but does not explain, the latter expression, which presumably means 'provided no higher bid is received within a week'.

[4] Locke does not explain how he came to get hold of this letter. According to E. P. Beaulieu (*Les Gabelles sous Louis XIV*, Paris, 1908, p. 69) the *bail* for the *Grandes Gabelles* was given in 1674 to Saunier for 17,650,000 l., that for the *Cinq Grosses Fermes* to the same person for 9,550,000 l., and that for the *Aides et entrées* to Du Fresnay for 18,800,000 l.

[5] *O.E.D.* gives for the expression 'than so' the sense of 'than that'.

of this country is very strong & very cheape, soe that to make Brandy they often buy of the strongest wines at the rate of 17 or 18s. or at dearest one livre per Muy,[1] a Muy containing 512 of their pots. Muy

   The goodnesse of their wine to drink seems to depend on two Vinum causes, besides the pressing & ordering the fermentation. One is the soyle they plant in, on which very much depends the goodnesse of the wine; and this is a constant rule, seting a side all other qualities of the soyle, that the vineard must have an opening towards east or South, or else noe good is to be expected. The other is a mingling of good sorts of wine in their vineyards, for they seldome make red wine of red grapes alone; it will be too thick & deepe coloured except the Spiran which, they say, will make good wine by its self, but to make their red wine pleasant & delicate, they use to mingle a good quantity of white grapes with the red.

SAT. 29 FEB. N.E. Fair. Very cold. Muscat they plant & presse Uva alone. It is ripe before the others. It will grow as well about Montpellier & make as good a wine as at Frontignan, but they dare not plant them because they would be stolen to eat & sell, being a pleasant grape & early ripe, but they are not thought so good as the Spiran, being apt to fume[2] to the head & make it ake.

   Spiran is a black, middle sizd, round grape, very sweet & very wholesome to eat, soe that physitians allow them in great quantitys, & the people think them the better because they are laxative. They also of all the red grapes make good wine by them selves, but they plant them not in so great quantitys as the others, because in hot & dry seasons they will dry up before they are ripe.

   There is a green grape also of this name, seldom used for wine, nor altogeather so good as the black for eating, but its chief excellency is that it will keepe long in the winter for eating.

   Marokin is a very black, fleshy grape, round & very large, very good to eat, but seldome used for wine. Terret is a black, very large, but not very sweet grape, & therefor used only for wine, wherein it gives a large quantity, but not much strength. Ramonin, a black, very sweet, midle sized grape, good for wine & eating. Pickapoul, black & very sweet, good for both uses.

---

[1] *Muid.*   [2] *O.E.D.* 'to rise as fumes'.

These sorts of red grapes, though all commended for wine, yet they are seldom used any sort alone or altogeather to make wine, without the mixture of these 2 sorts following of white grapes, without which the wine is too thicke & high coloured:

Picardan is a white, long, large, very sweet grape with a litle of the Muscat in it; makes very good wine alone or mingled.

Claret is white, midle sizd, longish, very sweet. These are both good to eat or for wine, alone or mingled, but the Picardan is the more commended.

Vinum   But to make their wine, they generally plant of all these sorts togeather (except the Muscat) in their vineyards, & upon the skilfull mixture of these, next to the property of the soile, the goodnesse of their wine does much depend, but the soile is so considerable that two fields which only a ditch parts, doe one yield good wine & the other constantly bad.

Vinea   They usually plant about this time of the yeare in the quarter before the full,[1] & their vineards will last 50, nay 100 years. The younger the vines, the greater quantity; the older, the better the wine. In hilly ground also the better, & spetially opening to South or east. In plains greater quantity.

They plant their rows in quincunx at the distance of 4, 4½ & 5 pans. Where they use ploughs to turne the ground, the rows are wider, where delveing, narrower, for they either delve or plough it twice every yeare, about this time of the yeare & again in May.

When their grapes are ripe, they cut them & as soon as cut, press them presently; any keeping spoyles them.

Besides the vines above mentioned there are other sorts here, viz. Corinth in their vineards. Indica or St. John's, ripe at Midsomer. Crispata, a good, sweet, ripe grape. These 2 later only in the Physick Garden.

Vinea   They plant, as they shewd me, their vines about 18 inches deepe, I beleive a spit deepe, & always leave 2 knots above ground.

For manure to their vines they esteme pigeon's or hen's dung to increase the quantity without injuring the goodnesse, but horse

---

[1] *Moon* understood (Locke uses exactly the same phrase 'before the full' in his *Observations*, p. 1).

dung or any beast's dung they think spoiles the goodnesse of the wine. This they have so strong an opinion of at Galliac,[1] a place about 30 leagues from hence, that if a peasant there should use any but bird's dung about his vines, his neighbours would burn his house, because they would not have the wine of that place loose its reputacion. They there marke all their wine casks with a cock burnt on, from Gal in pattoy being a cock. Rosemary flowers for making the Queen of Hungary's water[2] in great plenty already.

There are as many sorts of Olives as of grapes in this country, viz: *Olivae*

> Groosau, large.
> Pichulina, litle.
> Verdal, midlesizd.

These 3 sorts are good to eat & the last also is good for oyle & a good bearer.

> Olivera ⎫
> Corneau ⎪
> Salierna ⎬ bearer.
> Clarmontesa ⎪
> Redonau ⎭
> Bootiliau
> Argentau
> Moorau
> Marsiliensa
> Pigau

All these are litle olives & used only for oyle. They plant them promiscuously in their olive yards, & mingle the olives in making oyle. That which they principally regard in their plants is that they *Olea* be of the sorts that are the best bearers, & if they have not enough of those plants, they plant others & inoculate[3] them. Theyr plants have all roots which they get from ofsets, as I understand. Their time of planting is February, March or April. The olive trees last to a vast age, 200 years they say. When the old stocks are faulty, they let up young offsets from the roots round about, & when they

---

[1] Gaillac.

[2] Another important product of Montpellier in the seventeenth century. *O.E.D.* quotes the following definition from Chambers' *Cyclopedia*: '*Hungary Water*, a distilled water, denominated from a Queen of Hungary for whose use it was first prepared; made of rosemary flowers infused in rectified spirit of wine, and thus distilled'.

[3] *O.E.D.* 'to set or insert (an 'eye', bud or scion) in a plant for propagation'.

are grown up to any considerable bignesse, cut away the old stock, & when the remaining young trees have not roome to spread because of their neighbourhood, they transplant them till they leave at last but one standing. Divers examples of an old tree beset with these young ones we saw on the road between Avignion, Pont du Gard & Nismes.

They dig about their olive trees every year & lay soyle to them sometimes, & at the same time they dig their vineards, & sometimes at others, for all about this towne their olive trees & corne grow togeather, even where they are set at a distance of   [1] in Quincunx, & in some places they have olive trees scatterd up & down in their vineards.

Vinea SUND. I MAR. 167$\frac{5}{6}$. S.E. Very fair & cold. Vineard newly delved.

M. 2 MAR. S.E. Cloudy. Cold.

TUES. 3 MAR. S.E. Cloudy. Cold. At the Physick Schoole a Scholler answering the first time, a Professor moderating. 6 other professors oppose with great violence of Latin & French, Grimasse & hand.

Here passed through the towne 250 horse towards Catalonia. Very ordinary pret. medium 10 lb.

WED. 4 MAR. We went to Frontignan, 4 leagues. On the way we saw the Grotto of Madando,[2] something like Oakie hoale[3] with water in it. It is about 1½ leagues from Montpellier. From thence all the way to Frontignan we ride[4] in a Valley, having the Estang on one hand & barrain mountains on the other. All the way we ride through Vinea groves of large olive trees, in most places with vines or corne under them. The people all the way busy, some prueneing their vines, others ploughing, others houghing[5] their vineard. In some places Olea the earth was digd up about the roots of the olive trees, but not quite to lay them bare. The earth dug out lay in a circle round at the distance of 3 or 6 foot according to the bignesse of the tree. In this hole they put horse dung.

---

[1] Left blank in MS.   [2] Presumably the Grotte de la Madeleine.
[3] Wookey Hole (Somerset). In her *Journeys* Celia Fiennes spells the name 'Oacky Hole'.
[4] An old past tense of *ride*.   [5] *O.E.D.* 'hoe'.

Frontignan is a litle towne wald, the figure of the wall square, Frontignan
& is situated upon the Estang where it is a litle kind of a port. Here
we dind, but had but bad Muscat. From hence we went to Port
Cette.[1] Vineards by the way & some in ground soe stony that one Vinea
could see noe earth. Cette is 1½ leagues from Frontignan. The mole
at Port Cette is a mighty work, & far advanced according to the Cette
description of Froidour.[2] But the sand in the port now & the
breach made in the mole last winter shew how hardly one defends
a place against Neptune which he attaques with great & small shot
too. From hence we went to the baths at Balaruc[3] & lay there, Balaruc
where amongst other things we had served a plate of preserved
Haws which they call Pommett de Paradise.[4] There were 2 things
very remarkable in this new sort of sweetmeat, their ill taste &
largenesse which was about the bignesse of a Dutch Goosberry,
& before preserving they told us they were as big as Cherrys. In
a field of corne by the way we saw a great deale shot into ear.

TH. 5 MAR. The Bath at Ballaruc Is a pretty plentifull spring of
water which rises but a litle way from the Estang & the end of
a valley that opens upon the Estang, & the water in the bath is soe
neare the levell of that in the Estang that that in the Estang boys it
up. It rises in a roome 12 foot square, partly coverd with bords,
& hath roome only for 6 persons to bathe at once, each going downe
a pair of Stairs between 2 beams, & soe sit 2 & 2 opposite to one
an other. Here they bathe starke naked & often times men &
women togeather. The water is as hot as of the King's bath[5] & hath
a very salt taste. I had noe Galls[6] nor other things for experiments,
but they say it colours blew with Galls. From hence to the town of

---

[1] Known officially as Sète since 1927; cf. entry for 11 March 1677.
[2] Louis de Froidour, *Lettre...concernant la relation et la description des travaux qui se font en Languedoc pour la communication des deux mers* (Toulouse, 1672).
[3] Balaruc-les-Bains.
[4] Seventeenth-century and modern dictionaries are equally silent on this term. Littré gives only *pomme de paradis*, 'espèce de pomme rouge qui se mange en été' (cf. Appendix A, p. 279).
[5] At Bath.
[6] The aqueous extract of powdered gall-nuts, used as a reagent in testing for the presence of iron in waters. When this solution was added to a water containing dissolved iron salts a dark blue colour was added, owing to the presence of tannins in the original gall-nuts (cf. entry for 9 May 1676).

Ballaruc is about a mile, a wald towne on high ground on the side
of the Estang. It hath the shortest, narrowest, crookedest streets
that I ever saw any where, & I beleive never were soe few pitifull
& ill placed houses girt with a wall any where else.

   Round about the room where the Bath rises, are rooms for beds,
bad enough & fiter for an hospitall then receit of strangers that
come here for health or diversion. A good part of our way hence to
Montpellier lay through a large vally full of Corne, wine & oyle, &
in it by a litle river side more meadow ground then I had seen in
any part of France. By the way we saw beans blown.

Kermes FRID. 6 MAR. The plant that bears the Grana Kermes is a litle, low
shrub, growing much about the heigth of Juniper or furze in
England. It is a winter green, & the leafe with prickles like our
holly leaves, but not soe broad, thick nor stiff. . . .[1]

Milites SAT. 7 MAR. Four Luisdors to drink the King's health.

Mercurius SUND. 8 MAR. Dr. Barbeyrac told me that in diging cellars etc. they
often finde here in Montpellier great quantitys of running quick
silver, & that he hath often seen it him self amongst the earth.

M. 9 MAR. The Captain at Petit Paris telling the storys of his amours
(camp Laundresses) & rebuking the frier complaining of his
businesse & fatigue.

Vitis TUESD. MAR. 10. Vines newly pruned weeping. A peasant working
in the vineard said they were never the worse.

Sal SUND. MAR. 15. They sell at Montpellier a Minot of salt for £16 – 16
which at the salt pits about Aigues mortes, 4 or 5 leagues from
Mensura thence, costs them but £0 – 5. A Minot is a measure conteining
about 110 or 112 lbs. of Salt.

TUES. 17 MARCH. I sent the bill of ladeing for the vines to Mr.
Stringer.[2] They were shipd at Bourdeaux 5 March by Pierre
Rocaure on the ship James of Yarmouth, master Tho: Paris,
consigned to Mr. Kiffin[3] at London. Freight five shillings.

[1] There follows a long quotation on the subject from D'Albenas, *Les Antiquités de Nismes* (Lyons, 1559, folio), p. 47.
[2] The secretary of Locke's patron, the Earl of Shaftesbury.
[3] Also a member of Shaftesbury's household?

Spirits of wine burning away $\frac{4}{5}$ or more, the seller asked 4s. Vini spiritus
per lb.

Clysters are very frequently prescribd in the practise of physick
here & the Apothecarys' men administer them indifferently to men
& women. Only the meaner sort of women about Montpellier are
with difficulty brought to take them after this manner.

W. MAR. 18. The manner of making a doctor in physic was this. Doctoratus
First came in an officer with a mace on his shoulder, very much like
one of the squire bedles' staves in Oxford. On the end of it hung
a square, black cap such as the Doctors usually weare, but coverd
upon the top with Sleasie[1] silk, red, which was like a buff[2] rampant,
for it spread on each side as far as the edges of the cap. After him
followed one of the professors in his scarlet robes which were of
damask, & a black cap on, coverd with sleasy silk as the other.
After him followed the inceptor,[3] bare in a black gown like a
batchelor of arts. The Doctor ascended into the chair & sat him
downe. The inceptor followd him & stood just at the entrance. The
chaire is a large, stone pulpit much like that in the Divinity Schoole
at Oxford. As soon as they were got into that station, a company of
fidlers that were placed behind the company in a corner of the
room, strooke up. When they had plaid a litle while, the professor
made signs to them to hold that he might have oportunity to
enterteine the company, which he did with a speech against
innovation as long as an ordinary declamation. When he had don,
the musick took their turne, & then the inceptor began his speech,
wherein I found litle for edification, it being, I beleive, cheifly
designed to complement the Chancellor[4] & other professors who
were present. In the midle of his speech he made a pause, & then
we had an interlude of musick, & soe went on till he came to thank
us all for our company & soe concluded. Then the Doctor put on
his head the cap that had marchd in on the Bedle's staff in signe of

---

[1] *O.E.D. sleazy*: 'of textile fabrics or materials. Thin or flimsy in texture; having
little substance or body'.

[2] *O.E.D.* 'buffalo'.

[3] The Archives of the Faculty of Medicine give his name (Jodoun, of Auxerre), but
nothing further is known about him.

Michel Chicoyneau who held the office from 1667 to 1701.

his Doctorship, put a ring on his finger, girt him about the loins with a gold chain, made him sit downe by him that haveing taken pains he might now take ease, kissd & imbraced him in token of the friendship ought to be amongst them, & afterwards deliverd a booke into his hands, & soe the ceremony ended with the inceptor making legs[1] to each of the professors when he was come down into the midle of the roome, they sitting on both sides, & turning at every leg to salute them in their order. The professors are the Chancellor & 6 others.[2]

Beefe

Mutton

The ordinary rate for beefe in this towne is £0 – 2 – 4 per lb. & mutton £0 – 3 – 6 per lb. It is cheaper in the country round about, & therefor a coach goes some times to take the aire & bring in a sheep or peice of mutton. The reason of its being dearer is 6 deneirs per lb. paid to the towne for each lb. sold of beef, mutton, veale or porke, whereof ½ ought to goe to the maintenance of the

Protestants

Protestant ministers by the agreement of the peace, & they had it formerly paid them, but now they allow them but 1 d. per lb., nor doe they indeed pay them that, for 1 d. per lb. amounts in a year to between 5 & 6,000 livres & they pay them but 1,400 livres per annum.[3]

Homicidia

Monsieur Reniac,[4] a gent. of this towne in whose house Sir J. Rushworth[5] lay, about 4 years agon sacrificed a child here to the devill, a child of a servant of his, upon a designe to get the devill to be his friend & help him to get some mony. Severall murders committed here since I came hither & more attempted, one by a brother on his sister in the house where I lay.

Vine leaves out to-day.

---

[1] *O.E.D.* 'an obeisance made by drawing back one leg and bending the other: a bow, scrape'.

[2] Cf. entry for 20 March.

[3] Gachon (p. 173 n.) quotes a decree of 16 June 1682 taking away from the Protestants of Montpellier the sum of 1400 l. which they received out of the municipal taxes on meat.

[4] Rignac. This crime is related at some length by André Delort (I. 261–3) under the date of 1672. There is another version in Mme Du Noyer (Letter XIII).

[5] He does not appear in the reference books on baronets and knights, but Tufton several times refers to the presence of a person of that name at Montpellier in 1678 and the following years: for instance, he writes in Dec. 1678, shortly after Locke's second visit to Montpellier: 'Sir James Rusworthe [sic]...returns his service to you and is very sorry he had not the good fortune to meet you' (MS. Locke, c. 22, ff. 26–7).

Olive trees set both in corne ground & vineards in rows at the   Oliva
distance from 13 to 20 of my steps, i.e. 34 foot for 20 steps.

The husbandmen & country labourers in this country in diging,   Operarii
pruneing & other workes of husbandry work but till noon, wages
18s., but will doe as good a day's work in that time as in other parts
they do in a whole day.

Monsieur Puech for £46 – 12 – 5 Sterling paid in London had   Exchange
now a bill charged [sic] in Paris for 204 escus 50s. 10d., very
neare 1 escu & 6s. for every crown English, wanting but $\frac{1}{10}$ of
a sou in each crown.

THURS. MAR. 19. At the Physic Garden they make use of bislingua,   Hortus
which is a winter green, to set out beds. It grows thick quickly
& will be cut. It is raised by slips. But a better thing to me seems
to be Sabina baccifera which grows to a pretty high tree, but will
be kept cut at any heigth, as box, & endures the excessive cold of
the mountaines & is raisd by seeds.

FRID. MAR. 20. When the Doctor had don his speech,[1] he put on
the cap & ring & used the other ceremonys to the inceptor, & then
after that it was the Inceptor made his speech. When all was don,
they retird, professors & inceptor, into another room & there
the Chancellor, takeing the cap coverd with Slesy crimson silke
& in his crimson damaske robes, goes along with the inceptor
through the great streets to his lodging, the musick playing al the
way before, the other professors accompanying him & the schollers
following, where the dore was all hung round with bays. The
Chancellor enterd, where he & the rest of the professors dine with
the inceptor. Of the rest he took leave at the dore.

SAT. MAR. 21. The Archbishop of Lyons gives the King   Quater sols
1,000,000 Livres for the liberty of coyning 4s. peices for 3 years,   peices
& they coyn at Paris & Lyons 10 Kentals a day.

33 Companys quarterd at Moulin[2] upon free quarter, which the
people like not. Their companys are about 50 men a peice, officers
& all.

---

[1] Locke gives a cross-reference to the entry of 18 March.
[2] Moulins (Allier)?

Acetarium   Salade herbs used at Montpellier:

Lettice 8 days old.	Melissa.
Cerefolium.	Balsamum.
Eruca.	Capa Isalonica. Angl: Sithes.
Nasturtium.	
Prinpinella.	
Dracunculus.	

SUND. MAR 22. If one take the ashes of Sarments & put them in water about a day & half before the Aequinox, he shall finde them rise to the top of the water the very instant of the Aequinox. This was told Monsieur Regius[1] for a certain experiment, but he found it not succeed upon Triall.

Cartesiana   The New philosophie prohibited to be taught in universitys,
Philosophia   schooles & Academies.[2]

TUESD. MAR. 24. Sent the bill of Loading for the oranges to Mr. Stringer. Shipped by Pierre Rocaure on the Recovery of Yarmouth at Bordeaux, Nathaniel Locke, Master, consignd to Mr. Kiffin at London, 13 March 1676. Freight 8s.

---

[1] Pierre Sylvain Régis (1632–1707), one of the foremost popularizers of Cartesianism in the second half of the seventeenth century. He taught the new philosophy, first, at Toulouse, and then, under the auspices of his patron, the Marquis de Vardes, at Aigues-Mortes and, finally, from 1671 onwards, at Montpellier. Later he returned to Paris where he took over from Rohault the task of giving public lectures on Cartesianism, until these were banned. In 1690 he published his *Système de philosophie* and nine years later was elected to the Academy of Sciences. He was essentially an expositor rather than an original philosopher.

Locke evidently had contacts with him later in Paris, for his second note-book contains the following entry for 1678 (p. 92): 'Regis. proch la Greve a la rue de Tissandery a la test d'or St. Augustin place Daulphin'.

[2] Descartes's works were placed on the Index in November 1663. In 1671 the Archbishop of Paris communicated to the University of Paris a verbal ban on the teaching of Cartesianism there. 'Le Roi vous exhorte, Messieurs, de faire en sorte que l'on n'enseigne point dans les Universités d'autre doctrine que celle qui est portée par les règlements et les statuts de l'Université'. The rumour that the University of Paris was going to ask the *Parlement* for a formal ban on the teaching of Cartesianism in favour of the philosophy of Aristotle, led to the famous 'Arrêt burlesque' of Boileau. In 1675 the ban on the teaching of Cartesianism was extended to the University of Angers, and according to Bouillier (*Histoire de la Philosophie cartésienne*, Paris, 1854, 2 vols., I. 469) it was in the period 1675–90 that the supporters of the new philosophy met with most hostility from the authorities. It was not until 1690, for instance, that Régis was allowed to publish his *Système de philosophie*, and even then he was compelled to remove the name of Descartes from the title-page.

Dined at Pont Lunell, 4 Leagues from Montpellier. Pruneing   Pont Lunell
of vines by the way. S.E., very cold.

From thence to Aigues Mortes, 2 leagues, situated in a low   Aigues Mortes
plain with great washes[1] all around it, & soe is a very unhealthy
place. It is a litle square town, well walled, built by St. Luis[2] for
a port. The sea formerly washed the walls of it, but is now removed   Mare
a league from the towne, & there remains only a litle Estang that
comes up to the walls, which is navigable only to very litle boats,
as they told us, though when I was there, I saw not one boat all
over it. In the walls on the south side there is the mark yet of one
great gate between two towers, & 2 other lesse gates that opend
to the sea, but are now walled up, but there are some iron rings yet
remaining, & the signs of others that were fastened in the walls to
tie the vessels to.

The wals are about 8 foot thick of square stone cut every one
about the edg an inch or 2 in, soe that every stone hath its particular
eminency. The whole compasse of the walls is an oblonge square,
about 5 or 600 foot along the shore, & something about half or
$\frac{3}{4}$ of it the other way inwards towards the land, which is the whole
towne. There is a walk by the walls all round within & but one
gate, on the North west corner. In the wall there are severall
towers, some round, some square; and the towne within, to justify
the reput that it was built by St. Luys, is laid out into very strait,
faire street[s] which look most of them from one wall to tother, soe
that it seems to be designed at once. I have not seen in any towne
of France the streets soe regular.

They say there are 700 houses in this towne, though there be
some large gardens. There is a Temple & $\frac{1}{4}$ Protestants (they were
all formerly soe) & severall churches, but never a tower or steeple
in the towne but Constance's Tower, just by the gate as you enter,
a round tower of an ordinary steeple heigth, built, as they say, long
before the town. The walls of it are about 15 foot thick. From the
top you have a prospect all over the country which is a great plain
for many leagues about & very much coverd with water.

---

[1] O.E.D. 'a sandbank or tract of land alternately covered and exposed to the sea'.
[2] He embarked there in 1248 for the Seventh Crusade and in 1270 for the Eighth.

Just by this tower is the Marquis de Vards'[1] house, who is governor of the town & of the country about half a league about, as far as the tower called La Carbonier[2] where is a gard upon a passe over the washes, & we paid 4s. for passing. Between La Carbonier & the town we saw aboundance of partridges, and[3] they say there are plenty of hares & other game preservd there by the strict order & severity of the Marquis de Vards who, not long since, clapt a towns man up in a litle hole in Constance's Tower, where he had just roome to stand upright, but could not sit or ly down, & kept him there 3 days for committing some small trespasse on his game.

The town is a Garison & hath 3 companys in it, not amounting to 100 men, they having this last yeare lost 18 men out of a company that marchd in 30, a cleare argument of the good aire of the place. In the way from Pont Lunell the hedges are almost all Tamarisque, & about ½ mile from Pont Lunell is a Garden belonging to the Marquis de Lecai[4] wherein is a very long grasse walk of tall Cipresse trees on one side & bay on the other, & without the cipresse trees is a row of poplars, the handsomest & longest walke I have yet seen in France. The cipresse trees stood soe close togeather that they made a continued shade & touched one an other. There is noe thing else in the garden considerable for they were ploughing in it, which is usuall in their gardens, & taking care of the Kitching provision there. There is also a litle wood in it with some narrow walkes.

Vidor   This garden is on the banks of the Vidor,[5] over which is Pont Lunell.

Pecais   WED. 25 MAR. We went to Pecais, 2 leagues. The way lyes most of it through the marshes & washes of this low country, it being a great part water, & the remains of that which, 'tis probable, was heretofore a cleare Estang, but either by land flouds bringing down sand & earth or the south & the south-east winde driveing in sand, this way it is come in time to be pretty well fild up, & a great part

---

[1] François René du Bec-Crespin, Marquis de Vardes (c. 1621–88) was exiled from Court in 1664 for his part in various intrigues directed against *Madame*, Henriette d'Angleterre, the sister-in-law of the King. His exile in the South of France lasted until 1683.

[2] La Tour Carbonière.   [3] MS. has *as*.

[4] Marquis de Leques (?).   [5] Vidourle.

of it become firme ground, though it hath yet recoverd but a very course turf of rushes, sedge & a great many daffadils which we saw all along full blowne. But that it is earth made of sand cast up out of the sea is very probable, in that, though the salt water be interlaced with it all up & downe, &, in some places where we rode over, lay a litle above the surface, we found not any where any bogs, but the way was every where firme sand. Between those Marches & others that lye more inward towards the land & are fild with fresh water, there lyes all along, as far as I could see, & we crossed it between La Carbonier & Aigues Mortes, a tract of barren sea sand that lyes unequally in hillocks & higher then the marshes on Mare both sides. This, I imagin, was formerly a sea banke, such an one as is now the Fence between the Estang de Thau & the Mediterranean, a part whereof one rides on between Frontignan & Port Sette, & I believe the low, marshy land within this sandy ridg was formerly an Estang, as that of Thau now is.

At Pecais[1] is made all the salt that is used on this side France. Sal The manner is this. There is a great pond made in an oblong square. This is divided by litle banks into squares of about 40 steps of a side, & between every one of these squares is a litle chanell to bring in the salt water. These chanells run not of all sides, but only the crosse way of the great pond, about which also all round there runs a channell to bring the salt water to those other crosse channels. All these were now fild with rain water which, when the weather begins to grow hot, they let out, & then fill them with salt water, which they raise by wheels with wooden buckets fixed to them out of pits just by, which are supplied out of the Estang, for these salines are about a league from the sea. With this water they cover these squares or tables, as they call them, 5 or 6 inches deepe, & when the sun hath exhald almost all the moisture, they supply it with fresh, & soe continue to doe all the heat of the year till at the later end they have a cake of salt 3, 4 or 5 inches thick, according to the heat & drougth of the yeare. The last yeare was a bad one, for whereas they use to make 10,000 muids a yeare, they last yeare made but 1,000. The salt is very white. They that are the owners

---

[1] Peccais is still famous for its salt.

Minot

of the soile where the pits are, are at the charge of making the Salt,
& sell it to the Farmers for five sous per Minot, which is a measure
of 7 inches deepe & 23½ diameter. A Minot of salt weighs 120 lb.

The salt, when it is made, they lay up in great heapes & thatch it
over with reeds, much after the fashion of our wheat mows,[1] but
that the eves come quite to the ground. In one of these heapes there

Muyd
uses to be about 50 Muyds. A Muy or Muid is a grosse of, or 144,
Minots, & every Saline or worke, of which there are 18 at Pecais,
uses to make in a yeare 10 or 12 of these heapes.

Sal
The salt which the owner sels to the Farmers for 5 sous per
Minot, they sel again to others for £16–16 per minot; only the
inhabitants of Aigues Mortes have a priviledg to buy it for £1 per
minot.

For this farme of the Salines of Pecais they say the Farmers give
£2,200,000 a year to the King, & are at as much more charg[2] in
officers & guards imploid in the sale of it, they keeping constantly
in pay 18,000 men, & the stealeing the duty of this commodity is
of such consequence that, if a man should be taken with but an
handfull of salt not bought & paid for at this rate of the Farmers, he
would be sent to the Gallys.

In the granary of salt at Pecais you may see store of pouderd....[3]

Vinea
S. Hard. Very cold. Pruneing of vines as we passed. We lay at
night at Pont Lunell.

Castrete
THUR. MAR. 26. From Pont Lunel to Castret,[4] 2 long leagues. Here
on the top of an hil is the house of the Marquis de Castres. It was
begon to be built about 18 yeares agon by the late Marquis[5] who
was governor of Montpelier & one of the 3 Lieutenant Governors
of this province, who died two or 3 yeares agoe. His son,[6] about
17 year old, is now Governor of Montpellier, but the businesse of
it is managed by his unkle, Cardinal Bonzy.[7]

---

[1] *O.E.D.* 'stacks'.   [2] *O.E.D.* 'expense'.
[3] MS. appears to have something like 'S^t re wrences'.   [4] Castries.
[5] René Gaspard de la Croix, who died in 1674.
[6] Jean François de la Croix (1663–1728), who had a distinguished military career.
His wife is the subject of the famous portrait in Saint-Simon, beginning 'Mme de
Castries était un quart de femme, une espèce de biscuit manqué...'.
[7] The widow of the late Marquis was the sister of Cardinal Bonzi (see entry for
10 Feb. 1677).

64

The house[1] is 2 sides of a square, each about sixty steps long. An other side was designd to be built, but is left undon. The entrance into the court is in the midle of the dead wall, but into the house at the corner, where just before you is the great stair, which is neither large nor handsome, of stone (as they all are in this country) with 2 flights. It is a single building about 15 steps broad. All one side is a stable, & in the other is a hall, an ordinary roome, & from it runs an entry by which you are conveyd to severall other ordinary rooms. All this lower story, stables & all, are arched. Below the house lies a very spatious garden with a very large basin in it, but this house & all things about it are imperfect, except an aqueduct, which is a mighty work & too big, one would think, for a private purse, at least for one of about 1,000 lb. a yeare.

By this aqueduct the water is brought about a league off for the service of the house & garden, some part of it in a coverd trench on the winding sides of a mountain, some part of it on a wall 7, 8, or 10 foot high, as is occasion, & some part of the way over arches, some whereof are of a great heigth. To carry it from the side of a mountaine over one vally which is neare the house there are togeather 85 arches, which are each of them in the cleare $32\frac{1}{2}$ foot, but most about 30 foot & some under. The pedestals of these arches are some 8, some 12 or 13 foot & the severall measures between, but most about 10 foot or a litle more. From the end of these arches a wall takes it & carrys it to another row of arches, in number 25, of the same size with the former, soe that, allowing 40 or 41 foot to each arch, the whole length of the arches will be about 4,400 foot, which with 50 arches more of the same kinde that they tell us are near the source & we saw not,[2] will make 2,000 foot more, in all 6,400 foot of our English measure, for by the English foot I measurd.

The arches are some of them very high & are turnd all with stones of 4 f. 10 inches a peice, which is the thicknesse of the arch. The pedestalls below are thicker, most about 8 foot, & soe, just at

---

[1] Important additions were made to the château from 1656 onwards. The gardens were designed by Lenôtre, and Riquet, we are told, had a hand in the construction of the aqueduct.

[2] (Marginal note): 'I never could speak with any body that had seen these 50 arches.'

the abutment of the arches, are brought in & narrowed to 4 f. 10 inches, & some of them where the arches are high, are built wide at the ground & slopeing up like buttrices. Above the top of the arches is a wall which carrys the water, which is narrower then the thicknesse of the arches & is coverd all along a top & is here, I beleive, about a yard thick. Notwithstanding that the arches are all turned with long stones that reach quite through from one side to the other, yet severall of them leake already, & I believe Pont du Gard will stand firme when this aqueduct will be lost in its ruins, though that be 1500 or 1600 years older, & this be but yet 4 or 5 years old, if so much.

They say this & the house cost £400,000. The house stands upon the top of a hill & the gardens lye very low under it. The discents are not by stairs, but gentle declivitys turnd severall ways, very easy & handsome, with walls of squard stone on the sides just as high as the earth. At the end of one of them in an artificiall rock is a cascade of water of 4 falls.

Vinea   As we passd along, people were diging their vineards, some with triangular houghs & some with litle spades.

Agricultura   They weed their corne with little padles about 1 or 1½ inch broad at the end of staves 8 foot long or more.

Itinerantes   We met some travellers, few with boots, many with clokes, espetially purple, none without pistols, even those that rod into the fields to see their workmen.

The Envoys discourse with Mr. D^{sI} about alliance & assistance, besides severall others.

Lectica SAT. MAR. 28. 5 livres a day the usuall rate of an horse litter. Beauchattau alias Lusansy.^{2}

Funera   The Christenings of the Religion at Montpellier are about 300 & the Funerals about 260.

SUND. MAR. 29. Notes read in the Temple that one not of their communion desires their prayers, which they say is usuall.

---

[1] I am unable to offer the slightest hint as to the meaning of this entry (Does 'D^{s}' stand for Diggs, who seems to have had connexions with Geneva? See entry for 25 Jan. 1676).   [2] Another mystery.

MUND. MAR. 30. Pruneing of Olive trees.   Oliva

TUES. MAR. 31. Many murders committed here. He that en- Judicium
deavoured to kil his sister in our house, had before kild a man, & it
had cost his father 500 escus to get him off, by[1] their secret distribution gaining the favour of the Counsellors.[2]

WED. 1 APRIL 1676. An Irish preist[3] telling Mr. Bur:[4] that they
hoped they should have a body strong enough to support themselves.

1 Cane	a	8 pans.
1 Pan	–	9½ pouces.
1 Toise	–	6 pieds du Roy, ou pieds droits.
1 Pied	–	12 pouces.
1 Pouce	–	12 lignes.

Mensura

THUR. APR. 2. The papists visit all the Churches, or at least 7 or
eight, & in each say 5 Paternosters & 5 Ave Marias, in most of
which a crucifix is exposd on the railes of the alter which they kisse
with great devotion & give mony, there being persons of some
condition set at all the avenues of all the churches with basins to
beg.

GOOD FRID. APR. 3. To have violets etc. double. Sow the seeds Viola
& when the double one grows, let the single one that grows next
him seed, for the double one seeds not. Sow these seeds & you
shall have more double then otherwise. Jacques, the gardiner at the
Physic Garden, told me that he had tried it often.

SUN. EASTER DAY, APR. 5. S. Fair. Very hot.

MUND. APR. 6. To Pont Lunell to diner, 4 leagues. From thence
over the valy of Aigues Mortes 2 leagues, a deepe plain & rich
soyle, full of corne & hedgerows of willows & poplars & tamariske
for hedges. At Bauvair[5] we got up the hil & had there a very large Bauvair
& pleasant prospect to Aigues Mortes & towards Montpellier even
to the losse of sight, which was this day hinderd by a very hazy
aire. As soone as the ground began to rise above the levell of this

---

[1] MS. has *but*.   [2] I.e. the judges (*conseillers*).
[3] There was a monastery of twelve Irish monks at Narbonne, according to Basville.
[4] Perhaps the pastor, René Bertheau, whose name Locke spells elsewhere 'Birto'.
[5] Vauvert.

plaine, it began again to be full of pebbles & in some places was coverd with them, which yet hinderd not the planting of vineards, which in the rising of this hill we began to meet with again, besides some reall cherry trees planted up & downe from Bauvair which we left a litle on the left hand, seated on the side of this hill & overlooking the valley, the greatest part of the inhabitants Protestants (as of several of the towns here abouts).

Protestantes

To St. Giles 2 leagues more over unequall, pebly & in a great part very barren ground, coverd with Schesnes de Kermes, lavander, time & Cistus Leden, but noe grasse. Here I saw sheepfolds which, besides the hurdles, had a high fence of reeds, moveable & supported by forks as the hurdles, & set up on the weather side to shelter the sheepe.

St. Giles

Ovis

Here we saw the ruins of an old abby built by Charlemaine & destroyd in the late civil warres.[1] The front on the west end which hath not now half its ancient heigth, retains still its old imagery representing a good part of the Scripture story, & over the midle of the great gate of later addition & worse sculpture was the image of an old man siting with a globe in his hand, which he that shewd us the church, told us was God the Father, but soe ill work that, if the Scripture had not forbid it, the ill figure might have prohibited the use of it in religion. The Church is an Abby & the Abot's revenue worth, as we were told, 24,000 livres per annum.[2]

Deus pater

We saw upon the way several people in their holyday clothes which were but ordinary, espetially young wenches rideing upon asses & belabouring them with their boots, soe that one might say they went faster then their asses or the young fellows that accompanied them. At St. Giles a congregation of men & wenches danced heartily to the beating of a drum for want of better musick; nay, their naturall inclinations wrought so effectually that it helped them to dance even when the dubing of the drum faild them. 300 communicant Protestants in this towne, & the minister hath 200 crowns per annum.

Chorea

Protestantes

TUESD. APR. 7. From St. Giles to Arles 3 leagues. A litle mile from St. Giles we passed one branch of the Rhosne by a trill & here got

Arles

---

[1] In 1562.   [2] Basville gives 14,000l.

into a part of Provence, though we were but half over the Rhosne.
The other half, which washes the walls of Arles, we passed by
a bridg of boats. The Island between these 2 branches of the Rhosne   Camargue
is called Camargue. That which we passed over is a rich, deepe
soyle & plain, as Brentmarsh, for the most part imploid in tillage,
& bears very good corne. There we saw some plots of pasturage
& the turf good, but infested with tamariske & overgrown by it as
some of our pastures in England are with broome. The trill we
passed is 5 leagues from the sea where we saw some litle vessels of
20 or 30 tun, & the like at Arles. In Camargue, a litle before we
came to the towne, we found some vineards, which I believe by
necessity of the people rather then by fitnesse of the soyle placed
there. The Rhosne is kept out of Camargue with very high banks,
faced in some places with stone slopeing. A litle before we enterd
Arles, we heard the report of guns or something like it, which was
either guns or chambers fired as the Host was carried by.

In an opening before the Towne House is erected an Obelisque,   Arles
square & taper, 60 pans longue, found near the towne, not far from   Obeliscus
the Rhosne.[1] It was formerly all of a peice, but hath been broken
off about 18 pans from the top, but both peices are set togeather
& erected on a fair pedestall. It is of a kinde of blew stone,[2] which
is found, as they say, in this country. The Towne House is new
built,[3] & hath this remarkable in it that you enter into a pretty
large, vaulted roome where in are variety of very flat arches turned
in not an ordinary fashion, & in a litle roome of it an old famous
statue of Diana, that was formerly worshipd by the heathen here,
as they would have us beleive.[4]

East of the towne, just without the walls, lyes that which they   Coemeterium
call Coemeterium divi Petris de Campis Elysiis.[5] It is a large
circuit of ground, about a mile about, fild with large coffins of one
entire stone & great thick covers of stone upon many of them, a great

---

[1] It had just been moved to this position in the previous month.
[2] The stone (Egyptian granite) looks grey under ordinary conditions, but apparently
on wet days it takes on a bluish tint.
[3] It was built between 1673 and 1675.
[4] This is the famous *Vénus d'Arles*, discovered in 1651 and offered to Louis XIV by
the inhabitants of Arles in 1684. It is now in the Louvre.
[5] Known by the Provençal name of *Les Alyscamps*.

many of them above ground & entire, some half coverd & a great many, as they say, under ground. Some of them are Roman as appears by the inscriptions, & some Christian as appears by the inscriptions & crosses on them. By the side of this place & on some part of it stands a covent of the Minims,[1] where in we were shewd severall of these toombs, dug up in severall places hereabouts, of eminent saints, one whereof, as well as St. Denys, caried his head in his hands a good way. They shewd us also one of these toombs which was always wet on the outside & that under it always drie, for they piled them one upon another, & had always water in it which increasd & decreasd with the moon. This the Frier that shewd the toombs said was a constant miracle. He dipd in his cord at a litle hole to give us demonstracion, & I thought it noe lesse then a miracle to beleiv upon such a proof.[2] The Frier shewd us these & other things very courteously, & as civily at parting desired something to say Masse for our good journey, which a Swisse that was then there understood to be mony to drink our healths, & said it was the first Frier he had ever observed to aske mony to that purpose, & some thought his mistake not soe far out of the way, saying, soberly thinking of it, it was to aske mony to drink.

Mare

East of the towne, at a mile or 2's distance, lyes a litle hill called Montaigne de Cord, whither they say the sea formerly came & that there were iron rings lately found in it to which they tied their vessels. All round this hill is lowe ground & washes, & beyond them to the North & east at a pretty distance high mountains.

Arles itself stands on a hillock, & descends by degrees to the banks of the Rhosne, which divides itself just above it to make the Camargue. All towards the sea from thence, as far as one can see, is a direct levell &, I am of opinion, was formerly all sea,[3] & then perhaps this towne, at least the hillock it is situate on, was an Island.

Amphi-
theatrum

The Amphitheater here is more large, but more ruind then that

---

[1] Most of it is in ruins to-day, but the chapel, known as the *Chapelle St Honorat*, is still there.

[2] Skippon's comment (p. 723) is even more brutal—'probably a cheat of the monks and priests'.

[3] Or rather *étangs*. The marshes were drained in the Middle Ages and seventeenth century.

of Nismes, & had an aqueduct to it as that, vid. Guis who hath writt a booke of it.[1]

Remember the roofe of the church of the Peres de l'Oratoir,[2] which was in the outside noe thing but freestone, not plaine, but severall indentings rising from the sides to the ridg.

The town has a figure between ovall & triangular & is biger then Montpellier,[3] but not soe well built, but hath straiter & broader streets.

The seting up of the obelisque cost, as they say, 1,200 escus. Besides the amphitheater there are in the walls of the towne the remains of a very large triumphal arch,[4] & in severall parts of the citty severall imperfect peices of Roman architecture, as 2 very large pillars of Diana's temple,[5] neare the place where her statue was found in diging a well, another arch, etc.

WED. APR. 8. At the entrance of the Minims' covent are these 2 inscriptions on 2 monuments, in each of which is one of those stone coffins archd over. On the left hand of the entrance is this:

Ex hoc solo antiquitate collapso D. Andr.
Bertrandus regiae majestatis Arelatensis Quaestor hoc monumentum mente motu fecit erigi erectum propriis sumptibus jussit ornari ornatum sibi suisque voluit dicari. A. 1616.[6]

On the right hand is one of those stone coffins of Alablaster[7] with a great deal of imagery upon it & this inscription above:

sola † morte dividimur
Margarita de Quiqueran generali peste in Coemeterio B. Petri de Campis elysiis jam diu sepultas reliquias Franciscus Danthonella et Joanna de Cabanis gener et filia huic sepulchro ipsorum sumptibus restituto et condecorato inferri pietatis ergo curaverunt an.Dom. MDCXVI.

Without, against a wall, we saw one of those coffins archd over, which had this signification that, when any family was extinct, they buried the last of it in the coffin belonging to his family, &

---

[1] *Description de l'Amphithéâtre d'Arles* (Arles, 1629), 4°.

[2] Now the *Musée lapidaire païen.*

[3] To-day the situation has been reversed: the population of Montpellier is 93,102, while that of Arles is 20,138.   [4] Demolished in 1745.

[5] Apparently two pillars moved in recent times to the *Théâtre antique.*

[6] The tablet bearing this inscription is to be found to-day in the *Musée lapidaire chrétien.*   [7] O.E.D. gives this form of *alabaster.*

then put its cover on it, & built an arch over it soe as it could not be again opend.

Deus Pater   In the Minims' church over the altar is a picture of God the Father.

St. Martin   From Arles to St. Martins to dinner. 3 leagues to St. Martin de Crau. Descending from the litle hill Arles stands on & fills all but the Elysian Field on the east side, which is taken up with grave stones & windemils mingled, we passed a valley of low ground over which is a large aqueduct on arches. Water was formerly brought to Arles, but the great inundacion of the Rhosne in November 1664 which did such mischief about Pont St. Esprit, Avignion, etc., caried away several of the arches of this aqueduct, soe that the water which is brought hither from the River Durance, fals there into this vally & is lost in the estangs there. Geting up a little rise on the other side this valy you will see the road hath worne through a rock of pebles about 8 or 10 foot thick or more, which seemes to be the pavement of all the soile. When you are once got up upon it, from thence to St. Martin, but the infinite number of pebles that covers all the country, having some earth amongst them, affords rooting to olive yards (which we parted with beyond Pont Lunell & met not again till we came hither), vineyards & corne, & aboundance of rivulets bringing water out of the Aqueduct of Durance make this **Crau**   part of the Crau not wholy unfruitfull.

Salon   From St. Martins to Salon to bed, 4 leagues, a way as strait as a line all over the Crau, which is coverd soe thick with pebles that you can see scarce any thing else, & would wonder to see flocks of sheepe on it, & what they lived on, & yet they make a shift to pick up a living out of a litle grasse that creeps up between the pebbles. This pebly plain of the Crau reaches as far as the mountains under which the Durance runs, & soe quite to the sea, & the tradition amongst the people is that it was once sea. Out of the Durance they draw rivulets of dusty water which helps to make a little fruitfulnesse of grasse & in some places a litle corne.

At Salon in an old church of the Cordeleirs[1] in the wall lies
Nostradamus   Nostradamus with this inscription:

---

[1] Now the Église Saint-Laurent.

D   M

Clariss. ossa Michaelis Nostradami unius omnium mortalium judicio
digni cujus pene divino calamo totius orbis ex astrorum influxu futuri
eventus conscriberentur. Vixit annos 62, menses 6, dies 10. Obiit Salloni
anno 1566. Quietem posteri ne invidete. Anna Pontia Gemella Sallonia
conjugi OPT. V.F.

Above this inscription, which is in a long stone in the wall, the
lines running perpendicular, is his picture,[1] at the 2 upper corners
whereof 2 coats of arms with these 2 words in each, soli deo, & in
circumference: Clariss. Mich. Nostradamus, regius consiliarius et
medicus, annum agens 59. Caesaris Nostrad. filii patritii opus; &
in the 2 lower corners of the picture these 2 verses:

Inter et illustres semper memorabile[2] Michael,
Tu Gallis sydus tu decus omne tuis.

Beans boild in their cods.[3] Peas we had at Montpellier a fortnight
before.

THURS. APR. 9. From Sallon to the Griffon, 5 leagues, over rocky,
barren hills. From the Griffon to Marseilles 3½ leagues through   Marseilles
more rocky & barrener hills. About 2½ leagues from Marseilles
we began to have a sight of a large vally coverd over with country
houses, one of the finest prospects I had ever seen.

Between Sallon & the Griffon we rod along an inlet of the sea on   Sal
the side of which we saw a town cald Ber[4] by which there are
Salines as at Pecais, where they make salt for Provence. The salt
of these Salines is not, they say, soe white as that of Pecays, but
a little redish owing to the soyle.[5]

FRID. APR. 10. We went abord the Royal,[6] the Admiral Gally, the   Triremis
slaves clad in the King's livery, all in blew, the rest of the slaves in
the other Gallys in red. This Gally had twenty-nine oars of a side,

---

[1] This appears to be the portrait now preserved in the Musée Calvet at Avignon (see
Introduction, p. xxiii).
[2] The inscription on the picture at the Musée Calvet reads *venerande*, but there is no
doubt that the MS. has *memorabile*.
[3] *O.E.D. pods.*   [4] Berre.
[5] This paragraph comes two pages later in the MS., but Locke himself inserted
cross-references indicating that it should come here.
[6] Le Conte gives no such ship. The context makes it quite clear that it is the show
galley, *La Grande Réale* (built in 1675) which is meant.

280 slaves, 60 seamen, soldiers & volunteirs as many as added to the former make 500. They usually go victauld for 50 or 60 days. *Diaeta* The slaves are in very good plight. Their food is only 1½ lb. of bisquet per day & thrice a week beanes boild in salt & water, & their drink noe thing but water. They have sometimes tried what flesh & wine would doe with them, but found that with that food they were neither soe healthy nor strong.

Just at the end of the Key is a yard & 2 docks to build gallys. The docks are coverd to work out of the rain & sunshine, & lower then the sea water which they pump out, & when the gally is built, instead of launching her, they let in water at a hole which takes her off the stocks, & then open the gate & let her out. 3 sides of this yard are beset with buildings which with several other large, square *Arsenal* courts make the Arsenal, which is stord with all necessarys for the Gallys, every gally having its particular store house. Within this arsenall are imploid also smiths, sayle makers, carvers, joyners & all other trades necessary for the building & furnishing the gallys, great bake houses & large store houses fild with meale, bread & bisquit & a gallery in it, 120 fathom long, to make ropes & cables, an armory very well furnishd, & a large hospital for sick slaves, all very fit & magnificent.

There goe out 25 Gallys this year, the least hath 26, the bigest 29 oars on a side. There rides at the Key a very large Gally, cald also the Royal[1] of 32 oars, most curiously carved. All the carved work is to be guilt; the gold for the guilding it is agreed for already & will cost 36,000 livres. The Royal we were in carrys 5 guns, all before; that in the midle lyes in a case & is a very large one, cald the chase gun. Indeed all the buildings of the Arsenall are soe great, soe well contrived & made with soe litle saveing of charges that one cannot but thinke it is to carry on the businesse with great care & intention.[2]

The slaves when they row are stripd naked to the midle.

The cittadell lyes just at the entrance of the port which is always chaind & soe by severall fortified ascents rises to a heigth above the

---

[1] Another *Réale*, built in 1668.

[2] *O.E.D.* quotes a similar use of the word (='attention') in the *Essay on the Human Understanding*.

towne, which lyes on tother side the port & is about as big as
Montpellier.[1] There has been noe cost spared in the building of the
cittadell. In the midle of the town there runs along an high ridg on
which there are several windemils. The greatest & best part of the
town lyes on the south side of it towards the port. The Key is
handsome & long & full of people walking, espetially in the
evenings, when the best company, men & women, meet & walk,
which is not soe safe in other streets nor sweet, for the houses being
fild most of them with several familys living one over an other, have
no houses of offices, but instead of that all is don in pots & thrown
out of the windows, which makes the streets very ill sented always
& very inconvenient anights.

SAT. APR. 11. I saw the Towne House which is in the midle of the
Key.[2] The front of it is exceeding handsomely adorned with
figures of graved stone. A large roome below & an other over for
the administration of justice. The churches of the towne are not
very extraordinary. I saw part of the ceremonys of a christening at
Nostre Dame.

Round about the towne, in a vally incompassed round with high
hils or rather high rocks, are a vast number of litle country houses
which they call Bastites,[3] which stand within a bow shoote[4] one of
an other a league or 2 round about, & are, as some tell you, 22,000.
They that speake lowest say 16 or 17,000. They have most of them
litle plots of ground wald in about them which one can neither cal
a field nor a garden, for there are vines, fruit trees, artichoaks &
other garden hearbs, & olive trees & corne in most of them. In
Marseilleis there are about 50 familys Protestants, but they have
noe church in the towne[5] nor nearer then Cabanes de Berre, which
is 5 or 6 leagues out of towne, but have a minister in the towne to
baptise, visit the sick, etc.[6] We were here obleiged by the civility

---

[1] To-day Marseilles, with a population of 636,264, which makes it the second city
in France, has over six times as many inhabitants as Montpellier.
[2] Built in 1672, it was the only building left on the quay after the destruction of the
Vieux port by the Germans in 1943.
[3] *Bastides.*   [4] *O.E.D.* gives this form of *shot.*
[5] The Protestants of Marseilles and Aix had a *temple* at Velaux, as in neither town were
they allowed to worship in public.
[6] In 1674 the Catholics had complained of his presence there (*B.S.H.P.F.* 1922,
pp. 31–3).

of Mr. Tobie Sollicofre[1] who speaks English & Mr. Pasbon, Leiutenant of the Royal Gally, both Protestants.

Batallion   A batallion of foot is always sixteen companys & their companys usually about 50 men. The Regiment of Champain hath 100 companys.

SUND. 12 APR. We left Marseilles & the Hostel de Malt, the fairest *Maison brulée* inn I ever saw, & lay that night at Maison brulée, a single house near Castilet,[2] 6 leagues. We passed by several bastites. The walls *Murus* of severall of their gardens were spiked with glasse to hinder climbers, & soe in the vally of Marseille to Aubagne, 3 leagues, a litle beyond which we began to get in amongst the mountains which, though perfect rocky, were for a league or 2 of our way *Terebinthus* coverd with pines out of which they draw turpentine by cuting the bark & sap of the tree 7 or 8 rings deep, out of which the turpentine oozes & runs downe by the tree into a hole they cut at the bottom to receive it. We saw multitudes soe cut & runing. The wounds looked fresh, though the naked bodys of the trees shewd they had been soe used in former years, but where there were old scars, 'twas apparent they made the wounds in fresh bark, either above or by the side of the former scars, & soe contrived it by chanelling the edge of the wounded bark as to convey all the weeping into the receiver at the bottom, out of which they take it with iron spoons & boile it for rosin. When this treatment hath kild the trees, they make charcoal of them.

Bois de Conu   The wood of pines we passed through between Marseilles & Maison brullé is cald Boi de Conu.[3] The vallys here are fild with *Agricultura* corne, & in the corne olive trees, fig trees, pear, cherry, wall nut, hasel nut & other fruit trees. The corne & vines are set sometimes alternately like the corne & banks in Warwickshire, a ridg of corne & 4 or 5 rows of vines.

MUND. 13 APR. From Maison brullé to Toulon 3½ leagues, the way between high mountains of rocks, but where the vallys open or

---

[1] Tobie Sollicoffre (or Zollikoffer) was a Swiss merchant from Sankt Gall. He and his family and three other Swiss of the same name were still in Marseilles in 1685 after the Revocation of the Edict of Nantes (*B.S.H.P.F.* vol. LIV, p. 12).
[2] Modern maps give *Le Brûlat* and *Castellet*.
[3] This name does not appear on modern maps. Piganiol de la Force (III. 275) speaks of 'le bois de Coniols'.

there is any earth (which they endeavour to preserve by walls one
above an other on the side of the hils), it is full of corn, vines,
oyle & figs. About a league before we came to Toulon, we saw
gardens full of huge, great orange trees, & all along from Maison
brullé mirtle by the way's side, soe that such trees growing here
open, 'tis noe wonder we had green peas out of the Shells at
Marselles, where they say 'tis as hot as at Roome & would be
intollerable, were it not for the breezes that blow very fresh
constantly every day & rise about 9 or 10 o'clock. At Toulon   Toulon
usually in the faire weather of the spring the winde accompanys
the sun & blows east at morning, south at noon & west at night,
& in sumer about noone they have almost constantly a fresh sea
breez from the south.

In the afternoon we saw the Key & Port, v: Jouvin de Rochefort
en le voiageur d'Europe, Tom. 1, p. 122. In the Basin rode the   Navis
Royal Louis[1] which is admiral there, but was never at sea, but
serves for a receptacle for Soldiers & seamen as they are brought
thither for the maning of other ships. She is in length in the keele
137 f.; longeur de l'estrave à l'Estramberz 163 pieds; Largeur
$45\frac{1}{2}$ pied; L'hauteur de fond de Calle $20\frac{3}{4}$ pieds.[2] The Sterne is
mightily adornd with gilded figures. The guilding, as they say,
cost 150,000 livres. She hath portals for 120 guns, 8 foot one from
an other, but was never yet at sea, nor is never like to goe. The
Dauphin Royal[3] lyes by her, of 100 guns, but of noe more service.
By these lay the Monarque, Conquerant, Magnanim, Triumphant
& 2 or 3 other great vessels. Without in the port lay 9[4] vessels,
viz. Figue[5] Admiral 50 guns, Drol 36, Bijar[6] 40, Furieuse 44,
Indien 44, on which we were abord. There are at Messina[7] 35 men
of war & here about 20.

---

[1] Built in 1668.
[2] For the source of this information see p. 78 n. 2.   [3] Built in 1668.
[4] Though Locke only names five ships in this sentence, there is no doubt whatsoever
that the MS. has the figure 9. (For further details about the ships listed here see
Le Conte.)
[5] Le Conte gives no such name.
[6] *Bizarre* (the old form of the word was *bigearre*).
[7] When a revolt against Spain broke out in Sicily in 1674, French naval forces were
sent to aid the insurgents. On 22 April 1676 Duquesne defeated the Dutch and Spanish
fleets at Agosta.

The port is very large, capable of the bigest fleet in Europe & to spare, & in the basin its self roome for a great fleet. It is separate from the rode (as they call it) by a mole made within these 4 or 5 years, & hath a narrow entrance continually chaind. The water in both in most places deepe, the bottom mud with some shelves in it, the entrance wide between 2 castles at least ½ a league on sunder. To fortifie it more, there is another platform of 28 guns made on the S.W. side the whole port.

Arsenal   Adjoining to the port is the Arsenal, not soe fine as that at Marseilles, but every ship hath its particular store house, & there are within it offices for all that is necessary for the Navy: hemp dressers, cabels, smiths, bakers, etc. In the same place also is the dock where there are now 3 ships upon the stocks of 40 guns a peice, began last yeare, but at present goe not on very vigerously, & the timber they build with seems not to be very excellent.

Remember the crane with the worme. The towne lyes just under high rocky mountains & is extreamly well supplyd with water.

Hortus   Memo. Mr. the Intendent's garden, an oval in a square, & the way to preserve grass on the edges of gravel walks with litle cyppi[1] of sticks.

The towne is not strong nor like to be made soe, but the Arsenal as designd will be a magnificent thing. Fair, but only a very small mist for a litle while.

Antlia   TUES. APR. 14. Memo. a pump with balls instead of wind falls shewd us by Mr. Rodolphe Gedeon dit Corneille[2] to whom we were recommended by Mr. Tobie Sollicofry of Marseilles. Memo. to send him notice of what books of architecture or principally fortification in French or Dutch are to be had in London.

---

[1] 'posts, pillars' (Latin).
[2] The Lovelace Collection contains an account, written in French, of the measures and proportions of the *Royal Louis* and of the armament of other French ships at Toulon. It is signed 'Rodolphe Gedeon dit Corneille, Ingenieur a Toulon' and endorsed by Locke: 'Navis 78 [sic], Le Grand Louis'. There is also in the same collection another document, undated and not endorsed by Locke, entitled 'Table des Appointements et Solde des Equipages des Vaisseaux de guerre du Roy'. The name 'Jedeon Corneille' appears amongst the signatures of a petition addressed by Huguenot naval officers to the States-General of Holland in 1688 (*B.S.H.P.F.* vol. XXXVI, p. 199).

In the Grand Louis[1] is this inscription:

Je suis l'unique sur l'onde
Et mon roy l'est dans le monde.

From Toulon to Hyeres 3 leagues to bed. Hyeres is situated on   Hyeres
the south side of an high mountain looking in to a rode made by an
Island where the Gallys use to come. Below the towne the side of
the hill is coverd with orange gardens, in one of which we gatherd
& eat very good, ripe china oranges which were there in incredible
plenty & grew sometimes 9 or ten in a bunch. The garden, or
rather the 2 or 3 that are distinguished by several walls, was
capable, before applied to this use, of 36 charges[2] of corne. It is
now fild with orange & lemon trees. The colour of the fruit, leaves
& flowers mingled enterteind the eyes very pleasantly as well as
their smel & tast did the other senses, & it was one of the most
delightfull woods I had ever seen. There are litle rivulets of water
conveyd up & downe in it to water it in sommer without which
there would be litle fruit. This peice of ground thus cultivated yeilds
the owner 40,000 or 50,000 livres per annum,[3] who pays to the
King for tax 400 escus per annum. This fruit ripe at this time of the
yeare would make one think one should finde it very warme here, as
noe doubt it is in sommer, but in our way between this & Touloun
I found it soe cold that I was several times calling for my coat. The
vally between this & Touloun is coverd thick with huge, large olive
trees, but the tops of the hils are bare, barren rock.

For the best china oranges here we were asked 30 s. per cent.   Aurantia

Here we had for supper amongst other things a dish of green   Coquinaria
beans dressd with gravy, the best I ever eat.

Above the towne is a nunnery, of the order of St. Bernard, of
persons of quality. They all eat alone in their chambers apart,
& keepe a maid servant & a lacquey, & goe out of the Nunnery
& walke abroad when they please. The situation is very pleasant,
overlooking the towne, the orange gardens, the vally & the sea.

Here the peices of 4 s. goe not, noe more then at Touloun or   Mony
Marseilles, for feare forainers should import this base coin. Clouds.
Cold. E.

---

[1] Presumably the *Royal Louis*.   [2] A measure of weight of variable quantity.
[3] 'or rather 18,000' added above in the MS.

Maun WED. 15 APR. From Hyeres to Maun[1] to dinner, 4 leagues, through a very pleasant, but narrow vally counted the richest in Provence, fild with fruit trees, as wall nuts, pomigranets, figs, pears, cherrys, vines & some apples, above all olives, very large trees which, where there was earth, were planted to the very tops of the mountains. Where they faild & 'twas not perfect rock, there pines supplied their place & some schenes vert. The bottom had, besides corne & vines & some flax, more & better meadow then I had seen any where in France. All this plenty & beauty is owing to litle rivulets that come downe from the mountains, which are caried along the sides of the vallys to water the lower grounds. In the bottom of this vally runs a river, beset with poplars, Alder, some Ashes & Elmes. 2 leagues

Solier from Hyeres we came to Solier[2] & passed by the Marquis of Solier's house seated in the vally, one of the handsomest in the outside

Stoecas that I had seen in this part of France. By the way Stoecas plenty. From thence to Beaugency,[3] 1 league, where we saw the ruins of a very fine garden, full of fruit & rare plants, the strangest of all the

Ficus American fig tree that bears a flower as big as a rose, which are upon
Americanus the tree some white, some red & other colours, & if you gather it white, will change in your hand to red in walking 100 paces, et vice versa.

St. Baum   From Meaunes to St. Baum, 3 leagues, over very barren hils & extreme rocky, some pines & some shrub oakes, but most shene vert & sabina baccifera, rosemary, time, Lavender & Juniper. The covent of St. Baume[4] is placed in a cave in the midle of an extream high precipice, the Mountain 120 canes high, as Father Tho: Molineaux told us. Cold here as in England or colder as also the vally below.

St. Maximin THURSD. 16 APR. From St. Baume to St. Maximin,[5] 3 leagues. Under St. Baum is a grove of beeches & oaks, the only timber trees I had seen in all my journys since I took horse at Lyon. The

---

[1] Méounes.
[2] Solliès.   [3] Belgentier?
[4] Sainte-Baume. The 'Grotte de Sainte-Madeleine' to which the saint is alleged to have retired to do penance, transformed into a chapel.
[5] Formerly the site of a famous Dominican monastery. The church, built to contain the tomb of Mary Magdalen, is a famous place of pilgrimage.

way a good part rocky, but S. Maximin stands in a vally which,
they say, is never very hot. Here we saw the reliques, as at St.
Baum we saw the lodging of St. Mary Magdalen, both shewn with
great devotion. What they are, v: the book.[1] Cloudy, cold.

One that supd with us here told us that there were 16 companys,   Quarterings
i.e. about 850, coming to quarter in this town. The way of quartering
is this. The Consuls of the towne give them billets; the houses
where they are quarterd for lodging & diet have 2 s. per day per
man. The province pay this & deduct it out of their next tax.

FRID. 17 APR. From St. Maximin to Aix, 6 Leagues, the way pretty   Aix.
plain, but the country all along mountainous & for the most part
barren, the vallys themselves not over fruitful. N.E. Fair, cold.
Memo. the way at St. Maximins to beate haire with 6 whipcords
about 7 or 8 foot long. At St. Maximins we had grapes of the last
yeare preserved til now.

At Beaugency the gardiner grafted or rather inoculated an orange.   Aurantia
He cut of an orange branch of 2 years' growth & took out of it a   Inoculateing
bud, cut the bark sheild fashion, & then cut of a branch about the
bignesse of the other or a litle biger, slit the barke with his knife,
thrust in the sheild & left the top of it even with the stock, bound it
about & told us that the top of the stock & the lower part of the
slit was to be coverd with wax.

In the way between St. Maximins & Aix we met 3 or 4 women   Women
rideing along astride (a fashion very common all over France) &   rideing
behind one of them a lusty, tall fellow rid. This was to me a new
fashion of riding double.

As soon as you are unlighted[2] & got into your chamber at St.
Maximins, you will finde it fild with women offering beads &
medals to sell, who will pull you to peices almost with their im-
portunity to buy them. The reliques are kept with the greatest gard
of dores, grates, locks & bolts I had ever seen anywhere.[3] The
friers keep one part of the Keys & the town the other. He that shows
them habits himself first with a linin hood with a patch of green silk
just on his head, a surplice & a stole, & soe addressing himself to the

---

[1] I.e. Jouvin de Rochefort, *Le Voyageur d'Europe*, vol. I, pp. 108–13.
[2] *O.E.D. alighted.*   [3] MS. has 'any thing'.

reliques, & prefaceing all with a short prayer, he sheud us all with great reverence & dexterity. N.E. Fair, cold.

SAT. APR. 18. At Aix the Pallais[1] where there is noe entrance with swords, a roome well painted & a litle chappell over which Christ & 12 Apostles, which are the pictures of 12 of the Counsellors of this towne. Here are 70 counsellors.[2]

Musaea   Prior Borilly,[3] Mr. Sibon & Mr. Lohier's cabinets are furnishd well with medals & some other curiositys of antiquity & natural, & at Mr. Imbert's a collection of pictures. The day here was fair & in the sun very hot, in the shade the aire very cold.

SUND. APR. 19.[4] Aix, whilst we were there, was fild those 2 days

Processions   with processions of the villages round about, the Archbishop, Cardinal Grimaldi,[5] having obtain of the Pope the benefit of the last year's Jubilee to his diocesse, which they are to receive upon processions, soe that the whole towns come in these processions, scarce leaving people anough to look to their houses. From Brignole there will come 4,000. Some parishes come ten leagues, & severall of them in the processions walke bare foot with banners fild with pictures of Our Saviour, the Virgin & other saints, statues of saints & heads in silver, etc., & soe march through the streets with lighted tapers in their hands, 2 & 2, great numbers of them clad as Penitents Noirs, Blancs & Gris, etc.[6]

---

   [1] The *Palais de Justice*, demolished in 1786.

   [2] There were a *Parlement* and a *Cour des Comptes* at Aix.

   [3] Michel de Borilli, Prior of Ventabren, inherited from his father Boniface, who died in 1648, a fine collection of paintings, statues, vases, coins, medals, etc. There is a detailed account of it in Skippon (pp. 722-3).

   [4] Locke records here various medical notes obtained from Claude Brouchier, physician to the Archbishop of Aix. He was appointed to the Chair of Chemistry in the Faculty of Medicine at Aix in 1669. The original of these notes, in Brouchier's hand, is preserved in the Lovelace Collection (MS. Locke, c. 4, ff. 163-4), along with two letters from him to Locke. The latter evidently had a letter of recommendation to Brouchier from his friend Mapletoft, for the latter wrote to him on 8 July (o.s.): 'I am glad you found Dr. Brouchier so much the man I promised you; he expresses great satisfaction in you likewise' (ibid. c. 15, ff. 205-6).

   [5] Jérôme de Grimaldi (1597-1685). Born at Genoa, he was made Papal Nuncio first in Germany and then in France. He was made a Cardinal in 1643 and appointed Archbishop of Aix in 1655.

   [6] These religious organizations flourished in the South of France.

In Mr. de Mercoer's[1] garden are sicamores de Malt. They had
not yet put out, but had upon them bunches of fruit of the last
yeare. We were told they bore a very fine, sweet flower & were an
excellent shade. Over against this in a garden of Mr. Rimbaus was
a broome with white flowers.

Sicamores de Malt

Genista fl. albo

In this towne are 4 familys of Protestants, as there are 8 at
Touloun. They goe 3 leagues to church.[2] They had formerly
13 churches in Provence, but 9 of them have been puld down within
these 5 or 6 yeares, & they complain that those who are garantie of
the Edict of Nantes interpose noe thing in their behalf.[3]

Aix is a town seated on the N.E. side of a pretty large & pretty
fruitfull plain. It is round & something biger then Montpellier,[4]
but the streets much straiter, larger & handsomer then at Montpellier. The Towne House a pretty handsom building,[5] but the
Cours[6] is the handsomest place, being a long strait street, 70 steps
wide with two rows of trees on each side. That at Marseilles is not
soe long, but neare as wide, but much better built & hath but one
row of trees on a side. It is 30 steps between the trees & 18 or
19 between the trees & houses on each side.

Aboundance of Monasterys & covents in & about the towne.

Madam Elizabeth Dagut & Dorothe.[7]

Fair & cold in the shade.

MUND. APR. 20. From Aix to Lambesc 3 leagues, corne, some vines
& olives, but most Almonds which this yeare faild, the country not
over fruitfull.

Lambesc

From Lambesc to Cavaillon 4 leagues. A league short of Cavaillon

---

[1] Presumably Louis de Vendôme, Duc de Mercœur, who succeeded to the title of
Duc de Vendôme on his father's death in 1665. He was appointed Governor of Provence
in 1654, became a Cardinal in 1667 and died two years later.

[2] The Protestants had a church at Velaux, on the way to Marseilles; they were not
allowed to have one at Aix because it was the seat of an archbishopric.

[3] See entry for 3 June.

[4] With 14,556 inhabitants, Aix has to-day about a sixth of the population of
Montpellier.

[5] Built in 1658.   [6] To-day *Cours Mirabeau*.

[7] This entry stands quite isolated between a medical note concerning Dr Brouchier's
recommendation of *Le Médecin des Pauvres* and the note on the weather which follows.
There was in Aix in the sixteenth and seventeenth centuries a well-known family called
D'Agut, several members of which were *Conseillers au Parlement*.

Durance   we passed the Durance by a Trill. It was not there very broad, but the current quick, & the markes he had left shewd, as well as the informacion of the ferryman, that sometimes noe other banks then the mountains on both sides the vally, almost a league distance, can confine him.

Cavaillon   Cavaillon is but a litle, unhandsome towne, walled about & seated just under a high rode to the west. It is in the County of Avignion, & a Bishop's see worth 10,000 livres per annum. You enter into the County of Avignon as soon as you passe the Durance. The plain for a league or more about Cavaillon is very fruitfull & in very good corne, good meadow, & hath many orchards of apples, besides mulberrys & other fruit trees, but this fertility is owing to the water of the Durance which they convey in Channells & rivulets to water all the ground. All the places where I observed this to be donne in this part of France were fruitfull, but between Lambesc & the Durance we passed through but ordinary land. N.W. Fair, cold.

Vaucluse   TUESD. APR. 21. From Cavaillon to Vaucluse, 2 leagues, where of the greatest part through the pleasant, rich, waterd plain about Cavaillon till you come to the foot of the mountains. At Vaucluse is the famous fountain, just at the foot of an exceeding high rock. It is a basin, half a coit's cast over, which the water runs out of, & joyning with some other that runs out amongst the rocks below, is the source of a great river[1] in the vally below, which hath all its water from hence. The basin about Easter is usually a yard or 2 higher, as you may see by the marks, & soe will rise after 2 or 3 days' rain at other times. About August it sinks 25 cans below the heigth it was now at. They say they cannot find any bottom to it, having sounded with very long ropes, but finde a litle resting place about 32 cans deep.

Avignon   From Vaucluse to Lisle[2] 1 league, from Lisle to Avignon 4 leagues, through a rich plain, full of corne & Mulberry trees. Only one litle hill in the way hath the pebles of the Crau.

Danceing here by moonshine in the streets.

---

[1] La Sorgue.   [2] L'Isle-sur-la-Sorgue.

5 Companys of the Regiment of Champagne at Aix, poore, weak, tatterd fellows.

From Lisle to Avignon 4 leagues. Lisle (as Cavaillon) is a litle, walled towne, & is seated on the water that comes from Vaucluse which here makes a great river.

WED. APR. 22. At Ville Neuf over against Avignon[1] on the other side the Rhosne we saw the Charterhouse where are 60 Friers. Their chappell well adornd, their plate, copes & reliques very rich, amongst the rest a chalice of gold, given by Rene, the last King of Naples of the Anjou race.[2] I was going to take it in my hand, but the Carthusian withdrew it till he had put a cloth about the handle & soe gave it into my hand, noe body being sufferd to touch these holy things but a priest. In their chappell Pope Innocent the 6th lies interd; he died 1362, & in a litle chappel in their covent stands a plain, old chair where in he was infallible. I sat too litle a while in it to get that priviledg. In their devotions they use much prostrations & kisseing the ground. They leave no more hair on their heads but one very litle circle going round, which is cut as short as one's whiskers. After shaveing they confesse they finde it somewhat cold & inconvenient. The Cell we were in had 3 litle rooms below, a litle garden & a litle cloister on the far side of it. In the roome above we were not. Such an habitacion hath each of them apart. Their chappel, refectory & the Cell & other parts are all kept very cleane, & yet on the walls of one of their cloisters we saw a litle, black scorpion.

The walls of Avignon, were they all as fine as they are about the upper end of the Key & the north side, they would be the handsomest I had ever seen, but a good part of the South, east & west sides is soe plain that it yields to those of Aigues Mortes.

From Avignon to Tarascon 4 leagues, 1 league of it through the rich vally of Avignon which is very pleasant, being all either rich meadow or excellent corne & devided by rows of mulberry trees into squares of 4 or 5 acres apeice, some more, some lesse, which gives a very pleasant prospect to the passenger.

Ville Neuf

Carthusians

Avignon Walls

---

[1] Villeneuve-lès-Avignon.   [2] He died in 1480.

Vectigal   A league from Avignon we passed the Durance, & there leaveing the Pope's dominions, we found on the opposite shore an officer of the King of France who searched our portemanteaus & made us pay about $\frac{1}{2}$ a sol a pair for some new gloves we had, though bought at Marseilles, & gave us a ticket.

The rest of the way from hence to Tarascon was on the side of a not unfruitfull vally, but seemd not to be soe well cultivated as that of the County. Moderate taxes & a freedom from quarter gives the Pope's subjects, as it seems, more industry.

Mony   In the County of Avignon they count as in France by Sols & Livres, but 72 of their sols make a French crowne & consequently their cinque sols peices are but $\frac{5}{6}$ of the cinque sol peices of France. They have also a litle brasse coin cald patta where of 6 make one of their sols. The French mony goes here also as in France.[1]

Carthusians   Over the entrance into the Carthusians' cloister we saw this morning is writt: Janua Caeli. The Carthusian that shewd us the covent seemd not very melancholy. He enquird after their houses & lands in England, & asked whether, when we came to be papists, they should not have them again. I told him yes, without doubt, for there could be noe reconciliation to their church without restitution. He told me I was a very good divine & very much in the right. They have in their chappell severall pictures of the execution of some of their order in England in Henry 8's reigne.

THURSD. 23 APR. From Tarascon to Generat[2] 4 leagues, & from Generat to Pont Lunel 4 leagues.

Tarascon   At Tarascon we saw the castle seated on a rock on the brinke of the Rhosne, the ancient seat of the Counts of Provence who were some of them also Kings of Sicily. It is a very strong building, but not very regular, with large rooms in it, the upper rooms archd & the top of the castle paved with irregular, angld freestone, but yet soe, as they say, it never lets any wet through. The building is about an irregular square court in[3] which, as soon as you enter, you see in

---

[1] This information is repeated several times in the Journal.
[2] Générac.
[3] This word is not in the MS.

the wall the statues of Rene & Joan[1] don half way downe the breast with this inscription under that of the man:

Renatus D G Ierusalem
et Siciliae Rex.

& under that of the woman:

Dna Joanna Regina
Siciliae.

and under both:

Divi heroes Francis liliis cruceque illustres
incedunt jugiter parantes ad superos iter.

Yet notwithstanding this fair account on the outside of the wall, they shew within a litle chamber where her husband imprisond her for attempting upon his life, she having poisend a former husband.[2]

In the great church here[3] is kept, as they say, the head of St. Martha, inchasd in massive gold which is proportionable down to half of the breast, adornd with pretious stones & one very great emerald to a very great value: vid. Voiageur d'Europe.[4] All the other Saints we had made visits to, received us very civily & allowd time to our curiosity to survey them, but St. Martha allowd us but a short apparition. For the priest that shewd us these sacred things, first producing the arme in silver guilt, the fingers whereof were loaden with rings with stones of value on them, & holding it out to us, & discoursing upon it, but findeing we paid not that reverence was expected, he approachd it very neare the mouth of one of the company & told him again that the bones that appeared through the cristal were the bones of St. Martha, which not prevailing with the hardened heretick for a kisse, he turned about in fury, put it up in the cubbard, drew the curtain before all the other things, & with the same quicknesse he that had refused to kisse, turnd about, went his way, & the rest followd him.

---

[1] René d'Anjou, Count of Provence and King of Sicily, who died in 1480, and his second wife Jeanne de Laval, whom he married in 1454 and who died in 1498.

[2] Jeanne only appears to have been married once.

[3] Église Sainte-Marthe. The saint is alleged to have converted the region to Christianity and to have rid it of a monster called 'la Tarasque'.

[4] Vol. I, p. 141.

Provence   Here we passed the Rhosne again & left Provence, a country, however commended,[1] wherein I had seen more barren ground then fruitfull, & yet had passed the best part of it. The people too, if one may judg by their clothes & diet, had, like the country, 5 acres of poverty for one of riches, for I remember at Aix in a gardiner's house, where we found them eating, their Sunday dinner was noe thing but slices of congeald bloud fried in oile which an English gent. was with me would needs tast, though to the turning his stomach.

Mony   In Provence the Spanish silver as well as gold passes current, but with this abatement that their peices of 8 goe but for 58 sols & soe proportionably all the lesser parts of them. The Almonds in Provence faild.

Beaucaire   Just on the other side the Rhosne[2] stands Beaucair, a place famous for a faire there, & there we landed & soe through a good corne country went to Generat, 4 leagues, & from Generat over the vally of Aigues Mortes 4 leagues to Pont Lunel.

FRID. 24 APR. From Pont Lunel to Montpellier, 4 leagues.

Rates SAT. 25 APR. The rates we paid by the way were:

Pretium

At Maison brulle for supper & lodging	1 – 0
Toulon, 3 meales	3 – 3
Hyres, supper	1 – 5
Meonnes, dinner	1 – 0
St. Baum, supper & break fast	1 – 10
St. Maximin, supper & breakfast	1 – 15
Aix, 5 meales	5 – 0
Lambesc, dinner	1 – 0
Cavaillon, supper	1 – 5
Lisle, dinner	1 – 0
Avignon, supper & dinner	2 – 10
Tarascon, supper	1 – 7
Generat, dinner	0 – 17
Supper & dinner at Pont Lunel	2 – 5

---

[1] This seems to suggest that Provence was generally considered to be in a prosperous state, but reference to Colbert's correspondence for this period shows that there were constant complaints from the authorities on the spot about the wretched state of the province.

[2] From Tarascon.

WED. 29 APR. Snow on the hills beyond Peir St. Loup.[1]

THURS. 30 APR. A furnace at a Soap boyler's wherein they made
usually 100 Kentals & could make 150 Kentals of Castile soape at
one boyleing. The bottom that [sic] was narrow & a litle way up
only was copper; the rest of the sides seemed to be plaister, it
being set in a wall. They sell the soap at 3½s. per lb. They cut
it into peices with a brasse wire put through the sides of a bord &
slideing along a slit on both sides at fit distances one above an
other. Sapo
Soap

FRID. 1 MAY 1676. E. Fair. Warme, but snow lyeing on the hils
beyond Peire St. Loup.

The rents of Lands in France fallen above ½ in these few years
by reason of the poverty of the people & want of mony. Reditus

Merchands & handicrafts men pay above ½ their gain. Tributa

Noble lands pay noe thing in Languedoc in whose hands soever.
In some other parts of France Lands in the hands of the nobles, of
what sort soever,[2] pay noe thing. Those noble lands that are exempt
from taxes sell for ½ or ⅔ more then others.

The Protestants of France are thought to be $\frac{1}{16}$ part. In Languedoc
they are thought to be 200,000.[3] This yeare they have refused the
King's allowance of the meeting of their Synod of this province
of Languedoc because by it the ministers that live in noblemen's &
gentlemen's houses are excluded.[4] They have their agents at Court
solliciting to have it with its due freedome. It is referd to Villeroy[5] Protestantes

---

[1] Locke writes the names of this mountain (some 12 or 13 miles due north of
Montpellier) *Peir, Perre* or *Pierre St. Loup*. As the word *Pic* was not in use in this region
in the seventeenth century, it appears to have been known as *Puech St. Loup*.

[2] I.e. whether they were classified as *terres nobles* or *terres roturières*, the latter being
otherwise subject to the *taille*.

[3] Before the Revocation of the Edict of Nantes the *Intendant*, D'Aguesseau, estimated
the total number as 182,875; but in their fervour after the Revocation the Catholics
claimed 225,000 conversions! (See Roschach, XIII, 550.)

[4] Under the Edict of Nantes Protestant noblemen and gentry had the right to have
a pastor to conduct services in their private chapels on their estates. An *Arrêt du conseil*
of 15 April 1676 had forbidden these pastors, known as *ministres de fief*, to take part in
provincial Synods.

[5] Nicolas de Neufville, Duc de Villeroy (*c.* 1597–1685), *Maréchal de France*, had been
tutor to Louis XIV. He was made a Minister of State and President of the *Conseil des
Finances* in 1661.

& 3 others to examin & report to the King, & at the end of the yeare they expect the answer.[1]

Cerae
Albifactio

The way of blanching wax is this. They take the wax & melt it in a Furnace of a pretty large size. When it is melted, they take a part of it out thence & put it into a narrow, but deepe furnace in the midle of the room where with a litle fire they keepe it just melted. Then they take 3 wooden molds, just of the fashion of a sugar loaf, being each about 17 inches long & at the basis 7 or 8 inches over, with an handle in the midle of the basis. These they take & rub over with snailes beaten to a mash, houses & all, & so through them into a large stone trough of water that joyns on to the litle furnace & from thence reaches to the window of the roome. These 3 molds are imploid by 3 men, whereof one takes one of them & dips it down in the melted wax perpendicularly almost (i.e. within an inch or there about) as deepe as the basis, & haveing drawn it up, lets it run a litle & wipes of with his left hand the droping & congealing wax at the small end which is downwards, that it may be noe thicker there then by the sides. He throughs the mold, wax & all, into the water, which another there takes &, thrusting gently at the small end, loosens & soe turneing round in the water, draws it of from the mold & puts it on the ground, erect on its basis. The mold, as soon as free, the 3ᵈ takes, who sits on the other side the cisterne neare the furnace, & holds by the handle under water &, just as the dipper is ready for it, takes it up out of the water, & soe holds it erect on the small end upon a litle bord just on the edg of the litle furnace, where it is scarce rested but the dipper takes it by the handle & plunges it as before into the melted wax, & soe these 3 men & their 3 molds are constantly imploid.

Cera
dealbanda

The molds are rubd with snailes to keepe the wax from sticking to them. When after repeated dipings the mold & wax separate not well, they take 3 drye molds, rub them over with snailes & use them as the other.

These cases of wax which are thin, soe that they way[2] not each above 2 or 3 ounces, they clap one into an other for the convenience of cariage & soe remove them into an oblong square there by, which

---

[1] The Protestants for once won their case, as the decree was withdrawn in July of the following year.   [2] *O.E.D.* gives this spelling of *weigh*.

is paved all over with bricks & devided into squares with canes that lye horizontally about 7 or 8 inches from the ground. Each of these litle square divisions holds 16 of these wax cases erect upon their basis, which they squiz[1] a litle towards a square, there not being enough roome for 16 of these basises to stand in their full round.

Thus the whole pavement is coverd with these wax cases which stand there exposd to the sun which whitens them, but when the sun is soe hot that it threatens melting, they prevent it by throug[h]ing water on them, which to that purpose is conveyd all round in gutters in a litle wall, something higher then the wax cases, into litle square cisternes at fit distances to be sprinkled on the wax cases with a skoope, & for this reason it is that the pavements are divided into oblong squares with walkes between them that they may have convenience to scatter the water upon the wax.

The yellow wax they buy for 15 or 16s. per lb. & sel it blanchd for 20. It blanches sooner or later as it happens to be more or less clear sunshine. In some very cleare weather they say it will doe in a weeke. The usuall time they speake of is a month. When one end of the cases is blanchd, they turn the other upwards, & when it is all white, they melt it in earthen pots, almost like milke pans, & then with brasse things, some thing of the fashion of eurs or cruses, they power it into very fair water in a circle & soe make it into a figure of the fashion & bignesse of a Muffe. This they call granuling,[2] & soe set it abroad again in the sun upon coarse clothes to kisse away the remainder of its blushes, if there be any left.

A pair of partners in one worke house in Montpellier are said to blanch 500 Kentalls in a year.

At Toulon 3 ozs. of Essence of Jasmin Tuberos. etc., the 6 glasses   Jasmini ol.
it was in & the box for the glasses cost 4 livres.

WED. MAY 6. Set any peice of wood upright in an oven after the   Lignum
bread is out, &, according to the bignesse of it, you may drie it in   siccandi
¼ or ½ hower. You must set it upright, else it will warpe, & you must let it be round as it grew, or it will crack.

Queen of Hungary's water 40s. per lb. Mr. Puech.

---

[1] *O.E.D.* gives the verb *squize* (=to squeeze).
[2] *O.E.D.* does not give this word. Presumably, as Locke hints, it is the French *granuler* which is meant.

THURSD. MAY 7. How much doth the love of gaity prevaile when a journey man shoemaker who cannot reach the old, taudery ribbons set on top of his neighbour's old, greasy *cap*, *makes him a cap of coarsest*[1] *cards.*[2]

Vinea *They were this day digging their vineyards.*

Flos *Take grass, put sand in it and water* one finger's breadth higher *than the sand. Put stalks of berries or* flowers *in it, and they keep fresh longer than otherwise.*

Lignum The blacknesse *of walnut trees is from water soaking into them*
denigrandum *when they begin to* decay. *Lime water* colours Timber black, *so also* steep*ing of walnut* leaves, *but to let it deep in, heat the wood first: but to let in colour* deeper, *heat the wood and then rub it with* oyle of spike *to make it sink.*

FRID. MAY 8. A flock of sheep following the Shepheard apace in the highway.

Aurantia **SAT. MAY 9.** Twice a week they water their orange trees. Citron trees, if kept in winter in a place to close from the aire, will loose their leaves, but nevertheless will have flowers & fruit with new leaves the next spring. The fairest sort of oranges & largest flowers are Pome Adam.

Balaruc Mr. Upton tried Balaruck waters with galls & found them not
waters change colour *at all.*[3]

SUND. MAY 10. *Sent by* Mr. Nevock *to* Mr. Stringer some *seeds of*
Denier Sycamore of Malta & Sabina baccifera.[4] £10 in deniers weighes 12 lb. 10 ozs.

TUESD. MAY 12. A company of women riding out of towne, most on asses, *some behind men on* horses, *some with their faces to the far side.*

Sabina The seeds of Sabina baccifera may be sowne in September, it
baccifera being a winter plant; but if you feare a hard winter may kill it, sow it in the spring.

---

[1] This word is doubtful.
[2] *O.E.D.* gives *carde*: 'some fabric anciently used for canopies, curtains and linings' but does not quote a seventeenth-century example.
[3] See entry for 5 March 1676.
[4] He acknowledged their receipt in a letter of 5 June (o.s.).

WEDNES. 13 MAY. The leaves of 4 mulberry trees, some whereof   Silk
were not very large trees, sould for a pistol.

For returns of mony Mr. Younger found this train very good,   Returns of
& the men very ready & civil. Mr. Boverie, in St. Mary Axe, to   Mony
Madam Herinx et son fils á Paris. They to Mrs. Couvreur et
Hertener á Lyon. They to Senior Jacomo et Jovanni Moilives, at
Ligorne. They to their correspondents at Rome or other parts of
Italy, especially to Mr. Druyvestin at Venice who will give you
credit through all Germany & Holland.

To-day went by a large procession of severall orders of friers,   Rogation
litle children dressed up fine & carrying litle banners by some of   Procession
the crosses, & after the friers, following amongst the adults, a great
company of children, some walking, some carried, dressed up to
their best abilitys & hung about with little pictures, etc. This is
Rogation weeke & for a blessing on the fruits of the earth, which,   Prayers
though the children cannot pray for, yet the prayers being made in
their names & offerd up as from them by the parents or friends of
these innocents, they think will be more prevalent.[1]

THURSD. 14 MAY. Feed their horses & cattle in houses with green
barley in ear.

Bonfires all over the towne for the takeing of Condé.[2] The   Bonfires
Consuls walked about that cock[3] of brush before the Towne House
in their scarlet with drums, trumpets & violins before them & then
each with a torch kindled it. The other bonfires through the towne
not soe big. *One* fagot of sermans[4] often made *one. In other places
a little tod[5] of straw or* piece *of bedmat wherein* perhaps *some of their*
enemys[6] *were* destroied, *made a flame which sometimes an* unlucky
boy with one kick extinguishd. *I lost my way among these will-o'-the-
wisps, as soon out as in.*
Began again with Mr. Pasty.

MUND. MAY 18. The north wind they call in this towne trans-   Winds
montane, coming of the mountains. It is very cold in the winter
& exceeding hot in the sommer, & if it happens to blow & continue

---

[1] *O.E.D. effective.*   [2] On 26 April.
[3] *O.E.D.* 'heap of hay, wood, etc.'.   [4] =*sarments.*
[5] *O.E.D.* 'a bushy mass, especially of Ivy'.   [6] Their fleas?

long when the corne is blowing or kerning,[1] it does great dammage to their harvest & burns up their corne. This winde seldom brings rain, but the winds that bring rain here have usually some points of the south, but the most rainy of all is the south & south-east.

Protestants WEDNESD. MAY 20. Mr. *Bertheau told me that there was very little* piety *or religion among their* people *and that the lives of the* Reformed *was* [sic] *no better than that of the Papists: that in* Languedoc *men* Taxing *were taxed by their* estates, *in France by head,*[2] *at the* pleasure *of the* officers, *so that sometimes men pay more for their* estates *than the* real *income.*

Languedoc *alone pays yearly* 8,000,000 l., Paris 14 & Bourdeaux 4. Blended 8 ozs.

Kermes THURSD. MAY 21. At Mr. Puech's great quantities of the Grana Kermes which they by for about 16 s. per lb. They are litle red berrys *which* fasten themselves *to the* leaves *or stems of the* Ilex coccifera, a shrub *with* prickly *leaves like holly leaves, but little. The* grains *are red and about the* bignesse *of a small piece of* vetches. *They are* fastend *on to the plant by a little white matter which serves also for a* stopper *to the hole that is in this little grain. Without this white* stopper *lies* a great company *of very little red eggs, so small as little red sands in a small* hower-glasse. *These eggs are filled with red juice which is the greatest and best part of the* succus Kermes. *These seem by a* good microscope *to be of a* regular oval figure & in *the sun seem to* sparkle, & the shell *seems to be wrought with a most* delicate azure *and red* colour, interlaced *in* several wind*ings.*

Gentility FRID. MAY 22. *One that* gatherd *it, told us that he* collected *in* Bretaigne[3] 215,000[4] *for mulcts of those that* pretended *to* gentility *without title and* consequently *had worn swords.*[5] They paid 40 pistols *each, and on the same score the King had* 200,000 *out of* Languedoc. Trade Gentlemen *of* Bretaigne *have* liberty *to trade without losing their*

---

[1] *O.E.D.* 'of corn, to form the hard grains in the ear, to seed'.

[2] I.e. the *taille réelle*, based on the amount of land held, as compared with the *taille personnelle*, based on estimated income.

[3] Brittany.   [4] *Livres* understood?

[5] Colbert had waged war against the *faux nobles* whose exemption from the *taille* increased the burden on others, and diminished the amount of money coming into the Treasury. The poet, La Fontaine, was one of those fined for assuming noble rank.

gentility,[1] *only* ente*ring their names and laying by their* gentility *for a time, which they* resume *again when they leave trade, but the rest of France cannot do so, but if they once trade, they lose their* gentility.[2]

FRID. MAY 29. *Paid* Madame^elle3 Fisket for *lodging and washing for the month ending* 24th instant   9 – 10 – 0. *Paid my bill all I owed her.*

The varnish *wherewith they* varnish *their* earthen *pots, they grind*   Varnish
in a mill which stays deep in the ground, and there stays in a cask *wherein they put the* varnish *and a large quantity of water, and so a man turns it round with a handle like some* malt mils, *but the upper stone hath a good part of it broken away, I think to take the matter out.*
  Vineards *now digged.*   Vineards
  They use mules more than horses because they are more hardy, *both*   Mules
in their meat and labour.

SUND. MAY 31. Bonfires *for the taking of* Bouchain.[4]

MUND. JUN. 1. 1676. The Grana Kermes are fastend *on to the*   Kermes
branches and little sprigs of the Ilex coccifera, *but very seldom to the leaves. They are sometimes in clusters* 5 *or* 6 *togeather. They* contain
little eggs so small that there goes 4,300 *of them to* the weight of one   Eggs
grain. *In that is* conteind *the greatest part of the* succus Kermes.

TUESDAY JUN. 2. *This day* Mme. Fisket's *silk worms* began *some of*   Silk wormes
them to work. She took eggs and wrapped them up in a linen *cloth on* Good Friday *and so wore them in some warm place about her night and day till the Monday following they were* hatchd. *They* usually *put the eggs hatching in Holy Week, but that which best* governs *the time is the budding of the* mulberry trees, *that the worms, when hatched, may have food.*

---

[1] See De la Roque, *Traité de la Noblesse* (Paris, 1678), p. 454, chap. CXLIX: 'Que les basses charges et le trafic ne dérogent point en Bretagne'.
[2] In the rest of France noblemen forfeited their rank only if they engaged in retail trade (see entry for 1 Feb. 1676).
[3] *Mademoiselle* was often used for a married woman in the seventeenth century. Locke writes 'Mme.', 'Mlle' or 'Mrs.' Fisket according to the whim of the moment.
[4] On 11 May.

When they are hatchd, *they feed them with the leaves of the white* mulberry. *If there be any* yellow *leaves, they throw them away as not good. The leaves of young trees are best while the worms are young, but when they are grown pretty big, and towards the latter end of their feeding, they must be fed with the leaves of old trees, else they will not be strong to get up into the branches to work, but the leaves of young trees in the beginning makes the silk finer. Towards the latter end also they are not so* choising[1] *to pick out the yellow leaves, but they always take care that the leaves be not* witherd, *but to* avoid gather*ing fresh every day, they keep* 2 or 3 *days well enough in an earthen pot* coverd *or in a cellar.*

You must take care also that no wet leaves or moisture *come near to them, for that kills them. In feeding them also, they throw away the* tender, deepe coloured *young leaves at the top of the branches which make them very big, yellow and die without working.*

When they are young, you must coop them up in some box or chest from the cold which kills them. When they begin to work, thunder *kills them, as they say, but the thunder which was here last week hurt not those here.*

They change their skins 4 *times, from* 10 *days to* 10 *days or* thereabout. *This they call their sickness, for about this time they* forbear *to eat and therefore they feed them but once a day, but at other times they give them meat oftener. At the time also of their sickness they change them, taking away the cake of dry leaves and dung that is under them, by* removing *them with fresh leaves which they stick to: but after the* 4th *sickness is over, they change them every day till they begin to work, which is about* 10 *days* after.

They water their garden *here every day, raising water by mules, and* convey*ing it about by* trenches.

Cremor
Tartar   *They make at a house here* Cremor Tartar[2] *in great quantity out of* 2 Kentals of tartar.[3] *They* usually *make* ½ Kentall of Cremor. *They sell it for* £20 *per Kental. They have sold for* £50 *per Kental.*

Very warme, but since the rain that fell some *days* since, *it was very cool till now.*

[1] *Observations* gives *careful.*
[2] The old form, displaced by *Cream of Tartar.*
[3] Locke uses the old chemical symbol for this word.

WED. JUN. 3. Garanty of the Edict of Nantes, vid. Memoires de   Edict of
Sully Tom. 8, p. 219, 1672, & p. 267 in the History of Rochel.[1]   Nantes
Very hot. At sunset great lightening *in* several flashes. *There
seemed great* streaks *of fire in the sky. Some* thunder *at a* distance
and a very little shower of rain.

L sinke in well water 18 March, 4 p.m.; May 10, 8 p.m. swim
in W., sink in the water of Fountain Putanell,[2] & sometimes in the
night sinke also in W. May 15 swim in W. altogeather, but sink
in F.P. May 22 swim in F.P. May 30, the weather cooling a litle,
sinke in F.P. June 2 swim in F.P. March 15 sink in W. May 15,
9 a.m., swim in W., sink in F.P. May 25 swim in F.P. May 30
sinke in F.P. This day swim in F.P.[3]

THURS. JUN. 4. *When the* silkwormes begin *to work, they cull them*   Silkewormes
*when they are ripe, as they call it, from those that are feeding and put
them on* shelves *where they are to work. They know those that are ripe
or ready to work by their* clear*ness, for if you hold them up against the
light with their bellies upwards, you find them clear about the* fore*legs,
some yellow, some white, according to the several colours of the silk
they spin, and by this* clearnesse *you* easily distinguish *them from
those that are not ripe.*

The shelves *they put them on to work are thus made. They make*
shelves *of* deale boards, *one over another, as in* librarys. Mme.
Fisket's *are about* 30 inches *broad and* 22 *high. At a* distance *of
about* 9 *or* 10 inches *they set up* rows of *a small* brushy plant called
 ,[4] *which,* spreading *its branches at the top on one side and* tother,
touch those of the next row on each side so that those rows distinguish
the shelves, as it were, into so many little caves. Into these caves they

---

[1] See entry for 19 April 1676. The 1662 Paris edition of Sully's *Memoirs* (vol. VIII,
p. 219) contains the following passage under the heading 'Manifeste des Rochelois qui se
joignent ouvertement aux Anglois': 'Ce que le Duc de Rohan ayant sceu, il fit aussi sa
declaration, contenant les infractions aux deux Paix precedentes, le sujet qu'il a de s'en
esmouvoir et d'avoir eu recours au Roy de la Grand' Bretagne, *garend de la dernière*'.
The second reference is to the anonymous *Histoire des deux derniers sièges de La Rochelle*
(Paris, 1630), which reproduces on p. 267 Article IX of the 'Déclaration du Roi sur la
réduction de la ville de La Rochelle en son obéissance'. The marginal notes summarize
the article as follows: 'Abolition du crime de rébellion à ceux de La Rochelle', 'Liberté
de religion' and 'Eglise Cathedrale au lieu du Temple'.
[2] The Fontaine Putanelle is still in existence.
[3] Cf. entries for 19, 21 and 23 June 1676.   [4] Left blank in MS.

put the ripe worms who, creeping *up the branches, find among the little twigs places to work in. When one cave hath as many as it hath well room for, they fill the next, and so on.*

They *give them not the leaves of the red* Mulberry *in the* begining, *because it, being stronger* nourishment, *hurts them, but if you give them leaves of red* mulberry *towards the latter end, they will be stronger and* mount *the branches better, which, when they are weak, they cannot do, and the silk of those that eat red* mulberry *leaves is as good as the other.*

Feste Dieu.

This day being, as they call it, Feste Dieu, *the Host was carried about the town by the* Bishop, *the* canopy *over it carried by the* 6 Consuls. Several companys *of tradesmen, each with a* banner *wherein was a picture of their saint and some tools of their trade before them. After each banner followed* a piper, *or fiddlers played before them all the way, and after the* musick *followed a thing like a* garland dresd *up fine with* heron's *plumes etc., and after this* company *thus went all the* companys, *each with its banner,* musick *and garland, each* garland *having also* cakes *of bread about it. After the* company [sic] marchd *the severall orders of Friers, each with a cross before them. There were no* Jesuits *who, it seems, never use to* assist *at such* occasions. *After the friars followed a great many little boys in blue frocks with great white flambeaux* lighted. *After them the* Chainons[1] *of* St. Peter's[2] *here* in their surplices *who sung. Then came the* Bishop *and the Host, 2 in* surplices *going by it, one each side, with* censors *in their hands, every now and then* incensing it. After the Host followed Praesidents, Intendants, Conseilers, Treasurers, proctors *and other* officers *in their robes with lighted tapers in their hands, and after all a crowd of* people, *tradesmen of* company [sic] *and* [sic] *caried* lighted *tapers. In this order they set out for* St. Piere's *church and so,* fetching compasse[3] *through* several *streets of the town,* returnd *thither again, the streets all hung* where they *passed. This is the most* solemn *procession of the year, but if one judge either by the habits of the tradesmen or the hangings of the streets* which were in *many places*

---

[1] *O.E.D.* gives the once common form of *channons*, but this seems to be a misspelt version of the French *chanoines*.
[2] The Cathedral.
[3] *O.E.D.* 'make a circuit, detour'.

blankets & coverlids,[1] *one is apt to think that either their* fortunes *or devotions were very scanty.*

FRID. JUN. 5. Mr. Higham, an Italian, an excellent Gardiner, *lives somewhere near* Worcester, *where you hear of him or at* Sir Edward Seabright's.[2]   Gardiner

SUND. JUN. 7. Lightening in the evening. A procession of Penitent Blanchs *with* Host *and* canopy caried by the Consuls.

MUND. JUN. 8. *I* opend a cocon *of a silkworm that began to work on* 3 June, *and found all his work done and him turned into* an aurelia,[3] *the skin of his head and forepart, as far at least as his* 6 *forelegs, being slipped off and lying by him.*   Silkwormes

I also opened one that began to work a day or 2 after, viz. 5 June, *and found* [*it*] *quite at rest, but not yet changed into* an aurelia.

Looking to-day on some eggs of Grana Kermes *I had in a little* deale *box, I found them stir and, looking on them in a* Microscope, *I found among the eggs some little animals, in shape, bulk and colour like eggs themselves, only with* 6 *legs added to them,* 2 *horns before and* 2 *hairs behind.*   Kermes

I opened also some of the grana *wherein in the back part, I mean that opposite to the white spot by which it sticks on to the plant, I found some little flies about the* bignesse *of a little* flea *and leaping like them when touched, their wings hanging on by their bodies.* In the Grains, I beleive, *are bred 2 sorts of* animals, *for there are 2* sels[4] *quite* distinct, *without any* passage *from one to another, and when that behind was not quite* empty, *I found that* before full of *little red eggs which sometimes also were* hatchd *into such little* animals *as I* describd above, *and therefore that the hollow part* behind *serves for a storehouse for food for it* empty. *The hollow where the eggs lie is always just within the white spot and is of a* whitish *colour; but the other hollow where I found the flies, is always red and* polishd *where empty, and lie about the other hollow where eggs lie, but of this* amplius inquirendum.

---

[1] *O.E.D.* gives this form of *coverlets.*
[2] A Baronet (*c.* 1645–79), of Besford Court, Worcestershire. This entry is preceded by a medical note, derived from a 'Mr. Pean'.
[3] *O.E.D. chrysalis.*   [4] *O.E.D.* gives this form of *cell.*

Silke worme TUESD. JUN. 9. The *silkworm of* 5 June *that I* opend yesterday *had his head then pulled towards his forelegs, and they drawn close up together towards his head, and all, as it were, drawn in. To-day the skin of the forepart was slipped off, and he turned into a* perfect aurelia.

France WED. JUN. 10. *Wars are often* necessary *to the King of France to take away by this* fermentation *the scum of the people, for before these last wars* Montpellier *was so full of idle fellows that one was not safe in the evening going out in the streets, and he that carried out a cloak, was not sure to bring it home.* Mr. Magnol.[1]

Eclyps THURSD. JUN. 11. An eclyps of the sun begining 7 minutes before 8 in the morning & ending 15 minutes past, covering $6\frac{1}{2}$ digits, according to the observacion of Mr. Jolly.[2]

Another procession *with the Host, the* canopy caried by Consuls, *and a large train of people,* espetially *women.*

Asadarac FRID. JUN. 12. The seeds *of the tree we had at* Aix *in the* Duc *of* Mercur's garden *are of* Asadarac or Juiuba falsa, *though some call it* Sycomorus Malatensis. *It is a handsome tree, leaves much like* Ash. *It bears* a feather *of little flowers, each having* 5 *little, white leaves with a round thing standing up in the* midle, *in some of deep* purple, *others quite black.*

Kermes *The little* animals *of the eggs in* Grana Kermes *seen again to-day in a* microscop *are of the same colour and bigness as before, i.e. of the colour of the eggs and the same* oval figure, *with 2 horns before and 2 long hairs behind and 2 round, coal-black eyes. There are among them the shells or rather the skins of their eggs which are quite white and broken.*

---

[1] Pierre Magnol (1638–1715), a well-known doctor of Montpellier. His religion prevented him from being given a chair in the Faculty until after his conversion to Catholicism. He is chiefly remembered for his botanical studies (his name lives in *Magnolia*). Locke several times attributes to him various medical notes in his Journal. This entry is followed by a medical note at the end of which is written 'Mr. Gitto'.

[2] Another Protestant doctor of Montpellier (M.D. 1669), who, like Magnol, was converted in 1685. In 1686 he received a pension of 600l. (Haag, *France Protestante*). He seems to have been especially interested in astronomy, to judge from Locke's mentions of him in the Journal. Skippon (p. 715) describes him as 'a very ingenious person, and civil to the English'. Martin Lister also had dealings with him while in Montpellier.

I saw from Mr. Pueche's terras the Pyrenees, *white, which he told me were above* 100 English *miles off.*

The Eclyps *of the sun* yesterday, *according to the* observation *of* Mr. Jolly, *began when the sun's* elevation *was of* 34 degrees 30 m., *and when it ended, the* elevation *of the sun was* 61 d. 15 m., *and the* eclyps *of almost* 6 digits.   Eclyps

SUND. JUN. 14. Elders *of the church sent the clerk to remove some*   Protestants *women that were in the* Galery *among the men, but they kept their seats.*[1]

Risse[2] *baked with grease of mutton* Sunday's *supper for our family.*

MUND. JUN. 15. Shooting at Target.

TUESD. JUN. 16. Ml. Fisket took her Cocons *out of the branches and* Silkworms already *there were some* papilions *among them.*

I opend *some* grana Kermes *in the sun, but found only little red* Kermes *worms of the* bignesse *and colour of the eggs. In others I found only little white winged flies, but* 10 *times as big as the worms, and in some I found both worms and flies.*

One of the Confrery of the Penitent Blancs, *being dead, was* caried Burial *to his* interment dresd *up in the* habit *of that* Confrery *and so put into a* beere *like a* cradle *with his face* open *and his hands folded and a little cross held up in them. There* preceded *the corpse* several of the Confrery *in their* habits *and some friars,* and 6 *of the* Confrery *in their habits carried the corpse underhand as is the* fashon *here.* The *religious and people* followd.

Water in little glass tubes rises 11 inches *and no more.* Mr. Regius. Ascensus liquorum

WED. JUN. 17. Mm. Fisket *stripped off the loose silk from the* cocons Silkworms *and took as many as she thought fit for* breeding *and threaded them, but passed the needle so through the* cocons *by the side that it did not hurt the* aurelia *within. They allow* 1 lb. *of* cocons *for* 1 oz. *of* eggs.

THURSD. JUN. 18. Mrs. Fisket wound *her raw silk.*

25 pans *of holland to make* 2 shirts *at* 16 s. per pan *cost in all* 20 l. Linin

---

[1] In French Protestant churches the gallery was generally reserved for men.
[2] *O.E.D.* gives this spelling of *rice.*

FRID. JUN. 19. N.W. Clouds & some few drops of rain & soe coole these 3 last days *that the balls that had* swam *without any sinking for* severall weeks, *now sank again.*

Silkworms SUND. JUN. 21. The silk*worms that began to work on the* 3rd instant *came out in* butterflys *to-day. The males know the* females *at a good distance and* show a brisknesse *by stirring their wings and go to them, though covered with glass.*

Faire & soe hot that the ball L which had *sank for the* 3 *or* 4 *days last past in the* Fountain Putanel, *rose again this* evening *and* swam.

Bonfires TUESDAY JUN. 23. Bonfires *all through the* town *for* St. John's *day to-morrow, but* bonfires *made only by papists.*

Silkworms 8 lbs. *of* Cocoons *make* 1 lb. *of silk and* 1 lb. *of* Cocoons *make* 1 oz. *of eggs.*

Dying The berys of Solanum racemosum *dye a very red colour.* Jacques.

Nobility *The nobility and gentry have very little trust in the common people.*

Fair & very hot *so that my* 2 balls L *and* I *rose again in the* Fountain Putanel.

Bishop's THURS. JUN. 25. The Bishop of Montpellier[1] *died last night of* funeral Apoplex[y],[2] *about* 80 *years old. He was* exposd *to sight, lying in a great room,* 2 *storeys high, dressed in his* miter *and gown of purple stuff, his hands folded on his breast as low as they reached, holding a little* crucifix, *and his hat lying on his legs. He lay in a bed of black velvet in the middle of the room, at the head* 3 *or* 4 *priests* reading continually. *About the bed were* 12 tapers *burning. At the feet stood a little table, covered with linen, on it a* basin & eur *of silver. In the* eur *was holy water, and a branch of bay which papists of all sorts, as they came in took, and therewith* sprinkled *his feet. At the upper end of the room, in a kind of* alcove, *was an altar on which were* 6 tapers *burning.*

A Gent. at the Laboratory held a viper by the neck & opend his mouth with tother hand.

[1] Francis de Bosquet (1605–76) began his career as a judge, and rose to the position of *Intendant*, first of Guyenne, then of Languedoc. In 1649 he was appointed to the bishopric of Lodève and, six years later, to that of Montpellier.

[2] Locke invariably spells the word *apoplex*, a form unknown to *O.E.D.*

I paid Mr. Fisket £9 – 10 – 0 *for* lodging *and washing till that day and went to* Selneuf[1] *to* Mr. Michard's.

SAT. JUN. 27. Mr. Michard's Metery[2] *and the land about it cost him £4,000 to his predecessor and* 300 escus *to* Cardinal Bonzie *who is the chief lord or, as they call it*, Signieur. *The ground to be let yields about* 20 pistols per annum, *and for this he pays to the* King *about* 30 escus per annum *for taxes and to the* Cardinal *for rent about* £10. *For house pays nothing.*   Land   Taxes

SUND. JUN. 28. *Began with my* Barber *of* Selneuf *for* ½ Escu per month.

    Corn cut and made up in little stacks in the field where they watch it night and day till it be thrashd *there and so carried home.*   Harvest

    The Vineards *last well to* 70 *or* 80 *years, and still older vines' wine is better. Wine of young vines is commonly* green, i.e. sower.   Vineards

WED. JUL. 1. *Ripe figs at dinner.*

FRID. JUL. 3. *Their corn being cut, they carry it to some place in the fields and there put it together in little mows, and so, as fast as they can, thrash it in a round place about* 30 *or* 40 *steps* diameter, *made bare, or rather* tread *it out with mules and so* winnow *it on the place, and so keep it in* granaryes *all the year. Their way of* winnowing *or rather* raying[3] *is with a great sieve hung up with one rope* buckled *to it with* 3 *straps of* leather *and* supported *with* 3 *sticks* pyramidically erected. *The sieve is a yard or more over and* bottomed *with a thick kind of* parchment, *cut with round and long holes to let the other seeds and earth through, for by this way of* thrashing *there is a great deal of dust and earth mixed with the corn. If during their* threshing *there happen any rain to make their* threshing *floor smoother & harder, they cover it with* straw *and so* tread *it over with mules, which they do in this* maner. *They hoodwink their mules and so, taking a* halter *of about* 2 yards *long, they* fasten *one end to a mule's head and the*   Harvest   Thrashing

---

[1] Celleneuve, a village about six miles west of Montpellier.

[2] *Métairie*, a farm the produce of which is shared by landlord and tenant.

[3] The word does not appear to be in *O.E.D.*, but Wright's *English Dialect Dictionary* gives under *reeing-sieve* ('a fine sieve for riddling and cleansing corn, clover, etc.') the Somersetshire form of *raying-sieve*.

other end to an other like a long halter, *which is likewise fastened to the
other mule's head. To the mule thus* halterd *they tie about his neck
the other mule* halterd & blinded *that so they may go* 2 abreast *as in
a cart.* 8 *being thus fitted and all their long* halters fastend together,
*in the middle there stands a man who makes the mules trot about, and
so, as he pleases,* gently removes *them from one side to the other of the*
thrash*ing floor. They tell me one pair of mules thrashes in a day*
25 Septies *of corn.*

Essences SAT. JUL. 4. The *best* essences *to be bought at* Mrs. Bradshaw at
the French Arms in the Upper Walk in the New Exchange & at
Mr. Hanlock's at the Red Lion in the Old Exchange. Mr. Michard
used to sell them for 2 s. 6 d. per 1 oz.

SUND. JUL. 5. People at *reaping in the* evening. N.W. *all day, very
cool.*

MUND. JUL. 6. Mr. Michard *paid his reapers* 40 s. per diem.

Serge d'Uzes THURS. JUL. 9. *Paid for* 3 cans *and* 2 pans *of* Serge d'Uzes at
£5 − 5 − 0 per can £17 − 1 − 3; *for* 14 pans of *watered* tabby at
17 s. per pan, 11 − 18 − 0; *for* 7 cans *of broad green* ribbon at 12 s.
per can *and for* 2 cans of narrow *green* ribbon *at* 8 s. per can, 5 − 0 − 0.

Payments FRID. JUL. 10. *The King last year sent to all the* officers *of this*
province *to lend him* 2 years' *profit of their* offices. *Some were fain to
pawn their plate to have their money ready at the day. Otherwise they
had lost their places. This got him* 2 milions *out of this one* province.[1]

Vinum SAT. JUL. 11. *A little bread or oil mixed with must turns wine to*
vinegar, *and so does* thunder; *but iron* laid on barrels *keeps wine or*
bear *from* sour*ing by thunder, as also it does milk, if put on the thing
that* covers *it.*[2]

SUND. JUL. 12. *So cold that a fire had done no harm.*
Little boy with Mr. Gilminets[3] *borrowed chick*[4] *in street.*

---

[1] See entry for 15 Dec. 1676.
[2] Entry repeated on 14 Aug. 1676.
[3] Guilleminet was the name of a well-known Montpellier family.
This word is very doubtful.

THURSD. JUL. 16. The States of Languedoc consist of 22 Bishops, *States*
22 Barons, of 22 Consuls of the principal citys of each diocesse
& 44 Consuls of 44 other lesse towns.[1]
Fair *and so cold that one had wished it to be more warm.*

SAT. JUL. 18. The rathe,[2] *ripe figs they have about the* begini*ng of* Figues
July they call Gourran. *They are black, but not the best sort of figs.*
The same figtree bears another sort of figs later in the year.

A paisant rented a Metery & *the land* belonging *to it,* lying *between* Taxes
Sel Neuf & Montpellier *at halves,* the tenant *being at all* charge of
husbandry & Landlord *of tax. He counted this farm to be rented to be*
worth about £500 *per annum, out of which he thought the* Landlord
paid about £200 *for taxes. He had out of this farm, one year with*
another, about 500 Septies *of wheat and rye which he counted at* £3
per Septie, one time with another about 10 Muits[3] *of wine at* £20 *per*
Muit, *and*   [4] *charges of oil at* £40 *per charge. For the* management *of this farm he had* 6 hands, viz. 4 *men and* 2 women, *and*
2 mules.

A charge *of oil is* 360 lbs. In measure *of wine*   Measures

$$\left. \begin{array}{l} \text{1 Muit} \\ \text{1 Tonneau} \\ \text{1 Septie} \end{array} \right\} \text{conteins} \left\{ \begin{array}{l} \text{2 Tonneaux.} \\ \text{18 Septies.} \\ \text{48 pots.} \end{array} \right.$$

In measure *of grain* 1 Septie contains 2 minots.

Their usuall *increase of wheat* is 4 *for* one, *their greatest* 7 *or* 8 *for* Increase
one. Wheat worth now £4 – 5 – 0 *per Septie. As soon as they have*
reaped their corn, they make it up in mows by their threshing flore,
and there beat it out as fast as they can, which is done by trampli*ng of*
mules or horses. 4 men *and* 4 *mules will* thrash, cleanse & carry into
the granary about 40 Septies in a day. The hire *of these* 8 *costs*
£   [5] *per diem.* Wages of reapers is usually about £1 – 5 – 0 per
day.

Lammas wheat had media proportione 11 cornes per ear. Red Wheat
wheate 18 graines per eare. Lammas wheat 9 grains per ear.

Borrowed of Mr. George Wall £12 – 0 – 0.   Mr. Wall
Paid for a pair of silk Stockings £10.   Silk stockings

---

[1] These figures do not agree with others given by Locke.
[2] *O.E.D.* 'which ripen early in the year'.   [3] *Muids.*
[4] Left blank in MS.   [5] Left blank in MS.

Harvest **MUND. JUL. 20.** Harvest *was done here about the* beginning *of* July, *so that all was cut and* caried *by the middle of this month.*

Watering *Their great want in this country is of water which, when they have, they have grass and fruit, as at* Fontcaud, *about a mile from* Selneuf, *where is a* handsom garden *with grass, walks and fruit, being* waterd *by a cut from the* river.

Arbor *There I saw an* octagon arbor, 20 steps diameter, *of* cypresse trees upright, *kept and cut very* smooth, *with large openings like gates to the* several *walks that met* there. *Seats in* niches *in every corner. It looked very* handsome *and about* 20 *foot high, quite open to the air.*

Capers **TUESDAY JUL. 21.** Between this & Montpellier in holes of the garden wall, like scaffold *holes, there grew* capers, *whereof I* gatherd *some to-day as I went to* Montpellier. *They have buds of* floure *and have* tast a litle bitterish.

Soldiers *2 or 3 days last passed through* Montpellier *a regiment of horse and another of foot from Catalonia for Nîmes.*[1] *The horse were good men, but the horses poor and lame, but the foot* miserable *little boys.*

Colours **WED. JUL. 22.** *A solution of* silver nitrate[2] *turned* green ribbon *into* phyllymort[3] immediately *with a* circle *of blue about the edges of the* fyllymort. *Red* vinegar *turned grass green into willow green.* Verjuce *turned it into sky colour, and claret wine into willow,* aqua regis *into blue, and a solution of* silver nitrate *put on any of these* producd *still* phylimort.

Finger **THURSD. JUL. 23.** *Knot at the root of my middle finger first* observd, *but pain felt there 2 or 3 weeks before.*[4]

Mule **SAT. JUL. 25.** The price of an ordinary mule 20 or 25 pistols.
Paid Mr. Wall for mony laid out for me as followeth *and all* evened:[5]

---

[1] The shorthand stands for *Nis-may*, i.e. *Nismes*, i.e. *Nîmes*!
[2] This and *aqua regis* are expressed by old chemical symbols.
[3] *O.E.D.* '*fillemot* (from *feuille-morte*): dead leaf colour'.
[4] After this comes a fragment which is obviously part of the draft of a letter: 'The care and concernment for my health while abroad made me not wholly forget what I owed to our Lord (?) and to good manners. I thought myself bound, as others use to do, to bring home with me some presents to my friends as marks of my having been abroad, and in the first place not to fail....' This is nearly all in shorthand; the 'Lord' is presumably Shaftesbury.
[5] *O.E.D.* 'to settle an account'.

Morning goune	12 – 10 – 0
Stockings mending	00 – 05 – 0
Petty Paris	00 – 15 – 0
Letter	00 – 06 – 0
Black ribbon	00 – 02 – 6
Letter	00 – 05 – 0
Lent	12 – 00 – 0
Holsters	03 – 10 – 0
Letter	00 – 05 – 0
Letter	00 – 07 – 0
Lent	00 – 12 – 9
	30 – 18 – 3

Barons *that are of the Religion in this* Province *are not* permitted *to*   Protestants
*come themselves into the States, but may depute any one of the papists
and send him in their room.*[1]

SUND. JUL. 26. The marine winde is observd *here to have this*   Winde
quality, *that if one* skour *brass never so clean and bright, when that
wind blows, it tarnishes and grows dull in the hour, contrary to what
it does when other winds blow; and that it is moister than any other,
I find by* my thermometer.[2]

MUND. JUL. 27. Father Mage[3] *discoursed well of absolute monarchy*   Mage
and Ireland.

To make herb potage, cut the herbs and put them in a pipkin and   Potage
there boyl *them in* sufficient *quantity butter, and then after put water
to them and so* boyl *them yet longer, and when it is enough, beat some
egg in* verjuce *and mix with it, and you will have good soup. If you*
boyl hearbs *in water first and after add butter, soup not so good.*

SAT. AUG. I. 1676. Monsieur Regius *stung in the night in one eyelid*   Scorpionis
by a Scorpion. *It swelled as big as an egg by morning, but with no*   ictus
great pain. He only anointed *it with oil of* Scorpions *which took it
down and cured it quite without anything else.*

---

[1] Article XXVII of the *déclaration* of 1 Feb. 1667 (Pilatte, p. 20) banned Protestants
from the Estates of Languedoc. Gachon (p. 21) quotes a decision of the Estates in 1649
insisting that Protestant barons, who were entitled to a seat in their assembly, must be
represented by a Catholic deputy.
[2] The last word is in Greek characters.
[3] Presumably Magee (one of the Irish monks from Narbonne?).

SUND. AUG. 2. Thunder, lightening & hard rain the greater part of this morning. Thunder & hard rain a good part of this afternoon.

MUND. AUG. 3. Mr. Stringer *in his letter of* 15 June 1676 *writ me that he had received* £24 *of my* unkle[1] *and in his letter of* 8 July *that he had received* £24 more of my Unkle, *but nothing yet from* Oxford.[2]

Vintage   They cannot *begin their vintage here at* Selneuf *till* Cardinal Bonzi's officer *gives them leave, the tithes belonging to the* Cardinal.

Baucair TUESD. AUG. 4. *At* Baucair fair *but* 3 *barks this year whereas there used to be* 2 *or* 300.

Figues   WED. AUG. 5. One meets now the ripe Coucarelos,[3] a litle, red, round figue about the bignesse of a wallnut, wholsome much & sweeter then the Gourrans which are now gon.

Grapes THURSD. AUG. 6. Muscat grapes ripe the begining of this month.

Grapes SUND. AUG. 9. Spiran grapes ripe, *but yet* Dr. Barbyrac *thought it not fit to eat them.*[4]

Protestants   *This fortnight*[5] *Protestant ministers forbid to teach above* 2 *scholars at once.*

Catterpiller   *The great red* catterpiller *that fed on the* Spurge[6] *about the middle of* July *turned into an* Aurelia *out of which came a fine sort of* mothfly, *all the hinder part of* Dove colour, distinguishd *by white rings and, about the head, some* patches *of red.*

WED. AUG. 12. Thunder & hard shower of 2 howers. 2 or 3 days very hot.

TUESD. AUG. 18. Paid Mr. Michard 14 crowns due for my bord for a month ending 25th July last.

Prie Dieu SUND. AUG. 23. Prie dieu[7] catches flyes & eats them. He catches them all with his fore legs.

---

[1] Peter Locke (1607–86) who looked after his nephew's small properties in Somerset.
[2] For his Studentship at Christ Church.
[3] *Coucourelles.*   [4] *Yet* is repeated at the end of the sentence.
[5] Article XL of the *déclaration* of 1 Feb. 1669 (Pilatte, p. 24) reads as follows: 'Que les ministres de ladite religion ne pourront tenir aucuns pensionnaires que de ladite R.P.R., ni en plus grand nombre que de deux à la fois'. I have been unable to trace a similar decree for 1676.
[6] *O.E.D.* 'kinds of plant with acrid, milky juice'.
[7] In English, the 'praying mantis'.

TUESDAY SEPT. 1 1667 [sic]. *Scarce a cloud, the hottest day of the year hitherto. The last 7 or 8 days the hottest we had all summer.*

WEDN. SEPT. 9. N.E., fair, *cold. From hence I saw to-day the* Pyreneans, *but dimly. The other day I saw them as plain as* Pierre St. Loup. *They lie* S.W. *and are, as they say,* 50 leagues off.

THURSD. SEPT. 10. *Cold, fire* comfortable.

SAT. SEPT. 12. Nightingalls *singing in the King's Garden.* At Montpellier misty, rain, thunder & lightening, *and hard rain at night.*

MUND. SEPT. 14. Paid Mr. Du Bois £3 for 2 *months* ending 25 Aug. *for trimming.*

Men run[1] *at* Selneuf about twelve score[2] *or some thing more over* ploud land, very stony, *barefoot, and maidens the same, about half so far. There were also races of boys together and girls in other courses. He that won among the men had a hat, among the maidens a ribbon, and less fry* smaller *matters, all which were given at this* annual Olympiad *by the Cardinal who is the* Seignure *of the place, and was all tied to the end of a pole which was held up at the end of the race. The whole* prize *thus exposd was a hat,* severall *ribbons and tagged laces, 2 or 3 purses and a few pennies. Jumping also was another* exercise, *and after all, what never fails, dancing to* hoboy[3] *and tabor.*   Sports

TUESD. SEPT. 15. *Close.* Thunder, lightening & hard rain.

FRID. SEPT. 18. Paid Mr. Michard for 1 month 3 weeks board at £42 per mensem, £73 – 10, & for other accounts to make up the full £79 – 3 – 0. Came to Mr. Fisquet's.

TUESDAY. SEPT. 22. 1 Grape weighd 5 ozs. 1 scr. 3 grs. They call   Grape
them Grumaus. It was a black grape of the fashon of a peare, in compasse 3⅝ inches, wanting very litle, English measure, & in compasse long way 3⅝ Inch. They are very fleshy & the whole bunches are of this bignesse. *Fair, cold.*

SAT. SEPT. 26. Thunder, lightening & raine.
Deliverd to Mr. Hunt[4] 6 vipers for Dr. Thomas.[5]   Thomas

---

[1] Past tense?   [2] *Yards* understood?   [3] *O.E.D.* 'hautbois, oboe'.
[4] There are several references in the Journal to this person, and in a letter to Thoynard of 3 Sept. 1680 Locke refers to him as 'un de mes amis'.
[5] David Thomas, M.D. (Oxford, 1670), was one of Locke's closest friends. He practised at Salisbury.

Revenue TUESD. SEPT. 29. The Tail[1] *in France is* 45 millions per annum.
The Gabel, *which contains salt and* customs,[2] 40 millions. *King's*
Domain 15 millions. Casualtys, i.e. *selling of* offices, 10 millions.
All this exclusive of Languedoc, Britaigne & Burgundie, *yet they*
have States.[3] *The way of laying on the Taille is this. The King's*
Counsil *judges how much is needed. That being agreed, they send to*
every generality, v.g. Orleans, Com*missioners to levy their* quota.
The Intendant *of the place, with the* Elus *who are all* officers appointed *by the King,* assess the several parishes *within that* generality
and appoint collectors *in each* parish *who* assesse *the rest of the*
parish. *The* assessment *made, they bring it to the* Elus *who sign and*
so ratifie it *and give the* collectors *a commission to* collect *it, who are*
answerable *for the money. If any one find him* agreivd, *he* complains
to the Elus, *and if they right him not to his* satisfaction, *he must go to*
his Court of Aids[4] *at* Paris. *A Gent. pays nothing,* i.e. *he may keep*
in his hand as much land as he can manage *with* 2 *ploughs.*[5] *If he has*
any more, he must pay for it, but as well as they can, the burthen *is*
shifted off on to the paisants, *out of whose labour they wring as much*
as they can, and rot lights on the land. The Generality *of* Orleans *pay*
yearly 4 millions *for the Taille and* 4 millions *for salt. They pay at*
Orleans £44 *for a* minot *of salt, but are forced to take no more than*
they think fit, but near the salt works every house is forced *to take such*
quantity, whether they use it or no.

Besides this, the Church gives the King every now and then a round
sum.[6]

The King of France's revenue of 100,000,000 l., besides Languedoc, Britanny and Burgundy, is about £8,546,000 sterling.[7]

---

[1] The *taille.*

[2] The *Gabelle* could scarcely be said to 'contain' customs and excise duties, though
they were sometimes farmed out together.

[3] The total given by Locke comes to 110,000 millions, which seems slightly too high
a figure. Locke himself gives 100 millions—a figure slightly nearer the mark—in the
course of this entry.

[4] I.e. *Cour des Aides.*

[5] According to Clamageran (II, 620) Colbert limited the amount of land which nobles
and clerics could hold without paying the *taille* to four *charrues,* and for *bourgeois* to two.

[6] Its so-called *Don gratuit,* fixed by negotiation between the General Assembly of the
clergy and the government.

[7] This sentence is actually in the middle of the previous shorthand passage.

WED. SEPT. 30. Mony Laid out for me by Mr. Wall:

1 Letter	0 – 10 – 0
Essay morale[1]	3 – 0 – 0
Gloves	0 – 9 – 0
Letters	0 – 15 – 0
Messenger	0 – 02 – 6
Letter	0 – 5 – 0
To Mr. Cleves for a letter	0 – 5 – 0
Letter Aug. 22	0 – 6 – 0
Lent me	42 – 0 – 0
Letter Aug. 26	0 – 5 – 0
Paper Aug. 27	0 – 5 – 0
Letters Sept. 3	0 – 10 – 0
Gloves Sept. 5	0 – 9 – 0
Lent me Sept. 12	9 – 0 – 0
Letter Sept. 15	0 – 5 – 0
Lent me	0 – 4 – 0
19¼ escus 6 d.	58 – 10 – 6

Paid him this bill & 10 s. which he paid for me at Mlle Varshan's[2]
for dinner   59 – 0 – 6.

THURS. OCT. 1. Drawn a bill upon Mr. Stringer for 47 – 8 – 4 l. s. d. Stringer
sterling payable to Mr. Geo. Covart upon double usance.[3]

Grape stones they sell at 2 s. a bushell to be separated from the Pigeons
husks by the buyer. They feed their pigeons with them.

FRID. OCT. 2. The inscription upon a chapell dore neare Morat[4] where Inscription
in the bones of the Burgundians are heaped up that were killed there:

Deo opt. Max. Caroli Incliti et fortissimi Burgundiae ducis exercitus
Muratum obsidens ab Helvetiis Caesus hoc sui monumentum reliquit.
Anno 1476.

The country people about St. Martin le Chastille sur Soane[5] Damzen drink
seldom eat flesh, their common noriture being baked apples &
other sorts of fruit, pease, roots, cheese. For their drinke, it is

---

[1] Nicole's *Essais de morale*, four of which Locke translated or rather adapted (see
entry for 2 July 1678).   [2] Verchand? See entry for 17 Oct. 1676.
[3] *O.E.D. Usance*: 'The time or period...allowed by commercial usage or law for the
payment of a bill of exchange, etc.' 'Double usance' means two months.
[4] In Switzerland. Charles the Bold was defeated there in 1476.
[5] There is a Saint-Martin-le-Châtel (Ain), which is not far from Mâcon, but it is
several miles east of the Saône.

a certain liquor made of water & plumbs, not unpleasant, very wholesome, in this manner. They take a terse,[1] fill it with water, puting before into the vesselle about 2 bushells of damzens whole without bruiseing. After they have been about 5 or 6 days steepd there, they begin to drink it. This will keep good about two months. This is neare Mascon. It is a well tasted drinke. Mr. Charleton.

Stairs   At Sir Jo: Newton's,[2] 2 miles from Grantham, is a paire of staire [sic] that turns round with a pin. Mr. Herbert.[3]

Oake   At Bale in Norfolk an oake 24 fathom in compasse. ib.

Birds   At Fanly in Lancashire the variety of birds, the fat bird & catching
Dottrils   of Dotrills.[4] ib.

Dessigneing   Mr. St. Clar's short way of takeing Lanscapes or copys of pictures by his paralelogram.[5] ib.

Montpellier   Montpellier is about 43½ d. North Latitude. Dr. Jolly.

Olives   SAT. OCT. 3. The manner of pickleing Olives *is thus. They cut them in 2 or 3 plases to the stone and then lay them in water 7 or 8 days, changing the water every day. This is to take away the bitternesse. When that is done, they put them in a pickle of salt and water to keep. This is the time to do it, for now in a little time they grow black. To take away the bitternesse and keep them whole, they do thus. They soak them 6 or 7 hours in cold Soapboiler's Lye, this more or less, as they desire them more or less sweet, and soak them in fair water 7 or 8 days as the other, and then put them in pickle.* The Soapboiler's *lye* consists of lixivium alcolisatum, aqua coleis vivae & oyle of which they make their castile soap.

Cold   SUND. OCT. 4. Dr. Magnol assurd me that the winters here were sometimes soe hard *that* spitle would freez *before it fell to the ground, but that it* seldome *lasted above* 21 *days.*[6]

---

[1] *O.E.D. Terse* (or *tierce*): 'An old measure of capacity equal to one third of a pipe (usually 42 gallons); also a cask or vessel holding this capacity.'

[2] Not in the *Complete Baronetage* or lists of knights.

[3] Thomas Herbert (1656–1733), 8th Earl of Pembroke, was entered at Christ Church in 1672, and from 1690 onwards held various distinguished posts, including that of Lord High Admiral. It was to him that Locke dedicated his *Essay on the Human Understanding*.

[4] *O.E.D. Dotterels*: 'species of plover'. MS. has 'Lanchashire'.

[5] *O.E.D.* 'an old name for the *pantograph*, an instrument for the mechanical copying of a plan, diagram, pattern, etc. on the same or a reduced scale'.

[6] There is a long note on 8 October on the currency of Italy, on travel there and on what to see.

FRID. OCT. 9. Memo. to make candles put out them selves with a declineing socket & a bullet.

After a rainy day dancing along dirty streets in the night to a Danseing
hobboy.

My Unkle Locke in his of 22 June writes me that he hath paid Stringer
Mr. Stringer about £46.

The juice of Carduus stellatus takes away. Du Boys.

THURSD. OCT. 15. *For an* accidental *blow with a mall ball a* quarrel Fray
begun by the French, and 50 or 60 *set on* 9 *or* 10 English *with swords,
malls and stones.*

SAT. OCT. 17. Removed to Mr. Verchand's¹ & paid all at Mr.
Fisquet's.

TUESDAY, OCT. 20. A procession anniversary *for the* delivery *of this* Procession
town out of the hands of the Huguenots anno 1622.

The Marquis of Mealeauze² *whose* grand*mother was sister to* Protestants
Turenne, lives about Castres *in* Languedoc. *The young man hath
between* 40 *or* 50,000 *livres per annum. Served* 2 *or* 3 campaigns
and was buy*ing of a regiment lately, but the King refused to confirm
the bargain unless he would change his religion; but if he would do that,
he promised him great matters. He refused to change and was retired to
his estate. He is the most* considerable *man of the Religion in these parts.*

SUND. OCT. 25. *But* ⅓ *of any trade in any town suffered to pass
masters, i.e. to set up, of those that are of the Religion.*³

---

¹ According to the *Compoix* rolls for 1665 Henri Verchant, an apothecary, lived in 'la rue qui va au puits des esquilles'. He seems to have divided his time between Paris and Montpellier (see entry for 30 Oct. 1678 and Appendix B, p. 284). The list of Protestants and *Nouveaux Convertis* quoted above (p. 16, n. 2) gives for the same address, amongst the unconverted, 'le Sr. Verchant, appothicaire', and adds: 'est à Paris avec sa famille'. Is this the Henri Verchant, 'appothicaire de Montpellier', who appeared before the Parlement de Grenoble on 13 Oct. 1685, together with his wife and servant, on a charge of trying to flee abroad (*B.S.H.P.F.* VII, 135)?

² Guy Henri de Bourbon, Marquis de Malauze (1654–1706), began his military career under Turenne, his maternal great-uncle. It was, no doubt, pressure of the type described by Locke which finally drove him to 'conversion' to Catholicism. Bossuet received his abjuration in 1678. He served in the army until 1690 when he resigned on grounds of ill-health.

³ Gachon (p. 150) states that, by a decree of 24 October 1667, the Government, acceding to the request of the States of Languedoc, laid it down that not more than a third of the members of the guilds of the towns in the province, even where the Protestants were in an overwhelming majority, should be composed of Huguenots.

Dr. Thomas TUESD. OCT. 27. Paid Mr. Puech for 6 vipers 2 – 5 – 0.[1]

Measures WED. OCT. 28. 1 gallon English is 1⅛ quarte French
1 Tunneau contains 255 gallons.

1 Tunneau of Montpellier Brandy sold at London for ll. 40 sterling.

Olives THURSD. NOV. 5. The Olives *grow black about the end of* October. *A little before they grow black, they take green ones, pick out those that have worms and throw them away. The good ones they soak in the strongest lye they can get, to which purpose they buy it at the soap-maker's,* 4, 6, 8 *hours, according as they* designe *to eat them sooner or later. The longer they soak in the lye, the more the* bitternesse *is taken away, but they keep the less while. After they have been soaked in lye, they put them into water, and so for* 3 *or* 4 *days they change them* 2 *or* 3 *times a day and afterwards once a day, in all* 15 *days, this to take away the* tast *of the lye. The lye and water are both cold. When this is done, they put them into a* pickle *of salt and water and so keep them.*

SUND. NOV. 8. *As much coughing at church as ever I heard in* London.[2]

Epilepsia SAT. NOV. 14. Sir W. Waller *having had* Convulsive *fits....*[3]

States MUND. NOV. 23. *This day was the* ope*ning of the States here. When they were all sat and had been so a* pretty *while in expectation of the* Count de Roure[4] *and the* Intendant,[5] *in they came,* attended *by* severall *of the* Barons who, *on their* arrival *at the door of the* Town

---

[1] Locke gives a cross-reference to the entry of 26 Sept. 1676, and repeats this entry on 8 Nov.

[2] And Locke had come all the way to Montpellier to seek a cure for his cough!

[3] There follows a detailed account of his illness, in which Barbeyrac appears to have been consulted. Sir William Waller (d. 1699) is described by *D.N.B.* as 'an informer'. He played a prominent part in the politics of the time, and distinguished himself particularly by his activity as a Middlesex justice during the Popish Plot.

[4] Pierre Scipion Grimoard de Beauvoir, Comte du Roure, appointed a Lieutenant-Governor of the province in 1670. He died in 1733, aged 88.

[5] Henri Daguesseau (1634–1715), father of the more famous Chancellor, was *Intendant* at Limoges and Bordeaux before being appointed to Languedoc in 1673. He behaved with relative moderation towards the Protestants, at least compared with his successor, Basville, who took over from him in 1685.

House, *went down to meet them and* marchd *in before them. With them also came* two *of the* Treasurers *of France of this* province. *When they were* enterd, the Count de Roure, as one of the Leiutenants of the province, *took his seat in a* chair *under* the canopy *of state, next to him the* Intendant, *and next to him the* 2 Treasurers, *all* three *in* square, *black caps and black,* sattin gowns, *on* the Barons' *side or left hand of the chair.*

The first thing after they were sat, was the reading of the King's letter convocat*ing the States, the* Duke *of* Vernule's commission, the Count of Roure's *and* the Intendant's Commission. *This being done,* the Count of Roure *made a short speech and* concluded *with* refer*ing them to the* Intendant *who, as soon as he had done, began and made a long speech; and when he had done, the* Archbishop *of* Alby[1] (*for since last year* Alby *has been made an* Archbishoprick) *in the name of the States made a speech in* Answer *to the others. The* 2 *first, at the* distance *I stood, I did not hear, but the* Archbishop *was, in short, to this* purpose: *to* extol *their* happynesse *in that the* King allowed *them their* priviledges, *wherein he* mentioned par- ticularly *their* liberty *of talking* freely *of their* affairs. *Then he* mentioned the Duke of Vernule *as a great* preserver *of their* libertys, *and then* desird the Count de Roure to returne *the King the thanks of the States for those favours he* shewd *them and to tell him they make not ill use of the* liberty *he* allowd them, *and so ended.*[2]

N.B. *All* 3 *spoke sitting and* coverd.

The Open*ing of the States is* usually *by the Duke of* Vernules *who himself takes the* chair *and speaks in short to them, but he being now sick, it was* performed *by the* Count de Roure *who is one of the* 3 Leiutenants *of the* province *of* Languedoc, *a very* proper, *handsome* man.

---

[1] Hyacinthe Serroni (1617–89), an Italian protégé of Mazarin who employed him in various diplomatic missions, was Bishop of Mende and *Premier aumônier* of Anne of Austria before being made the first Archbishop of Albi in 1676. He presided over this session in the absence of Cardinal Bonzi who was in Rome for a conclave.

[2] The *Procès-verbal* of this session of the Estates adds little to Locke's account. Apparently the theme of the Comte du Roure's speech was 'les motifs qui doivent en- gager cette province à persévérer dans le zèle qu'elle a toujours eu pour le service du Roy afin de se rendre digne des graces dont Sa Majesté continue de la combler'. The *Intendant*, we are merely told, made 'un discours fort éloquent' on the same lines.

Taxes   *Before the* Duc de Vernule *was their* governor, Languedoc *used to give the King by the States yearly about* 200,000 livres, *and now they give him as many* millions, *and still increase every year, beside that* 2 *or* 3 *years since the King* borrowed *on the* credit *of this* province 1,600,000 livres, *whereof he promised to pay the use,*[1] *and at the next* assembly *of the* States, *beside what they gave him of* supply, *he* demanded 100,000 l. *of them to pay the use of that debt, which they were fain to give him.*[2]

Salt   SUND. 29 NOV.   Salt *here is* £18 per minot, *at* Paris 48£ per Minot, *which is here and at* Paris *just of the same* bignesse. *They talk that* Taxes   *the* States *this* session *will lay on salt* 30s. *more* per minot. *Besides* 3,000,000£ *are* demanded *of them.*[3] *Land whose* product *is worth* 1200 *crowns* per annum *pays out of it to the King about* 1,000 livres, *so that the owners, by that time* taxes, servants' *wages and all other things are paid, have not above* 4 *or* 500£, *at most, clear.*

MUND. NOV. 30.   *Fair, hard frost.* About the later end of this month they begin to gather their olives.

Grievances   WED. DEC. 2.   Mr. Perota of Uzes *put in the* Bastil *in* November *for going to the King as* Deputy *with the* grievances *of this* province.[4]

---

[1] *O.E.D.* 'interest'.

[2] These grumblings which Locke has faithfully recorded for us, contain, as so often, a certain element of exaggeration. It is true that the amount of the *Don gratuit* of the province had been stepped up rapidly in recent years, partly on account of the war. In 1675 the sum demanded was 2,100,000 l. and in 1676 three millions, and both these sums were eventually granted by the States, though in each case they received eventually a rebate on them (100,000 l. in 1675 and 300,000 l. in 1676). In the earlier years of the personal reign of Louis XIV there had generally been a considerable gap between the sum demanded and the sum granted by the States, e.g. in 1662, while the Prince de Conti was still Governor, the King demanded 2,500,000 l. and finally accepted 1,500,000 l. But one would have to go well into the first half of the century to find a *Don gratuit* as small as 200,000 l. The loan of 1,600,000 l. (for the Canal du Languedoc) had been raised in 1672: the Commissioners had promised a reduction of 100,000 l. in the taxes of the province, if the Estates agreed to pay the interest. (Roschach, XIV, 1118–19.)

[3] As *Don gratuit*.

[4] This entry raises problems to which I have been unable to find a solution. It is highly probable that Locke spelt the name wrong, and M. Gouron, *Archiviste en chef du Gard*, suggests that it should be Perroutat, since at that time there was at Uzès a certain David de Perroutat, seigneur de Saint-Victor-des-Oules et de Saint-Quentin-la-Poterie. The Archives Nationales possess three dossiers on him (TT. 190, No. XIII; 229 D, No. XXXVI; 457, No. 64), all belonging to the period after 1685. He was converted to Catholicism, though his wife and three daughters took refuge at Lausanne, and his

THURSD. DEC. 3. Hard snow. *Their way of making wine is thus. They* Wine
gather the grapes when ripe and so in a kind of grate over the cuve[1]
men *tread them till they are all broken and then throw them in, husks,*
stalks and all, into the cuve, and thus till all the grapes are trod.

When all the mass is in the cuve, they let it work there 1, 2 *or* 3 *days*
as they think fit. The longer it works and the more stalks are in it
(for sometimes they put them not all in), the rougher and deeper-
coloured will the wine be, but keeps longer.

When it has wrought its time in the cuve, they put it into butts and
there let it work as long as it will, filling up the working vessel *every*
day with some of the same must, kept on purpose, *for it wastes much*
in working. What remains of the husks and stalks in the cuve, they
press, which makes a worse, coarse sort of wine for the servants.

When they have a mind to have their wine fine sooner than ordinary,
they put in a cask a pretty *good quantity of shavings of fir, and, in some*
places, of hazel, and with it they sometimes put some whole white grapes.

The cuve is a place made in the ground in some part of the house,
proportionably *big according to the quantity they make, and lined*
with plaister *of* Paris *to keep it from leaking. In this, which is made*
use of but once a year, and all other parts of their making wine they
are sufficiently *nasty, according to their manner. The grapes are often*
very rotten and always full of spiders. Besides that, they say they put
often salt, men's dung and other filthinesse *in their wine to* help, *as*
they think, its purging.

FRID. DEC. 4. *Very fair and very cold.* Ice & snow lying.

SAT. DEC. 5. Ice & snow lying & extrem cold.

SUND. DEC. 6. *Very fair, very cold, snow lying.* Ice *of one night's*
freezing *above* an inch thick, *near* 2 inches.

MUND. DEC. 7. *Cloudy, snow lying.*

TUES. DEC. 8. *Rain all day.*

---

two sons were killed at Athlone in 1691 in the army of William III. However, there was
nobody of that name or of Uzès among the deputies whom the province was allowed to
keep at Court to represent its interests there. Moreover, there is no trace of any such
person in the Archives de la Bastille, or in the lists of prisoners given by Ravaisson and
Funck-Brentano. On the other hand, these papers are notoriously incomplete, and if one
cannot confirm this entry, neither can one reject it as false.

[1] *O.E.D.* 'cask, vat'.

Wine THURSD. 10 DEC. The wines of Languedoc about Montpellier will not endure the Ocean, but spoile if caried upon it, but endure the Mediterranean & become the better by that Navigation. Mr. Puech hath tried it, & soe have severall other Merchants to their great losse. Muscat must be excepted, espetially that of Frontignan which mends by cariage into England.

Montpellier Montpellier lies in 43 d. 40'. Mr. Reyly.

Capuchins SAT. 12 DEC. The Capuchins' covent *here, which is but an* ordinary *one of 30 monks, cost* 50,000 *escus, but it was much of it to buy and pull down houses to make their garden.*

MUND. DEC. 14. Hard snow,[1] *and then the wind coming about to* E.S., *it turned to rain.*

TUESD. DEC. 15. *The King has sent this year to the* Primier President *of this place for* £32,000, *to the other* Presidents *for*   [2] apeice, *and to each* Counsellor *for* 1,000.[3] The Primier President's *place is worth yearly* £10,000.

WED. DEC. 23. Capuchins *cheated of their pot which was sold for* £9.

Young SAT. DEC. 26. Sir Wm. Waller & Mr. Grenvil[4] desird *to borrow each* £1,000 *of* Mr. C. Young.

SUND. DEC. 27. Witnesse to Mr. Charles Younge's will.

---

[1] Delort (I, 294) records for this day an extremely heavy fall of snow which drove in the roofs of sixteen houses by its weight, and caused several deaths.

[2] Left blank in MS.

[3] This is a reference to one of the numerous devices used by the Crown to raise money to carry on the war. According to Delort (I, 285–8) the King, by an edict of Jan. 1674, demanded that the judges of the higher courts of law should pay 14,000,000 l. in return for a so-called *augmentation de gages* of 1,000,000 l. The share of the *Cour des Aides* and *Cour des Comptes* of Montpellier came to 450,000 l. Their members negotiated with the Treasury to secure a reduction in this amount, but at the last moment the government refused all concessions, and they were thus left seven days to pay the money, which they just managed to do. Delort calls the rapidity with which they raised the money 'une chose qui paroit incroyable ou du moins bien difficile'.

[4] Denis Grenville (1637–1703), Jacobite divine. Appointed Archdeacon of Durham in 1662, he took the degree of D.D. at Oxford in 1671 and was appointed Dean of Durham in 1684. Because of his strong Jacobite sympathies he fled to France in 1688 and died in Paris fifteen years later. There are 23 letters from him to Locke in the Lovelace Collection, and it was for him that the latter composed various dissertations in the Journal, published very inadequately by King (pp. 113–15, 323–5).

THURSD. DEC. 31. Memo. that Sir Wm. Waller made a bill for Young
1,000 £ which he borrowed of Mr. Young to which Mr. Wall &
I were witnesses, which he said he would give into Mr. Grenvil's
hands, & which Mr. Grenvil acknowledged he had receivd of him,
as he did also that he had received of Mr. Young the 1,000 £ which
he had desird to borrow of him. vid. Dec. 26.

1677[1]

MUND. JAN. 4. Hard snow for 3 or 4 hours.

TUESD. JAN. 5. *The* Bishop *of Alet,*[2] *for speaking in the States in* States
behalf of the province *about* 10 *years since, has been ever since by the*
King's order excluded *the States and his* vicar *comes in his room.*

The King has lately laid £1½ *more per minot on salt in* Languedoc. Salt
For this augmentation *of this one* province *the Farmers give him*
£1,100,000 *per annum more than their former rent. This was done*
without asking the States' consent.

WED. 6 JAN. *Fair,* very hard frost.

THURSD. JAN. 7. *Fair, very* hard frost.

FRID. JAN. 8. *Fair,* freeze in my chamber.

SAT. 9 JAN. Freez in my chamber.

SUND. 10 JAN. Fair. N. Freez hard in my chamber.

MUND. JAN. 11. Freez hard in my chamber.

> Sabina baccifera. Seeds
> Ilex arbor.
> Azaderac.
> Ilex coccifera.
> Acasia.

---

[1] An almanac is bound in with the Journal for 1677—*Le Grand Almanach Journalier
pour l'an de grace 1677. Calculé par Mr. Claude Trenet, très-Docte Mathematicien.
A Lyon. Par Jean Malpech, Imprimeur, en rüe Noire, à l'Enseigne des bons Enfants.*

[2] Nicolas Pavillon, Bishop of Alet from 1637 to his death in 1677, was one of the four
Bishops who resisted the attempts of Church and State to stamp out Jansenism in
France. Roschach (XIII, 407) states that he had received a broad hint that the King did
not wish him to be present at the meetings of the Estates.

Lotus arbor.
Jujubae.
Jonquille.
Cyanus fl. albo et fl. rub.
Convolvulus Asareus.
Balsamina Cucumerina.
Astragallus Africanus Luteus odoratus.
Limonium Elegans.
Juniperus major bacca ruffescente.
Lachryma Jobi.

Hogs   The acorns of the Ilex arbor, i.e. shene vert, are the best of all others to feed hogs.

Cheez   If cheez *be over dry by keeping, sprinkle it with a* decoction *of* chestnuts *and wrap it up in a cloth soaked in same, and lay it in a cellar and it will* recover.

TUESDAY JAN. 12.   Freez in my chamber in the night.

Funerall   FRID. JAN. 15.   This *day was* celebrated *in* Nostre Dame the obsequies of   ,[1] one *of the* 3 Deputy Governors *of this* province. There *was* erected *a* herse *for him at the west end of the church, not very* stately, *set round with a great* number *of tapers. The* Bishop of Nismes[2] *said Mass, who put on his* sacerdotal habits *under a* canopy *of state on the north or left side of the altar, kissing some of them as they were putting on, and towards the latter end of Mass changed a good part of them. The Mass being done, he, with a cross before him, in a little kind of* procession *went to the* herse, *whither his* chair *was carried after him, and there, setting him with his face towards the* herse *and his back towards the* high *altar, after a little while began some* office *there*, sprinkled *with holy water and in*censed *the* herse, *and, all the office being done, he had no sooner turned his back on the* herse *but they began to put out the tapers, to pull down the* herse *and to show to all the world that this* pageantry *was only about a little frame of wood, without a* corps *or so much as a* coffin.

SAT. JAN. 16.   *Cloudy, very warm.*

---

    [1] The name, left blank in the MS., should be that of Jean François de Tremolet de Bucelli, Marquis de Montpezat, appointed *Lieutenant-Général* of Bas Languedoc in 1674. He had a distinguished military career and was due for promotion to the rank of *Maréchal de France* when he died.

    [2] Jean Jacob Séguier de la Verrière, who occupied the see from 1671 to 1687.

MUND. JAN. 18. *Very hot. The States sent to* complement *the* Marquis de Caveson's[1] *wife* (*who is one of the* Leitenant [sic] *of the* province, *a dull man, but of great state,* i.e. 20,000 escus per annum, *lives about* Nismes) *who came to* town *by chance.*

FRID. JAN. 29. *I ate of a trout brought from* Geneva *to* Montpellier,   Trout *white, but well tasted, that was* 3 foot 4 inches *long.*[2]

MUND. FEB. 1. *I saw* La Princesse de Cajetan, a Spanish *woman*   Spanish Lady *whose dress was very odd.*[3] *Her petticoat was as other women's. On that she wore a black,* velvet *coat embroiderd, which came down half way her petticoat and reached up half way her back. Round about the top of this was something like a scarf, but by the thinness of it seemed to be of black lace, for one could see her skin very plainly. This scarf reached above the top of her coat about a finger's breadth or two. All above this was naked except her head, which had a little, black hat on it, covered with a plume of white feathers which had one red one among them. This little hat was turned up on the left side, on which side* almost *all her hair was coiffed and plaited into one tress which was tied full of knots of* limon coloured twopenny *ribbon and hung down* carelessly *almost to her middle. At the* beginning *of the plaiting a knot of* diamonds. *Beside this* braded *lock, she had* several *small, long tresses, very little curled, which hung down* carelessly *on her breast, and an even row of thin curls laid all* along *her forehead. Her hair was of brown* chesnut. The sleevs *of her coat reached to about her* elbows *and were at the end laced about with double, silver bone lace, and from that part came out, or at least were fastened on there,* two sleeves *of* lemon *coloured* tafata *which were fastened close about the wrists, but between that and the end of the coat the sleeves were very large and hung like bags or like half shirt sleeves pulled out.*

---

[1] Jean Louis Nogaret de Louet, Marquis de Calvisson (1630–1700), was appointed *Lieutenant-Général* of Haut Languedoc in 1669.

[2] In a medical note in the entry of 30 Jan. there is a reference to Sir John Chicheley, a rear-admiral (1673) and later (1675–80) Commissioner for the Navy. He was afterwards an M.P. and died in 1691. Judging from an entry in the Journal, dated 5 April 1677, Locke appears to have treated Sir John for a wound while he was at Montpellier, for on that date he wrote down a note on 'a wound drink I prescribed Sir John Chichley at Montpellier which I think contributed much to his cure'.

[3] Locke's surprise at her costume was no doubt due to the fact that while down to about 1630 Spanish fashions were dominant in Western Europe, after that date they became isolated from the main trend of fashion, now increasingly directed from Paris.

White gloves and muff. She had 2 or 3 knots of diamonds on her coat before, and Jewels in her ears which hung down very low; no necklace, but her neck bare half way down her back, for one could see her skin, which was very white, above a hand's bredth below her armpits behind and a great part of her breasts before, which seemed to hang down lower than those of our women and to be but little. She was handsome enough, had very little or no red in her face. She spoke French and in this language enterteind the Dutchesse of Verneule who made her a visit at the inn where she lodged, and at this interview I saw her.

WED. FEB. 3.

Madam de Montespan au Roy.

Verses

Tout se destruit, tout passe et le Coeur le plus tendre
Ne peut d'un même object se contenter toujours.
Le passè n'a point veu d'eternelles amours,
Les siècles àvenir n'en doivent point attendre.

La raison a des loix, que l'on ne peut entendre.
Jamais de ses desirs on n'areste le cours.
Ce qu'on aime aujourdhuÿ deplait en peu de iours;
Notre inegalité ne se scauroit Comprendre.

Touts ces defauts, grand Roy, sont ioynts a vos vertus.
Vous m'aimiez autrefois et vous ne m'aimes plus.
Ah! que mes sentiments sont differents des vostres.

Amour de qui depend et mon mal et mon bien,
Pour quoi n'a tu pas fait son coeur comme le mien,
Ou que ne faisois tu le mien comme les autres?

Responce du Roy a Madame de Montespan.

J'ay le coeur, belle Iris, aussi constant que tendre;
Ce que j'ay droit d'aimer, ie laymeray touiours,
Mais des que mon devoir condamne mes amours,
De ma fidelitè on ne doit rien attendre.

L'honneur a des raisons qu'un prince doibt entendre.
Quoique de mes plaisirs elles rompent le cours,
J'immole à ce tiran le reste de mes iours
Par un effect [sic] sur moi que je ne puis comprendre.

Je renonce à l'amour qui ternit mes vertus.
N'allegues point les loix, jè ne les conois plus.
La gloire a des apas qui triomphent des vostres.

Apres tout, belle Iris, ne scaves vous pas bien
Qu'un heros dont le coeur est si grand comme le mien
Done à l'amour des lois que l'amour donne aux autres.[1]

THURSD. FEB. 4. A nun this day professed at the Nunnery of St. Maria.[2] *After Masse, she being stood in their choir within, a priest sitting in a chair near the* altar *made a speech to her*, recommending *to her the* 3 *parts of her vow*, i.e. poverty, chastity *and* obedience, *wherein he* misapplyd several *places of* Scripture. *When that was done, the office for the purpose was read, and the most* considerable ceremonies. *These were*: 1° *the* priest *that read the* office, incensed *and* sprinkled *with holy water the* silver *cross and* vail *she was to wear, and put them both on her.* 2° *he told her she was now to die to the world, and then she retired into the* midle *of the* quire. *She kneeled down and then, some of our nuns* throwing a pall *that lay ready there, on her, she fell all* along forwards *and so lay* a pretty while, *two nuns* standing, *one on one side, the other on the other side, with tapers in their hands, and a* 3ᵈ *behind which, I think, was the* Abbesse, *reading some part of the* office, *and after some time the* preist, *sprinkleing some holy water, bid her rise, and so she did.* 3° *after she was thus risen from the dead, they led her out of the choir and brought her in again* perfectly dressed *like the rest, with a* garland *of* flowers *on her head.* 4° *she went and kneeled down to the* Abbesse, *making first a low* reverence *to her who* imbraced *and kissed her, and from here she went round to all the rest of the nuns who all* imbraced *and kissed her, but she only bowed to the rest, but knelt only to the* Abbesse. *They had all burning* tapers *in their hands, which were lighted about the middle of the* office.

Nun professed

---

[1] By a curious coincidence Leibnitz's Paris correspondent, Hansen, sent him these two sonnets in a letter of 1 March 1677 (*Sämtliche Schriften und Briefe*, ser. 1, vol. 11, pp. 253–4); but the two poems seem to go back to a period roughly ten years earlier, and though several contemporary sources connect the poems with Madame de Montespan and Louis XIV, they seem to belong to the La Vallière affair. (See J. Lair, *Louise de La Vallière et la jeunesse de Louis XIV*, Paris, 1907, pp. 224 and 454–6.)

[2] The convent of the order of La Visitation Sainte Marie. The seventeenth-century buildings are still occupied by nuns of the same order.

Burthens WED. FEB. 10. 500 escus *made a year by Mme*. de Castres[1] *for a* dispensation *to* tip*ling* houses *for breaking the rules of the town, which are that no* towns*man eat or drink in* cabarets *which are for* strangers, *and if anyone be drunk or found in these houses on holy days in time of* divine service, *to pay so much.*[2] *The* Capitaine du Guet *was the* officer *that looked after these* formerly *and was* annuall *and put in by the first* Consul, *but now by the* Governor *has been made* perpetuall. *She also makes a* profit *of the* stores *of the* Cittadell *and allowing bakers to sell light bread; and besides ploughing up the* Splanade, *which* formerly *belonged to the* officers *of the* garison, *she also sells the mud of the town ditches.*

Queen of Hungary's Water — SAT. FEB. 13. Paid Mr. Upton for 2 botles of a pint peice of the Queen of Hungary's water £5 – 9 – 4, which he sent into England in his case. We paid to La Faveur[3] 50s. per lb. Others sel it for 40s.

Dr. Thomas — FRID. FEB. 19. Mr. Hoskins, in his letter of Dec. 10th, tells me that Dr. Thomas has sold my mare for 9 – 5 – 0 sterling to Parson Horler.

Toilet — MUND. FEB. 22. *Paid for my* parfumed Toilet £9 *to* Mademoisell Verchant.

Pezenas — FRID. FEB. 26. From Montpellier to Zizian[4] 3 leagues, from Zizian to Pezenas 5 leagues. *Beside corn, wine and oil,* the ordinary & great product *of this* province, *between* Zizian *and* Pezenas the

---

[1] Élisabeth de Bonzi, sister of the Cardinal, married in 1644 the Marquis de Castries, who later became Governor of Montpellier. When her husband died in 1674, her son, aged eleven, was allowed by the King to succeed to this post, but inevitably the running of it was in the hands of his mother and uncle for some time. In 1692 the *Intendant* Basville accused the son, as well as the lady friends of the Cardinal, of corruptly deriving a large income from the town of Montpellier (*Correspondance des Contrôleurs-généraux*, ed. A. de Boislisle, vol. I, Document 1150).

[2] In the MS. 'to pay so much' comes immediately after 'if anyone be drunk'.

[3] This La Faveur, whose name occurs several times in the Journal in connexion with various medical notes, was probably Sébastien Matte La Faveur who in 1675 was given the post of *démonstrateur royal de chimie* at Montpellier in recognition of his work in that field.

Another medical note under the date of 17 Feb. mentions 'Mr. Paul', presumably the Paul who took his M.D. in Montpellier on 7 October 1677, and is several times mentioned as sending greetings to Locke in the letters of W. Charleton of 1680 and 1681. (MS. Locke, c. 5.)

[4] Gigean.

ground *much broken into* irregular, scatterd *hills and full of* Garigues,
i.e. uncultivated ground *with trees nothing but* ilex coccifera, ros-
mary, lavender & some *such* uselesse *plants among stones. The
country all so till we came into the* valey *beyond* Montaniac,[1] a mile
or 2 from Pezena, *which is a broad, fine* valey *washed by the river*
Lirau[2] *running in the middle of it; and about a* mile *from* Pezenas,
on the edg *of that valley, on the west side of the river, is the house of
the* Prince de Conty, *called* Grange,[3] *well* situated, *and seems at a*
distance *very large. It is talked of as the best house in* Languedoc.
  Rosemary *bloom on* Garigues *as we passed.* N.E. Misty, rain Spring
all day.

SAT. FEB. 27. From Pezenas to Beziers 4 leagues, *the country more
sandy and barren than* about Pezenas. *Close all day and some little
rain. South.*

SUN. FEB. 28. Beziers stinking, *dirty streets, ill-built houses, but*
pleasant situ*ation. Air* Subtil, *but marine burning in summer.
Several* scatterd remains of Roman buildings & inscriptions, *among
the rest of an* ancient Amphitheater *which is now* the garden of the
Croix blanc *where we lay. There are yet to be seen the* remains *of* an
archd vault, *as it seems to be, which runs all along one side of the*
garden *which, though it leans over about* 8 or 10 *foot* in the maner
of a half arch thus, ⌒, *yet it* supports *a vast* weight *of earth and
trees that are on it.*
  On the west side of Beziers *runs the River* Orbe *just below the
walls, on which side the town stands very high on* a precipice *and hath
a fine and large* prospect. E. *Rain and misty all day.*

MUND. MAR. 1. From Beziers to Pisariay[4] 2 leagues, the country Pisariai
like that about Montpellier. From Pisariay to St. Chignan de la St. Chignan
Corne[5] 2 leagues, all mountainous Garigues. From St. Chignan

---

[1] Montagnac.   [2] L'Hérault.
[3] La Grange-des-Prés, now a ruin, belonged to the brother of the Grand Condé who,
after acting as patron to Molière, whose company frequently performed there, turned
over a new leaf and died there in the odour of sanctity in 1666. He was the predecessor
of the Duc de Verneuil as Governor of Languedoc. Locke met his son, who died young
in 1685, during his stay in Paris (see entry for 13 March 1679).
[4] Puisserguier.   [5] St Chinian.

St. Ponx to St. Ponx[1] 3 leagues, *all* over & amongst high, steep, rocky mountains *among which we saw one little wood of* oaks & beech, *all the rest nothing but rocks and* shrub box. St. Ponx is a bishoprick *worth* 45,000£ per annum.[2]

Arpan An Arpan[3] is a square of 24 perch each side, i.e. 576 square perch, each perch being 14 pans Montpellier measure. By this they measure their woods here in Languedoc, as they doe all their land in France; but in Languedoc they measure their arable & Seterys vineards, etc. by Seterys[4] which are different almost in every parish, v.g. a Setery at St. Ponx is a square of 32 cans each side, at St. Chignan 38 cans 4 pans 2 pous.[5] *Fair all day.*

Wine *At* St. Chinian de la Corne *we drank the best wine I have met with on this side* Paris, *which yet they sell for* 2 sols the pot, *which* conteins each 2 pints *of* Paris measure, *and at* St. Ponx *they sell their wine for* 4 deneirs the lb., *i.e. about* an English pint.

The coach *way that has been made from* St. Chinian to St. Ponx over the highest mountains *I ever passed,* cost 22,000£ Tournoys. *From the top of the hills we go down to* St. Ponx, *about* 2 Leagues, *a very plain and easy* discent *by a little river's side full of* cascades *with vast high and* exceeding *steep, rocky* mountains *on each hand, so that it is a way in a deep winding* gutter, *just room enough for the way and water. On the* edges *of this* brook, *wherever the ground is not too steep and that they can come to water it, they* produce *good* medow *and plenty of grass.*

This way was made at the charge of the province *by the* procurement *of the* Bishop *of* St. Ponx, *but yet, when it was made, it served only to bring his coach to town, whose streets being* proportionable *to its* compasse, *were not large enough for his coach to pass, so that he was fain to cut a house in some places to widen the streets.*

St. Amand TUESD. MAR. 2. From St. Ponx to St. Amand[6] 4 leagues, *all along in a* valley *between* mountains, but the valley larger & the mountains lower *and less steep than* yesterday, *and all along the* valley *plenty of* pasture ground *and watered meadows. Hills coverd with woods, and,*

---

[1] St Pons. [2] Basville gives the figure of 33,000l.
[3] *Arpent.* [4] *Séterées.*
[5] *Pouces.* [6] St Amans.

lower in the valley, hedg rows *of* oaks. *This country had some* re-
semblance *with some hilly countries of* England. *The people of*
St. Amand *and so up this* valy *most of the* Religion.   Protestants

Between 9 *and* 10 a clock *we saw* 4 parelia[1] *in a great white* circle,   Parelias
2 neare the sun & the 2 others at a great distance in semicircle, the
sun being also in it. We seemd to be in the center of the circle
which, towards the south west, was some what imperfect & that
sun the faintest. Through the 2 parelia nearest the sun ran also the
archs of an other circle, but not very clear, of which the sun
seemed to be the center & beyond that, at a great distance of each
side, two short arches of a greater parabol circle where of the sun
was the center, of the colour of rainbows. The two parelia nearest
the sun were red on one side, as I remember, of that farthest from
the sun, & white on the other, the two remoter only white & pretty
bright light & not round, but shooting out into a more then ovall
length, perpendicular to the white circle they stood in, which also
was the figure of the two others.

From St. Amand to Castres 4 leagues, the greatest part of it in   Castres
same valley still widening. In this valley, a league or 2 from St.
Ponx, rises the River Thoré which passes by Castres into the
Ocean.[2] In this Valley they are most of them Protestants. 2 *or*   Protestants
3 *little towns walled, but one would think rather to keep in* poverty
than to keep out enemies, *for they seem very poor and* miserable.

About a league *before we came to* Castres *we passed by a fine house*
belonging *to the* Countesse of Viole.[3] *It is well* situated *on the south
side of a hill, woods on each side and a little river below it, with the
finest* medows *I have seen in* France.

ASHWEDNESDAY, MAR. 3. Castres situated *on the River* Agout   Castres
which passes through the middle of it and, about half a league *below
the town, joins with* the Thoré. *They are about making it* navigable
quite to Castres. *The* Bishop's *see is* worth 40,000 £ tournois per
annum.[4] *It is about half as big as* Montpellier *or somewhat more.
Streets large, but* buildings *very poor and* decaying, *and* droops *for*

---

[1] *O.E.D. Parhelia*: 'mock suns'.
[2] MS. has *Oceans*.   [3] Comtesse de Bioule?
[4] Basville gives the figure as 35,000 l.

want of the Parliament miparty,[1] removd 6 *or* 7 *years agon to* Castelnaudary. *They of the* Religion, *who are above half the inhabitants, have 2 temples and have a bell to call them to* church, *not* usually allowd. *The town walled about, with much wall faced with stone, in some places coverd with a* penthouse, *so that it is a walk in the dry all round the town. The* Bishop's Pallace *is a building 3 sides of a* Square *and 2 storeys. It is of stone and looks well. Cost, as they say*, 100,000 crowns, *to which the* province *has given* 20,000. The churches *in the town very* inconsiderable, *and that which serves for a* cathedral *like one of our* London Tabernacles.

Since the removal *of the Chamber to* Castlenaudary *they have found a way at* Castres *to* imploy them selves *in making* Crapon,[2] *so that the* Bishop *who caused the* removal *of the Chamber, would now get it back again.*

Convents   The Covents *in* Italy & Spain *are much richer than in* France, *because the monks there are* permitted *to in*herit *the goods of their* freinds, *but in* France *they have no in*heritance.

Revel   THURSD. MAR. 4. From Castres to the Reservoir neare Revel[3]
Reservoir   4 leagues through a valley, most corne. The dam of the Reservoir *is a great work, but seems not to be so big as* Froidour[4] describes[5] it. The vault *which runs through the thickness of it is of my steps* 188. From thence to Castle Naudary 3 leagues.

---

[1] The *Chambre de l'Édit* (or *Chambre mi-partie*), set up under the Edict of Nantes to try cases in which Catholics and Protestants were concerned, was removed from Castres (with its predominantly Protestant population) to Castelnaudary, a Catholic stronghold, in 1670. It was finally abolished in 1679.

[2] *Crêpon.*

[3] Here Locke began his examination of the Canal du Languedoc, the greatest engineering achievement of the reign of Louis XIV. He had long been interested in the Canal, as is seen from an earlier reference to Froidour's book on the subject. The edict entrusting the work to Riquet (see below) was signed in October 1666, and work had already begun by January of the following year. Riquet carried on the work of construction in the midst of all sorts of difficulties (the enterprise was not popular in the province and the Estates first refused and then gave only grudgingly their share of the necessary funds). The Canal was still not finished when he died in 1680, but it was brought to a successful conclusion and officially opened to traffic in May of the following year.

The Basin of St Ferréol, near Revel, where Locke began his tour of inspection, stores the waters collected from the streams of the Montagne Noire. From there the water is taken to the basin at Naurouze.

[4] See entry for 4 March 1676.   [5] MS. has *describles.*

FRID. MAR. 5. From Castlenaudari *on the* Canale's side to the Basin[1]   Castle
2 leagues. *The earth of the bank falls in, but not much.* At the Basin   Naudary
a water mill with *an only water wheel of this* fashion, *with* 16 spokes   Water mill
in the bigger wheel and 14 *in the* lesser, *for there were two mills.*

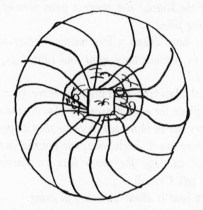

The bredth *of the great wheel* in diameter 6 pans *and the* diameter
of the little wheel 5 pans. From the center *of this wheel goes up a*
beam directly *into the mill stone and turns it. This beam is one* pan
diameter. The mill with the lesse *wheel goes the better of the* 2. *The*
thickness of the water wheel is about 7 inches. *On this water wheel the*
water falls obliquely through a trunk, the opening *whereof is one*
pan, *but the* Miller *told us if it were less, it would be better, and*
6 inches *would be enough. The water wheel lies* horizontall.

The beame or spindle is 7¼ inches diameter.[2] In the draught all
within the inward circle is solid. From the spindle to the outside
of the solid part of the whole 11½ inches. The semi diameter of the
wheele 2 foot 1½ inch, & the diameter of the milstone the same with
the wheele.

The trunke that lets the water in upon the wheele seems to be
raisd above the plaine of the horizon about 35 or 40 degrees, & the
opening of it, where the water shoots out upon the wheele, is

---

[1] The Col de Naurouze is at the watershed between the Atlantic and the Mediterranean coasts of France, and here is situated the basin which feeds the canal with water.
An obelisk commemorating Riquet is to be found there.
[2] This paragraph and the following one occur in the MS. two pages later, but with
a cross-reference to this page.

about ⅓ longer in the perpendicular then the horizontall, soe that it makes an oblong square.

Basin Each sid[e][1] *of the* octogon of the Basin about 200 of my steps. The depth *of* the water in the Basin about 6 *or* 7 pans, *but, where it comes in out of the* Rigol,[2] *not above* 2 pans now *of water, the sand brought in having filled it.*

Canale The pacquet bote *draws* 3 foot *water. Other boats of* burthen need 5, *which in summer they want and cannot go,* but *the* packet *boat goes always.*

From[3] Castel Naudary *to* Tholouse *there goes a* pacquet *boat every day, the* price *for each* passenger 30s. *he and his* portmantue. *Goods they carry not in that boat, because they change boats at every lock, whereof there are* 3 single *ones, one* double *and one* treble.

The price of carriage *for goods between* Castle Naudary and Tholouse 7½s. per Centall.

The pacquet *boat is about* 12 *hours in going.*

Half an hexagon *with* six sluses[4] *to work dry, deep in water where* sluses *are at the locks. The use of it is to clap it close to the side of the wall, draw the* sluse *of the lock and the water holds it close.*

The wall of the Basin is of ill stones which decay apace. *It is about* 6 *foot thick.*

From the Basin at Narouse[5] *back to* Castlenaudary, 1 league.

Scripture An advocate *we met at supper who is judge of the place where he lived, being asked,* could *not tell what was the* Second Commandment, *and confessed he had never read the* Scripture.

Castle Naudary stands *high, is ill built, all papist. The* Canal *runs just by the town. Rain all morning.*

Carcasson SAT. MAR. 6. To Carcasson, 6 leagues. *There are, as it were, 2 towns. That which they call the* Citty, *which stands high on the east side of the* River Aude, *a very* ancient *town,* double *walled and a strong* cittadell, *at least for a war of bows and arrows. There one may see some of the* ancient crosse bows *yet, which are very large and stiff. There is but one gate into the town on the east side and so into the*

---

[1] Locke frequently uses this spelling of *side*.
[2] The channel which brings the water from the reservoir at St Ferréol.
[3] MS. has *between* in place of *from* which has been erased.
[4] *O.E.D.* 'sluices'.   [5] Naurouze.

cittadell *where it joins on to the hill. All the rest is high and steep.
The other part on the west side of the River* Aude *is in a plain, a little
rising towards the west: is called* the Bourg. *'Tis larger than the
other, walled and much more* moderne *than* the Citty. *It seems to
have been built all at once, for the streets are* paralell & perpendicular
one to another and sufficiently *wide, with a large,* square market
place, *so that at every* crosse *street one may see the walls on all
4 sides. Were it as well built as is it laid out, it would be the* prettyest
town in France.

Here is a great manifacture *of cloth, and they use a great deal of*   Cloth
Spanish *wool which comes without any imposition. The finest* medlys
they sell for 30 escus *per* can *and the finest black* £40 *per* can.   Kan
1⅔ aune de Paris *makes just one can which is the can of* Montpellier.   Aune
One clothier there whom we talked with, makes 1200 *cloths* per annum.
They pay no other tax but 5 s. tournoys *per cloth for laid mark.*[1]
They have got into this way of making fine cloth by means of
80 Hollanders *which, about* 5 *or* 6 *years since,* Mr. Colbert *got hither.
They are all now gone but about* 12, *but have left their art behind
them.*[2]

A house in Carcasson *of* 100 escus *rent pays* 200 l. per annum   Taxes
to the King, but their land pays but about 1/10.

Instead of fuller's earth they use soap for their cloths.   Clothing

In the way between Castlenaudary & Carcasson *in a little* vilage
this inscrip*tion on a cross:* O crux Christi salva nos.

A Toyse *is* 9 *pans* Montpellier measure.   Toise

SUND. MAR. 7. *At the* Cathedrall *at* Carcasson *which is a* pitifull
one, a friar preach*ing with great action.*[3]

The States of Languedoc *consist of* 22 Bishops, 22 Barons *and*   States
the Deputys *of* 44 towns. *Each town sends* 2 deputys *which between*

---

[1] The *droit de marque* was a payment made for the placing on the cloth of a sign that
it conformed with the regulations laid down by the government. Cf. *O.E.D. mark*: 'A
particular character imprinted by public authority upon several things, either for the
payment of duties or to prevent adulteration.'

[2] The *manufacture royale* for the manufacture of cloth, set up at Carcassonne in 1666,
and the use of Dutch skilled labour to set the industry going, are typical features of
Colbert's economic policy.

[3] *O.E.D.* 'gestures, oratorical management of the body and features in harmony with
the subject described'.

them make but one voice and, if they agree not together and consent not in the vote, their vote goes for nothing.[1] The Deputy of each town is the Primer [sic] Consul of the present year and Primier Consul of precedent, and have each a Luidor per diem counting still part of a month for the whole. In the town where the States sit, all the Consuls of the town, which are usually at least 4, enter, but the 2 deputys only have votes. In their summons under the great seal for their assembly is still continued the old forme, viz. to agree or disagree, consent or dissent to what the King by his Commissioners proposes to them, and in their grant of mony to the King they always add that they have freely given so much, and that it be not drawn into a praesident[2] for the future.

One of the States told me that he was at an Assembly 20 years agon when, the King asking 7 or 800,000 livres Tournois, they thought it too much and gave nothing at all, but that they dare not do so now.[3]

Carcassone   The Citty and Bourg are two destinct corporations, independent one of another, each having 4 Consuls. The Bourg sends deputys to the States, the Citty none, being noble and paying nothing to any of the taxes of the province.

States   The Baron that hath the right to enter into the States, if he be not homme d'espé, but homme de la robe,[4] loses his right for his time, but this prejudices not his son, if he professe armes.

In the Citty of Carcasson there is a garison of 115 men. Their pay is 2 sols marques per diem. Besides this, the townsmen of both towns and 2 or 3 other little neighbouring vilages watch in their turn every 8th night.

MUND. MAR. 8. From Carcasson to Narbone 8 leagues. In this
Olive trees   day's journy we began to see olive trees again, which in all this tour we

---

[1] See Roschach, XIII, 156.

[2] O.E.D. gives this form of precedent.

[3] It was at the session of March–May 1653—just at the end of the minority of Louis XIV and of the civil war of the Fronde—that the Estates kicked over the traces. The Commissioners asked for a sum of 1,800,000 l., and, according to the Procès-verbal of the session, the Estates stubbornly maintained until they finally broke up that unless the troops in the province were removed, they would pay nothing. However, at the next session, which began in December and lasted until March 1654, they finally gave way. Twenty years later, resistance to an absolute monarch at the height of his power was, of course, unthinkable.

[4] I.e. not a soldier, but the holder of some higher judicial post.

had not seen. From[1] St. Chignan *all the way at the foot or among* mountains. *Very little fruit.*

The Trinity *at the* Cathedrall represented *thus.* A statue of an old   Trinity
man siting *for the Father, holding a* crucifix *down between his legs for the Son, and a dove with it, tall to his chin and the head towards the top of the* crucifix, *for the Holy Ghost. Of this* church *the* quire *only is built and no more. That is stately. Those that* officiated *at* Matins, *whether* Chanoins or singmen, *had a fold or* lappel*ing of their hoods that came down to almost their paps, and* coverd *them all before, faced with* purple, *reaching close up under their chins, which looked strangely, having never seen any such anywhere else.*

At Carcassone *I saw a wheel, turned by one ass, which* twisted &   Clothing
wound *at the same time* 64 threads *of yarn.*

Narbone *stands on the side of a very low,* Marshy *flat and is very* unhealthy; *is* 3 *leagues from the sea; hath a* navigable canale *that goes to it, which runs through the town. It is strong, hath but 2 gates, a bell at each, where always stands a watchman who, for every horseman that* approaches *the gates, gives a* knock *on the bell; is* noe garaison, *but the townsmen keep guard.*

The Archbishop's Pallace[2] *is a very old, large, strong house, well suited to its* revenue *of* 100,000 £ *per annum.*[3] Narbon *wants ⅓ or more of the* bignesse *of* Montpellier. *The streets narrow and ill-built, but a wide and* handsome opening *on the* canale *within the walls.*

TUESDAY MAR. 9. From Narbon to Beziers 4 leagues. N.W. *Very*   Beziers
fair and very warm. West side of Beziers *is very* pleasant, *standing high over* the river.

WED. MAR. 10. From Beziers to St. Ibery[4] 3 leagues, from St. Ibery   St. Ibery
to Loupian 3 leagues, from Loupian to Ballaruke baths 1 league.   Loupian
S., *very fair and very warm.*

THURD. MAR. 11. From Balleruk to Port Sette[5] 1½ leagues. The   Balleruk
long arme of the mole, *which is that on the west side, runs out* near   Sette

---

[1] MS. has *for.*
[2] The palace, still extant, dates back to the thirteenth and fourteenth centuries.
[3] Basville gives 90,000l. (See note to 14 Feb. 1676.)
[4] St. Thibery.   [5] See note to 25 Jan. 1676.

east, *as I think. It is now as far out into the sea as it is to be, as* Mr. Ricquet[1] *himself told me on the place. The farther end of it, which stands out into the sea, is of* semented *work, which is let down their quays. There were* 2 *others of like*[2] *of each side of this that is now standing, but the sea last* December caried *them both away, and they lost there by the weather* goods *to the* value *of* 100,000 £ Tournoys. *They are now busy about* repar*ing it by throwing in great stones on both sides, and so raise it of a* breadth *big enough to make a* platforme *on the top to be a* fort *for the* defence *of the* port. *This* arm *of the* mole *is* about 1040 *of my steps long and about* 30 *broad at the top. At the end of the mole they have* 40 *foot of water; farther in, where the* vessels *ride,* 12 *or* 14; *near the shore one or* 2 *where, when the mole began to be built, they had* 18 *or* 20, *and* [we] saw *men* [who] *told us that it fills every year with sand* mightily.[3] *The other arm of the mole which runs* near *south, as I think, is not above* ¼ *or* ⅓ *so long as the* other. Ricquet's *draft in the* printed *book*[4] *agrees well with it, but that arm* that points south *is in* print *much longer than in* port. From the Basin[5] to Port Sette *they have* 80 Toyse fall & to Tholouse 40. *The length of the* Canal *from* Sette to Toulouse *is* 30 leagues *and the* passage *will be of* 4 *days. The Canal is* passable already *from* Toulouse *to* Castlenaudary & from Sette to Beziers. *That of it which is yet to* finish *will not be done yet these* 3 *years.*[6] 1 Toyse is 6 foot of Paris & one league of Languedoc 2 of Paris. *All this*, except *the* in*crease of sand, I had from* Ricquet *himself, and also that they hope not to have it for*[7] vessels *above* 100 tun. *We saw about* 12 *of such or* lesser *in the port.*

Frontignan   From Sette to Frontignan 1 league. From Frontignan to Montpellier 3 leagues. E. *Fair and so hot that it was* trouble-som.

---

[1] Pierre Paul Riquet (1604–80), was the son of a *procureur* of Béziers (though descended, like the Mirabeau family, from the Florentine noble family of Riquetti). He gradually worked his way up in the administration of the *Gabelle*. It was as a tax-farmer, who acquired his wealth by somewhat dubious means, rather than as a successful engineer that he appeared to most of his contemporaries in seventeenth century Languedoc.

[2] 'Size' omitted?

[3] This has always been a problem at Sète.

[4] Froidour, op. cit.   [5] At Naurouze.

[6] It was in fact to take four altogether.

[7] MS. has *from*.

SAT. MAR. 13. A salade of Mr. Jacque:

Lactuca, young lettice.
Melissa, Balme.
Dracunculus, Taragon.
Pimpinella, Burnet.
Eruca hortensis, Garden rocket.
Eruca asinina, wilde rocket.
Apium, Smalage.
Nasturtium hortense, garden ⎫
      aquaticum, water ⎭ cresse.
Cardamine, ladys smock.
Aliaria, Sauce alone.
Saepa escalonica.
    estirillia.
Faba hortensis, garden bean leaves.
Atriplex, spinage.
Valerianella, lambs lettuce.
Acetosa trifolio, wood sorrell.
    hortensis, ordinary sorrell.
Caerifolum, Cerfoil.
Myrrhis odorata, Sweet ferne.
Portulaca, purcelane.
Rapunculus.
Ocymum majus ⎫
    minus ⎭ basill.

Dans les illustrations des Gaules vieux livre imprimé a Paris   Prophesie
1521 au mois de Septembre il y a ces vers

Floribus adiunctus Ranas per prata vagantes
Arctabit Coluber proprias remeare paludes.[1]

SUND. MAR. 14. The Bishop of Lodeve[2] *and two others* prohibited States
to come to the States and confined to their diocesses *for* contesting

---

[1] Jean Lemaire de Belges's *Illustrations de Gaule* appeared in three parts between 1511 and 1513; there was, however, an edition of 1521. Neither an edition of 1528 nor the modern edition of Stecher which I have carefully examined contains these two lines. The *couleuvre* (*coluber*) was the emblem of Colbert.

[2] Charles Antoine de la Garde de Chambonas, Bishop of Lodève from 1671, succeeded his uncle in the see of Viviers in 1690. This quarrel between Cardinal Bonzi and certain bishops over the right to have a crimson carpet in the Church of Notre Dame was solemnly remitted to the King for his decision. The dispute took place during the 1674 session of the Estates, and the *Procès-verbal* of the 1675 session gives the King's decision, which was in favour of the Cardinal. The quarrel gave rise to a satirical fable entitled *La rose et la violette*, the text of which is reproduced in *Monspeliensia*.

with the Cardinal for a crimson carpet *at prayers at* Noterdame. *The* Bishop of Vivares[1] *never comes to the States but when he hath a* particular *command from the* King, *he liking not their* proceed*ings.*

Cardinal's Mis[tress]   50 pistols *the way to have a* captain's *place in the new* regiment *of dragoons.*[2] Mistresses *get money all the world over. This made men of worth and good* soldiers *miss places.*

Vines   SAT. MAR. 20. *They prune their vines one year in the new of the moon and the other in the old, else they say they will grow too much to wood.*

Q. Moon   Q. *also whether, as they say here, linen washed in the old of the moon will be stiffer than what is washed in the new?*

Corall   WED. MAR. 24. At Marseilles they make corall things. The ordinary red corall polishd they sell for 4 l. tournois per ounce.

Minot Septier   A Minot or Septies is a measure of nineteen inches diameter & ten inches & a quarter deepe, English measure. A pan of

Pan   Montpellier is neare about 10 inches English.[3]

Loupian   THURSD. MAR. 25. From Montpellier to Loupian 4 leagues. 20 s. *for dinner.*[4] From Loupian to St. Iberi 4 leagues. Au Tapis vert, 20 s. pour couche.

Beziers   FRID. MAR. 26. From St. Iberi to Beziers 3 leagues. 20 s. diner.

Olive trees   In prune*ing their olive trees, which they do about the* begin*ning of* March, *they cut the top* branches, *I* suppose *to make them spread.* From Beziers to Pusol[5] 5 leagues. 25 s. couche, a Nostre dame. *Ill* treated.

Pecheuri   SAT. MAR. 27. From Puzol to Pecheuri[6] 3 leagues. *Very cold.* 15 s. diner & ill treated at the Trois coffers.

States   *In the time of* Henry IV *the States of* Languedoc denyd *him*

---

[1] Viviers? The latter see was occupied from 1621 to 1690 by Louis François de La Baume de Suze. He was succeeded by his nephew, the Bishop of Lodève.

[2] We have seen how in 1692 the *Intendant*, Basville, complained of the corrupt practices of the Cardinal's lady friends. No doubt Jeanne de Gévaudan (prudently designated in the margin of the MS. as 'Cardinal's Mis.') had a rake-off from the selling of commissions in the regiment of dragoons which the King had demanded from the province during the 1676–77 session of the Estates.

[3] Here follows a list of books left with G. Walls (see *The Library*).

[4] On 22 Feb. (o.s.) (=4 March) Sir John Banks had written to Locke to tell him he was sending his son to Paris and asking him to meet him there (MS. Locke, c. 3, ff. 66–7). Locke answered his letter on 23 March (ibid., ff. 74–5).

[5] Pouzols.   [6] Puichéric.

100,000 escus *that he* desird *for to make the* Canal *which is now making, and they* denyd *it him.*[1]

To these 2,700,000 £[2] *which this* province *is to pay this year* land *of* 100 escus per annum *will pay about* 130 l. The ter[re] noble *which is about* $\frac{1}{20}$th, *pays nothing. What was not* anciently noble, *but* ennobled *by grant, pays* 1 *year's* value *every* 20 *or* 30 *years, but the* ancient *doth not, and* [if] a Roturier *or* Commoner *buys it, it pays this year's* value. *Monks, when they get land by gift or* purchase, *if the* Estates *do not spare them, they* usually *get the King to en*noble *them and so the* burthen *still increases on the rest.* Taxes

The States give a sum and proportion *a* share *to each* diocesse. A Commissary *named by the States, with the* Bishop *or* his vicar general, *some* consuls, etc. distribute *it on the* parishes *in each* diocesse, *and if anyone be over*chargd, *they apply to them, and if they do not* Justice, *the* party appeals to *the* Commissarys of *the* States, *which are the* Intendant *of the* province *and* 5 *others named by the States.*

Mr. Riquet *was a* proctor's *son of* Beziers, *not worth a* farthing. *By being an* officer *in the* Gabel *of salt and afterwards a* Farmer, *and now the* Canal, *has* maried 3 *daughters and gave each* 50,000 escus.[3] Riquet

From Pecheuri to Carcassone, 3 leagues. *Very cold. At* the Ange 25 s. pour couché & well treated. Carcassone

SUND. MAR. 28. From Carcassone to Villepinte 4 leagues. At the Cheval blanc an ill collation 10 s. From Villepinte to Castelnaudari 2 leagues. At the 3 pigeons 25 s. *Very* ill treated. *As cold as it could be* without freezing. Paid for my horse from Montpellier for 4 days & 4 days return, meat & all, at 40 s. per diem, 16 £. Villepinte
Castelnaudary

---

[1] Though plans for a Canal were made as early as the reign of Henry IV (or even earlier), the scheme never seems to have been placed before the Estates and rejected, though a request from the King to contribute 30,000 l. towards the construction of a port at Sète was so rejected in 1602 (see *Procès-verbal*, 26 Feb. 1666).

[2] The King had originally demanded 3,000,000 l., but later remitted 300,000 of that sum.

[3] The modest beginnings of Riquet and the wealth which he amassed as a tax-farmer are established facts, but it seems doubtful whether he had more than two daughters and no mention of the dowries he provided them with appears in any biography of him. However, the passage is interesting as showing contemporary gossip in Languedoc about his rise to wealth.

Montesquieu MUND. MAR. 29. From Castelnaudary to Montesquieu by the Canal
Tholose 5 leagues. An extream ill diner 15 s. From Montesquieu to Tholose
5 leagues by the Canale. The price of passage from Castelnaudari
to Tholouse by the Canale 30 s., you & your portmantue, but it is
a very incommodious passage if you have any cariage, for there is in
this day's passage 17 Locks, & at each the goods are to be caried
from one boat to an other, for at each lock the boat is changed.
Very hot all day, so various the weather here as well as in colder
countrys.

Taxes   *When the King* remitted *to this* province 100,000 escus *of the*
3,000,000 £, *the States gave him*, he demanded of them *a regiment
of dragoons, the raising whereof cost* 120,000 £, *and the yearly charge
of keeping them will be* 240,000 £, *so that the* province *may well have
gained by the King's bounty.*[1]

Tholose TUESDAY MAR. 30. At Tholose at the Carmes' Church[2] a statue
of a man over one of the Altars holding a girle in his armes with
this inscription: Sum pater matris Dei, and neare it eastward in the
Grand rüe a statue of an old man, his breast open & a face there.

Reliques   At the Church of St. Sernin *they tell us they have the bodies*
entire *of* 6 *of the* Apostles *and the head of a* 7th. *This is much,*
consider*ing what need there is of such* reliques *in other places, but
yet notwithstanding they* promise *you* 7 *of the* 12 Apostles. *They are
not half so* liberal *as* the Count de   [3] *who in*vited *the* Duke *of*
Vernule *to* Tholose *and told him he would see there* the 100 Apostles.

Pies   *He thought the* Apostles *perhaps as common as* pies, *whereof he*
presented *a whole horseload to the* Duke, *because he heard he used to
hawk them.*[4] *We saw not these* Apostles, *but being told by a* spiritual
*guide of the in*falible *church, we believed, which was enough for us.*

L'Eglise de la Daurade *was* anciently *a* temple of Diana. *There
are in it at the* upper *end* 12 Patriarchs *and* 12 Apostles, *as big as life,
in* Mosaick *work. It now belongs to the* Benedictins.[5]

---

[1] This seems a somewhat strange calculation, unless one takes it that only the
immediate cost of 120,000 l. should be set against the King's remission of 300,000 l. But
the amount to be paid by the Estates in succeeding years had still to be fixed, and might
be more than the 2,700,000 l. paid in this year as *don gratuit*.
[2] Now demolished.   [3] Blank in MS.
[4] The Duke was extremely fond of hunting.
[5] The present Church of Notre-Dame-la-Daurade was built in the eighteenth century.

At the Dominicans[1] *is the* finest *altar I have anywhere seen, and before it, or rather in the middle of it, for it stands in the middle of the* Church *and has an altar on both sides, is the head of* Thomas Aquinas. *In a corner of the cloister is a* statue *of the* Virgin *holding her son in her arm and looking on him,* pretty. *Several* with this *in*scription: Impera et impetra.

Virgin

Over the Jesuits' *door*[2] *this in*scription: Jesu Christo et Xavirio Indiarum Apostolo.

At the Cordiliers[3] *in a* vault *we saw* several *dead bodies, which were very* intire, *that have been dug up* severall *years after their* buriall *in their church and cloister, I believe between* 20 *and* 30 *that we saw standing round the sides of the* vault, *besides others that lay heaped one on another. A grave was making in the church when we were there, and a coffin was dug up as fresh as when laid in. They said it had lay* [sic] *there* 8 *or* 10 *years.*

Corps

Maison de ville is very handsome.

At the Grand soleil 30s. per diem, ordinary treatment.

WED. MAR. 31. From Tholouse to Verdune[4] 5 leagues upon the Garonne. *Some* pretty *houses on the river,* Mr. Riquet's son in law, a Consilier of Tholose, one of the prettyest.

Verdune

THURSD. APR. 1. From Verdune to Avillar[5] 6 leagues. Vines prund *and one branch left tied to* a *stake, round like a hoop, and the little end down: this, I suppose, that the vine branch, being turned round, may shoot at the divers joints.*

Avillar
Vines

At Avillar *an ill* dinner 15s. From Avillar to Bouér[6] 4 leagues, a rascally litle village, the couché at the master *of the boat's* house 15s., ordinary.

Boüe

FRID. APR. 2. From Boüe to Agen half league. *We paid each from* Tholouse *hither* 30s., *our* portmanteaus caried *into the bargain.*

SAT. APR. 3. *At* Agen at *St.* Pierre 20s. per repas. Moderate treatment. Agen a Bishoprick,[7] *but a poor town, ill built and but one*

Agen

---

[1] *Église des Jacobins.*

[2] This early seventeenth-century doorway to the Jesuits' school, though mutilated during the Revolution, is still in existence.

[3] Cf. Arthur Young's description (14 June 1787). The church was destroyed by fire, all but the tower, in 1871.   [4] Verdun.

[5] Auvillar.   [6] Boé.   [7] MS. has *Bishoprock.*

street in it of any bigness. All the rest little lanes. A very fine walk without it in a meadow between it and the river.

Tonneins   From Agen to Tonneins 4 leagues. *At* au cheval Blanc 15 s., well treated. Almost all of the Religion.

Cadiliac   SUND. APR. 4. From Tonneins to Cadiliac 7 leagues. *We hired*
Langon   *a boat with 4 watermen to* Langon, 2 leagues *above* Cadiliac *for 12 £ and gave them 3 £ more to carry us to* Cadiliac. *At the* Chappeau rouge, *the most cut-throat house I ever was in, I paid* 20 s. *for 3 roast apples and a little bread and water boiled. Here is the brave, but* decay*ing house of* Cadiliac, *belonging to the* Duke *of* Espernon.[1]

Bourdeaux MUND. APR. 5. From Cadiliac to Bourdeaux 5 leagues. 7 s. 6 d.
Revenue   There are 4 *branches of the revenue of France*: La gabele, les entres, les aides et la Taile. Les entres[2] *are the same with our* Customs, i.e. *a tax on* merchandise *in motion.* Les aides *are excise on wine sold in* caberets *and, as I think, retail of* tobaco, tin *and* perhaps *some other* commoditys. La Gabelle *is a tax on salt. These together are farmed at* 50 millions per annum *and the taile yields as much more.*[3] The Taile *is something like a Land Tax, but it is laid at the* King's *pleasure who every year takes as much as he thinks fit. The sum being agreed on in the* Counsel, *the share of each* province *is sent to the* respective Intendant *and there* proportioned *to each* generality *its share, and so to each* parish *where the* Consuls[4] *make* writ. *Where anyone find himself overcharged, he hath* recourse to *the* Commissioners *to that purpose.* Terre noble *pays no* taile nowhere in the *owner's* hand, *but if it be let, the* renter pays it. *In some parts land of a* noble*man, whether noble or not, pays nothing, but in other parts their noble land only is* excepted, *but the other pays.* Church land not noble pays as well as the other.

Things sent   A yard & almost half of course, coloured, stiffend canvas which
home   I served me for a twoilet. Recd.[5]

---

[1] See the long description of this château in the entry for 26 Sept. 1678.

[2] Generally known as *les traites*.

[3] According to Clamageran (II. 599 f.) the total revenue from the *gabelle, traites* and *aides* amounted about this time to some 50,000,000 *livres*, but the total amount collected from the taille in 1677 came to 40,421,000 l.

[4] Presumably the *Élus*.

[5] These 'recd.'s were added, of course, later. After the first item there comes in the MS. a long list of books, to be published in *The Library*.

A little box of sweet oyles, not being in all 3 ounces.
A couple of ordinary combs.
An palpitationi cordis spiritus salis armoniaci conveniat^c. [sic].
A peice of Seneca [sic].
Andr: cissars.
A Hammer.
A case with 2 rasors & a paire of cissars. recd.
12 pair of cissars. recd.

These things all packd up in a litle deale Box marked M H &
put into Mr. Sauvage's hands at Bourdeaux 10 Apr. to be sent
away to Mr. Hunt. They were shipd on the Edward & Elizabeth
of Dover $\frac{6}{16}$ April, bound for London & consignd to Mr. Hunt.
The master Charles Mantell.

Take 2 eggs, the raw livers of any poultry or, for want of that,   Cookery
some liver of veale or mutton, mince the livers very small with
some good suet or, for want of suet, with the fat of bacon, mixing
crumbs of bread with it. Make up this with the egs beaten into
a past & in the flap of a breast of mutton or the belly of a boild hen
it makes a very good puding.

Cut chickens in peices, par boile them in as little water as may
be with onion or chalot. In the same liquor frie them in a friing
pan. A litle nutmeg with some time & other sweet hearbs cut
small & mixd adde a relish. An egge or 2 beaten with this liquor it
is fried in compleats the sauce & makes a good fricacy.

Take Spinage q.v., boile it in water s.q. When it hath boiled a   Herb potage
while, put to it a good peice of butter. When it is sufficiently boild,
take the yolkes of 2 or 3 eggs, beat them well with a litle vinegar, &
when they are well beaten, take a litle of the liquor where in the
spinage is boild & mix with the egs, continually stiring them that
they curdle not, & when you have thus mixed a pretty good quantity
of the liquor with the eggs, then pour the egs into the bullion, &
soe pour the bouilon, egs & all, forwards & backward in two vessells
till they are well mixd & then put all into a dish where slices of
bread are, & this is noe ill soope. This may be donne with other
hearbs, as lettuce, purslane & divers others which, put togeather in a
good mixture, may produce a very good taste. They say that if the
butter be put to the hearbs first, & soe set to stew gently togeather
before the water be put to them, they will eat tenderer & better.

Wine   A tun (i.e. 4 hoghead English or perhaps 4 or 5 per Cent. more) of the best wine at Bourdeaux, which is that of Medoc or Pontac, is worth, the first penny, 80 or 100 crowns. For this the English may thank their own folly for, whereas some years since the same wine was sold for 50 or 60 crowns per tun, the fashionable sending over orders to have the best wine sent them at any rate, they have, by striveing who should get it, brought it up to that price. But very

Brandy good wine may be had here for 35, 40 & 50 crowns per tun. A tun of Brandy is worth at Bourdeaux about 115 crowns.

     For the buying of these they are obleiged to[1] make use of brokers to whom the King of France allows 18£ for every 21 tun of wine they ship, which is constantly allowed them when they come to pay the custome at the custome house.

SUND. MAY 9. The Duke of Rauclaure,[2] Governor of Guienne, made his entrance into Bourdeaux to take possession of his government. In favour to the town he would have it as private as might be, soe that there was noe thing but the shooting of the guns of the Castles & some fire works at night.

Stringer MUNDAY MAY 10. I receivd of Mr. Tho: Arundell at Bourdeaux 255£ or 85 escus upon a letter of Credit of Sir Patience Ward's[3] for 20 ll. sterling, & according to the direction of the letter & Mr. Arundell's demands who writ the bills, signed two bills upon Sir Patience Ward himself, but however writ away the same day to Mr. Kiffin to desire him to repay the 20 ll. to Sir Patience Ward & take his discharge.

Roper WED. MAY 12. Lent then to Mr. Sam Rooper half the mony I receivd of Mr. Arundell for which he gave me 2 bills of Exchange upon Mr. Ed. Barkly in Angell Court, Throgmorton Street, for ten pounds sterling.

Pontac wine FRID. MAY 14. I rode out & amongst other things saw President Pontac's[4] vineard at Hautbrion. It is a litle rise of ground, lieing

---

[1] MS. had originally 'they generally' which is erased.

[2] Gaston Jean Baptiste, Duc de Roquelaure (1615–83), appointed Governor of Guyenne in 1676.

[3] Sir Patience Ward (1629–96), a London merchant, who was knighted in 1675 and became Lord Mayor in 1680. He took a prominent part in politics, as a strong Protestant.

[4] Arnaud de Pontac (1599–1681), a member of a famous Bordeaux family, was *Premier Président* of the Bordeaux Parlement from 1653 to 1672.

open most to the west. It is noe thing but pure, white sand, mixd
with a litle gravell. One would imagin it scarce fit to beare any
thing. Some of the vines are about 4 or 5 foot high & have stakes.
Others are direct along upon the ground, not above a foot from it,
between litle, low stakes or laths, soe that the old branches stand
on each side the root like a pair of armes spread out towards the
south. The reason of this different way of culture I could not
learne of the work men for want of understanding Gascoin. This
ground may be esteemd to yeild about 25 tun of wine. However,
the owner makes a shift to make every vintage 50, which he sells
100 escus per tun. It was sold some years since for 60, but the
English love to raise the market on them selves. This, however,
they say, & that men of skill & credit, that the wine in the very next
vineard, though in all things seeming equall to me, is not soe good.

 Frid. Apr. 2 I was taken ill at Agen,[1] feaverish & an extraordinary Tertian
pain in my head, haveing between Tholose & that had a very cold
& untoward passage by water, & a great pole haveing fell upon my
head in the boat. Not knowing which to impute it to, but willing
above all to secure my head as much as I could, if that had receivd
any harm, I tooke a clyster in the afternoon, & the next morning,
the pain in my head continueing with great violence, I bleeded,
I believe, between 11 & 12 ozs. It proved afterwards a tertian
ague....[2]

TUESDAY 18 MAY. From Bourdeaux to Blay 7 leagues by water. Blay
We hired a boat for 1 Escu. At the Lion d'or well treated, *but paid
dear*, viz. 30s. pour couche. There is a castle of the old way of
fortification.

WEDNESDAY 19 MAY. From Blaye to Petit Niort 5½ leagues. At Petit Niort
the Fountain well treated, 20s. From thence to Pons 4½ leagues. Pons
At the Escu d'Albret *well* treated for 20s. pour couché.

---

 [1] He nevertheless continued his journey, as we have seen, and arrived at Bordeaux
on the 5th.
 [2] There follow three pages of notes, of purely medical interest, on the course of his
illness. It lasted well over a month, and when Locke left Bordeaux on 18 May, he had
still not fully recovered (cf. the end of the entry for 22 May and that for 24 May). There
is a gap in the entries between 5 April and 9 May, and another from 14 to 18 May, both
due, no doubt, to this illness.

This day's journey through a country much like some parts of
England, the soyle deep & inclineing to clay in many places, few
vineards, some meadows, a great deale of wood land & most corne.
Hedgrows all along, fruit trees scatterd up & down in the hedgrows
Oakes   & fields. The woods most of oak where of there are 2 sorts, one like
ours in England, & the other that puts out much later, soe that
some of them had not yet spread their leaves. They put out their
leaves hoary & tender & like young ferne, & their leaves are much
more indented like then the other. They many of them also beare
large apples, & ruddy on one side, but are very soft & shrinke
mightily after haveing been a litle while gatherd.

Vines   To make vines beare in a barren ground, put a sheep's horne to
the root & it will doe wonders.[1]

THURSD. 20 MAY. From Pons which is a pretty big towne, but very
Escouyaux   ill built, but hath a Temple, to Escoyaux,[2] 6 leagues. About the
Charante   midle of the way we passed the Charrant,[3] 2 leagues from Xantes,[4]
a very deepe & slow river, & the ferry a very ill one. The meadows
on its sides very course grasse as being all the winter overflowd,
the country much like that we passed yesterday. At Escouyaux at
the Escu de France excellently well treated, 25 s. the couché.

Villedieu   FRIDAY 21 MAY. From Escouyaux to Villedieu[5] 6 leagues. Here
we enterd into Poictou, as at Petit Niort we enterd into Xantonge.[6]
At the Palme 20 s. dinner, but not too good. From Villedieu to
St. Leger   St. Leger de Mel,[7] 4 leagues. In the midle of the way at Briou[8]
a Douan[9] where my portmanteau was searchd. The country we
passed like some of the champain[10] countrys of England, almost all
corne feild, but barren land with some woods scatterd up & downe,
& litle parishes in the bottoms with trees about them. At St. Leger
at the St. Martin 30 s. pour couché, the treatment not answerable.

[1] Cf. Observations..., p. 7: 'I have been told that a sheep's horn buried at the root
of a vine will make it bear well, even in barren ground. I have no great faith in it, but
mention it because it may so easily be tried.'   [2] Écoyeux.
   [3] Charente.   [4] Saintes.
   [5] La Villedieu.   [6] Saintonge.
   [7] St Léger-lès-Melle.   [8] Brioux.
   [9] A douane (customs-post). The customs-barriers which existed between different
provinces or groups of provinces inside France were not swept away until the Revolution.
   [10] O.E.D. Champaign: 'flat, open country, without hills, woods or other impediments'

SAT. 22 MAY. From St. Leger to Lusignan, 7 leagues, a pretty big   Lusignan
bourg. All the other places between this & Pons have been but
vilages. The country more inclosd & more pasture then I have seen
in France. At the White Horse 25 s. pour couché, ordinary treatment. Here are some of the walls remaining of the prettyest parke
I ever saw, which would deserve a description, were I in health
& humor.

SUND. 23 MAY. From Lusignan to Poictiers 5 leagues. The walls   Poictiers
are of a great circuit, but the towne is shrunke from them & seems
by the houses & people in a deep consumption. Within these
2 yeares there is a tax of 5 s. per charet[1] for all the wood is brought   Taxes
into towne.

MUND. 24 MAY. *I took 2 clysters....*

TUESDAY 25 MAY. From Poictiers to St. Genai[2] 5 leagues. By the   St. Genai
way, 2 leagues from Poictier, we saw the fine Chasteau de Bonivet,   Bonivet
well situat & a fine house.[3] From St. Gené to Richeleiu 4 leagues.
By the way, about a league from St. Gené, we saw an other handsome Chasteau, de Pigarrau,[4] with a parke well wooded joyning to   Pigarrau
it, & large gardens. The country corne feilds set with wallnut trees
even amongst the corne, as well as by the sides, vineards & plenty
of woodland, all of oak. In this day's journey also we saw more
chasteaux & handsome gentlemen's seats then I have seen in
5 in any other part of France &, to compleat all, in the evening we
saw the exactly regular and magnificent house of Richleu,[5] to which   Richlieu
I think noe thing is wanting but a more healthy aire, for the flat it
stands in is not without morass ground &, I thinke, is not over
healthy. In this country they make their mules & asses draw by
their heads, as all over Xantonges & Poictou they do their Oxen.

The prospect of Richleiu from a hill about a league to the north
appears in a great flat & incompasd [sic] all round with woods,
except in the North side on which stands the towne. The plain it

---

[1] *Charette?*   [2] St Genest.
[3] This magnificent Renaissance château was demolished in the nineteenth century.
[4] Puygarreau. Considerable parts of this sixteenth-century château are still standing.
[5] Only the park of the château and the town still remain.

stands in is noe very fruitfull sand, & it[1] stands in the very bottom
of it where runs a litle river, which furnishes the moats of the house
& gardens. The town is very litle, but neat & regular, & from the
farther gate one looks through the street which is exactly strait
& uniforme to the other, & soe into another gate which opens into
a walke that leads to the house, passes between the base court &
offices & fine house, & soe into a walke in the parke, soe that this
vista is above a league long.

Pont Roan   WED. MAY 26. From Richleiu to Pont Roan[2] 7 leagues. About
Vienne   3 leagues from Richleiu we passed the River Vienne by ferry [at]
Bouchard   l'Isle Bouchard, where the Duke of Richeleiue hath an other
chasteau. The Vienne is handsome, clear, broad river. At Pont
Roan au Cheval rouge good wine & all the rest indifferent. Here
was passed an other river called   .[3] On the sides of the hills
bounding the valleys where in these rivers run we saw severall very
handsome seats. The country much the same as the day before.
Tours   From Pont Roan to Tours 4 leagues. These 2 days' journey I saw
more handsome Chasteau then I had seen between Montpellier
& Poictier.

Tours stands upon a litle rise between the Loire & the Cher. It
hath very good medows on the south side, but the standing water
in washes & ditches neare the town stank horridly. It is a long
town, well peopled & thriveing, which it owes to the great mani-
Silk   facture of silke is there.[4] Few gentry in the towne. They talke of
10,000 have gon soldiers out of this towne since the war.

Taxes   They gave the King this year 45,000 £ to be excused from winter
quarter, which came to $\frac{1}{10}$ on the rent of their houses. Wine, wood,
etc. that enter the town pay tax to the King. Besides he sends to the
severall companys of trades men for soe much mony as he thinks
fit.[5] The officers of each corps de mestier[6] taxes every one according
to his worth, which perhaps amounts to about 1 escu or 4 £ to a man

---

[1] MS. has *in it*.   [2] Pont de Ruen.
[3] Blank in MS.: 'the Indre'.
[4] Locke gives a rather different picture of the state of the silk industry at Tours in
the entry for 10 Aug. 1678.
[5] Boissonnade (pp. 251–2) mentions a sum of 45,000 l. paid by the guilds of Tours in
this period.   [6] Guild.

counted worth 100 escus. But a bourgeois or trades man that lives in the town, if he have land in the country, if he keep it in his hand or set it to rent, which is the common way, that pays noe thing; but the paisant who rents it, if he be worth any thing, pays for what he has, but he makes noe defalcation of his rent, for the manner of taxing in the country is this. The tax to be paid being laid upon the parish, the Collectors for that year assease every one of the inhabitants or house keepers[1] of the parish, according to his proportion as they judg him worth, but consider not the land in the parish that belongs to any one liveing out of it. This makes them say that the taile in France is personal, but in Languedoc sur le fonde, i.e. Land tax, which there always pays where it lyes. This is that which soe grinds the paisant in France. The collectors make their rates usually with great inequality. There lies an appeale for the over-taxed, but I finde not that the remedy is made much use of.

Passer maistre or to have a licence to set up any trade, for haveing servd an apprentiship (which is usually but of 2 or 3 year) gives not that priviledg, but it comes from the King, & they must have letters for it. The severall trades have severall regulated prices, & whereas about Tours & Amboise a Silke worker pays 100 escus for his freedome, a baker 50, those that would set up in the woollen manifacture pay but 6 livres.[2] Marke the incourage-ment. The Cigoni at Tours a good house, 22 s. pour couché. *Trades' freedome*

Woollen manifacture

THURS. MAY 27. From Tours to Amboise 6 leagues through a sandy vally by the side of the Loire, full of rie and poplar trees: are not 12 ordinary English miles.[3] Amboise is a litle, stragleing towne. There is a manifacture of woolen stuffs, an old Chasteau, built by Dogabert,[4] which stands high over the towne, wherein is a chappell where are hung up the mighty paire of Stag's hornes, 15 foot high & 7½ broad, the stag, they say, kild in the Forest of Arden[5] in Francis the Ist time, & a round tower where, in a spirall ascent, *Amboise*

---

[1] *O.E.D.* gives the sense of 'householders'.

[2] Locke gives in the margin a cross-reference to the entry of 6 March 1677 in which he describes the woollen industry at Carcassonne.

[3] This is all one sentence in the MS. Guide-books give the distance as 25 kilometres, i.e. some 16 miles.

[4] This appears to be a pure legend, though the château originally dates back to the fourth century A.D.					[5] Ardennes?

a coach may drive up to the top. In the midle or nave of this winding ascent is a well, & a cart might goe down the same way to fetch up water. The ascent not very steep, nor the tour very large. A la Corne excellent coole wine, but make your bargain before hand or expect an extraordinary reconing.

Blois FRID. MAY 28. From Amboise to Blois 10 leagues. We rode it at a litle more then foot pace in 4½ hours, soe that I beleive it scarce 15 English miles.[1] The way al along upon the bank of the Loir,[2] the vally much the same as that between Tours & Amboise. Several chasteaux on both sides the valley on the riseing ground. Bloys stands high upon the north side the river & seems to be a very healthy place. The Three Merchants a good house, but 30s. per repas.

Clery SAT. MAY 29. From Bloys to Clery 12 leagues. Here Lewis the 11 lies buried.[3] Here is a sort of wine cald Genotin[4] which is not bad.
Taxes At the Ange ill treated for 25s. per repas. In Angolmois[5] 100 escus pays at least 20 taile. In Normandie they often pay more for the taile then their land is worth to be lett, but this lights heaviest on the poor & lower sort of people, the richer sort befreinding & easeing one an other. The collectors are answerable, wether they can get the mony or noe.[6]

Orleance From Clery to Orleance 4 leagues. Betwix[7] Bloys & this we rode on the South side of the Loire, the greatest part of the way through vineards. Orleans is a large, fair towne with large & broad streets & a great many fair buildings. It stand[s] upon a litle rise on the north side the Loir. At the Trois Rois for 25s. per repas not over excellent treatment. Here we dischargd our horses which brought us from Blay. For the 3 horses we paid 3£ per diem for hire & 3£ more per diem for their meat, & to our guide that rode one of them 10s. per diem for his hire & 10s. per diem for his meat, & the same rate of 7£ per diem for their returne, counting 8 days from Orleance to Blay.

---

[1] The guide-books give 34 kilometres, i.e. about 21 miles.
[2] Loire. [3] In the *Basilique Notre-Dame*.
[4] Jennetin. [5] Angoumois.
[6] If they did not produce the money, they went to prison.
[7] *O.E.D.* gives this spelling.

SUND. MAY 30. The peare Moule-bouch[1] an excellent peare about   Pears
Christmas & one of the best pears of France, & the peach de Pau
the best peach & the smooth[2] peach.   Peaches

MUND. MAY 31. Very cold, soe that I crept to the fire, though the   Weather
4 days we spent between Poictiers & Bloys were the hotest I ever
rod in.

TUESDAY JUN. 1. From Orleance to Toury 10 leagues. At the   Toury
Escu de France ill treated for 23 s. at dinner. From Toury to
Estamps 10 leagues, all the day's journey over a very large plaine   Estamps
all of cornefeilds.[3] Estamps is a large, raggd towne, placed at the
opening of a fine valley bottom upon a litle river & but poorly
built, soe much as we passed through of it, which was above half
a mile long. At the Pety Paris cut throat.

WED. JUN. 2. From Estampes to Chatres 6 leagues. From Chatres   Chatres
to Paris 8 leagues. By the way we saw the fine house of Chily[4] & the   Chily
new house of Mr. Colbert a Sau:[5] 4 pavilions, at each corner one,   Seau
tacked together by 2 cowhouses of each side that hath no windows
into the court, & a pavilion in the midle opposite to the entrance.
Paid to Mr. de Voulges for a letter from Sir J. Banks 1 – 0 – 0.   B.[6]

FRID. JUN. 4. Paid for letters from England to Montpellier & thence   B.
to Paris   2 – 1 – 0.

SAT. JUN. 5. *Beaver*   £25 10 – 0.
3 auns *of cloth*   £51 – 0 – 0.

WED. JUN. 9. Recd. of Mr. Pelletier upon a bill of Mr. Kiffin's of   Stringer
13 Sept. 1676 £315 – 15 – 9 for 25 ll. sterling (v. leger, p. 89) paid
by Mr. Stringer.
Peruque   £36 – 0 – 0.
Memo. *loop to hold fast in coaches.*   Coaches

---

[1] Furetière gives *Mouille-bouche*.   [2] For *smoothest*?
[3] The Beauce.
[4] The château of Chilly-Mazarin, demolished in the early nineteenth century.
[5] Sceaux. The estate was bought by Colbert in 1670. He began the construction of
a new château which was demolished about 1800.
[6] 'B' and 'C.B.' stand for Locke's pupil, Caleb Banks.

Stringer   SAT. JUN. 12. Mr. Stringer in his of 9 Apr. 1677 tells me that he hath received 50 ll. for me of Mr. Thomas.[1] Sent to Mr. Stringer Mr. Rooper's bill upon Mr. Ed. Barkly for ten pounds which I lent him at Bourdeaux.

B.   Recd. of Mr Banks[2] £631 – 18 – 0, the value of 50 ll. sterling

Sir Jo: Banks   which Sir John presented me.

B.   SUND. JUN. 13. For lodging & diet from my comeing to Paris till I removd to Mr. de Launay's,[3] June 10, £15 – 6 – 0.

B.   Diner   1 – 0 – 0.

B.   MUND. JUN. 14. Supper   2 – 0 – 0.

B.   WED. JUN. 16. Supper   0 – 10 – 0.

Goblins   THURSD. JUN. 17. We saw the hangings at the Goblins.[4] It being Fest Dieu, they remained exposd all day. Very rich & good figures. In every peice Lewis le Grand was the hero, & the rest the marks of some conquest, etc. In one[5] was his makeing a league with the Swisse where he lays his hand on the booke to sweare the articles with his hat on & the Swiss Ambassador in a submissive posture with his hat off.

B.   Dinner   1 – 0 – 0.

Cypher   A secret way of writing invented by Cardinal Richeleiu which was then counted soe rare & of such dangerous consequence, if ill

---

[1] I.e. from Christ Church.

[2] A draft of a letter of Locke to Sir John Banks, dated 9 June (MS. Locke, c. 24. ff. 20–1), shows that Caleb was rather slow in obeying his father's instructions to give Locke this money.

[3] Among the numerous books which Locke packed up before he left Paris in July 1678 (see *The Library*) were copies of four works attributed by him to 'De Launay': his *Logique* (2 copies), *Cosmographie*, *Introduction à la philosophie* and *Essais de la physique universelle*. The third and fourth of these works are attributed by the catalogue of the Bibliothèque Nationale to a certain Gilles de Launay. Although dictionaries of biography are silent on this man, he is mentioned in a letter of Bayle of 24 June 1677 (*Œuvres*, La Haye, 1737, 4 vols., folio, I. 49) as teaching in public lectures the philosophy of Gassendi and as the author of the *Introduction à la philosophie* (cf. G. Reynier, *La Femme au XVIIe Siècle*, Paris, 1929, p. 162). Bayle links his name with Bernier, another popularizer of Gassendi's philosophy with whom Locke had personal relations in Paris. Was this the 'De Launay' with whom Locke lodged in 1677?

[4] The workshops at the Gobelins were founded by Colbert in 1662.

[5] This tapestry, known as *Le Renouvellement de l'alliance avec les Suisses*, depicts a ceremony which took place in 1663. It is part of a series on the reign of Louis XIV designed by Le Brun.

imploid, that it was death in his army to make any use of it. It is
to be found in a MS. in the library of St. George's in Venice....[1]

[SUN.] 20 JUNE. Diner at Charenton[2]   2 – 4 – 0.   B.

To melt silver quickly & in an ordinary fire put with it a small   Silver melt
quantity of corrosive sublimate[3] and antimony: v.g. take argent.
1 oz., corrosive sublimate   ,[4] antimon. gr. 2. Mr. Herbert.

The building at the Observatoire[5] is 131 stairs up & the descent   Observatoire
underground 160 stairs. Down each stair being 6 inches or something better, makes from the bottom to the top 186 foot.[6]

WED. 23 JUN. From Paris to Versales 4 leagues. The Chasteau[7]   Versailes
there a fine house & a much finer garden,[8] situated on a litle rise of

---

[1] There follows an account of this cypher, and after that 10 pages on a 'delineating
parallelogram' (=pantograph) and 5 pages (with illustrations) on the subject of
'designeing'.

[2] No doubt, Locke and Caleb Banks attended the service at the Protestant *Temple* of
Charenton, frequented by the Huguenots of Paris, who were not allowed to have a church
in the capital. It was demolished in 1685. On 23 July (o.s.) Sir John Banks wrote:
'I cannot advise my son's goinge often to the Embassador's, but constantly to the
Protestant church, and to eat at ordinarys where he hath opportunity of conference of
all sorts' (MS. Locke, c. 3, ff. 86–7).

[3] MS. has the chemical symbol.   [4] Left blank in MS.

[5] The Paris Observatory, an offshoot of the foundation of the Académie des Sciences
in 1666, was constructed between 1667 and 1672. It was used not only for astronomical
observations, but also for other scientific experiments. The staircase which extended
from roof to cellar was of use for the study of falling bodies.

[6] Medical notes bearing the name of Charas occur at this point. Moïse Charas
(c. 1618–98) was a well-known pharmacist who held the post of demonstrator in
Chemistry at the Jardin des Plantes. Being a Huguenot, he retired to England in 1680
and was appointed Apothecary to Charles II. Later he travelled in Holland and Spain,
having in the latter country unpleasant adventures with the Inquisition. Finally, he
was converted to Catholicism, returned to Paris and was elected a member of the
Académie des Sciences.

During his stay in Paris most of Locke's letters were addressed to him 'chez Monsieur
Charas Apothicaire rue de Boucherie Fauxbourg St. Germain'. There is some evidence
to show that Locke lodged in his house during at least part of his time in Paris. Thus
a letter of Dr Brouchier of Aix, dated 2 April 1678 (MS. Locke, c. 4, ff. 165–6) explains
that he had sent his agent in Paris to collect a book at Locke's lodgings, but that Charas
had told him 'que vous ne logies plus ches luy'. A series of letters from Jacques Selapris
of Lyons, written between November 1678 and the end of Locke's stay in France, are
addressed to him care of Charas, but four of them, written between 23 Nov. 1678 and
14 Jan. 1679, are more explicit, bearing after the usual 'Monsieur Locke, Gentilhomme
Anglois', the extra words 'Logé chez lui' (MS. Locke, c. 18, ff. 75–82).

[7] In 1677 Versailles was still far from having achieved the final form given to it by
Louis XIV. The Château that Locke saw was that of Le Vau who was responsible for
the second phase of its construction, and whose work was to be superseded, in part at
least, by that of Mansart, who began operations in 1678.

[8] Designed by Le Nôtre.

ground, haveing a morasse on each side of it, & though a place naturally without water, yet hath more jet d'eaus & water works then are to be seen anywhere, & looking out from the King's Apartment, one sees almost noe thing but water for a whole league forwards, this being made up of severall basins, supplied by jet d'eaus, & a very large & long canale at the end of a broad walke (which is soe conceald by the hanging of the hill that one scarce sees any of it, but the severall basins seem almost contiguous to one an other & to the canale) in which there rides a man of war of 30 guns, 2 yatchs[1] & severall other lesse vessels. The jet d'eaus, basins & cascades in this garden are soe many, variously contrivd & changed in a moment that it would require a great deale of time to describe them. We had the honour to see them with the King, who walked about with Madam Montespan from one to an other, after haveing driven her & 2 other Ladys in the coach with him about a good part of the garden in a coach & 6 horses. The rooms at the Chasteau are but litle, & the stairs that goe up into the house seeme very litle in proportion either to the greatnesse of the house or the persons are to mount by them.

The King *seemed to be* mightily *well pleased with his water works and* severall *changes were made then to which he himself gave sign with his cane, and he may well be made merry with this water since it has cost him dearer than so much wine, for they say it costs him* 3 s. *every pint* (i.e. 2 lbs.) *that run there.*

The great men's houses seem at first sight to stand irregularly scatterd up & downe at a distance, like cottages in a country village, amongst which the Chasteau, being higher & biger then the rest, looks like the mannor house, but when one takes a view of them from the entrance of the Chasteau, they appeare to be ranged in very good order, & there is an exact uniformity even in them on every side, & they make a prospect very pleaseing, which is soe much the more soe because all this finery & regularity is found in a place where Nature seems to have designed & observed none, it being an uneven country, broken into severall noe very great hills, which are most of them coverd with woods (copice woods), & the country in

---

[1] The two yachts were built in England.

it self looks naturally very wild & seems to wonder how all this bravery come there.

About ½ league from the Chasteau is the Menagery where amongst other strange beasts & birds we saw the two bigest in each kinde, an Elephant of 15 years old, a vast mountain of an animall, & severall ostriches which seemd to have very litle heads to soe great bodys. The contrivance of the appartments for the birds, in answer to an octogon roome that stands in the midle of an yard on which they all a but, & from which roome they may all easily be seen, is very fine & commodeous. The elephant eats 50 lb. of bread per diem & 16 lbs. of wine with rice.

At the same distance from the Chasteau, but on tother side the Canale, lies Trianon,[1] a very extraordinary house of pleasure in a very fine litle garden wherein are aboundance of orange trees. The lower part of the roof of this house is coverd with aboundance of wood work carvd & painted in the figure of China pots of severall fashons with severall birds & beasts among, which gives a very odde prospect to the eye. The Chasteau, Menagery & Trianong make an unequall triangle, the short side whereof is between the Menagery & Trianon. The great Canale runs in the midle between them & an other crosse that lies in the line between them, soe that at either of them there is a fine prospect, but the best from the Chasteau.

Coach from Paris to Versales.   3 – 0 – 0.   B.

THURSD. 24 JUN. We saw the house & lodgings. The King & Queen's apartments are very fine, but litle rooms, near square, all of them about 16 steps over & archd. The roome where the King eats about the same bignesse. In the new lodgings they are some what biger, 18 or 19 steps square. There are 6 of them, one within an other; the innermost of all is the same breadth, but about 32 steps long. All the rest are neare a square & all vaulted roofs, a litle freted.[2] The great walke that gives a view from the house to the Canale is about 70 steps wide & the canale broader.

---

[1] Not the present Trianon, which was built in 1687, but an earlier building put up between 1670 and 1674, and known as the 'Trianon de porcelaine' because of the plaques and other ornaments in faïence.

[2] *O.E.D. fret*: 'to adorn (esp. a ceiling) with carved or embossed work in decorative patterns'.

The King's Cubberd[1] is without the roome, on the staire's head in the passage, & stands in [sic] hollow of a window, & soe was the Dauphin's on the other side the court on the stairs that goe up there. Both the King & hee eat in rooms next the stairs & have no antychambre to them.

The water that is imploid in the garden is raised into a reservoire over the grotto out of a well by 10 horses that turn two spindles & keep two pumps continually goeing, & into this well it is raised out of an estang in the bottom by winde mills. Out of the works in the garden it falls into the canale, & from thence by a windemill it is raisd again into the estang, soe that all these fountains & jets d'eaus are kept in play only by the same water circulateing.

The garden lies west of the house, & the canal of the garden, & beyond the canall the prospect is extended in a valley a great way, but on the other sides it is at a litle distance shut in with hills.

B.   Expenses at Versales & returne   8 – 11 – 0[2]

B. FRID. 25 JUN. Supper at the Ville de Stockholme   1 – 4 – 0.
              Limonade   0 – 5 – 0.
              Plays   4 – 10 – 0.[3]

B. SUND. 27 JUN. Supper   0 – 7 – 0.

Jacobines MUND. 28 JUN. The Jacobines in Paris fell into civill war one with an other & went to gether[4] by the ears, & the battail grew soe fierce between them that the covent was not large enough to contein the combatants, but they severall of them sallied out into the street & there cuffd it out stoutly. The occasion, they say, was that the Prior endeavourd to reduce them into a stricter way of

---

[1] *O.E.D. cupboard*: (1) 'a sideboard, buffet'; (2) 'a set of vessels displayed upon a cupboard, a service of plate'.

[2] Locke evidently incorporated some of these details about Versailles in a letter which he wrote to his friend, James Tyrrell, on 23 June, for in an undated letter of that year the latter wrote: 'I must tell you that I was extremely pleased with the account you give me of Versales, which is a great deal in a litle' (MS. Locke, c. 21, ff. 36–7).

[3] On this day the Théâtre Guénégaud performed *La Comtesse d'Orgueil*, a comedy of Thomas Corneille. We have unfortunately no similar records for the other Paris theatres, the Hôtel de Bourgogne and the Théâtre Italien.

At this point in the Journal there begins a dissertation in French on artificial wines (pp. 181–5, 187–8).

[4] MS. has *to gather*.

liveing then they had for some time past observd, for which in the
fray he was soundly beaten.[1]

TUES. 29 JUN. Collation   0 – 7 – 0.   B.

THURSDAY 1 JUL. Lent to Mr. G. Walls   Wall

    A bag of 4s. peices content   100 – 0 – 0
    Escus 29   087 – 0 – 0
    12 peices of 4s.   002 – 8 – 0
    1 sol marque   000 – 1 – 3
            In all   189 – 9 – 3

For which he gave me two bills to pay Mr. Stringer 15ll.   Stringer
sterling in London at sight, where of I sent one to Mr. Stringer by
Mr. Wall inclosed in a letter.

SAT. JUL. 3. A play   1 – 10 – 0.[2]   B.

SUND. JUL. 4. Dinner   0 – 15 – 0.[3]   B.

WED. 7 JUL. Mr   [4] garden at the end of the Cour de la Reine is Orange trees
full of Orange trees. There are in all 2,600 & odde, as the gardener
told us. They are all set in square cases & are a great many of them
biger then a man's thigh, but most of them with litle heads, haveing
been lately transported i.e. 2, 3, 4, 5 or 6 years since. They bring
them, as he told me, from Italy to Rouen by sea, big as they are,
& the better to transport them, cut of the stock where it is entire &
not spread into branches, & cut of (as the Gardener told me) all
the roots. I beleive they are[5] most of them cut of, for the boxes
seeme not capeable to hold the roots which are necessary for a tree
of that bulke as many of them are, & soe, root & branches being
cut off, they bring them exposd to the aire like soe many stakes at
all times of the yeare without dyeing, but I am afraid in this later
part of the story the gardiner made bold with truth.

---

[1] A letter of Colbert, dated 22 June 1677, to the Archbishop of Paris refers to 'le
désordre des Jacobins de la rue Saint-Jacques'. Some twenty monks were expelled from
Paris as a result of this affray (Clément, VI, 116; cf. Depping, IV, 120–3).
[2] Nothing at the Théâtre Guénégaud.
[3] Here begins an essay in French entitled 'Remarques sur les Eaux minerales des
Bains de Baleruc' which runs from pp. 195 to 197 and is continued on pp. 199–205. It
concludes thus: 'p. Monnier, Dr. en Medecin de l'Université de Montpellier et professeur
aux Mathematiques'.
[4] Blank in MS.   [5] In the MS. are is repeated after them.

B. THURSD. JUL. 8.   Collation   o – 9 – o.
                          Play   1 – 10 – o.[1]

Louver SAT. JUL. 10. The bredth of the rooms in the Dauphin's apartment in the Loover is about 18 or 19 steps, the length of his guard chamber which is the first roome, something more, that of the presence neare about as much,[2] his bed chamber about 9 & his closet within it about 7. The Queen's apartment which is just over it lies just soe, & the rooms about the same scantling.[3] The King's bedchamber also a narrow, long thing, but the rooms without on his side much larger. The painting, guilding & finishing of all these rooms very rich.

Politia MUND. JUL. 12. *In France there are* Governors *of* provinces *as*
Galliae *formerly, but they have no power at all.* Leiutenants *of* provinces *are watch and guard upon them and on the least* occasion *can seize them, and the King's* man[4] *is spy and guard on them both. Besides the* Intendant *gives* constant intelligence *of all things to the Court.*

Regements   *The regiment of* Picardy *hath* 230 companys *in it, but this, as well as the* 5 *other great regiments which they call the* "*old bodies*",[5] *are never all together, but scattered here and there.*

Prince of   *Formerly great numbers of coaches used to wait on the Prince.*[6]
Conde   *Now nobody goes to him unless it be some few* Vertuosi, *for no* officer *can go to see any of the Princes of the Blood* except *he ask leave, and he* promotes *not his* interest *by it.*

B. TUESD. JUL. 13. Supper   1 – o – o.

B. WED. JUL. 14. Collation   o – 10 – o.
                 Supper   1 – 10 – o.

---

[1] Nothing at the Théâtre Guénégaud.

[2] Added above in the MS. are the words: 'as I remember 15'.

[3] *O.E.D.* gives the original sense as 'builder's or carpenter's measuring-rod'. Here the meaning is 'measurements'.

[4] The *Intendant*. Locke seems to exaggerate the power of the *Lieutenants-Généraux* who had been established in the provinces to further reduce the importance of the Governors. But he brings out clearly the latter's loss of all effective power and its transference to the *Intendant*, the new agent of the central government in the provinces.

[5] The term *vieux corps* was applied to the six oldest regiments: Picardie, Piémont, Champagne, Navarre, Normandie and la Marine.

[6] The 'Grand Condé' (1621–86). He had fought his last campaign in 1675 and was now living in retirement, mainly at Chantilly. The Duc d'Aumale, in his *Histoire des Princes de Condé*, vol. VII, paints quite a different picture of the last years of the Prince.

THURSD. JUL. 15. *The King of France is so far* aquainted *with the* grant of all* offices *that the hangman's place of* Tours *hath his hand in the* margent *to the grant of it, there being a* register *kept in a book of all that are* proposd *to him to pass, and if it hath not* name *in the* margent, *passes no farther.* — Politia Galliae

FRID. JUL. 16. For the cuting of milstones they were wont to loose a great deale of time & stone by separating soe much as would serve for one milstone from the rest of the rock that was under. To remedie this inconvenience this was found out. They bored holes all round at the thicknesse they desird, & then drove into these holes stick of willow (Salow) that had been very well dried in an oven, just fit to the holes. The moisture of the aire swelling these sticks, forced the stone from the remaineing rock, & when they had it thus loose, they managed it at pleasure. — Milstones

6 Inch English make of the French $5\frac{7}{12}$ inches. — Measure

MUND. JUL. 19. At the Academy for Painting & Sculpture[1] one sees in the great roome severall peices done by the cheif masters of that Academy, & here it is they meet once a month. They are about 80 in all. Out of them are chosen 2 every two months to teach, each one his month, those[2] young lads who are admitted. They pay here for their being taught but 10 s. per week, which is meant not for a reward, but as a meanes to excite emulation for those that doe very well pay noe thing at all. Every yeare they trye for the prize which the King gives by the hands of Mr. Colbert, who is Protector of this Academie. The prize is worth about £400 & is 3 or 4 medalls of gold. Those usually who get it are also sent into Italy & mainteind there at the King's cost to perfect them. Thus this Kingdom is like to be furnishd with excellent masters in painting & sculpture. — Painting

Laundresse   2 – 5 – 0. — B.

TUESD. JUL. 20. At the Invalids *they had at the first* Institution 1 pint of wine, $1\frac{1}{2}$ lbs. of bread per diem & half a pound of flesh per meale, but now it is abated *and they have but half so much. They have a new suit of clothes and 2 pair of shoes once every 2 years and a half.* — Invalids

---

[1] Founded in 1648, the *Académie de Peinture et de Sculpture* was reorganized by Colbert in 1664.   [2] In the MS. *those* is written between *teach* and *each*.

B. THURSD. JUL. 22. Diner   1 – 0 – 0.

Benedictins' Library **FRID. JUL. 23.** In the Benedictyns' Library at the Abbay of St. Germains[1] 800 old manuscripts where one may observe that about the time of Lotharius, the Emperor, they writ without distinction of points or soe much as words, all their letters, whether the same or different words, being set equidistant. There are also a Testament & some other books writ in golden letters upon a kind of murry parchment;[2] and an old manuscript of the Romans upon tables spred over with wax; and the late testimonys of the Armenian & Easterne churches of their beleife of transubstantiation, etc.

B. TUESD. JUL. 27. Collation   0 – 3 – 0.[3]

Invalids **SUND. AUG. 1.** There are at the Invalids 5 courts. The lenth of the whole building in front from East to West 360 steps,[4] in depth from

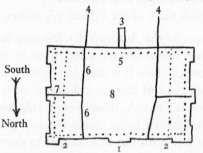

1. The great gate in the midle of the front.
2. Two gates of each side.
3. The chappell.
4. The preists' lodgings.
5. The great stairs & besides in every corner a paire of stairs & 2 other paire in the front between the great & litle gates on each hand.
6. Two long halls for eating, painted with the King's victorys.
7. The Kitching.
8. The Court royall.

---

[1] Many manuscripts of this famous library were destroyed by fire during the Revolution, in 1794, but some 10,000 were saved and transferred to the Bibliothèque Nationale where they now form a special section.

[2] *O.E.D. murry*: 'a colour like that of mulberry: a purple or blood colour'. Germain Brice (II, 151) describes a manuscript in this library, the *Psautier de Saint Germain*, as being written in gold and silver letters 'sur un velin de couleur de pourpre'.

[3] On 29 July there is a medical note with 'Dr. Donalson' at the end of it. According to *D.N.B.* Walter Donaldson (*c.* 1575–*c.* 1630), the Scottish Principal of the Protestant College at Sedan, had a son, Alexander, who became a physician. In the first note-book occurs the following entry, on the subject of Locke's financial relations with Caleb Banks: 'To the Surgeon for bleeding him, 29 July. 3 – 0'.

[4] Apparently Locke's steps had become shorter since November 1675 when he measured the front as 320 paces.

North to South 240, besides a chappell & loging for[1] preists that
run out beyond the square of the courts south ward. The front
stand[s] North ward towards the Seine, & the building is 5 storys
high, besides sellars, & the forme of the whole as you see.

The prickd line a long entry or vista from one end of the building
to the other with lodging chambers on both sides numberd. These
entrys or gallerys are both below & in the 3d story & are open at the
two ends like cloisters into the Court royal which, both above
& below, hath a cloisterd walke on the sides, soe that one may walk
round it in the drie.

In the gallery from North to South, which is 240 steps long,
there are of each side 33 chambers, each haveing 5 beds, in the
length, which is 360 steps, a proportionable number, soe that,
without takeing in the crosse partitions where the Kitchings stand,
the number it will hold, considering that there are 5 storys &
5 soldiers in each chamber,[2] will be 1155, but then, deducting out
of this the halls marked 6.6, which run all along the side of the
Court royall, which halls also in their length take in 2 storys, adde
to this the Chappell in the front, the Apartments both of the
officers belonging to the house & of the officers of the army receivd
into it, & that, as I remember, the building round about the Court
royall is single & soe there are not chambers double as in the other
parts where the gallerys have chambers on both sides, the number
will be a great deale lesse. But the building not being yet finishd,
nor the passages all open, one cannot yet come to see the whole
soe particularly. Q. the use of the 5th story which is cocklofts?

They say there are at present about 15 or 1800 in it.

MUND. AUG. 2. Dinner   1 – 0 – 0.   B.

TUESD. 3 [AUG.] Mr. T. Stringer by his of July 13 tells me that he   Stringer
hath receivd the bill of ten pounds on Mr. Berkeley & the bill of
15 ll. on Mr. Wall.   Wall
              Dinner   1 – 0 – 0.   B.
              Collation   4 – 0.

WED. AUG. 4. Dinner   1 – 0 – 0.   B.
The broad walke answering that of the Tuilleries is at the end by   Walk

---

[1] MS. has *from*.
[2] MS. has at this point the words: 'the number it will conteine', which are superfluous.

the Cour de la Reine about 37 yards broad & the other two lesse
on each side are about 17 yards, & the trees which make these
walks are about 4¼ yards assunder. They are witch elms.

B. THURD. AUG. 5. Dinner   1 – 0 – 0.

Pendulum FRID. AUG. 6. The length of a pendulum of seconds[1] according to
Mr. Hugenius's[2] computation (Journal des Scavans, 1 Jan. 1674)
being 888 demy lines or, which is the same, 3 foot 8½ lines of the
foot of Paris, & the proportion between 3 foot Paris to a pendulum
of seconds being as 864, which are the demy lines of 3 foot, to 881,
it follows that the pendulum being divided into 1000 parts, a foot
of Paris is $326\frac{874}{881}$, i.e. very near 327 of them. And the English
yard, supposeing it be   [3] lines of the Paris foot will be   [3] of
1000 of a pendulum of seconds.
Cloudy. Very cold. Rain in the afternoon.

King's   At the King's Library[4] *we saw a very old* MS. *of* Livie;[5]
Library   Henry 4th's love letters in his owne hand; the first Bible that ever
Printing   was printed, which was in the year 1462, upon velum; but that
which seemed of all the most curious was 18 large folios of plants,
drawne to the life in miniature, and 6 of birds, soe exactly well
donne that who ever knew any of the plants or birds before, would
there know them at first sight, the figure, proportions & colours
being all soe lively & naturall. They are donne by one Mr. Robert[6]
who is still imploid to goe on with the same work which, if he could
live to finish, would certainly be the best of this kinde was yet ever
seen. They are drawn upon velum. There is Mr. Silvester[7] & others

[1] The length of a seconds pendulum was determined by Mersenne in 1644, and thirteen
years later Huyghens invented the first successful pendulum clock.
[2] Christian Huyghens (1629–95), the famous Dutch scientist, worked in Paris for the
greater part of the period 1666–81.
[3] Left blank in MS.
[4] In 1666 Colbert had moved the Bibliothèque du Roi to a house in the Rue Vivienne,
behind the buildings at present occupied by the Bibliothèque Nationale.
[5] Presumably an eighth century MS. of the third 'decad' of Livy, preserved to-day
in the 'Réserve' under the number 5730.
[6] Nicolas Robert (1614–85), a painter who specialized in plants and birds (he was
responsible for the flowers in the famous *Guirlande de Julie*), had as patron Gaston
d'Orléans and then, on the death of the latter, was attached to the King's service by
Colbert.
[7] Israël Silvestre (1621–91), the famous engraver, was appointed *graveur et dessinateur
du Roi* in 1662.

who are also imploid in drawing & graveing the King's 12 houses.
The library keeper told us there were 14,000 MSS. The books are
set round severall pretty large rooms, one within an other.

SAT. AUG. 7. 1 foot of Paris conteins   12 Inches   Measures
              1 Inch. . . . . 12 lines
              1 Line divid [sic] into.   12 primes

soe that 1 pied de Roy ou de Paris being divided into primes
conteines 1728 primes. The philosophical foot[1] or pes universalis
conteines of those primes 1762. Soe that the philosophicall foot Pendulum
being divided into 1000 parts which one may call grys, the foot of
Paris is 981 grys, wanting about ⅓ of a gry.

Mr. Colbert's son[2] Answerd in philosophie at the Cordeleirs, his Colbert
brother moderateing over him, where were present three Cardinals,
Boillon, D'Estre[3] & Bontzi, the Primier President of the Parlement
of Paris, a great number of Bishops & clergy & of the long robe,[4]
a state[5] being erected for the Dauphin to whom his theses was
dedicated.

At Mr. Butterfield's[6] au Roy d'Angleterre, rue de Fosse, I saw Levell
a levelling instrument,[7] made to hang & turne horizontally like
a mariner's compasse. The sight was taken by a perspective glasse

---

[1] The unit of a new decimal system of linear measurement proposed by Locke:
1 philosophical foot = 10 inches; 1 inch = 10 lines; 1 line = 10 grys (see entry for 29 Jan.
1678).

[2] Jules Armand, Marquis d'Ormoy (1663–1704), who was appointed in 1674 *Surintendant des bâtiments en survivance*; after his father's death he took up a career in the army.
The brother mentioned was no doubt Colbert's second son, Jacques Nicolas (1655–1707),
later Archbishop of Rouen.

[3] César, Cardinal d'Estrées (1627–1717), was a typical *grand seigneur* in clerical garb.
He is the hero of Saint-Simon's story of Louis XIV complaining at dinner of the inconvenience of having no teeth left, to which he replied: 'Des dents, Sire? Eh! qui
est-ce qui en a?'

[4] I.e. of the *noblesse de robe* (members of the Parlements and high civil servants).

[5] *O.E.D.* 'a canopy or raised chair with a canopy'.

[6] Michael Butterfield (his name is not in the *D.N.B.* and he is described in the
Biographie Universelle as being of German origin!) was an instrument-maker who was
several times employed by Colbert (see the *Comptes des Bâtiments* for 1679 and 1680).
He published several books and papers (two of the latter in the *Philosophical Transactions*)
on his inventions. He died in 1724. His shop was in the Rue Neuve des Fossés,
Faubourg Saint-Germain.

[7] There is a detailed description of this instrument, with illustrations, in the *Journal
des Savants* of 1677 (pp. 227–8) and another of an improved version of it in the volume
for 1678 (pp. 440–3).

of four glasses, about a foot long, & between the first & 2nd glasse was placed one single filament of silk strech [sic] horizontally by which the levell was to be taken. This silke haire was soe orderd that it might be removed forwards or backwards soe as to fix it just in the focus of the eye glasse, & set higher or lower soe as to place it just in the levell. There was an heavy weight of lead hung down perpendicular about a foot long to keepe the telescope horizontall.

Italici scriptores   SUNDAY AUG. 8. S.W. Misty rain. The Italian authors of the 14th age are the best. Mr. Falaisau.[1]

B.   MUND. AUG. 9. Dinner & supper   2 – 0 – 0.

B.   TUESD. AUG. 10. Lawndresse   2 – 9 – 0.

B.   WED. AUG. 11. Paid Mr. De Launay for my lodging at his house for two months ending 10 Aug.   44 – 0 – 0.[2]

Cartesius   Videre est Cartesii vortices apud Jordanum Brunum, de immenso et commensurabili; Ejusdem doctrinam de lumine et coloribus apud Jo: ab Indagine de Iride et refractis coloribus. Et materiam subtilem apud Diogenem Laertium quae idem plane est cum fragminibus Empedoclis et Ramentis Heracliti.[3]

B.   THURSD. AUG. 12. Dinner today & yesterday   2 – 0 – 0.

Thuillerys   FRID. AUG. 13. The length of the Twillerys is thus. From the Louvre to the first basin 234 steps, the circumference of the basin 228. From the first basin to the second 595. The Circuit of the second basin which is an octagon, 360. From the second Basin to the end 190, soe that the whole length of the garden is about 815 steps.

St. Clou   SAT. 14 AUG. The great roome at St. Clou[4] 14 French yards long & about 10½ broad. The walks in the garden set with witch elms

---

[1] There were at least two families of this name, both from Touraine, who were prominent amongst the Protestant community in Paris at this period; but for lack of any further detail it is impossible to identify this particular Falaiseau.

[2] A list, with prices, of ten volumes in the series of works of Classical authors of the edition *ad usum Delphini* is given before this entry.

[3] This passage on the alleged sources of Descartes's system presumably derived from a conversation, for Locke is always very careful to give precise references to books from which he copied passages.

[4] The château was bought in 1658 by Louis XIV for the use of his brother, Monsieur, and was greatly enlarged. Only the park remains to-day.

about 12 or 15 foot English asunder & honey suckles let up about
the bodys of them. The cut hedges of beech or hornbeame. Apple   Apple trees
& pear trees spred just above ground & well loaden with fruit,
though not soe high as goosbery bushes. Long ally arbres turnd   Arbres
with an arch, the support of the work of Iron at about 8 or 9 foot
distance, the bottom coverd with beech or hornebeam & the top
with honey suckles.

The way of parfumeing gloves in a cubbard with several shelves   Parfumeing
to draw out & put in at several distances, these shelves made like
rackets, but with the smallest lute strings, & on them to lay orange
flowers or ranunculus tuberosus or other sweets[1] & the gloves on
an other over them without touching, & thus S.S.S.

TUESD. AUG. 17. From St. Clou to Meudon 1 league, where is   Meudon
a decaying Chasteau of the house of Guise.[2] It is situate upon a hill
from whence is a good prospect over the Plaine de Grenell to
Paris which from hence is seen very well. The house & gardens are
very much out of repaire. Behind it, as we were told, is a great
parke.

From Meudon to Isis[3] 1 league. Here are fine walks in a garden   Isis
or wood & severall handsom jet d'eaux, basins & ponds. It belongs
to one Mr. Brasiere[4] who, haveing been once SurIntendant de
Finances, made here this garden & laid the foundations of a great
house, but the sunshine of that place lasted only long enough to
make this building appeare a litle above ground, where it stands,
never like to grow higher. Here are some jet d'eaux which through[5]
the water very high, but not comparable to that at St. Clou, which,   St. Clou
they say, mounts it in a continued streame 90 foot high &, when
they let it goe with a jerk, 120.

---

[1] O.E.D. gives this word in the sense of 'substances having a sweet smell'.
[2] The Guise family had sold the château in 1654. In 1679 it was purchased by Louvois
and was later acquired by the Dauphin.
[3] Issy. Contemporaries apparently offered this derivation of the name. Only the
gardens remain to-day.
[4] Or rather, Macé Bertrand, seigneur de La Bazinière, who succeeded his father as
Trésorier de l'Épargne (and not Surintendant des Finances) in 1643. He was involved in
the fall of Fouquet in 1661, and was both imprisoned and compelled to pay a fine of
6,000,000 livres. He died in 1688.
[5] O.E.D. gives other examples of this spelling of throw.

B. WED. AUG. 18. Candles   0 – 7 – 0.

B. THURSD. 19 AUG. Dinner to day & yesterday   2 – 0 – 0.

MUND. AUG. 23. *Rain* Saturday & Sunday. Dinner for Mr. Banks & me, Tuesday Versailles   2 – 0 – 0.

Versailes WED. AUG. 25. Leaden pipes at Versales 16 or 17 Inches diameter, & indeed there needs pipes of that bignesse to convey water enough to that which they call the Treefountains[1] & the Triumphal Arch. In the first there rises a sheaf of water made of 173 jet d'eaux joynd close togeather in a bunch, besides severall other great jet d'eaux of great bores riseing high 6 in one basin, playing crosse, 3 of a side, & in the 3d of these Trois Fountains 6 or 7 great jet d'eaux riseing neare one an other, divergeing one from another to a great heigth in figure of a bell, the brims upwards. The Triumphal Arch is yet more magnificent where, besides a vast number of cascades to a great heigth & jet d'eaux, there are two great mountains or wears, as it were, of water & 4 pyramids of water neare 30 foot high, in all which there runs water enough to drive a mill. The aboundance of water, variety of shapes it appears in, the magnificence & artifice of the whole is very surpriseing.

In an other quarter of the garden is found a large statue, guilt, in the midle of a very big basin, blowing a trumpet out of which a streame of water mounts to the heigth, as they say, of 70 foot. This basin is encompassed with raile. The raile is of white marble and the pillars or square peirs that uphold it at severall distances admirably carvd with trophies, foliage, imagery etc. of admirable worke & the pilasters between the peirs of Iron cut through & guilded. This fountaine is of an Extraordinary charge. In the same quarter is Enceladus, a vast statue guilded, lying amongst rocks in the midle of a great Basin. To set down the particulars of all these would require a volume.

The alleys of the garden are large, laid with sand instead of gravell which coache & horses goe, & are raked over every day to destroy the ruts & keep them even. On each side of these great alleys are litle alleys of about 9 foot wide for walkers, separated

---

[1] Trois Fontaines.

from the great alleys by a hedg or wall of beech trees, set close to
geather in a line, & 20 or 30 foot high & green from top to bottom,
kept shorne even on both sides soe that they are not above half
a foot or a foot thick, but green from top to bottom. They are the
finest hedges I ever saw. In some places I saw hedges of Maple
set, but they were all very young, soe that I know not how they will
thrive, & they being set under the sides of high grown cops woods,
perhaps they make use of this tree, though of a duller green, because
it is able to endure & get up under the dropings of other, sed super
hac re melius inquirendum.

The contriver of all the waterworks is Mr. Fracin, a French son
of an Italian.[1]

The water that runs in the severall water works is one & the
same. The lowest part is the canale; from thence a winde mill
returns it into the Estang; from the Estang it is raisd into the Tour
d'el eaux by 5 winde mils where 18 horses are night & day at worke
to raise it into the reservoire by the Chasteau, & there 10 other
horses continually working raise it to the reservoire over the Grotto
of Thetis.

THURD. AUG. 26. The Arch du Triomphe is an oblong square, at   Versailles
the upper end whereof there are three Arches of Iron work, & over
them the roofe hath over the very ridgh one jet d'eau and a litle
basin about 3 foot diameter elevated above the roof about a foot or
more, & from thence on each side 8 others like the first, which make
soe many cascades. On each side of the 3 dore[s] are contrivances
to make the water fall en nape from about 18 inches to 18 inches
which, when it plays, seemes to make soe many, i.e. 4, pillars of
water. In each of the dores or gates is a basin about a yard diameter
with each a jet d'eau in it above an inch diameter.

All the water of these severall jet d'eaux falls down into a narrow
cisterne of this figure ⌒, which is about 22 steps long,
& soe by 6 severall falls comes into a cisterne which by 3 pipes of
8 or 10 inches diameter a peice is caried away under ground. The
cascades of these six severall falls are the whole length and of

---

[1] François Francine (1617–88), son of Tommaso Francini, a Florentine engineer who
came to France during the reign of Henry IV.

severall heigth, the highest about a yard & the 3 lowest about 6 or 8 inches apeice. On the third, fourth & fifth of these cascades are severall jet d'eaux of above an inch diameter.

On the 4 corners of this square are[1] 4 pyramids which, when they play, make, as it were, 4 pyramids of water of about 20 foot high, about a foot diameter at top & 2 foot at bottom, the water falling from space to space about 18 inches distance en nape.

On each side of the square in the midle is a cascade about 12 steps long in front & about 6 in depth. Here are eight falls about a foot a peice & soe it rises like a paire of staires both on front & by the sides. In every other of these descentes there are jet d'eaux of about an inch diameter. From the lowest of these it falls about 4 foot into a cisterne that goes all round it, & soe is convey [sic] away underground. These two cascades, when they play, look like 2 great mountains of water or weares. On each side of these cascades & of the pyramids stands a basin, *about* 3 foot diameter, elevated on a pedistall about 7 foot high, each basin haveing it[s] great jet d'eau in it. At the lower end of the square goes down an alley, on each side of which are two water courses broken into severall falls. At the upper end of these a great streame of water rises & sinke[s] away agen at the lower end, all the whole passage being made of lead. At the end of this alley is an other cascade with very great jet d'eaux where the water run[s] & falls in a very big streame. The water that runs in this one place is enough to drive a mill.

On the west side the Alley d'eaux, over against the Arc de Triumph in an other litle wood, is the Trois Founteins where are 3 great fountains with jet d'eaux, cascades, etc., but it is too long to describe them particularly, being all full of charge, vanity & magnificence.

Windemils to raise water

The water of all these works is noe thing but the rain water of the winter stopd by dams made in the vallys on both sides the Chasteau. From thence it is raisd by 10 winde mills, 5 on a side, to the reservoire by the Grot de Thetis in the garden. Besides these 10 windemills there are 120 horses kept on purpose to raise water also, where of 40 are always at worke night & day. They worke

---

[1] The word occurs twice in MS.

2 hours & rest 4. One of the winde mills we were in was built high, 7 storys, a balcony round above the second story whither the ends of the vanes reach. The water is raised by a chain of copper bucket[s],[1] holding each 16 pints of Paris. There are of the bucket[s] upon one chaine 72. The linke of the chaine each bucket is fastend to, is about 2 foot long & that which brings them up is the square of the crosse peice of timber they turne on, which is as broad as each linke is long. The roof, milworke etc. of this mill is turnd with a litle wheel of rounds which take hold of cogs that are set all around on the top of the wall on the inside, & 134 in number, each one, with the space belonging to it, being about 6 inches.

When the winde is strong, the same mill turns two chaines of bucket[s], the wheele that brings them up on one side being made soe that it may be brought to take in the cogs of that which turns the other or be removd out of their reach, as is occasion. It worked only at one well whilst we were there; the other stood still. There is one of these mills with 6 vanes which hath by that means an addition of strength with the same winde. This is the best sort of windemills I have seen anywhere, it being capeable to be made very high, because there needs noe post to come down from the top to the ground to turne it to the wind.

Robinets a foot French diameter, one where of cost £2,000.

WED. SEPT. 1. These 2 or 3 last days of August very cold.

Le Quai de Peletier[2] projected beyond the perpindicular of the wall a yard, 4 or 5 foot as I guesse, in arch worke without any thing to susteine it & running thus all along from Pont Nostre Dame to the Greve. The author of the Journal de Scavants, 13 Avr. 1676, says thus of it: Cette avance forme un quart de cercle en l'air de 5½ pieds. {.sidenote: Quai de Peletier}

Mr. Oury, a watchmaker upon that Quay, tells me they have given off the way of makeing watches with very great ballances in imitation of pendulum because, by the severall jogs in one's pocket, they are apt some times to stand still, the ballance being too big to be set a goeing by the main spring. {.sidenote: Watch}

---

[1] Locke three times uses this form as a plural.
[2] Named after Claude le Peletier (1631–1711), then *Prévôt des Marchands* of Paris, who was *Contrôleur-Général* from 1683 to 1689. The *quai* was finished in 1675.

C.B. THURSD. SEPT. 2. Mr. *Banks received* 100 ll. *from*[1] Herinks. *In* July *he received* 100 ll. *of* the....[2] *and in* June 100 ll. *of* de Voulges *on a letter of credit.*

Diner today & yesterday   2 – 0 – 0.

Walk SUND. 5 SEPT. The long terrasse walke on the south side the Twilleries is from the wall to the rowes of trees on both side[s] about 6 yards broad, & the midle walke between the trees about 15 yards broad. The trees are witch elms, new planted & cut off about 8 foot high, planted about 15½ foot asunder, & in the midle between each two a fir tree which, beginning to spread at the very ground, grows up like a piramid which in the midle walk of the Twillerys where they are grown, keep 8 or 10 foot high & grow between horse chestnut trees. They look very finely.

B. MOND. SEPT. 6. Lawndresse   2 – 10 – 0.

Hedges of TUESD. SEPT. 7. At the Tuilleries the hedges that divide the com-
Maple   partments of the garden are most of them of maple whereof some only are cut up the sides & soe let shoot up. Others are shorne also on top & kept soe & grow & looke very well, being green quite to the bottom.

Chantilly THURSD. SEPT. 9. From Paris to Chantilly 10 leagues. *An* irregular *building, the rooms some of them large, but not very handsome nor well contrived and worst of all* furnished, *it being all very old.*[3] The garden *very fine and every day making finer,* £100,000 *being* alloted *to be spent on it every year. Water works there* designed, though *it be full of* Jet d'eaux & basins already. *In the* garden *is a* canall, 1400 toise long & 30 broad *and* a great stream *falls into it in a great* cascade, at the upper end out of a round basin, 60 toise diameter. The forest that comes downe quite to the garden's side is large & full both of high & coppice wood & cut out into severall pretty walkes. In it is a litle Trianon & menagery where are to be seen vultures, eagles, a very tall Ostrich & severall other strange birds, but amongst the rest one they call a true pellican, biger then a rooke, not soe big as

---

[1] MS. has *for*.   [2] MS. has '....' (= 'the same'?).
[3] After his return from exile Condé set about improving the estate of Chantilly. He began with the gardens and the construction of cascades, fountains and a canal, and finally, towards the end of his life, turned his attention to the château.

a raven, of a colour a litle sadder[1] then the back of an hobby,[2] a hawking bill, but white as ivory. They say it has been here this hundred years.

FRID. SEPT. 10. From Chantilly to Liancour[3] 4 Leagues, a place **Liancourt** with a very large garden & very many water works. Here in the garden are the highest & straitest fir trees I have seen any where. From Liancour to Verneuile[4] 2 leagues, a house standing high & **Vernuile** well near the Oyse, very regularly & handsomely built. From Verneuile to Chantilly 2 leagues. The Duke & Dutchesse of Vernueile came in the evening from Verneule to Chantilly to visit the Prince, & at the play which they were at (the Prince's players[5] being in the house & playing every night) had this of particular to enterteine them that severall pots of African marigolds [were] set before the scenes which were two screens, as a particular marke of their reception.

SAT. SEPT. 11. From Chantilly to Champlastreux 4 leagues. 'Tis **Champlast-** a litle & ordinary house belonging to a President of that name,[6] the **reux** garden large & ordinary where we found, as is ordinary, the walkes harrowed up to keep away the grasse, gravell walks being unknown in France.

From Champlastreux to Equan[7] 2 leagues, a house belonging **Equan** formerly to the family of Montmorancy, standing on a hill on the edg of the vally of Montmorancy. It is now very much decaying. The motto one finds up & down in severall places of this house is this: Arma tenenti omnia dat qui justa negat. From Equam to Paris 4 leagues.

The predecessors of the King of France have upon occasions to **Revenue** raise present sums sold annuitys at 12 years' purchase. Of these **Annuities**

---

[1] *O.E.D. sad*: 'dark, deep (of colour)'.

[2] *O.E.D.* 'a small species of falcon'.

[3] The château of the Duc de La Rochefoucauld, demolished in the nineteenth and twentieth centuries.

[4] A sixteenth-century château, now in ruins.

[5] The company of actors which bore the title of 'Troupe de Monsieur le Prince' toured the provinces when it was not performing for Condé.

[6] Louis Molé, sieur de Champlâtreux (1644–1709), a member of a famous family of judges, was *Président à mortier* in the Paris Parlement. The present château seems to have been built in the eighteenth century.

[7] Écouen. This magnificent Renaissance château is still in existence.

were £10,000,000 payable to the Chamber of Paris[1] who were, as it were, trustees for the particular persons that had purchased these annuities. These 10,000,000 have been by several abatements since this rain[2] reduced to 5, soe that now there is paid ½ of the value of these annuitys. This King hath also within these 3 years sold annuitys at 14 years' purchase to the value of 5,000,000[3] which is yearly paid in to the Chamber of Paris out of his revenew soe that his revenew is chargd still to the Chamber of Paris 10,000,000 per annum. Besides that he is now selling annuitys for life at 8 years' purchase to the value of   ,[4] if he can finde purchasers, which I doe not heare come in very fast, there being but   [4] yet contracted for.

B. MUND. SEPT. 13. Supper   1 – 0 – 0.

B. TUESD. SEPT. 14. Supper   1 – 0 – 0.
                              Candles   0 – 7 – 0.

WED. SEPT. 15. Very hot these two or three days.

B.   Play   1 – 10 – 0.[5]

Peaux   THURSD. SEPT. 16. Three men swiming in the Sein with cinctures
impenetrable   de peaux impenitrables blown up about their midles.[6]

B.   Supper   1 – 0 – 0.

B. MUNDAY 20 SEPT. Play   1 – 10 – 0.[5]

Fonteinbleau   THURSD. 23 SEPT. From Paris to Ysole[7] 7 leagues, from Ysole to Fontaine bleau. It is situate on a litle, open plaine incopped[8] with rocky & woody hils in the midle of the great forest of Fontaine bleau. One passes 3 or 4 miles through it in the way from Paris hither before one comes to the towne. Here at night we saw Alceste, an opera,[9] where the musique, both vocal & of instruments, was very good. At the opera the King & Queen sat in chaires with

---

[1] By this Locke no doubt means the *Hôtel de Ville*.

[2] *O.E.D.* gives this spelling of *reign*. Colbert's reductions in the value of the *Rentes* made him extremely unpopular in the years after he came into office in 1661.

[3] One of the measures taken by Colbert to finance the war.

[4] Left blank in MS.

[5] Nothing at the Théâtre Guénégaud on these two days.

[6] See the *Journal des Savants*, 1678, pp. 39–41 (*Experience curieuse faite à Paris sur la riviere de Seine l'esté passé*) which gives an account of experiments with waterproofed leather.   [7] Essonnes.   [8] *O.E.D.* gives *incoop, incoup*: 'enclose'.

[9] By Lully and Quinault, first performed in 1674.

armes. On the right hand of the King sat Mme Montespane &,
a litle nearer the stage on her right hand, Mademoiselle, the King of
England's neice.[1] On the left hand of the Queen sat Monsieur,[2]
& of his left hand, advanceing towards the stage, Madame,[3] & soe
forward towards the stage other Ladys of the Court, all on
Tabourets except the King & Queen.

FRID. 24 SEPT. We saw the house at Fontaine bleau, whereof there
being a description in print, I refer to that. At night we saw a ball
where the King & Queen & the great persons of the Court danced,
& the King himself took pains to cleare the roome to make place
for the dancers. The Queen was very rich in Jewells & there needed
her stiffness to support soe great a treasure, & soe were severall of the
Ladys. The King, Queen etc. were placed as at the Opera. The Duc
d'Anguien[4] sat behind the Daulphin on that side.

SAT. 25 SEPT. Le pain le plus blanc appellé le pain de Challis   Rates
        7 onces cuit et rassis 1s.   Bread

> Le pain noir appellé pain de bis ou de brode   13 onces 1s.
> Le paine jaunett appellé pain bourgeois   10 onces 1s.
> Le paine mollet   5 onces 1s.
> Le vin la pinte du meilleur du pais   6s
>   du meilleur du Bourgogne et Champagne 12s. la pinte.
>
> Viande.
> 1 Livre de boeuf   3s.
> moutton   4s.
> veau   5s.
> Lard a larder   7s.
> petit lard   6s.
> Chandelle   7s.
> Foine 100 lb.   20s.
> Le Septier de vieille Avoine contenant 8 boisseaux mesure de ce
> leiu dont 17 font le Septier de Paris £3 – 12s.

This with other rates affixed to one of the back gates of the
Chasteau.

---

    [1] Marie-Louise, the daughter of Monsieur and his first wife, Henrietta, the sister of
Charles II, was born in 1662 and married in 1679 Charles II of Spain. She died in 1689.
    [2] The King's brother, Philippe d'Orléans (1640–1701).
    [3] Monsieur's second wife, Charlotte Elizabeth, a German princess, famous for her
vast correspondence.
    [4] Henri Jules de Bourbon, Duc d'Enghien, son of the Grand Condé.

There are in the house 5 large courts, but variously & irregularly enough built. That side which is towards the garden looks like a company of litle tenements set one by an other, some 3, some 4, some 5 storys high, & soe is the first court you come into. On the farther side the parterre is a moat which bounds the garden which would be very fine, were it not turned into filthy suds[1] by those that continually wash there. The gardens are everywhere full of nosegays, espetially all along under the long gallery windows, & there was *one laid on* Monsieur's *back stairs to mark, I suppose, the good housekeeping rather than the* cleanlynesse *of the place, and at all the stairs one is sure to meet with a parfume which yet hath nothing of* Vespatian's *good savour.*[2]

Trinity

At the foot of the great staire, which is a very large & fine one, is a fine chappell where the Altar peice is God the Father, painted at large in the forme of an old man clad in azure, a dove by him & Our Saviour below. The altar &, I beleive, the chappell, by the inscription on the top of it, is dedicated to the Trinity, & soe here they are represented in painting, & this donne lately by Mr. Duboys, one of the present King's painters.[3]

Veau MOND. 27 SEPT. From Fountain bleau to Veau[4] 4 leagues. The entry in to the house is first into a vestibule 15 steps square & thence into an ovall 30 steps long & 22 broad. This is the thicknesse of the house & something more, because one side of the ovall stands out towards the garden without the front of the building. The lower flore, soe much of it as is finishd, is very handsome & exceeding rich in guilding & painting donne by La Brun,[5] & I think better or at least as good as any I have seen in the King's houses. The garden you descend into from the house by severall descents of stairs & over a moat which invirons the house. It is large & very well contrivd & adorned with very magnificent & costly water works.

---

[1] *O.E.D.* 'dregs, leavings, hence filth, muck'.
[2] Vespasian laid a tax on urinals.   [3] Jean Dubois (1604-79).
[4] Vaux-le-Vicomte, the magnificent château constructed by Nicolas Fouquet before his fall in 1661.
[5] Charles Le Brun (1619-90), *Premier peintre du Roi* and the leading official painter of the reign.

At Fontain bleau yesterday the King & Court went a stag hunting in the afternoon, & at night had an opera, at all which Madame appeard in a peruke & upper parts dressed like a man.[1]

I saw there a cubberd made about the bignesse & of the fashon of a chaire[2] as far as it is square. This was divided into five shelves of grates, the first of Iron (under which they hang a pan of live coles), all the rest of wood, upon each of which they place dishes of meat & then, shuting a slideing dore that is before each shelf, two men cary this just as they doe a chaire, & thus you have your dinner served up hot whose lodgings are in the court far removed from the kitchin, a useful contrivance.

There are 5 large courts of buildings at Fountain bleau, the lodging richly guilded & painted. Severall fine gallerys, amongst which is one which they say is 106 toise long.

There are in the parterre two large basins, one square, in which is a rock, etc. with a jets d'eau & cascades, the other round, 70 toise in compasse, at the side of the parterre that looks along the canale into the parke at the head of this canale, where run 450 pouce d'eau & below 170 Jet d'eaue. The Canale is 600 toise long & 20 broad. In it is a barge of pleasure & a boat to tow it.

The second story at Veau le Viscount is but very ordinary & therefor the stairs that goe up to it but ordinary neither. The 3d story is all lodgings for servants.

Before the hou[s]e you have a litle court within the moat, & without a large, square one separate from the high way that passes just by it, by 3 Iron gates & between them grates of upright barrs of Iron set on a wall about 4 foot high, as I remember. On each side this first large court on both sides are two other as large square courts of stables, barnes, etc. which, bounding the approach to the house on both sides, make the entrance very handsome.

At the ball at Fountain bleau when we were there the Queen & Ladys were very rich in Jewells.

The Gards du corps are 1600, divided into 4 companys, over each of which there is one Leiutenant, 2 Exans[3] & 2 Brigadiers.

Fontaine-
bleau

Veau

Gards du
corps

---

[1] Cf. Arvède Barine, *Madame mère du Régent* (Paris, 1911), pp. 111–13, for confirmation of this statement.

[2] A sedan chair.   [3] *Exempts.*

There is going to be added to them 400 more. Their pay is 40 s. per diem & a coat once a yeare, their armes sword, pistols & carbine. The King himself makes choise of every one that is put in. They are presented to him by some great man of the Court, & then he him self examins them about the service they have been in, for none but tried men are put there.

E[arl of] Shaftesbury

THURSD. 30 SEPT. For my Lord Shaftesbury:[1]

Maps of Lorrain
Luxembourg   } 1 – 4 – 0.
Campagne [sic]
Haynault } 1 – 4 – 0.
Namur

B. FRID. 1 OCT.[2] Play   3 – 0 – 0.[3]

Monsieur We saw Monsieur at Supper with Madame. There was but litle company & that very ordinary. Musique all the while.

SAT. OCT. 2. Sent the maps by Mrs. Armstrong.[4]

SUND. OCT. 3. Very faire & warme *as it was almost all* September.[5]

Library MUNDAY OCT 4. At the King's Library we saw, besides the books in the cabinet, an excellent collection of Coyns. The cranium of a bore out of whose upper jaw on each side grew out a long but slender horne or tusk which turnd round almost like a ram's horne, but made only one turne which was a good, large one. We also saw the seale & sword & other reliques of King Childeric, most of them gold & enamell, which were some time since found in his tombe.[6]

---

[1] The Shaftesbury Papers in the Public Record Office show that in 1679 Locke received the sum of 3s. 10d. in payment for these maps. In 1677 Shaftesbury was imprisoned in the Tower, and Stringer wrote to Locke on 16 August (o.s.) to ask him to get these maps 'because the war in all probability will come there again' (Christie, II, 248).

[2] Before the next entry are some notes on Descartes's geometry, furnished by Mr Herbert.

[3] The Théâtre Guénégaud performed on that day Molière's *Fourberies de Scapin* and *Monsieur de Pourceaugnac*.

[4] On 5 October (o.s.) Stringer wrote to Locke: 'I will take care to inquire after the maps you have sent by Sir Thomas Armstrong's daughter' (Christie, II. 250). Sir Thomas Armstrong was executed in 1684 for his part in the Rye House Plot.

[5] Here is a table of coins of the ancient world with their equivalent in *livres tournois*; and under it: 'This communicated to me by Mr. Falesau who tooke out [sic] of Vitry's Bible.' (See note to entry for 8 Aug. 1677.)

[6] It was discovered at Tournai in 1653.

The seale was very massive, graved with his image in very ordinary graveing & these words round it: Childerici Regis. His sword which was about 18 inches long was blunt at the end, strait & the handle coverd with thin plates of gold, and enamell upon it which was pellucid & lookd like glasse, which they told us was enamell, it lying upon some part of the worke in large peices over litle hollows.

Play   1 – 10 – 0.[1]   B.

WEDNESD. OCT. 6. At Versailles The new staire a makeing very *Versailles* magnificent both for largenesse, marble & painting. The walls about the Bassin of Latona which make the half moone of the ascent *Garden* to the Chasteau & which are some of them high, are coverd with yew which proves an excellent thick green.

In the compartment of the Trois Fontaines the Gerbe at the upper end makes a mountain of water which, falling downe through the cascades below, makes a river. The 6 great inclineing pipes make an high arch in the 2d, & the 4 great ones at the 4 corners send great quantity of water very high. And in the 3d the feather in the midle, which are 8 great pipes neare to geather in a round which, a litle inclined outwards, through[2] the water in great quantity very high, which makes a kinde of feather or bell inverted, & round about there as many upright great pipes which spout water to a wonderfull heigth, & all these when they play togeather with severall lesse ones, make a deluge which yet you stand by without being wett. The orifices of all these great pipes are coverd with brasse peirced with regular holes bigger then those of a skimmer.[3]

THURSD. OCT. 7. Mr. Justell[4] told me that the Duke of Hanover has *Coach* a coach he travaild in lately to his army which at night he turnd

---

[1] Nothing at the Théâtre Guénégaud.   [2] *throw*.

[3] *O.E.D.* 'a shallow utensil, usually perforated, employed in skimming liquids'.

[4] Henri Justel (1620–93), who succeeded his father as *Secrétaire du Roi*, is chiefly remembered for the meetings of learned men which took place at his house, and which Locke—in a modest capacity—appears to have attended. Being a Huguenot, he fled from the increasing persecution in France and came to England in 1681. He was naturalized, elected to the Royal Society and appointed Librarian of St James's Palace. He spent many years collecting material for a work on what he called 'les commodités de la vie', i.e. all sorts of inventions which contributed to making life easier and pleasanter. Several of Locke's notes on his conversations with him will be seen to come into this category—as for that matter do many of his own notes on things which he observed in France.

into a tent & which will serve also for a boat to passe a river.[1] He
shewd me also a leafe of Palimpsestus or in French peau d'asne.
It is of a yellowish colour, very smooth. What is writ on it with inke
may be blotted out again. It comes from Neurimberg. In German
it is called Esselhaut which is the same with peau d'asne.

Palimpsestus

Esselhaut

Maps
They make in Holland maps upon tafety that one may carry
about in his pocket like an hand kercheif.

Tablebook
To blot out what is writ on ordinary table books take pouder of
pumice stone in a fine rag & soe rub it out.

Observatoire
At the Observatoire we saw the moone in 22 foot glasse & Jupiter
with his 4 satellites in the same. The most remote was on the east
& the other 3 on the west. We saw also Saturne & his ringe in
a 32 glasse & one of his satelites on the west side, almost in the line

Declination
of the longer axis of his ring as it then appeard. Mr. Cassini[2] told
me that the declination of the needle at Paris is about 2½ degrees to
the westward. 'Twas between 8 & 9 at night that we saw these
planets, but Saturne last of all & after 9.

Table book
FRID. OCT. 8. Take Aqua fortis[3] q.s., dissolve in it bookbinder's
starch till you bring it to the consistence of milke, then strain it
through a cloth. Adde to this cirussa alb. pulveris: till it be of the
consistence of soft butter. With a pencil or the like spread over one
side of your paper. When it is drie, which will be in 3 or 4 hours,
spread in the same manner the other side of your paper. When
both sides are thoroughly drie, take a course cloth & rub it smooth.
For greater perfection beat it as bookebinders beat their bookes to
make it smooth. This one may write on with a silver pen. Mr.
Brisban.[4]

---

[1] In a letter of 1707 concerning his relations with Justel Leibnitz wrote: 'Je me souviens
que je lui envoyai la description d'un coche inventé par feu Monsieur Ernest Weigel,
qui pouvait être changé en bateau et en tente, comme on en fit l'expérience assez
promptement; il se trouve présentement à Wolfenbutel' (Ancillon, *Mémoires concernant
les vies et les ouvrages de plusieurs modernes célèbres...*, Amsterdam, 1719, p. xxx;
cf. letters of Justel to Leibnitz of 4 Oct. 1677 and 7 March 1678 in the latter's *Sämtliche
Schriften und Briefe*, ser. 1, vol. II).

[2] Jean Dominique Cassini (1625–1712), an Italian by origin, came to Paris in 1669
and was virtually director of the Observatory there. In 1672 he had discovered the
second known satellite of Saturn and later discovered two more (1684). At this time he
was studying with Römer the eclipses of the satellites of Jupiter.

[3] Locke uses the old chemical symbol (cf. entry for 22 July 1676).

[4] In Firth & Lomas (p. 24), John Brisbane is described as 'agent marine' at the

Mr Bernier[1] told me that the Heathens of Indostand pretend to great antiquity; that they have books & historys in their language; that the nodus of their numbers is at 10 as ours & their circuit of days 7. That they are in number about 10 to 1 to the Mahumetans & that Aurang Zebe[2] had lately ingagd him self very inconveniently in wars with them upon the account of religion, endeavouring to bring them by force to Mahumetanisme; & to discourage & bring over the Banians[3] or undoe them, he had given exemptions of Custome to the tradeing Mahumetans, by which meanes his revenue was very much lessened, the Banians makeing use of the names of Mahumetans to trade under & soe eluding his partiality.

SAT. OCT. 9. Esselhaut is to be had also at Strasburg & other towns in Germany.

At St. Geneveve le Pere Molenet[4] sheud us, besides a great many other naturall & artificiall curiositys, a stone about 10 or 11 inches long & thicker then one's fist which was made up of severall stones soe lockd one into an other that though they were perfectly distinct stones, yet they hung fast all togeather, but yet were loose enough to shake & suffer the whole to bend like the inarticulations[5] of the back bone. There were also cut in onyxes

(right margin notes) Indostan / Antiquity / Arithmatique / Weeks / Esselhaut / St. Geneveve

---

British Embassy in Paris. He was appointed to this post in 1676 and when, in 1678, the Ambassador, Ralph Montagu, was recalled, Brisbane became Secretary to the Embassy. After his recall in June 1679, he eventually became Secretary to the Admiralty.

[1] François Bernier (1620–88), doctor, traveller and philosopher. After taking his M.D. at Montpellier, he spent thirteen years (1656–69) in Oriental travel. In 1670–1 he published his *Histoire de la dernière Révolution des États du Grand-Mogol* which Locke made notes on during his stay in Montpellier. In 1678 he published his *Abrégé de la philosophie de Gassendi* which Locke had amongst a large collection of books which he packed into boxes before setting out on another tour of France in July 1678. This and another conversation (see entry for 20 June 1678) which he had with Bernier, were concerned, so far as the record of the Journal goes, only with the latter's travels and not with his philosophy. For another conversation with Bernier (in March 1679) see Appendix B, p. 282. In Locke's second note-book (p. 60), under the heading '1679', there is the following entry: 'Bernier. Q. What he knows of the Mazlach of the Turks. v. Turneisserus. pp. 156, p. 120. Whether of the...(?) women drew her dead husband, i.e. to bury him in holy ground & burn her self with him.' (The whole of the entry is crossed out, and the second sentence is practically illegible.) Of some slight interest is another entry (p. 169): 'May 26. Sent Mr Toinard by Mr Romer...3 tortis shell knives & forks, 1 for him self, one for Mr Bernier & one for l'Abbé Fromentin. 3 s 6 d a peice.'

[2] The Mogul Emperor of Hindustan (1619–1707).   [3] *O.E.D.* 'Hindoo traders'.

[4] Claude Dumolinet, Librarian of the Abbey of Sainte Geneviève from 1673 to 1687.

[5] *O.E.D.* 'the jointing of one thing into another'.

very finely in releife the heads of all the French kings, in all 61.
A great collection of ancient & moderne medals & coins, and amongst
As   the rest the As Romanum which was a pound of brasse stamped with
Janus on one side & an ox on the other & Roma subscribd, semis or
Mony   6 ozs., triens or 4 ozs., dodrans 3 ozs., sextans or 2 ozs. & 1 oz.
Denarius   These were all of brasse. Of Silver there was a denarius where of
seven weighd 1 oz. & 'twas cald denarius because it was worth
Quinarius   10 Asses; Quinarius, the half of the other, markd with an V for
Sestertius   5 & Sestertius which was half the quinarius, markd S L L which
signified it to be worth Libras duas cum semisse. These were all
Congius   fine silver. There was also a Congius which, as the Father told us,
Sextarius   conteind 3 Paris pints, a Sextarius which was the 6th part of that,
etc. And amongst other moderne medalls this insolent one:
Cromwell's head on one side & on the reverse an olive tree with
lesse[1] about it, etc. with this inscription: Non deficient oliva.
3 Sept. 1658.[2] There were also medalls of all the Popes.

B. SUND. OCT. 10. Diner   1 – 0 – 0.

Versailes   TUESDAY OCT. 12. At Versailes saw all the water works of which to
me the Renommè seems the finest as it is the most chargeable,[3]
spouting water through her trumpet to a vast higth (though the
highest & bigest of all the jet d'eaux is that in the Fountain of
Dragons), & into the basin wherein shee stands, falls a nape of
water all round from a guilded trough, brest high, which is supplied by severall large jet d'eaux riseing about a foot high at fit
distances.

B. WED. OCT. 14. [sic] Lawndresse   3 – 12 – 0.
B.   Fuel   0 – 8 – 0.[4]
B.   Supper   0 – 4 – 0.

---

[1] I.e. smaller ones.

[2] This medal (along with one or two others which derive from it) was struck after the
death of Cromwell in September 1658 to insinuate that there was another Cromwell to
succeed him. The inscription means: 'They (i.e. the people) shall not lack an olive-tree.'
(Cf. Edward Hawkins, *Medallic Illustrations of the History of Great Britain and Ireland
to the Reign of George II* (London, 1885), 2 vols., I, 433–5).

[3] I.e. 'costly, expensive'.

[4] Here occurs a note on tooth-ache, followed by the name of 'Mr. Scawen'. In
a letter to Mapletoft of 19 Oct. 1672 Locke, who had just returned from his first visit
to Paris asked for his regards to be given to 'my brother Scawen'. Nothing else seems
to be known of him.

TUESD. OCT. 19. Paid Mr. de Launy for my Lodging   £28 – 15. B.
For removeing my things   0 – 12.[1]
⅔ aulne of Point d'Espagne   £20 – 0.

Point
d'Espagne

WED. OCT. 20. At Val de Grace the altar dressed in mourning & at   Val de Grace
one side the Chappell, on the left hand as one looks up to the
Altar, in a litle roome within the grates a herse dressed up &
a solemn aniversary masse said for the soule of the late Queen
Mother of France, foundresse of that monastery,[2] at which
Monsieur & Madame were present.

THURD. OCT. 21. At the Mint at Paris. My Guiny weighd just   Guiny
2 gros 13 gr. & was valued at £13 – 7s.   Weights

                  8 gros make   1 oz.
                  8 oz. . . . . . .   1 marc.
                  2 marcs . . .   1 livre.
                  24 deneirs . .   1 oz.
                  24 gr. . . . .   1 deneir.

The finesse of gold they count by carats, where of 24 make fine gold.   Mony
The gold of England, France & Espagne they say is of the same
finesse, i.e. 21$\frac{26}{32}$ carats.
   The finesse of their silver they count by deneirs, calling perfect
fine silver of 12 deneirs. . . .[3]

SUND. OCT. 24. We saw the Palais Mazarin,[4] an house very well   Pallais
furnishd with pictures, statues & cabinets in great plenty & very   Mazarin
fine, & the roofs of the rooms extreme richly painted & guilded.
Amongst the pictures there we saw that of old Par who, as the   Par
inscription of it says, was

        borne   anno 1483
        died an. 1635
soe that he lived years 0148.[5]

---

[1] In Locke's first note-book (p. 140) there is the following entry: 'Nostre Dame.
Removed thither Monday 18 Oct. 1677.'
[2] Anne of Austria, the Queen Mother and former Regent, died in 1666.
[3] There follows a long list of weights of various coins, English, French and Spanish.
An entry in the first note-book (p. 40) reads: 'La Montagne taken into service
21 Oct. 1677 at 28 escus & a livery coat per annum. Turnd away 29 Dec.'
[4] Now part of the Bibliothèque Nationale.
[5] The figures are those given in the MS., but the arithmetic is peculiar.

Pes philo- **MUND. OCT. 25.** Mr. Butterfeild brought me home my rule.
sophicus

V the universall foot.
P pes parisiensis.
D...of Denmark.
L of Leyden.
E of England.
P.R. Palma Romana.

Gard de   At the Gard de Meubles at the Louvre we saw aboundance of
Meubles   riches, both in Agots, gold & silver vessels. Amongst others there
were 2 frames of looking glasses newly made, each whereof weighd
in silver 2,400 marck, each marck soe wrought costing the King
52£. There were also candlestick[s] much weightyer then these,
& beds exceeding rich in imbrodery, amongst which one which
was begun by Francis 1st & which Cardinal Richeleiue got finishd
in his time & presented the King, which cost 200,000 escus. The
way of keepeing these beds is very fine, they being hung all upon
a kinde of turning jibbets, 5 or 6 of a side, in a presse where the
imbroiderd curtins hang at length & bredth. The presse is about
8 steps long & of an heigth proportionable, & these jibbets turne in
one after an other on each side alternatively, they being set one
within an other not in a parallell line to the side of the presse, but
in a peice of wood both above & below that is diagonall to the square
of the presse. Of these presses there were severall in one roome.

Versailes **TUESD. 26 OCT.** At Versailes The water works at the Menagery
where litle jet d'eaux throwing water in very small streames through
pin holes makes a perfect rain all over the court.

C.B.   Mr. Banks receivd yesterday upon credit of Madame Herinx
£1324 for 100 ll. sterling to be paid in England at double usance
which was 54¾ pence English for an escu French. If the bills had
been to be paid at 8 days' sight, we should have had it at 54⅛ which
is ½ per cent. more. The reason of the exchange being soe high on
the French sid[e] at this time was the great need of mony they had
at this time in England, either for the East India sales or some other
occasions.

Exchange   In the businesse of Exchange between Paris & London that side
that first pays the mony upon credit takes the exchange about

2 per cent. higher then the other, & soe make their profit upon
credit.

SUNDAY OCT. 31.[1] Sent to Mr. Stringer by Mr. Charas for my   Books
Lord S[haftesbury]:

> Methode pour commencer les humanites p. le Fevre.
> 12⁰, Saumur, 1672.
> Examen d'enseigner la Latin etc.   − 0 − 15[2]

TUESD. NOV. 2. At Ruell 2 leagues from Paris, a fine cascade,   Ruell
a triumphant arch in perspective so natural that they say birds have
mistaken the painting of the gate for a passage & flown against it.
'Tis certainly very apt to deceive the sight of one who comes in
view of it at a fit distance unawares. The garden is large &, like
others here, consists principally of woods & walks. The wood in it
is all beech & the ground unequall. The armes shews the house to
be built by Cardinal Richleiue in which family it is still.[3]

WED. NOV. 3. Supper   6 − 0.   B.

THURD. NOV. 4. *The Duke of Hanover hath* 50,000 crowns *a month*   Hanover
for his neutrality.[4]

SAT. NOV. 6. Play   3 − 0.[5]   B.

MOND. NOV. 8. There is a sort of down to be got in Norway a pound   Ederdons
whereof put between two Sarcenets[6] is enough to make a coverlet,

---

[1] The entry for 30 Oct. consists entirely of a long document in French (pp. 305-15)
entitled 'Manifeste du Duc de Villa Hermosa'. The Duke of Villahermosa was Governor
of Flanders and commanded the Spanish troops on that front.

[2] In his letter of 16 Aug. (o.s.) (Christie, II, 248), after asking Locke to send certain
maps to Shaftesbury (cf. entry for 30 Sept.), Stringer went on: 'Likewise he desires you
will inquire and let him know what books the Dauphin was first initiated in to learn
Latin. He apprehends there are some books, both French and Latin, either *Janua
Linguarums* or Colloquies, and also he desires to know what grammars; this he conceives
may be best learnt from those two printers that printed his books' [i.e. the editions of
Classical texts *ad usum Delphini*]. Shaftesbury's interest in the question was due to his
preoccupation with the education of his grandson, the philosopher, then a boy of six.
(Cf. entry for 6 July 1678.)

[3] The Château of Rueil was destroyed during the Revolution. On the triumphal arch
see Piganiol de La Force (II, 264): 'La perspective est des plus belles, et le ciel y est
peint avec des couleurs si naturelles qu'on assure qu'il y a eu plusieurs oiseaux qui s'y
sont trompés et qui, croyant voler en plein air, s'y sont tués ou cassé le bec.'

[4] Presumably Johann Friedrich, Duke of Brunswick-Lüneburg (Hanover), a pen-
sionary of Louis XIV.

[5] Nothing at the Théâtre Guénégaud on this date.

[6] *O.E.D.* 'fine, soft silk material now used chiefly for linings'.

which is very light & very warme & may be caried in a very litle roome. It costs 12 or 15 £ Tournoys per lb. They call it Ederdons. Mr. Justell.[1]

Bellonius   Bellonius,[2] says Mr. Justell, gives a good account of Turkie & espetially takes notice of the conveniencys of life.

Sir Thomas Banes[3] way of refuteing Ricaut is admirable according to what Monsieur   [4] says of it.

B. THURD. NOV. 11. Play   3 – 0.[5]

SAT. NOV. 13. S. *close, warm; all the fore part of the week* N., *very cold and very hard frost.*

Taxes   TUESD. NOV. 16. *They who have* terres nobles *may, if they have* 2 *or* 3 terres, *i.e., as I suppose,* manners, exempt *any one of them while they keep it in their hand from paying tax, but the rest must pay.*

A rear band   *The King having this present war raisd the* arrear band,[6] *took*[7] occasion *to* exempt *all that would for* 100 crowns apeice, *which* stands establishd *for all that think not fit to go to war* hereafter in *any such* occasion.

Soldiers   A gent. *that goes to war, while in* service, *cannot be sued, but a* commoner may.

Febris   Monday night goeing to see Mr. Herbert I found him in bed a sleep & in a litle sweat with a feaverish pulse he had taken the Saturday before. . . .[8]

---

[1] After this follows a dissertation in French on verdigris (pp. 321–36).

[2] Pierre Belon (*c.* 1517–64), whose *Observations de plusieurs singularités*...appeared in 1553.

[3] Sir Thomas Baines (1622–80) accompanied his friend, Sir John Finch, to Constantinople where he died. Sir Paul Ricaut (1628–1700) was the author of *The Present State of the Ottoman Empire* (1668). I can find no trace of a printed refutation of Ricaut by Baines.

[4] Left blank in MS.

[5] Nothing at the Théâtre Guénégaud.

[6] The *arrière-ban*, the summoning of those nobles who did not regularly serve in the army, had last been tried out in 1674 and was such a fiasco that in the following year the King demanded a money payment in its place, in order to pay for the raising of regular troops.

[7] MS. has *take*.

[8] An account of the progress of his illness (in Latin) takes up most of the entries from 17 to 25 November.

MUND. NOV. 22. Sir Jo: Heyward of the life & reigne of K. Edw.   Heyward
& the beginning of Q. Eliz: 12º, London, 1636. pp. 494. Q. what
he means about abaseing the mony, p. 280? Mr. Briot.[1]

FRID. NOV. 26. Charles, Duke of Cambridg, borne Wednesday
7/17 Nov. 1677, hora 10 p.m.[2]

MOND. 29 NOV. Mr. Banks received 100 ll. sterling at the rate of   C.B.
54½ d.[3] for 1 crown Tournoy which amounted to £1321 – 2 – 0
Tournoy & gave a bill home for 100 ll. sterling, this being taken up
upon credit.

Received of Sir J. Banks *by hands of his son for my winter* conveniencys £400 – 0 – 0.

Of the Musquetairs there are 500 in two companys, of each of   Musquetairs
which the King is captaine. Their ordinary pay is 40 s. per diem
whereof 5 is defalced[4] for coats etc. They wear red coats, ride on
horse back, cary phusees, fight on foot & are most gentlemen.

The exchange about a month since for mony taken up upon   Exchange
credit here was 54⅜ pence for 1 escu.

TUESDAY NOV. 30. Play   03 – 0 – 0.[5]   B.

THURSD. DEC. 2. About 6 or 7 a clock I was cald to my Lady   Countesse of
Ambassadrice whom I found crying out in one of her fits....[6]   Northumberland's Case

---

[1] Pierre Briot, who translated various English works, including Ricaut's *Present State
of the Ottoman Empire*. The Journal supplies the date of his death, apparently unknown
up to the present, for after giving an account of Briot's ailments and the treatment he
followed, Locke added later between the lines: 'Mr. Briot died the beginning of the
following winter of an apoplexy.' (In a letter of 21 Nov. 1678, MS. Locke, c. 21,
ff. 7–8, Thoynard informed Locke of Briot's sudden death.) Locke asked Stringer to
procure certain books for Briot (cf. the latter's letter of 5 Oct. 1677: MS. Locke, c. 19,
ff. 137–8).
Under the same date in the Journal there is also an entry concerning the weight and
value of various coins, French and English, associated with Briot's name.

[2] Charles Stuart, son of James, Duke of York, and his second wife. The child died
when five weeks old.

[3] MS. has '54½ s.' which makes nonsense.

[4] *O.E.D.* gives the word as *defalk* (=*defalcate*).

[5] The Théâtre Guénégaud gave Pradon's *Tamerlan* and Molière's *L'Amour médecin*.

[6] The treatment of this patient apparently absorbed all Locke's attention from this
date until 16 December, as every entry in that period is concerned with the case.
There are further entries on the subject on 17 and 20 December, and others in January.
(Details of the case are also given in letters to Dr Mapletoft for the same period, published
in the *European Magazine*, vol. xv.)
Elizabeth Wriothesley (1646–90) was the daughter of the Earl of Southampton. In

B. FRID. DEC. 17. Received of Sir J. Banks by the hands of Messrs Moreau & Dusault 444 escus & 26s., it being in exchange for 100ll. sterling.

Velvet MOND. DEC. 20.   3⅞ Aulns of Velvet at 21   £81 – 7 – 0
Satin   4 Aulnes of Satin at 8   32 – 0 – 0
                                                                                      ‾‾‾‾‾‾‾‾‾‾‾‾‾
                                                                                      113 – 7 – 0

B. TUESD. DEC. 21. Opera   5 – 10 – 0.[1]

1678[2]

B. WED. JAN. 5. Supper   5 – 10 – 0.[3]

Pay MOND. 17 JAN. A Captain of English foot 2 Escus, of French 1s. for each soldier he hath in his company. An English foot soldier in winter quarter 7s. 6d., a French 5s., a French Leiutenant of foot 7s., an horseman 9s.

1662 she married Jocelyn Percy, 11th Earl of Northumberland, who died in 1670. Three years later she married again, this time Ralph Montagu (later Duke of Montagu) who was several times sent as Ambassador to Paris. This particular mission lasted from September 1676 until his recall in July 1678. Locke appears to have known the Countess in 1672 when he paid his first visit to France.

The Lovelace Collection contains letters from Mapletoft as well as one from Sydenham, and the opinion of three London doctors, all concerning her case. There is also a note from Mrs Blomer (MS. Locke, c. 4, f. 12) summoning Locke to the Embassy: it is wrongly dated in his handwriting '3 Dec. 78'.

[1] On 25 December there is an entry on tooth-ache to which the name of Hubin is appended. The latter, whose name appears several times in the Journal after this date and also in Locke's correspondence, is described by Lister as an eye-maker. He was presumably the author of *Machines nouvellement exécutées et en partie inventées par le sieur Hubin* (Paris, 1673), a copy of which Locke possessed (see *The Library*).

The volume concludes with an essay (pp. 391–401) entitled: 'Memoire ou instruction des termes usites au Royaume de France en ce qui regarde le fait des monnoyes et prix du marc d'or et d'argent, p. Mr. Briot.'

[2] Bound in with this volume of the Journal is an almanac entitled *Ephemeris ou Almanach historial pour l'an de grâce mil six cens septante-huict...avec l'Almanach du Palais*, A Troyes et se vendent A Paris chez la V. Nicolas Oudot, rüe vieille Bouclerie.

[3] Most of the entries for this month consist of notes on reading and philosophical dissertations. In addition there are: (1) a note on Turkish coins, followed by the name of 'Mr. Robinson' (possibly John Robinson, 1650–1723, who after a diplomatic career became Bishop of London. He was made a fellow of Oriel in 1675 and was given leave by the college to go abroad in 1677). (2) A question of Locke's own on the medicinal use of mercury. (3) On 30 January he began to treat 'Mr. Robinson' for an illness and there are a large number of entries on his case in the following weeks.

FRID. 21 JAN. Amianus Marcelinus for D. Thomas   10 – 0 – 0.[1]   D. Thomas

WED. 26 JAN. Midle walk 50 steps broad, side walke 19 steps broad.   Walk
This is a walke newly set by the Invalids.
Play and supper   4 – 10 – 0.[2]   B.

SAT. 29 JAN.   Leiden foot 948.   Measures
                Paris foot 980.
                Denmarke foot 955.
                English foot 920.
                Roman palme 672.

A pendulum of seconds being divided into 3 equall parts, each   Pendule
of them makes that which may be cald the philosophicall or universall foote, the 10th part of which foot I call an inch, the 10th
part of that inch a line, & the 10th part of a line a gry: soe that the
English foot is 9 inches 2 lines 0 grys of the philosophicall foot &
consequently the English inch 7 lines & $6\frac{2}{3}$ grys.[3]

TUESD. 1 FEB. I saw[4] the review of the Gards du Corps, the   Revieu
Musquetaires & the Grenadiers in the Plaine de Duile[5] neare St.
Germains. The Gards du Corps were 11 or 12 squadrons & might
be about 12 or 14 hundred men, all lusty, well horsed & well clad,
all in blew, new & alike[6] even to their hats and gloves, armed with
pistols, carebins & long back swords with well garded hilts. The
Musquetaires were 4 squadrons, about 400 men, clad all alike in
red coats, but their clokes blew, but with distinction from those of
the Gards du Corps, but half (i.e. all one company) horsed on black
horses & half on grey, their coats & belts laced, the grey with gold
galoon & the black with gold & silver, their hats & gloves to all the
same, even to the ribbans on their hats & crevats. At least, I am
sure the Gards du Corps were soe, some squadrons haveing all

---

[1] David Thomas had asked him to procure this work for him in a letter of 21 July 1677
(MS. Locke, c. 20, ff. 11–12).
[2] Nothing at the Théâtre Guénégaud, but quite possibly a performance of Thomas
Corneille's tragedy, *Le Comte d'Essex*, which was first given at the Hôtel de Bourgogne
on 7 January and had a successful run.
[3] See the *Essay on the Human Understanding*, Book IV, chap. x, para. 10.
[4] MS. has *say*.   [5] Plaine d'Ouilles.
[6] Locke's interest in the dress of the troops of the Royal Household is no doubt due
to the fact that uniforms were only just coming in. They had been adopted first for these
troops, and the rest of the army gradually followed suit.

yellow ribbans & others all skie. The Grenadiers were but one squadron of the same size neare with the others, but their clothes different, their coats being red, but with loops distinguished from the Musquetars, & soe their blew clokes too, but that which did most soe, was an odde fashon cap that was the cover of their heads, made of red cloth turnd up with fur, the fashon, when on, something like a Mountro,[1] but standing out much more before & behinde, & standing up with a peake upon top [sic] of their heads which turnd backwards. These caps both soldiers & commanders all wore & which seemd an uniformity. More particulars. They all wore great wiskers & I think they were all black, whether to make them look the more terrible, I know not. Their arms were pistols, carebines & short, broad hangers & pouches, & other things fit for the cariage & management of their granados.

The King[2] came to take a view of these troops between 11 & 12, which he did soe narrowly that he made them, squadron after squadron, march in file, man after man, just before him, & made the number in each squadron, as they passed, be counted, takeing in the meane time a strict survey of their horses & them. The King, when he light out of his coach, had a hat laced about the edg with gold lace & a white feather. After a while he had been on horseback, it begining to rain, he changed it for a plaine hat that [had] only a black ribbon about it & was, I think, by the Audace a Cordebec.[3] The Queen towards the latter end came in a coach & 8 horses. The King led her along the head of all these squadrons, they being drawn up all in a line 3 deepe with litle intervals between each squadron. At going off the feild, which was about 3 in the afternoon, the Grenadiers were made exercise before him, which was to face about, not as horse usually doe, fetching a compasse[4] & the same ranke always keeping the van, but as foot, by turning their faces & making the van the rere, which they did very readily, though on horseback, by wheeleing every 4 men of the same rank

---

[1] *O.E.D. Montero*: 'A Spanish hunter's cap, having a spherical crown and a flap capable of being drawn over the ears.'

[2] Louis's love of such occasions earned him the nickname of 'le roi des revues' (Saint-Simon).

[3] Caudebec was famous for the manufacture of hats.

[4] *O.E.D.* 'to take a circular or circuitous course'.

togeather, by which meanes they, without any disorder or confusion, faced about & were immediately in ranke again. When this
was don, the King went alone into his chariot, takeing his best
hat again, & soe returnd. There were at this muster 2 Marshals
of France, viz. Luxembourg[1] et Lorge,[2] each of them Captain of
a company of Gards du Corps, at the head of which each of them
took his place & saluted the King as he returnd after his first time,
haveing passed all along the front of all these squadrons.

Mr. Stringer Cr. by a knife bought by my order & presented to   Stringer
Mr. Charas, vid. his letter 20 Dec. 1677 £1 – 2 – o.

Lawndresse   7 – 9 – o.

MOND. 7 FEB. King of France passed through Paris to go to   .[3]   King
He was in the Queen's coach with 8 horses. In the coach with
the Queen Madam Montespan, & before the coach marchd the
Musquetaires, the 2 companys about 260 men, & behinde the
coach, which was alone, the Gards du Corps, not an hundred, all
their swords drawn.

TUESD. 8 FEB. Lord Blany[4] 60 *yards at* 20 *jumps and will* 155 *yards at*   Jumping
60 *jumps.*

THURSD. 10 FEB. The two theorems in Euclid that, applied to   Algebra
Algebra, make it soe much shorter are 28th of 2d & 17th of the 6th.

Water sealed up in a glasse tube out of which the aire is drawn,   Water in
being shaked, strikes against the end of the tube & gives a knock   vacuo
as if it were a solid body, but if it be let stand still a while, the first
time you shake it, it makes noe more noise then that wherein the
aire is included. This I tried at Mr. Hubin's in the Rue St. Martin
over against the end of the Rue aux Ours, in glasses about 8 or 9 or
so inches long & about an inch diameter. The cause he assigned was

---

[1] François-Henri de Montmorency, Duc de Luxembourg (1628–95), appointed in
1673 one of the Captains of the Gardes du Corps and, in 1675, *Maréchal de France*. He
was soon to be implicated in the *Affaire des Poisons*.

[2] Guy de Durfort, Duc de Lorges (1630–1702), a nephew of Turenne, was appointed
to this post and made a *Maréchal de France* in 1676.

[3] Left blank in MS. The King's ultimate destination was secret. He travelled first
to Metz, and then moved rapidly north to besiege Ghent which was captured on
9 March.

[4] Henry Vincent, Lord Blaney, a zealous partisan of William III. He died in 1689.

the parts of the liquor turnd into aire & upon shakeing returnd into the liquor again. Q. whether this will doe in all liquors & in longer tubes (they were above half full) & in all weathers alike? This was a moderate day for this time of yeare.

Mapletoft   Paid Dr. Blomer[1] for Dr. Mapletoft's[2] Tully of Stephen's edition

20 – 0 – 0.

And for my Twoilet   07 – 0 – 0.

C.B.   TUESDAY 15 FEB.   Mr. Banks receivd upon a letter of credit £1297 – 5 – 6 for 100 ll. sterling, i.e. at the rate of 55½ d. English for a crown French, of Mme. Herinx.

FRID. 18 FEB.   The danceing master broke on the wheele.[3] Chamber
B.   room   3 – 0 – 0.

Stringer   SAT. MAR. 12.[4]   Sent Mr. Stringer a bill drawn on Mr. John Cholmeley at the Golden Anker over against St. Dunstan's Church

by Mr. Herbert for 18 – 15 – 0. v. May 2. Sent also by Mr. Herbert, directed to Mr. Hoskins, Dassie's Architecture navale[5] for my Lord Shaftesbury   80 s.

E[arl of]   Sent also by Mr. Herbert, directed to Mr. Hoskins, 383 cuts at
Shaftesbury   2½ a peice for Mr. Tyrrell[6]   47 – 0 – 0. which my Lord Shaftesbury had.

And in the same pacquet 12 cuts of Turkish habits for Mr. Anthony.[7]

---

[1] Thomas Blomer, M.A. (Cambridge, 1660), was at Westminster School with Locke. He became chaplain to the Earl of Northumberland; and his wife (who appears to have been Locke's cousin) was in attendance on the Countess.

[2] John Mapletoft (1631–1721), took his M.D. at Cambridge in 1669. He was also at one time attached to the household of the Earl and Countess of Northumberland. In 1683 he was ordained and held various livings. He had asked Locke to get him this edition in a letter of 25 July 1677 (MS. Locke, c. 15, ff. 20–1).

[3] No doubt a well-known criminal case, but I have been unable to trace the details. Locke and his pupil evidently shared the contemporary taste for witnessing public executions.

[4] On 7 March Locke acquired a new patient, a Mrs Sandys, whose illness occupies much space in the Journal for the next few weeks.

[5] Paris, 1677.

[6] James Tyrrell (1642–1718), historian and political writer, formed at Oxford a friendship with Locke which lasted down to the latter's death. Both men wrote a refutation of Filmer's *Patriarcha*.

[7] Anthony Ashley Cooper, third Earl of Shaftesbury (1671–1713), the philosopher. After his return to England in 1679 Locke superintended for a time the child's education.

Paid for a Plutarch's Works in 2 vol. for Dr. Mapletoft   Mapletoft
                        £30 – 0 – 0.
        Supper   5 – 10 – 0.   B.

TUESDAY MAR. 22. At St. Germans Mademoiselle, the Grand Versailes
Dutchesse of Tuscany,[1] Madame de Guise,[2] Madame de Bouillon[3]
& Madame   [4] at dinner with the Dauphin. The company &
attendance there but litle.
            Expences there   3 – 4 – 0.   B.

WED. MAR. 30. This day I saw the water drinker who drank at once,
as fast as he could pour them in, 16 or 17 ordinary glasses of warme
water & then spouted them up again & this he did 5 or 6 times
whilst we were there, i.e. lesse then ½ hour. The last time he drank
25 & says he could do 40 or 50. He shews this 2 or 3 times a day
& oftener if one will. He has used this this 40 years & is, as he says,
very healthy, has not been sick these 18 years, has a good stomach,
but eats not but at nights when he has donne his drinkeing, & then
eats what other people doe. When any thing makes him sick in his
stomach, he voluntarily spews it up as he does the water, & then
washes his stomach with warm water & is well.

THURSD. MAR. 31. To die red haire browne: Dans une livre de Capillus rufus
poudre ordinaire un quartron de mine de plomb et un once de
Cray de Brianson.[5] Cela donne la couleur brune a la poudre
blanche. Mr. Lambert, Rue d'arbre sec.

TUESDAY APR. 5. At the Arsenall, as they told us, always armes for Arsenal
100,000 men, though there seemd not half soe many. They now
make their musquets 3 foot 10 inches longe in the barrell & of Musquets
18 bullets to the pound. They are well wrought & are made at
St. Etien in Forez & deliverd here at the Arsenal for £8 – 10 – 0
a peice. The carbines of the gardes are scrued.

---

[1] Marguerite Louise d'Orléans (1645–1721), the stepsister of Mademoiselle, both
being daughters of Gaston d'Orléans. She married the Grand Duke of Tuscany in 1661,
but in 1675 she left her husband and children and returned to France.
    [2] Elisabeth d'Orléans (1646–96), a sister of Marguerite Louise, married in 1667 the
last Duc de Guise.
    [3] Marie Anne Mancini (1650–1714), a niece of Mazarin, married the Duc de Bouillon
in 1662. She was implicated shortly after this in the *Affaire des Poisons*.
    [4] Left blank in MS.   [5] I.e. *craie de Briançon*.

C.B. Mr. Banks received upon credit of Mme. Herinx £1250, the
Exchange exchange runing at 58 d. sterling for 1 crown French, by which
account £1241 Tournois make 100 ll. Sterling.

Revenue TUESDAY 12 APR.   Revenue
                            Grose ferme   40 m.
                            Taile   40 m.
                          Depense.
                            de la Reine   2 m.
                            du Monsieur   2 m.
                            du Dauphin   1 m.
                            de la guerre 50 m.
                            de la marine 10 m.[1]

Drabicius TUESD. APR. 19.[2] Drabicius[3] *put to death at Presburg in* 1669 *for his*
Prophesie *book,* Lux in tenebris, *writ many years before in* Bohemian *and trans-*
lated into Latin by Comenius. *He there foretells the conquest and*
quitting of Holland; *that* Holland *would make peace with France,*
assist it and be happy; that the King of France would be King of the
Romans and Spain and would have in his possession all the riches of the
House of Austria and of the other who thinks himself a greater
monarch,[4] except Bohemia *and* Silesia *which his allies would have;*
that the Emperor, by the many wives he should have, would leave no
issue male and would be the last Emperor made by the Electors; that
to do all this, the King of France must make an alliance with Pologne,
Suede, Danemark, Brandenbourg, Saxe, Palatin, Brunswick,
Lunebourg & Holstein.

---

[1] Clamageran (vol. II) gives the total of all taxes farmed out as 60,457,000 l. and of the
Taille as 40,421,000 l. for 1677. The *Cinq Grosses Fermes* seem to have produced about
20,000,000 l. He gives the total expenditure on Army and Navy as 83,350,000 l.

[2] On this date there are notes on an operation for the stone performed by Jérôme
Collot, a member of a distinguished family of French surgeons who specialized in this
operation from the sixteenth to the early eighteenth century.

[3] Nicolas Drabik (or Drabitius), born in 1597 in Moravia, was executed in 1671
(not 1669) for his prophecies of the downfall of the House of Austria. His *Lux in
Tenebris*, in the Latin version produced by Comenius, appeared in 1657. The Lovelace
Collection contains a 13½ page letter in French, unsigned and not in Locke's hand,
addressed to Louis XIV, which gives an account of the prophecies of Drabicius and
appeals to him to direct his policy in accordance with them. It is endorsed by Locke
'Drabicius, 25 Apr. 1678'.

[4] The MS. mentioned in the above note has: 'Que V. Mté doit estre Roy des Romains
et Roy d'Espagne et qu'elle aura en sa possession toutes les richesses de la Maison
d'Autriche et d'un autre qui s'estime plus grand monarque....'

A Muy conteins 1400 pints of Paris, & of wine pays entry there £20.

Muy
Taxes

THURD. APR. 21. Mr. Toinard[1] sheud me his Harmony of the Evangelists printed in a new method which I thinke may be very usefull.

Guns also of severall fashons, all to charge in the breech, one about carbine bore, 16½ long in the barrell, that would carry point blank 82 toise. He says when the barrell is thick, it will carry farther, truer & not recoile. By this contrivance of chargeing in the breetch which is by puting in, as it were, a litle, false gun which is chargd before hand, he will discharge 4 times for one.

Guns

The proportion of chargeing any gun is this. Take the bullet that is just of the bore & weigh it against its weight of shot, which they call in France plumb de seize where of 340 by take weigh 1 oz. pharma: de Paris. A thimble that will hold just that shot is the charge of your gun of good powder, supposeing the barrell to be of 4 foot long. If your barrell be 5 foot, add ⅕ to the charge of pouder. If your barrell be 3 foot, deminish your charge of pouder ¼ & soe in proportion, addeing or takeing away from your charge of pouder proportionably as you make your barrell longer or shorter then 4 foot.

Charge

To make your bullets well, you must make a litle pin hole by the side of the great one in your mold where you power in your lead, to let out the aire as the lead runs in, & soe your bullets will be without holes or blebs.

Bullet
moulds

To polish the inside of your mold well when it is made, take led & cast a bullet in it, then fasten a peice of iron in the bullet soe cast & with this leaden bullet & emery polish the inside of your mold. Hactenus Mr. Toynard.

---

[1] Nicolas Thoynard (1629–1706) with whom Locke later kept up a long correspondence only begins to appear in the Journal at this point. He was born at Orleans, and came to Paris in 1652 to pursue his scholarly interests. He was a member of the circle of the Dupuy brothers. He travelled fairly widely—to Spain, Portugal, Holland and England in turn—and then settled in Paris where he pursued his biblical researches and at the same time showed an interest in scientific and technical problems. He was very keen on guns, as we shall see. His *Evangeliorum harmonia graeco-latina* appeared post-humously in 1707, but as early as 1669 he had printed some parts of it which he presented to his friends. Locke was one of those who received a copy.

Fermentation   At his chamber I saw by chance an experiment which confirmed me in an opinion I have had a long time, viz. that in fermentation new air is generated. He produced a large bottle of Muscat or Jenetine wine of Orleance, stopd with a glasse stopper. The wine was cleare when he set it on the table, but as soon as he had drawn out the stople,[1] there rose such a multitude of litle bubles that they sweld the wine above the mouth of the bottle & made it run over, & also raised the lee[2] with them soe that the wine grew thick & troubled. When the violent ebullition was a litle abated, the wine sank again, but there still continued to rise a great number of those litle bubles very fast. I then stopd the botle again & the bubles continued still to rise as before, but lessend by degrees in number & quicknesse of motion. After the bottle[3] had stood thus for some time well stopd, & the litle bubles had very much ceased riseing, I opend it again & presently upon opening they rose thicke again, which comes from

Aer   this that the aer which was included & disseminated in the liquor, had liberty to expand it self & soe to come visible &, being much lighter then the liquor, to mount with great quicknesse.

Q. Whether this be aer new generated or whether the springy particles of aer have,[4] in the fruits out of which these fermenting liquors are drawn, by the artifice of nature been pressed close togeather & there by other particles fastend & held soe, & whether fermentation does not loose these bonds & give them liberty to expand themselves again? J.L.

Take a botle of beare as soone as it begins to worke in the kyve,[5] or of mustum,[6] tie a bladder on to the mouth. Q. how much new aer it will produce? Q. also whether this has the qualitys of common aer?

Taxes SAT. APR. 23. Taile 1678 44 millions.[7]

Guns   Take old German hors shoes & of these make the barrell of a gun. To make a good one, German hors shoes are best because the iron is soft. If you have not them, take a bar of the best Iron you can, cut it all the length & beat it into a plate of a convenient breadth

---

[1] *O.E.D.* 'stopper'.   [2] *O.E.D.* 'sediment of wine'.
[3] MS. has *bottled*.   [4] *have* is repeated after *are drawn* in MS.
[5] *O.E.D.* *kive* or *keeve*: 'vat, tun'.   [6] Latin for 'must, new or unfermented wine'.
[7] Clamageran gives the figure of 40,480,000l.

& thicknesse; then take another of the same & beat it into a plate
as the former. Cut this into peices of a fit length to laye crosse the
other, soe that the lines that went the length of the iron when it was
in the bar, may in those litle peices lie crosse to the lines that goe
the length of the plate above mentiond. Then of an other length of
the bar make an other plate & lay along upon the other crosse peices.
Heat & incorporate all these togeather & make thereof one solid
peice of Iron to make the barrell, & in forgeing your barrell make
the caliver or bore as litle as you can, the reason whereof is 1°
because that, by takeing away a great part of the inside of the Iron
by boreing it to the bignesse you desire, you take away the flaw
that always remains in the inside of the barrell in forgeing, the
inside of the lips of the plate out of which you forge your barrell
never shuting soe well or soe firmly as that of the outside; though to
make them shut & close the better, it would doe well to file them
even before you turne the plate into a tube to forme the barrell.
2° because by boreing away a great deale of the inside you leave
very litle or noe thing of the inner plate whose veine run [sic] the
length of the barrell, for it is to be remarked that in all bars of Iron,
as in wood, the veines run according to the length &, as in wood,
Iron is much more apt to split that way then crosse, & in the barrells
of the guns the cracks that goe along the barrell are much more
dangerous & like to flie then those crosse, the stresse in dischargeing
being streching the barrell that way, & therefor 'tis to strengthen
the barrell & make it lesse apt to split the long way that these plates
are put in the midle with the grain crosse that soe they may hold the
faster, the fibres or veyns of the Iron being by that means turnd
round the barrell & not runing the long way, which makes the
barrell less apt to split.

One ought also to forge the barrell soe that, it being neare true
from the hammer, the file may take away very litle of the outside,
because the joynt or seame which, in turneing the plate into a tube,
runs all a long the barrell, is much better closed & shut in the
outside then in the inside of the barrell.

A thick barrell, though it be heavyer then a thin one, yet it shoots
much farther & truer then a thin one, & recoils not at all. Hactenus
Mr. Toinard.

Iron   Capon's grease rubd on Iron keeps it from rusting. He supposes it may doe better if it be purified in MB.[1]

Bras   Lead rubd on brasse instruments keeps them from rust or cankering. ib.

Memoranda his guns that are chargd at the breech.

Stringer   MUND. MAY 2. Mr. Stringer in his letter of 15 April 1678 tells me he has received of Mr. Cholmeley the 18 – 15 – 0 which I returned to him by a bill of Mr. Herbert's. v. March 12.

Window   MUND. MAY 9. Memo. The two slideing Iron bars that come downe in the insid of the wooden shuts[2] to fasten them in the night at Mr. Brisban's. The way is this. A bar of Iron standing clear from the wall goes crosse at the top of the window. Upon these are hung two slideing bars which in the day time hang downe behinde the shuts in the corners, on each side one, but in the night when the wooden shuts are closed, they are slid out & soe hang downe on the midle of each of the shuts & are fastend below by a bolt into a staple on purpose & also into the crosse barre of the window, where there is a forke of Iron just fit to receive one of them, & into that, by a pin runing crosse from one to an other side of the forke through loops made in each end on purpose, they are pind in.

Coach   In the yard of the King's Library in a coach house was an hanging cover of canvas made for the coach that stood in there, much like the tester[3] & curtains of a bed, a very good way to keep off dust.

Bisieule   We saw also Mr. Bisieul's house[4] in the Veile rue du Temple where was an apartment of 7 or 8 rooms togeath[er], not very large, but the fine guilding, painting, inlaying & exquisite finishing the richest that ever I yet saw, the very frames of the window shutters being richly guilded & painted with excellent pictures in miniature, & every part coverd with rich treble guilding by an Italian Master & the floors of the alcoves very finely inlaid. We were told there

---

[1] The old chemical symbol for *Balneum Mariae* or *water-bath*.
[2] *O.E.D.* 'shutters'.
[3] *O.E.D.* 'canopy over a bed'.
[4] The Hôtel Amelot de Bisseuil, now No. 47, Rue vieille du Temple, was bought in 1638 by the Amelot family, and came in 1655 into the hands of Jean Baptiste Amelot, Vicomte de Bisseuil. It is now generally known as the *Hôtel des Ambassadeurs de Hollande*.

that it cost 1,000,000 £. I'm sure for soe much it is far the most costly that ever I saw any where. It was finishd thus about 17 years agon, & the goold & pictures very fresh yet, as if new don.

WED. MAY 11. Dr Mapletof [sic] Dr. for Xenophon's Works, Gr. Lat. fol. Paris, 1625.   £10 – 0 – 0.   Mapletoft

FRID. MAY 13. Exchange 56½ pence sterling for un escu Francois,   Exchange
i.e. Mr. Banks had chez Madam Herinx 1275.   C.B.
    Aune de Paris contient 3 pied 8 pous du Roi. This measure taken   Aune
chez Mr. Butterfeild upon a tradesman's aune.
    People of good condition serveing the sick in the Hostel de Dieu.[1]

SAT. MAY 14. Wild succory is good in Salads, but to take away the   Salade
bitterness of it, it must be soaked 3 or 4 howers before in faire
water. The buds of Tragopogon or asparagi are also very good in
Salades, wholesome & diuretick. Mr. Frelin.
    Sir J. Chichley gave Mr. Hubin a note to pay him the 1300 livres   Hubin
he had of him some days before either in Paris or in London.

MUND. MAY 16. To my Laundresse   £6 – 0 – 0.   B.
    I saw to day at Mr. Fobert's[2] Academy a beast got between a bull   Jimar
& a mare. About the head, espetially the mouth, it has something
of mixture in the make between horse & bull, & just at the foretop
it had two litle hornes which one might easily feele with one's
finger. The taile also had a mixture of both species, & the teeth in
the lower jaw over reachd those of the upper. It was but litle, but
very hardy & laborious. They are never big. In Languedoc they
are often to be found & they call them Gimar.[3]
    The aune of Paris is precisely 3 pied 8 pous du Roy.   Aune

---

[1] For some considerable time both before and after this date the Journal is filled with medical notes, entitled 'Salivatio': perhaps a case which Locke was observing at the Hôtel-Dieu?
[2] Salomon de Foubert, *écuyer du Roi*, ran an *Académie*, i.e. an establishment in which young noblemen learned riding and other accomplishments. As he was a Protestant, his Academy was closed down in 1679 and he took refuge in England where he was naturalized in 1685. His son, Henri, became an aide-de-camp to William of Orange. The Academy was in the Faubourg Saint-Germain. On 9 June 1677 (MS. Locke, c. 24, ff. 20-1) Locke informed Sir John Banks that his son had decided not to 'put himself into an Academy', but that 'he rides in one of them'—presumably Foubert's.
[3] *Jumarts.*

$\frac{0}{0}$ $\frac{0}{0}$ cent, i.e. $\frac{0}{0}$. This marke stands for an hundred in merchants' books in France.

TUESDAY MAY 17. Till the beginning of this weeke the weather hath been wet, cold & winterly. Now it begins to be warme.

Versailes SAT. MAY 21. At Versailles in the garden at Trianon there was a coverd walk all of Orange trees & mirtles, but it was sunke above half its heigth below the plaine of the garden that borderd on it, which was, I suppose, contrivd that the whole walke might be the better coverd in the winter to preserve the trees from the injurys of that season. It was broad enough but for 2 persons a breast, & the higth of the arch or frame of the arbor proportionable, but it was not yet quite coverd with green.

In a roome on the right side of the garden as one enters, there was some reall china & some painted & all the sides of the rooms fild with drawers about 18 inches square & from 8 to 10 inches
Parfumeing deepe, each divided horizontally at equidistant spaces by small net worke of treble lute strings of which the meshes were too small for an orange flower to fall through. This is a way to perfume gloves or any thing else with orange flowers.

St. Clou I saw at St. Clou the jet deau which throws up the water 80 or 90 foot.

Seau SUND. MAY 22. We saw Mr. Colbert's gardens at Sau.[1] There are now makeing the best cascades, I phansy,[2] in France. There are 18 or 19 falls of water, each 17 steps a sunder, & empty them into a very large basin in the bottom. The house is but litle, but the gardens very large. We could not see the house.

Walk Here is a walke of great elmes set & have been transplanted
Elmes thither when their bodys were about a yard in girt.

Guns MUND. MAY 23. The reason why most barells cary not true, but scatter the shot, is because the bore is taper, i.e. wider at the mouth then in the midle, where commonly it is narrowest, & soe widens from thence to the britch & to the mouth, which is occasiond thus: that commonly in boareing the barrells, the boriers not being long

---

[1] See entry for 2 June 1677.
[2] O.E.D. gives this amongst other exotic spellings of *fancy*.

enough, they begin at one end & bore to the midle & then turn tother & bore to the midle, by which meanes the bore of the barell is thus ⊂==========⊃ viz. wider at both ends then in the midle, the reason where of is this, that the borier makes it always widest in that part which it passes over most, which is the end where it enters; & therefor in boreing of guns great care must be taken to enter the borier only at the britch, espetially the last, fine, polishing borier, which must be an exact, true square of steeles 6 or 8 inches long, the longer the better. By thus boreing the barell from the britch quite through, it will be taper in the bore from the britch to the mouth, which will make it carry the shot round togeather.[1]

THURSD. MAY 26. At the Garde de meubles noe increase that I found of silver vessells, but rather a diminution since I saw it in October last. That which looked freshest & newest were the 2 looking glasse frames I saw there before, which weigh each of them, as they say, 2,300 marke. Francis the First's bed of £800,000 was there still, & they told us of the silke & imbroiderd sailes & furniture & cordage for the Grand Luis,[2] which they say cost as much, but we saw in the presses only the standard, the rest being, as they said, rolled up among the tapistry. The presses were 10 paces long. *Garde de Meubles*

FRID. MAY 27. Sent to Dr. Blomer by Dr. Mapletoft's order Xenophon's works which cost me ll. 10, he haveing before Tully's & Plutarch's works according to Dr Mapletoft's directions.

Play   £3 – 0.[3]   B.

SAT. MAY 28. The Memoires de Sully are full of falsitys & self flattery, concluded by the company chez Mr. Justel (the same which Mr. Falayseau had before told me). Those of the Duc de Guise[4] a Romance, but those of Modena[5] concerning Naples good. ib. *Sully* *Guise Modena*

---

[1] Here (on 24 May) occurs a description of a case observed by Locke at the Charité, which is reproduced in a letter to Boyle of 6 Aug. (Boyle's *Works*, London, 1744, 5 vols., v, 569) and in the *Philosophical Transactions*, vol. XIX (1697), pp. 594–6.

[2] Cf. entries for 13–14 April 1676.

[3] The Théâtre Guénégaud gave Molière's *L'Étourdi*.

[4] *Les Mémoires de feu M. le Duc de Guise* (Paris, 1668).

[5] *Histoire des Révolutions de la ville et du royaume de Naples* (Paris, 1665–7), 3 vols.

Houses SUND. MAY 29. Il y a á Paris 22 belles maisons qu'on peut voire:

Luxembourg
l'Hostel de Guise
de Soissons, quoique vieux et beau [sic]
l'Hostel Salé
de la Baziniere
de la Ferte
de Grammont
de Mr. Colbert
Mr de la Vrilliere
de Mazarine
Mr de Lyonne
Mr de Bretonvilliers
de Mr Justin
de M. Lambert
des Chamont
de Lesdiguiers
de Conti
de Mrs de Lamoignon
de Jars
de Turenne
M. Amelot Bisieule
La Maison de Mr. de Boisfrane
de Vendosme
d'Espernon
de Longueville. Hactenus Mr. Justel.[1]

Stringer SAT. JUN. 4. Sent Sir John Chichley's bill for 9 – 13 – 4 sterling,
drawn on Mr. Charles Beaumont & payable to Mr. Stringer, to
Mr. Hoskins to be deliverd to Mr. Stringer.

Gravier Mr. Gravier hath writ a booke of the building, equipping &
sayleing of ships & all other things belonging to the sea, the most

---

[1] This list, in Justel's handwriting, is in the Lovelace Collection (MS. Locke, c. 12,
f. 56) and is preceded by (1) *Mémoire de ce qui merite d'estre veu à Paris* (ff. 47–53), and
(2) notes entitled *Commodites de France* (ff. 54–5). The first of these two documents also
contains a list of books recommended by Justel.

In the entries for 2 and 3 June there is an account of a fever which 'Mr. Auzot' had
had ten years earlier. Adrien Auzout (1622–91), one of the leading French mathematicians
and astronomers of the time, was a foundation member of the Académie des Sciences, but
quarrelled with Colbert and Perrault, and withdrew to Italy in 1668. He later returned
to France, and Locke seems to have encountered him frequently from this point onwards.
Auzout visited England in 1682 and three years later retired to Italy.

exact & perfect of the kinde that ever has been. It is not yet printed
& 'tis to be doubted whether ever it will be. Mr. Toynard.[1]

SUND. JUN. 5. One double p. lib.[2] amounts to £1,700 per diem for
the building the Invalids.[3] Abbays & priorys & monastarys were
formerly obleiged to enterteine, some one, some 2, some 5 lay
brothers which were maymd soldiers. This maintenance in kinde
came to be changed into a pension of 100£ per annum for each
person. This, some few years since, was augmented to 150£ per
annum & presently after taken from the present possessors & applied
to the Invalids,[4] besides which all the maladries[5] or lands & revenues
belonging to the hospitals for leapers are appropriated to the said
Invalids, & whatsoever accrues from the Knights of St. Lazar, an
order newly revivd. *Invalids*

TUESD. JUN. 7. Play   £3 – 0 – 0.[6]   *B.*

THURD. JUN. 9. A gent. of Auvergne told me at Mr. Justel's that
at Pont gibault,[7] about 5 leagues from Clermont in Auvergne, there
is a spring that is hot in winter & soe cold in sommer that there is
ice at the bottom of it, & this, he said, of his owne knowledg. *Pontgibault* *Spring*

SAT. 11 JUN. Supper   1 – 10 – 0.   *B.*
The gazets[8] of this weeke tell us of the abatement of 6 millions
per annum in the taxes, & invites all them that have lent mony,
i.e. bought rent charges at 14 years' purchase (of which there was
to the value of 40 millions) to come & receive their mony if they
please. *Revenue*

SAT. JUN. 18. Given Mrs. Ann Osby[9] Voyage de Pyrard & Sagesse
de Charron to carry for me into England. Recd. *Osby*

---

[1] It does not appear to have been published.
[2] I.e. 1 *double pour livre*.
[3] A royal decree of 12 March 1670 which dealt with the finances of this new foundation imposed a payment of 2 *deniers* (=1 *double*) out of each *livre* of the expenses paid out by the *Trésoriers-généraux de l'Ordinaire et de l'Extraordinaire des guerres* (for further details see R. Burnand, *L'Hôtel royal des Invalides*, Paris, 1913).
[4] See edict of 24 Jan. 1670 (Burnand, op. cit. p. 100).
[5] Originally *maladeries*; the more modern form is *maladreries*.
[6] The Théâtre Guénégaud gave Scarron's *Héritier ridicule*.
[7] Pontgibaud.   [8] See the *Gazette de France* for that date.
[9] See entry for 6 July.

Podagra MUND. JUN. 20. Mr. Bernier told me that in the East Indies the
Calculus
Quartan gout & stone are diseases scarce knowne & a quartan very rarely.
Febris The endemial diseases of the country are burning feavers &
Dysentery dysenterys.[1]

Gun THURSD. JUN. 23. Mr. Toynard shewd me a new fashon gun to
charge behinde, which had this also peculiar in it, that the bore was
oval & the oval had one turne in the whole as scrued guns use to
have. It was made of very soft Iron which is best.

The way to have a gun cary shot true is to have the bore a cone
from the britch half way the barrell & the other half perfectly
cylinder, if one can, & the way to have it soe is to bore the barrell
always that way which one begins, quite through from one end to
the other, & to begin always at the britch.

Bonfires Fire works at the Greve & bonfires all the town over as it is always
Midsomer Eve in all Catholique countrys.

Exchange FRID. JUN. 24. The exchange on Tuesday last chese Mme. Herinx
55$\frac{3}{4}$.

Hostel de We saw to day l'Hostel de Guise,[2] a house not uniform nor of
Guise a beautiful outside, but large. The stairs good, which leade into
2 or 3 large rooms &, beyond that, Mademoiselle de Guise's[3] own
apartment which consists of 6 or 7 litle roomes, all in a vista, in
which there were the greatest collection of litle pictures in miniature
that ever I saw. Mademoiselle's bed chamber is a litle roome, not
hung, but the floore, sides & roofe coverd with cedar & wood of
Santa Lucia interlaced one with the other in handsome figures
which looked very prettily. This with some boxes, stands & a litle

[1] The entry for 22 June which begins, 'Mr. Duclos at the King's Library…', is
followed by a regular spate of medical notes. Samuel Cottereau Du Clos (d. 1715), was
a foundation member of the Académie des Sciences. A Protestant convert to Catholicism,
he was appointed physician to Louis XIV and ended his career as a Capuchin. His
principal writings were *Observations sur les eaux minérales* (Paris, 1675) and *Dissertation
sur les principes des mixtes naturels* (Amsterdam, 1680). The reference to the 'King's
Library' is probably explained by the fact that the Académie des Sciences met there at
this period.

[2] L'Hôtel de Soubise, now part of the Archives Nationales, was built on the site of
the Hôtel de Guise.

[3] Marie de Lorraine, Duchesse de Guise et de Lorraine (1615–88), known as
Mademoiselle de Guise', the last representative of the House of Guise.

table of Collan bark¹ made a very fine smel in the roome. At the end of this apartment is a litle galery which has in the midle of it a litle closet wherein is a very fine artificial rocke of marble, agates, cornelian & fine branches of Corall, & in the midle of this grotto a litle jet d'eau.

SUNDAY JUN. 26. We saw l'Hostel de la Ferte,² a very large house with a handsome garden to it for a citty. The apartment below, paved with marble, good, & the gallery above wel painted & the guilding hath not been spared. [margin: Hostel de La Ferte]

TUESDAY JUN. 28. In Canada the Lake Eryé falls in one cascade 120 fathom perpendicular & makes the great River St. Laurens. It fals at Ontario & above is the vast, unfathomeable Lake of Erye, 2 or 300 leagues longue, of fresh water, & beyond that is another Lake. [margin: Cascade / Lake of Erye]

Mr Duclos tels me that the best water about Paris is at Auteuil, a litle towne upon the Sein below Paris neare the Bois de Bologne, & next to that is Luxembourg water. With that of Auteuil he hath cured diseases....³ [margin: Water / Aquae minerales]

That the soule quits not the body presently upon the disorder of the organs necessary to the motion of the machin is his opinion, & upon this occasion he tells this story whereof he himself was an eye-witnesse. There was a young fellow hanged himself who loved & was exceedingly beloved by his father. The father came into the place where the body lay good while after he was dead, upon which the bloud came fresh out of his nose. After he had left the body, there was an occasion that made him returne again, & upon his approaching again the dead body, fresh bloud boubled a fresh out of his nose, which being taken notice of, the experiment was tried over severall times by makeing the father goe & returne, & always succeeded. What love did in this, other passions will doe in the like occasions. Hactenus Mr. Duclos. vid. his booke [margin: Soule / Clos]

---

¹ These two words are none too clearly written and might be deciphered as *Collau back*. In neither case is their meaning clear.
² Hôtel de la Ferté-Senneterre.
³ A long list of the diseases follows.

of Salts[1] which is now going to be printed. Mr. Duclos *great liar*, Br:.[2]

THURSD. JUN. 30. Crucipotens[3] et Jupiter plane idem ibunt iter.

Poland 80. *France* 81.[4]

Deliverd Mr. Poulin for Sir John Chichley a box   £1 – 10

wherein:

Sanson's booke of maps	77 – 0
2 sets of buckles for bridles of coper guilt	£33 – 0
A set of brass hinges & hapses[5] for a Coach guilt	20 – 0
Delphineis for Mr. Stringer	01 – 0
Bought Sanson's & Duval's maps of Canada	00 – 18

SAT. 2d JUL. Put into a black trunck to be left at Madame Herinx's:

> 2 Wastcoats white woollen.
> 1 Mild Flanel Drawers.
> Essay de Intellectu fol.[6]
> a Black velvet cap.
> perfumed Toylet cloth.
> A box with coyns & bagatels.
> 1676 & 1677. 1678[7]
> Brasse ruler of the universal foot.
> Essay de Morale. Eng.[8]
> Chagrin table booke.
> Paire of perfumed gloves.
> 2 Rasors in a case.
> 1 Gilt spoone & case.
> 1 Gilt spoon, forke & knife in a case.

---

[1] This would seem to be his *Observations sur les eaux minérales*, but this work appeared in 1675; on the other hand, his *Dissertation sur les principes des mixtes naturels* did not appear until 1680.

[2] There is no doubt that this stands for Briot, whose name is given in full in an entry for 22 June where he is reported to have made the same remark about Duclos's claim to have effected various cures.

[3] No such word appears in the Latin dictionaries, but it perhaps stands for *crinita stella* (a comet), since on that date a comet was near the ecliptic and approaching Jupiter. (For this explanation of the sentence I am entirely indebted to Professor Bonno, Professor Stratton and Dr G. Merton of the University Observatory, Oxford.)

[4] The meaning of this entry is a mystery. It is followed by a long list of books, reproduced in *The Library*.

[5] *O.E.D. hasps.*   [6] The MS. of his *Essay on the Human Understanding*?

[7] The Journal for these three years?

[8] Locke's translation of four essays of Nicole, dedicated to the Countess of Shaftesbury, first published in 1828.

shamway[1] drawers.
1 pair wollen stockings milled.[2]
2 Flanen[3] shirts.
box ruler.
purple cloke.
velvet coat.
muffe.

The best edition of Castalio's translation[4] is 1567. Mr. Toynard.   Castalio
Bosius[5] super epist. Ciceronis Atticum. Mr. Toynard.   Bosius

SUND. 3 JUL. Left with Mr. Brisban Sir John Chicheley's sword.
Mr. Banks paid Mr. Baber for me

8 escus	£24 – 0
Dr. For spoon, forke & knife	24 – 0
Dr. for Puffendorf, Officium hominis	01 – 10
Cr. by 2 escus lent me	06 – 00
Dr. for paid him	04 – 00

MUND. 4 JUL. The way to have fat rabets is to gueld them young   Rabets
& let them run & this will make them excellent. Mr. Toynard.

WED. JUL. 6. Writ to Mr. Stringer to take Pyrard's Travells &
Charron de Sagesse of Ann Osby, Maurice Hunt's maid.

l.   s.   d.
Sent him also a bill on Sir John Chicheley for 10 – 14 – 0 sterling   Stringer
for £131 – 10 – 00 Tournois laid out by me for him here, which,
at 56 pence in Exchange for an escu de France, amounts, as I cost
it, to that sum.

First tried by speakeing Latin, & when that would not doe,   Daulphin
grammer, & then talkeing on a theme in Latin of which was
afterwards given in French to translate of the discourse as many
words as he could remember, & the rest he sought in a dictionary.
On the other side he translated out of Latin into French Caesar's
Commentarys.[6]

THURSD. JUL. 7. Left with Madam Herinx 4 boxes of books baled,   Herinx
marked C.B. No. 1, 2, 3, 4. A 5th, corded, marked C.B. No. 5,[7]

---

[1] O.E.D. gives this spelling of *chamois*.   [2] O.E.D. 'ribbed'.
[3] O.E.D. gives *flanen* as well as *flanel*.
[4] The Latin translation of the Bible by Sébastien Castalion (1515–63).
[5] Siméon du Bois (1536–81). This work appeared in 1582.
[6] Cf. entry for 31 Oct. 1677 and note.
[7] For lists of the books in these boxes see *The Library*.

& a black trunke wherein several things above mentioned. Recd. all these things of Madame Herinx.

Brisban **FRID. JUL. 8.** Left with Mr. Brisban a paire of silver candle sticks & a silver standish[1] with inke box & a sand box & a Silver bell, all weighing 7 Marke 2 ozs., given me by my Lady Ambassadrice. Recd.[2]

Left with Mr. Marshal[3] the key of my trunck at Madame Herinx's. Recd.

A note of linnen taken with me:

Half shirts 4.	Cufs 3 pair.
Handkerchiefs 4.	Woolen stocking 3 pair.
Sleeves 5 pair.	
Crevats lace 4.	
Drawer 2.	
Quilted caps 3.	
Holland caps 2.	
Necks 5.	

Banks   Lawndresse   6 – 2½.

Stringer   Mr. Hoskins in his of 14th June writes me that he had deliverd my bill of exchange to Mr. Stringer, which was Sir John Chicheley's bill on Mr. Beaumont for 9 – 13 – 4.

C.B.   Mr. Banks receivd of Mme Herinx £1,900, the exchange being

Exchange   at 56.

---

[1] O.E.D. *inkstand.*

[2] A letter dated 1 Aug. from Mrs A. Beavis (she signs herself 'your humble servant & Governesse A.B.') informed Locke that she had collected these articles from Brisbane in order to send them to England with the Ambassador's plate. (MS. Locke, c. 3, ff. 162–3).

[3] Locke's second note-book (p. 46) contains the following entry: '1679. Mr. Marshal a la ville de Venise rüe de Bussy.' A sentence in a letter addressed to Locke from Paris in May 1680 by his cousin, Mrs Anna Grigg (MS. Locke, c. 10, f. 123) would suggest that Locke lodged with him during at least part of his stay in Paris. 'Mr. Marshall', she wrote, 'is your servant and punctually observd all orders, so that *I am in your lodgings* and have in the honest Scotchman a diligent and usefull acquaintance'. Yet Locke's note-book has only two entries (p. 186) concerning financial transactions with Marshal (given in connexion with Caleb Banks):

'29 April [1679]: Cr. by given Marshals man   0 – 7 – 0.
2 May   — by paid Mr. Marshal   5 – 0 – 0.'

Unfortunately these note-books and the Journal throw singularly little light on Locke's various addresses in Paris.

SAT. JUL. 9. At Hostel Notre Dame   I – 10 – 0.   B.

From Paris to Longemeaux[1] 4 Leagues, about a mile from which   Longemeaux
on top of the hill is the Chasteau de Chayly[2] belonging to the
Marquis de Fiate,[3] a handsome built house of the figure of a Gr.
⌐Ⴈ, & that which is very convenient in it, from the gate of entrance
up to the house are 4 courts, separate one from an other by a litle
ascent, on both sides of which are built the stables & other out offices
etc., which are all to be seen from the house, which is separate
from them by a dry graffe[4] & draw bridg ⌐‥⌐‥⌐‥⌐‥ ⌐ .

MUNDAY JUL. 11. From Toury to Orleans 10 leagues. Well lodged   Toury
at Toury, but horrid deare, au Grand Cerf.

At Orleans in a table on the town wall by the water's sides under   Orleans
the statue of the Virgin with Our Saviour in her armes & two other
statues, one of each side of her, this inscription in golden letters:

> Prions Jesus et la Reine de gloire   Virgin
> Les Sts. Patrons St. Nicolas et St.
> Clement afin qu'ils nous preserve
> sur Loire de tous perils, &c.

Bought Plutarch's Works, 4 vol. 4to, translated by Amyot.   Plutarch
£3 – 0.

TUESD. JUL. 12. Sent Plutarch to Mr. Hubin by the Orleans Coach.
Recd.

We see [sic] the Glashouse where they made glasse bottles with   Glasse house
glasse stoppers that scrued in, the invention of Mr. Toynard.[5]

Upon the bridg is the Pucelle etc. as described by Verdier,[6] only   Pucelle
there is this more to be remarked, that Charles 7th's sheild has the
coller of the Order[7] about it, which was not instituted till after his
death by his son.

The town abounds in lame & crooke backed people.[8] Dr.   Lame &
                                                          crooked

---

[1] Longjumeau.   [2] Chilly (see entry for 2 June 1677).
[3] D'Effiat.   [4] O.E.D. 'moat'.
[5] See his letters to Thoynard of 14 July 1678 and 15 Nov. and 13 Dec. 1680 (in
Ollion).
[6] Gilbert Saunier, sieur du Verdier, Le Voyage de France (Paris, 1673), p. 83.
[7] 'L'Ordre du Saint-Esprit', instituted in 1578 by Henry III.
[8] Cf. La Fontaine's remarks on the same subject in his Relation d'un voyage de Paris
à Limousin (Œuvres, G.E.F. edition, IX, 241–3).

Tussis Godfroy,[1] a physitian of the town, imputed the crooked backs to the coughs the children are apt to have here when they are young, & the coughs to the subtilty of the aire & strength of the wine which, making the young children cough, puts out their backbones when they are yet tender. Their lamenesse he imputes more to the negligence of nurses then any thing else, carrying them always wraped up & on one side, & he thinks this to be the cause, because this lameness lights more on girles that are tenderer, then boys who are stronger & sooner out of their swadleing clouts.

Town House WED. JUL. 13. We saw the Town House, an old building of noe great importance. From the tower of it we had a prospect of the whole towne, which is large, but if one will judg by the houses & buildings to be seen in most parts of it, it seems decayeing & not over rich.

Hand mill I saw at Mr. l'Abe Gendron's[2] Mr. Thoynard's mill that would grind corne enough in 24 howers for 100 men. It was in diameter from outside to inside 300[3] & about 240 or 250 long & all to be put in a litle box & set up in an instant.[4]

Loiret THURSD. JUL. 14. We were at the source of the Loiret which is the bigest I ever saw make a great & navigable river as soon as out of the ground. There are two of them a litle distant one from the other. In the great one they say they can finde noe bottom. It is in the midle of a large poole & rises like the boileing of a pot. The house just above it belonging to Mr. de la Source is a very pleasant situation. It is about 1 League from Orleans. That which makes this source the more strange is that there is noe hills any where within view of it, nor any where there about that I can heare. It is in a flat which extends from thence to Orleans neare (as I beleive) the levell of the Loire, & rises at the foot of a litle brow about the heigth of a house of two or 3 storys, which ranges all along that

---

[1] Dr. Godefroy furnished a large number of medical notes during Locke's stay in Orleans.

[2] The Abbé François Gendron (1618–88), a friend of Thoynard, enjoyed a great reputation as a doctor and was sent for to treat Anne of Austria for cancer in her last illness. He was given an abbey as a reward for his services.

[3] Most of the measurements on this journey were taken by Locke's own system.

[4] Locke gives a reference to the entry for 23 July which contains a detailed description of this mill (not reproduced here).

way from east to west & terminates a large plain which, as soon as
you are up the brow, you see a pert de vieu.[1] From hence to Olivet   Olivet
which is[2] about ⅓ the way to Orleans, the country is very pleasant,
being all inclosures of vineards, mingled with fruit trees & houses
scatterd up & downe among. At Olivet is the house of Mr. de
Coeur, excellently well situate on the Loirett, according to the
description in Verdier. The Loiret, 2 leagues from its source, after
it has given motion to about 30 mills, looses its self in the Loire.

SAT. JUL. 16. Take[3] the leaves of kidny beans (phaseolorum) & put   Puneses
them under your pillow or some convenient place about your bed.
They will draw all the puneses[4] to them & keepe you from being
bit.[5]

THURSD. JUL. 21. Mr. Stringer tells me in his of July 3 that the   Stringer
silke is at use & that he hath received my bill on Mr. Beaumont,
9 – 13 – 4.

    The Taile in France they count personal upon the paisants, for   Taxes
in a parish where the taile is to be paid, which is a certain some[6]
appointed, one of the paisants is appointed Collector who assesses
all the Paisants of the parish as he thinkes fit. If any one findes
himself agreivd, he may have recourse to the Elus[7] & thence to the
Generality. Where any one pays not, the Collector may seize [h]is
goods, all except his bed & the utensills of his calling. If any one
be found non solvendo, his taxe is laid upon the rest of the parish.
If the Collector pays not in the mony to a farthing by the day, he
goes to prison. He has $\frac{1}{40}$ for his pains. The inhabitants of free
towns, as Paris, Orleans, etc., where of there are many in France,
are not taliable, & sometimes the Land adjacent, as the land a league
about Orleans, is free. The inhabitants of other townes, if they
be not gentlemen or gens de letres,[8] are Taliable. The inhabitants

---

[1] *A perte de vue.*   [2] This word is missing in the MS.
[3] MS. has 'thake'.   [4] *punaises.*
[5] The next entry relates how a certain 'Mr. Labdonier' asked Locke to examine his
wife who was suffering from kidney trouble.
[6] *O.E.D.* gives this spelling of *sum.*
[7] Officials concerned with the assessment of the *taille.*
[8] The term *gens de lettres* was used in a much wider sense in the seventeenth century
than to-day. Furetière defines it as 'ceux qui s'appliquent à l'étude'. It might be rendered
very roughly here as 'members of the liberal professions'.

of free towns that have land in the country perswade them selves that they nor their land pay not, because 'tis the pore tenant that pays, but yet according to the increase of their taxes their rents decrease; & if their tenant leaves their land, they may keepe it in their hands for one yeare without paying anything, to have time to provide a new tenant; but if in that time they finde not one, they shall be obleiged to pay as much taile as their last tenant did.

A paisant that has land of his owne or otherwise, if he leaves his land & lets it to an other & goes & lives in a free towne, he shall be obleiged to pay every year as much taile as he did the last year of his living in a tailiable place & this for 10 years togeather, his tenant paying neverthlesse as much taile also as he is assessed or judged able, but after ten years liveing in a free towne, a paisant becomes free of Taile unlesse he returne to his husbandry again. This makes all these people, as much as they can, send their children to live in free towns to make their persons free from taile.

Burthens   The town of Orleans, though a free towne & by particular priviledges exempted from quartering any soldiers, yet the last winter, to be exempt from winter quarters, though noe soldiers were neare, were [sic] fain to compound at the rate of 52,000 £; & Poictiers, a towne of extraordinary merit towards this very King,[1] by whom it had that amongst other priviledges granted it, was fain also the last winter to buy its exemption at a round sum.

Charcoals   THURSD. JUL. 28. Put a peice of Iron amongst burning charcoales & it hinders the malignity of the smoke & fumes. This is constantly practised in France by those that make use of such fire. Dr. Godfroy.

Gardening   Steepe tobaco leaves in water & there with sprinkle the plants that you would preserve from being eat by wormes or other vermin, etc., for it keeps them off & hurts not the plant. ib.

Acquirenda I saw there in the Capucines' garden a sort of sage of a larger &
Salvia   thicker leafe & stronger smell then the ordinary with a fringed edg.

---

[1] Presumably because of its fidelity to the Crown during the civil wars of the Fronde.

I saw there also Caprifolium semper virens which P. Ange[1] told   Caprifolium
me kept green all the winter & bore a sweeter flower then the   semper virens
ordinary honysuckles, & sometimes flowerd in winter. I saw there
also several sorts of basil (ocymum), some almost of a quite deepe   Ocymum
purple colour. Of all these he promised me whatever I desired in
the fit season, or any thing else there.

There was also the mervaile of Peru which Dr. Godfroy says is   Jalap
the true Jalap.

Left with Dr. Godfroy Horatios Vario:, Test. Gr. Sedani &   Godfroy
l'Hist. de Canadas directed to Mr. Charas to be sent to him by any
convenient oportunity. Recd.[2]

SAT. 30 JUL. From Orleans to Avery[3] 8 leagues, for, the winde being   Avery
against us, we could not get to Bloys & therefor Mme de Richmond
who went in our boat, would stop here, being afraid of the waves,
& caried us to Mr. d'Avery's, a person of quality, where we were
well received & lodgd. It is a house half new built, the other half
old, in forme of ☐ when finishd, incompassed with a very large
moat, fed with springs riseing in it, full of large carpes. He is
a gent. of 20,000 £ per annum & has 2 very handsome daughters,
his sonne now in the army. He has a very good garden full of fruit
trees, but very litle fruit this yeare, as al along the Loire, some fogs
in Lent haveing spoild all their fruit.

---

[1] There are also medical notes associated with this name.

[2] In a letter of 14 July, to Thoynard, Locke informed him that he intended to leave
Orleans that day for Blois. The reason why he spent another sixteen days there is not
explained in the Journal except that an entry dated 22 July, and entitled 'Vertigo',
contains a reference to the fever from which Caleb Banks suffered in this town. A letter
of Sir John Banks, dated 25 July (O.S.), refers to his son's 'well recovery' and expresses
the hope that Locke and he will 'returne before winter, for the last news of his not being
well makes his mother more desirous of his coming home and we feare his travell this
warme weather'. (MS. Locke, c. 3, ff. 106–7.) Locke's second note-book (p. 195) gives
the following items paid by him for Caleb Banks:

'19 Jul.	pro medico	5 – 14 – 0.
24	Paid the Apothecary	6 – 14 – 0.
25	to the Physitian	5 – 14 – 0.'

A bantering letter from Mrs Beavis (see note to entry of 8 July), addressed to Locke at
Orleans on 1 Aug., contains the following passage: 'My Lady [the Countess of
Northumberland] says you are very lazey to be noe further then Orleans all this while.
She hopes to be in England long before you get to Bloys if you make no more hast then
you have yett'. (MS. Locke, c. 3, ff. 162–3.)

[3] Avary.

Here I was told that the best peares are in the ordere as follows:

Pears

Moule Bouche
Virgoleuse
Martinsec
Double fleure
Rouselet
Colmar
St. Marsiac
Vert et long

Plumbs

Plumbs.
Perdrigon

de Ste. Katherine which are the plumbs of Tours, a white plumb which they drye in ovens, & takeing out the stones, put one in an other & soe they are excellent.

Bloys SUND. 31 JUL. From Avery to Bloys[1] 7 leagues. By the way, 2 leagues short of Bloys on the right side of the river, is the house

Menars of Mr. de Menars,[2] Intendant of Orleans, which presents a faire frontespice to the river from a litle riseing it stands on.

MUND. AUG. 1. In the late Duke of Orleans'[3] garden here which is now run to ruin, there is a gallery built by Henry 4 591 foote longue.

Chez roulant[4] From the Axel to the Standard behinde 1700. Heigth of the standar [sic] 2200. From the axel to the midle of the supporte before 4000. From the midle of the supporte to the end of the shaft about 6000. Higth of the supporte about 620. Length of a plate of Iron lyeing a long the shaft over the axel & set on with screws 2400. Length of the shaft behind the standard about 1500. The bottom of the chez above the shaft 300. The hinder edg of the chez or body of the chariot hung very near, just over the Axel. The supports I call two knobs of timber, almost semicircles, fastend on

[1] Locke's correspondence gives his address at Blois as 'chez Madame Vefuve de Mr. Simon Fesneau'. His second note-book gives this address with the addition of 'banquiere'.
[2] Jean Jacques Charron, Marquis de Ménars (1644–1718), married a sister of Colbert. He was appointed *Intendant* of Orleans in 1674 and *Intendant* of Paris in 1681.
[3] Gaston d'Orléans (1608–60), the younger brother of Louis XIII and, until the birth of Louis XIV in 1638, heir-presumptive to the throne. He was responsible for the building of the seventeenth-century wing of the château.
[4] *Chaise roulante.*

upon the shafts on which by litle short braces the fore part of the chez was supported.

This was the forme of a chez roulant, the lightest & easyest I remember to have seen. It is not drawn by the shafts which reach but to the midle of sadle which the horse weares & there by a leather trace goeing crosse the sadle is held up, but the chese is drawne by a trace which on each side is fastend under the shafts a litle behind the horse breech. The shafts were very light & slender.

TUESD. AUG. 2. Left with Mme Brunye for my Lady Northumber-   Brunye
land's 2 dozen of gloves £51. Recd.[1]

WED. AUG. 3. To make good oyle of sweet almonds, pound the   Oleum amyg
almonds well in a mortar & then thrust them up to the side of
the mortar with the end of the pestle & presse out the oyle with the
pestle. By this means you avoide both fire which spoiles the oyle,
& linin also, which gives it an ill relish & corrupts it, unlesse it be
new lining. P. Ange.

Take horse haire, either of the taile or mane, twisted up into   Shoes
litle cords & soe boile it about an hower or an hower & half. Let it
coole & drye. This gives it a curle that it will keep. This is good to
make a lineing between the inner sole & sole of thin sheep's skin
or the like in one's shoes to make them easy & coole in summer

FRID. 5. AUG. We saw Menars, a fine house belonging to Mr.   Menars
de Menars, Intendant of the province, exceeding pleasantly situated
2 leagues above Bloys upon the north side of the Loire. The gardens
are fine &, lyeing upon the edg of the river, very pleasant.

We also saw Chambort, a house of the King's, about 3 leagues   Chambort
from Bloys, about a league distant from the Loire on the left hand.
It is situate on the edg or in a morasse & has by it the Forest of
Bologne.[2] The structure of the house is very particular, being
a square with a round tower at each corner, noe court in the midle,
but in the center of the square goes up the great staire which is

---

[1] In the Lovelace Collection (MS. Locke, c. 4, ff. 193–4) there is a letter from Mme Brunyer, dated 22 Aug. and addressed to Locke at Angers ('chés Monsieur de la riviere Huet') informing him that she has executed his commission to buy gloves for the Countess.

[2] Boulogne.

a double windeing staire. The landing place in each story is on the opposite sides of the staire case in a space that goes clear round the staire case, upon which open 4 great sales about 26 ft. broad &

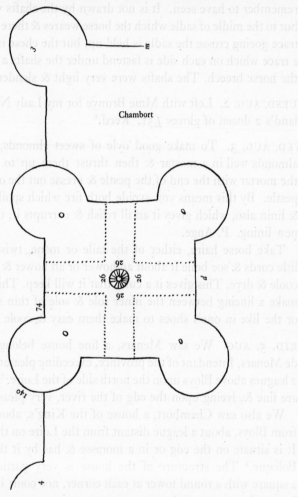

Chambort

about double as long, & out of which, on each side, goes dores into lodging[s] that take up all the space between the sales in which the towers are also.

The staire case in the midle is about 16 ft. diameter with a hollow in the midle about 2½ diameter with windows in it. There are in this

one staire case two paire of staires which one begins to mount on
opposite sides, & each landes you in the opposite sales marked
16 [sic] between the pricked lines, one in the sale leading to the front
& the other in the opposite. Each of these sales is 26 ft. broad &
about twise as long. The distance between each tower in the outside
is 74 ft. & the arch of each tower as it stands in the building is 140.
All the space between the sales marked o is taken up with lodgings.

Of these sales there are 3 story, the first you come in even with
the ground & 2 others, & over the 3d is an open terras of freestone
just of the same breadth with the sales, but the spaces o & the
towers are built 2 or 3 storys higher, but the parts of them of
unequall heigths with turrets & pinacles & great high chimnys,
which makes the roof of a very various, irregular figure.

The dore is at d into one of the sales that leads to the staire case.
The opposite front of the house is extended soe as to have 4 towers
in it, that marked 3 is finishd, from which there goes a range of
buildings to m, which was to have been continued all round the
house at that distance from the pile that is finished, as appears by
the foundations that are laid & raisd almost to the 2d story. The
other tower in the front, marked 4, is of a pretty good heith, but
was never finishd.

'Tis a house that has, I beleive, the most lodging upon the least
area that ever was built, but for the conveniency of it I can say noe
thing, haveing not had time enough there to consider all the rooms,
though they seemd to me to be very irregular. It is mighty strong
built & makes a great show at a distance, being full of turret[s],
pavilions & chimnys like turrets & the great staire case runing up in
the midle higher then all.

We also saw Beauregard, a litle house, but haveing very large & Beauregard
fine gardens, about 1½ leagues from Bloys. In it is a gallery where
are the picture of most of the considerable personages of these later
ages, but not extremely well donne.

On one side of the court as you enter, is a very deepe well where Well
in are severall things very well contrived. 1. a chaine & two
buckets. That that draws is a litle wheele about 1 ft. or 1400 diameter, wich is turned by a winless, at the opposite end of whose
axis are 3 armes of Iron about 2½ long, at the end of each of which

is a great knob of lead, weighing, as I judg, about 25 lib. which, when by turneing the handle they are made to goe apace, by their owne weight continueing the motion, make the weight of the bucket of water almost insensible. Perpendicularly over the mouth of the well are two other wooden wheels, biger then the former, whose planes are not parallel, but point both to the line of the litle wheele below & soe divaricate[1] on the farther side that they keepe the buckets at such a distance that they justle not in their meeting. Each of the buckets [h]as a ring of iron about the thicknesse of a curtaine rod that runs about 50 clear of the brim, the use where of is that, there being a cisterne placed about 4 or 5 foot above the mouth of the well, hangeing a litle over the mouth of the well, there hang out, over the side which is towards the buckets, 2 iron hooks which are fastend to a bar of Iron by hinges soe low in the cisterne that they are each from the hing [sic] to the hooke about 2½ foot long, soe that when they have a minde to fill this cisterne, 'tis but drawing up the buckets (the wheels wherein the chain was, hanging a good deale higher) & when the bucket comes to the edg of the cisterne, it lays hold on the ring & soe puls downe one side of the bucket & powers the water into the cisterne, & when that is donne, leting downe the bucket. The hooke, when it is fallen soe low as to rest upon the brim of the cisterne, lets the bucket goe again & soe the cisterne is filled without any other pains but bare drawing up the buckets.

Memo. that 'tis the universal foot here measured by.

Janison   Janison, one of the ministers of Bloys, a very ingenious & civil man.[2]

Poinson   SAT. AUG. 6.   1 poinson of wine conteines 220 pintes.
Brandy   1 poinson of brandy . . . . 210 pintes.

Wine   It was worth here formerly 80 or 90 £ & now since the warre it is worth but 30 £; and their wine here now they sell by retaile for 18 d. per pinte.

1 Tunneau of wine contains 2 poinsons or 440 pintes. Their pintes here are the same with those of Paris. 1 pinte of water

---

[1] O.E.D. 'stretch or spread apart, diverge'.
[2] Michel Janiçon was minister at Blois from 1657 to 1685 when he took refuge in Holland. He then became a pastor in Utrecht where he died in 1705.

weighes 2 lbs. of 16 ozs. to the pound, 8 gros the ounce and 72 grains the gros, Apothecarys' & goldsmiths' weights, soe that their scruple here is 24 grains, equall to 24 grains of barly.

MOND. AUG. 8. From Bloys to Tours 16 Leagues, but very litle (£11) for our passage by water in a boat to ourselves.   Tours

TUESD. 9 AUG. From the top of the tower of St. Gratien[1] we saw the town of Tours which is strechd a great length on the left side the River Loire, but is not very broad. The Capucins have a covent on the other side of the river, situated very pleasantly on the brow of the hill from whence also one has a very good prospect of the town.

The Gardiner of the Covent gave us off the trees a plumb or   Plumbs 2 which he called prune d'Apricot, a yellowish, round plumb, a litle ruddy on one side & came cleane from the stone, hard & juicy, & of an admirable tast. He told me that the best plumbs were

> D'Apricot.   Plumbs
> Perdrigon.
> Diapré.
> St. Katherine.
> Verte et longe.
> Damar Violetes.

Above the town, a litle on the right side the river, is the great Monastery de Marmoustier.[2] The Abbay there is an handsome &   Marmoustier very high church. The new buildings which are not finished, very handsome, the gardens large, but the cellars much larger, being cut in under the side of the hill into the rock. They had the last yeare there 1,380 peices of wine. We saw there the great cuve which, they say, will hold 200 tun of wine. The grapes being all every where   Grapes else very green, this year being backward, we saw there in the garden a sort of red grapes, pretty ripe, which they called Raisins de St. Magdalene, because they use to be ripe about that time, which is 22 July.

Poire de Buré Blanche[3] is a good sort of peare, as we were told   Peare there.

---

[1] The modern form is *Gatien*. Varennes in his *Voyage de France* speaks of 'saint Gratian, vulgairement saint Gassian'.

[2] Very little now remains of the old buildings.

[3] Furetière lists a pear called *beurré blanc*.

We were told that the revenue of this Benedictine Abbay was £500,000 per annum. This I'm sure, 'tis in a very pleasant place. This Abbay with its dependence is worth £400,000. Mr. Bon.[1]

Verret   **WED. AUG. 10.** From Tours to Verret[2] 2 leagues, a house[3] situated pleasantly on the left side the Cher upon a litle heigth of a steep ascent. The house is pretty & well furnishd, & has to it, as all the great houses in France, a pretty parterre with knots & flowers, an orangery & a wood walled in, divided into walks with arbors & seats. It belongs to the Abbé Defiat, son of the Marshal Defiat.[4] He hath several Church benefices which with his temporal estate Architecture makes him a great revenue; they talke of £90,000. The house is a square with a court in the midle. Only in one corner (i.e. opposite to that where one enters) they have clapd the staire case, which conteines a windeing staire which, though it spoiles a litle the uniformity of the square, saves a great deale of roome & uniformity [sic] to the house & seems noe ill way of building. Though this be but the last day of July in England, yet these Weather 2 or 3 days past I found the weather soe cold here that I found it convenient to get on my flanen shirt, & should not have been Winde troubled with a wastcoat. Ever since we came to Orleans, the winde has been west, & commonly rises & sets with the sun.

We saw here Mr. Gill, the son of an English man, that speaks himself good English, a merchand of Silke that hath a very fine house & garden. Mr. Barkestead, a silke merchand in London neare Smithfield, hath married his daughter, & Sir Patience[5] Ward is his correspondent, a fit man to procure fruit trees & grafts.

Silke   Where as there were lately 6,000 silke weavers here in Tours,
trade   there are now but 1,200, & those that could gain 50s. an aulne for
Wages   weaving of figurd silkes have now but 30s. or 35s. There have broke here since Easter last for above 6,000,000 £.[6]

---

[1] Neither this second estimate (which appears to have been added later) nor the first seems near the truth; at least Piganiol de la Force (VI, 66) gives the Abbot's income as 16,000 l. a year, and that of the monks as 18,000.

[2] Véretz.   [3] Now in ruins.

[4] The Abbé d'Effiat (1622–98) was exiled there from Court from 1674 to 1678. Mme de Sévigné visited him in 1675 when she travelled by boat down the Loire.

[5] MS. has 'Patient'.

The silk industry at Tours appears to have reached its period of greatest prosperity

The best sort of plumbs, both to preserve & to eat green or Plumbs dryed:

> Perdrigon.
> Lisle vert.
> St. Katherine.
> D'Apricot, which I eat there dried of this year, very good.

THURSD. AUG. 11. We saw the weaveing of figured silks. The worke Silk weaveing men complain of want of worke, decay of trade & abatement of wages. In the house we saw it, were lately 12 looms & there are now but two.

We saw also the way of Calandering[1] & watering their silks which Calandering gives them a glosse & the water by drawing on them, being wound upon a rouler,[2] a weight of 650,000 lib.

A day's worke of figurd silke is about an aulne. We saw also the weaveing of velvet, the cuting whereof upon a litle brasse wire with a litle grove or noch[3] in it all the length is very dexterous.

We saw also the twisting & windeing of silke in one of their mills, which is drove about by a maid & turnes at once above 120 spooles & windes the silke off them. The maid works from 5 in the morning till night, only rests twice in the day an hour at a time, & has for her day's work 5 s., a small recompence for drawing such a weight 7 leagues, for soe much they say she goes in a day. The wages was formerly greater.

Monnoye de France.

> Le Denier vaut 2 oboles.   Mony
> l'Obole 2 pites.
> L'obole et la pite ne sont pas monnoyes reeles.
> Le Liard vaut 3 d. Il n'est pas aujourd hui monnoye reele.
> Le Blanc vaut 5 ds. Il n'est pas monnoye reele.
> Le sol vaut 12 d. il n'est pas monnoye rele.
> Le sol marquè – – – – – – 15 d.
> La livre Tournois – – – 20 s.

---

at the time of Richelieu, but had greatly declined by the end of the century. Boisson-nade's claim (p. 178) that, while it lost ground compared with Lyons, 'sa chute ne date que de la période postérieure à Colbert', is certainly not borne out by Locke's observations in 1678.

[1] O.E.D. calender: 'to press cloth etc. between rollers for the purpose of smoothing'.
[2] O.E.D. gives this form of roller.
[3] O.E.D. gives these forms of groove and notch.

L'escu d'argent – – – – – £3 or 60 s.
Le demy escu 30 s.
Le Louis de 15 s. d'argent.
Le Louis de 5 s.
Le peice de 4 s. d'argent.
La peice de 2 s. d'argent.
Le Louis d'or vaut lb. 11.
Le double Louis £22.
Le quadruple £44.
Le double quadruple £88.
La Pistole d'Espagne qui à cours en France vaut £11.
Le ½ Louis & ½ pistole vaut £5 – 10 s.
Le Lis d'or vaut £7.
L'ecu d'or vaut £5 – 14 s.
Le ½ ecu d'or vaut 57 s.

Mesures

De la Mesure.

Le pied de Roy ou pied de Paris contient 12 pouces.
Le pouce 12 lignes.
La ligne 6 points.
Le pas Geometrique 5 pieds.
Le pas commune 3 pieds.
La demarche 2½ pieds.
L'aune 3 pieds 7 pouces 8 lignes.
La toise 6 pieds.
La Chaine du Comté de Blois pour mesurer les heritages 4 toises
  ou 24 pieds.
La petite lieüe ffrancoise 2000 pas geometriques.
La Lieüe commune 2500.
La grande Lieüe 3000.
Le Tour de la Terre 10,800 lieües communes.
Le Muy de blé ou autre grain contient 12 Septiers.
Le Septier 2 mines.
La mine 2 minots.
Le minot 2 boisseaux.
Le boisseaux 4 quarts.
Le tunneau de Vin mesure de Blois contient 2 poinçons.
Le poinçon 2 quarts.
Le poinçon mesure de Blois contient 220 pintes mesure de Blois.
La pinte 2 chopines.
La Chopine 2 Septiers.
La fourniture de vin contient 42 poinçons.
Le cent de fagots, harengs, pommes, clouds, &c. contient 104.

Du Poids.

La livre de France contient 2 Marcs.
Le Marc 8 onces, l'Once 8 gros, &c.
La livre des Marchands de Soye contient 15 onces.
La livre de Medecine contient 12 onces.

Hactenus Mr.   ,[1] Mathematique Master at Blois.

FRID. AUG. 12. From Tours to Saumur 17 leagues, cariage by water   Saumur
in a boat by our selves £9. From Orleans to Blois we paid £11
& from Blois to Tours £11, a litle too deare. By the way we saw
several gentlemen's seats, most of them rather beareing the marks
of decay then of thriveing & being well kept.

At Langer,[2] 6 leagues short of Saumur, we went a shore to seek   Langer
Mellons, this being the place of France where they are counted   Melons
best & from whence they are sent to Court & to Paris, but we found
none yet ripe.

MOND. AUG. 15. At Orleans 3 Empereurs, 60 s. per diem, well. Bloys   Rates
at the Galere 50 s. per diem, very well. Tours at St. Marthe 50 s. per
diem, ordinary. Saumur at the Trois Mores 40 s. per diem, well.

The best plumbs to drie are: Plumbs

1. Roche Corbon, red & large. The next are Ste. Katherine,
large & yellow. These two are the best because they are large &
fleshy. There are two others which they use to drye also which are
good, but are lesse. They are the Mirabel & Catalane, both white.
All these 4 sorts are also very good raw.

The way to drye them is this.   Plumbs
drying
1. They must be soe ripe that they drop of the tree of themselves, which is best, or else fall with a litle shakeing.

2. The best way (which is not always observed) is to put them
2 or 3 days in the hot sun shine, which will drie up gently some part
of the superfluous moisture.

3. When they have been thus a litle dried in the sun, you must
heat the oven gently (one litle brush fagot is enough the first time),
& haveing placed them single upon wicker driers about 2 ft. broad
& 4 or 5 ft. long (or of a figure round soe large as will goe into the
oven's mouth), put them into the oven & soe let them drie there

---

[1] Left blank in MS.   [2] Langeais.

till the oven is cold, & then they must be taken out & turned whilst the oven is heating. The oven may be thus heat twise a day at 6 in the morning & 6 at night. The 2d time the oven may be made a litle hotter then the first, & soe repeated till they are drie enough, which is when they are of a due consistence & brown colour. When they are soe far dried as to be capeable of presseing, the best way is to presse them gently with the fingers not into a flat, but round figure, for that way they keepe best. The great care to be taken is, in the first puting them into the oven, that the oven be not too hot, for if it be, it makes them crack their skins & run out, which makes them much worse.

Peaches drying

After the same manner one dries peaches, with this difference that after the first time they have been in the oven, one peeles them with a knife, for then the skin will easily strip, & the stone then is to be taken out, & if one will, a litle peach thrust into its place, which makes the other larger & better.

Pears drying

Thus also peares are to be dried (the Roussette de Champane is the best), but that the oven may be a litle hotter for pears then plumbs. They are to be stripd also after their first comeing out of the oven.

This was taught me by Madame de Superville.[1] My Lady Milles hath seen her doe all these & hath of the trees in England.

Pears

The best summer pears are:
La Rousselette de Champagne.
La poire de Citron.
La Citron des Carmes.
la poire de Monsieur.

The best winter pears:
Virgoleuse.
La Verate.
L'Amadote Musqué.
la Muscate d'Almagne.

[1] No doubt the M. and Mme. de Superville mentioned here were the parents of the Protestant theologian, Daniel de Superville (1657–1728). His father was Jacques de Superville, a doctor at Saumur, who died in 1679, and his mother Marthe Pilet, the daughter of an apothecary, who appears to have taken refuge in Holland after the Revocation of the Edict of Nantes. (See P. Fonbrune-Berbinau, *Daniel de Superville*, Chambéry, 1884.)

The best peaches:
>   La Belle Chevereuse.
>   Le Gros pavy d'Italie.

Hactenus Mr. de Superville a Saumur.

They set their melons here in the common earth of their gardens **Melons**
without dung, & use no other art to them but to nip the tops of the
branches when the young melons are knit to hinder them from
runing into branches, & those here & at Langer are the best melons
in France.

THURSD. AUG. 18. In the Recolets' garden here is aboundance of **Pears**
good fruit, amongst the rest a sort of peare which they call poire
sans peau which are ripe at the same time that cherrys are. It is,
as they told me, a very great peare & a great bearer. They were all
ripe & gon. They have there also a peare which they call poire de
jasmin which, as they say, hath something of the flaver of Jasmin.

The white wine here of this towne is very good & wine soe plenty **Wine**
here that they sell it for 18 deniers la pinte at their boushons,[1]
i.e. where people in privat houses sell their owne wine by retail,
& of these 18 deniers per pinte the King hath 10 deniers for excise **Taxes**
& the proprieter 8 d. for his wine.

At the 3 Mores 40 s. per diem, well.

FRID. AUG. 19. From Saumur to Angers 10 leagues, to Port a Cé[2] **Angers**
by water £7 – 10 – 0, from Port a Cé to Angers 1 league. We paid
15 s. a peice for our horses for this league; the usual price is but
10 s. at most, but they made use of our necessity.

SAT. AUG. 20. At Angers at the Minims' church[3] hang up several **Prayers for**
tables in brasse with the pictures buy [sic] of the devout women **the dead**
(for I saw noe men there soe pious) who made the donations. In
these tables of brasse are mentioned certaine masses, some to be
sung, some á base voix, to be celebrated on certain days to

---

[1] Hatzfeld & Darmesteter give under *bouchon*: 'Bouquet, faisceau de feuillage qui,
placé au-dessus de la porte, indique un cabaret': cf. *bush* (*O.E.D.*) 'bunch of ivy as
ancient vintner's sign'. (Locke has some fuller comments on this subject in his
Observations, p. 23.)

[2] Ponts-de-Cé.   [3] Demolished during the Revolution.

perpetuity pour le repos de leurs ames, for the founding of which masses have been given by some £400, by others £600 & by others almost £1000, & in some 'tis pour le repos de leurs ames et de leurs parents deja decedes, and in one of them is purchasd also the exposeing of the Host on certaine days. Soe that if there be any benefit to be had from these things, it is, it seems, only for those who have faith & mony enough to pay for them.

Salt   MOND. AUG. 22. Here a boisseau of Salt costs a Luis d'or & about 10 livres of it is sold for 10 s. This makes them here very strict in examining all things that enter into towne, there being at each gate two officers of the Gabelle who serch all things where they suspect may be any salt.[1] They have also in their hands iron bodkins about 2 foot long which have a litle hollow in them neare the point, which they thrust into any packs where they suspect there may be salt concealed, & if there be any, by that means discover it. The penalty for any one that brings in any salt that is not a Gabeller,[2] pays 100 ecus or goes to the gallys. It is also as dangerous to buy any salt but of them.

Boisseau   A boisseau of salt weighs about lib. 24.

I saw a Gabeller at the gate serch a litle girle at her entrance, who seemd only to have gon out to see a funerall that was prepareing without the gate, which had drawn thither a great number of people.[3]

TUESD. AUG. 23. We saw by the river's side, a litle above the towne, a place which they say was formerly the house of pleasure of the Kings of Sicily.[4] They shew a litle, ordinary roome which they call the Sale &, as they say, painted with his owne hand, for soe it is,

---

[1] There was an obvious temptation to attempt to smuggle in salt from neighbouring provinces where the price was much lower.

[2] *Gabeleur.*

[3] On this date Locke wrote to M. de Juigné, to whom he had been recommended by Thoynard, asking advice about the best route to La Rochelle. 'Je veux bien employer mon voyage à conaistre les provinces où je seroy passé et ne pas négliger ce qu'elles ont de curieux et de rare...' (Ollion, p. 19).

[4] This manor house, known as 'de Reculée' from the part of the town in which it is situated, is still in existence. It was built in the fifteenth century by René, Duke of Anjou and King of Sicily. Many paintings have been attributed to him, though without any certain proof.

all the roof of it, with vines & grapes, but with a sort of painting better fitting a cabaret as it is now then a pallace as they say it was. At least in those times the buildings & paintings that served princes was very ordinary. By it is a litle, low, long building like a shed or cow house which they say was his galery, suteable indeed to the magnificence of the Sale, where in were some touches of painting of the same hand, but soe litle reverence was now paid to this royal workmanship that it served only to enterteine a cow that was lodgd at that end, the rest being full of wood & straw. That which gives the greatest credit to this building, is the armes of the Kings of Cicily, graved in stone, appeareing still to passengers in the wall of the Sale.

We saw also at St. Maurice, the Cathedral of Angers, aboundance of reliques, the tooth of one Saint, the bone of another, etc. whose Reliques names I have quite forgotten as well as he had, of some of them, that shewd them us, though they were his old acquaintance, but it served our turns as well when he put St. Martin for St. Moril; but the things of most veneration were a thorn of the crown of Our Saviour, some wood of his crosse which I beleive was there, though I saw noe thing but the gold & silver that coverd it. There was also some of the haire, a peice of the petticoat & some of the milke of the Virgin, but the milke was out of sight; and one of the water pots wherein Our Saviour turnd water into wine. That which made this morcell pretty hard of digestion was that it was porphyre, a sort of furniture a litle to costly in all appearance for the good man of the house where the weding was kept, & which made it yet worse, was a face in demy releive on that side that stood outwards, a way of ornament not much in use amongst the Jews.[1] However, I could not but wish for the pot because of its admirable effects to cure Miracles diseases, for once a yeare they put wine into it, consecrate it & distribute it to beleivers, who there with cure feavers & other diseases.

WED. AUG. 24. In the Church of St. Maurice this also is remarkable that, there being 3 towers at the west end all of a front, that in the

---

[1] 'Thou shalt not make to thyself any graven image, nor the likeness of any thing that is in heaven above, nor in the earth beneath, or in the water under the earth....'

midle has noe other foundation then the arch of the great window,
& it is hard to conceive how it supports its owne weight & that of
the two great bells that hang in it, the highest whereof is neare
7 yards about.

Organ · I saw today at the Cordeliers le P. la Motte who is makeing there
a new organ which he pretends will have something more then is
usuall in other organs, as a viol stop etc. The fingering of the Keys
he makes of the bones of horses instead of ivory, which he says

Ivory · will never grow yellow as ivory doth; but to whiten them he puts
them in water with quicklime & soe boiles them 3 or 4 howers over
the fire, which takes out all the grease, soe that they are as white as
snow & will never turn yellow. Oxe bones will not keepe nor be
made soe white.

Writeing · Belonging to the Church of St. Maurice is one Mr. Chollet[1] who
is makeing a booke for the church service writeing in velom, the
best writ that I have seen, with excellent miniature[s], but it is
rather a way of printing then writing, for, cuting the alphabet in
litle brasse plates, he lays on the letter he has need of upon the
line & then rubs upon the plate with a brush dipd in ink & soe
leaves the forme of the letter on the velum. His great secret is his

Ink · several inkes. The best he says for writing with a pen is wherein
there is as litle coprass[2] as possible, but aboundance of galls which
the newer the better, because they have then a gum in them which
is much better than gum arabique, which ought not to be put into

Parchmin · inke. When his velum proves any where greasy, he rubs it with the
pouder of egshells, which he says is the best thing to take out
grease. Mr. Chostart l'ainé[3] who was there with me told me that
the pouder of egshels dried in the sun, pouderd again & sersed,[4] is
the best for hower glasses. He esteems his book at 25 escus per leafe.

Macres · THURSD. AUG. 25. They have a sort of fruit they sell here 100 pour
1 s. that grow in the water. They are of an irregular figure of severall

---

[1] Gervais Chollet (1639–1706), a priest who, apart from two years in Rome, spent
most of his life in Angers and earned a considerable reputation for his skill in writing
on vellum.

[2] O.E.D. *copperas*: 'Proto-sulphate of iron'.

[3] Jean Chostart and his son, Jacques, were well-known architects of Angers. Locke
had been recommended to the father by Justel (second note-book, p. 38).

[4] O.E.D. 'sieved'.

points & of a sooty colour, the meat within very white, but of a very
ordinary tast, much worse then chesnuts. They call them macres.[1]

The forme of Our Saviour sepulcher as it is at Jerusalem, figure, *Sepulchrum*
cover, proportion & all, is shewn at Bamete,[2] a covent of Recolets[3] *Christi*
½ [league] below Angers upon the river.

FRID. AUG. 26. We saw the quarrys of Ardoise.[4] They employ about *Ardoise*
100 men in diging, spliting & cuting these stones. Formerly there
were 200, but the war as on other parts hath had an influence on
this vent to. The best workers in the quarre[5] have about 13s. a day, *Wages*
& the others on land that split & square them have 30s. per
thousand, at which rate they earne about 10s. per diem.

The stones are dug out of the rock in great & large peices, but
to make them more portable they break them into peices of a fit
largenesse & soe with chisels they split them into that thicknesse
they finde fitest for use & cut them square, those for Paris about
a foot long & 8 inches over. The vaine of the rock runs towards the
north east & lies perpendicular. That part of the rock that lies
nearest the surface of the earth is not good, though it be also of
a stone whose veine lies the same way & will split, but not soe well
as that which lies lower. When they are come to the good, the lower
they goe, the better, but they cannot worke it to the bottom of the
rock, being dround out before they get soe low.

It splits best as soon as it comes out of the quarre. After it is
dried a month or two in the aire, it will split noe more. In frosty
weather it splits best, but in a thaw they cannot worke it. One may
have tables of it almost what largenesse or thicknesse one will.[6]

The wine that was formerly sold here for 4s. per pinte is now *Wine*
sold for 1s.

---

[1] *macre* or *macle*: 'water caltrop'.
[2] La Baumette.
[3] This monastery, the buildings of which are still in existence, is supposed to have
been the one where Rabelais was a novice.
[4] There are well known slate quarries at Trélazé, some four miles S.E. of Angers.
[5] *O.E.D.* does not give this form of *quarry*, but it is to be found in Coryate (*Crudities*,
Glasgow, 1905 edition, vol. 1, p. 170).
[6] Here come some medical notes, furnished by 'Mr. Beaumont'. (According to these
some extraordinary ailments seem to have been cured by tobacco-chewing in seventeenth-century France!)

Figues SAT. AUG. 27. In the garden of the Chanoines regulaires de St. Augustin whose church they call de Touts saints[1] or, if you will, the garden á touts saints in Angers, are severall figue trees of the white fig of Provence, the fullest of fruit I ever saw any [where]. They are large trees & standards.

Kitchen   In the Kitchen there also there was set in the back of the chimny a great caldron, the side where of ranged along with the wall of the chimny & was defended from being hurt by the fuell by some bars of Iron that were set up perpendicular before it. Into this caldron was cold water let by a cock conveniently placed on one side the chimny, & by an other cock on the other side hot water was let out of it, by which meanes there was hot water always ready for all uses of the kitchen without any charge of fuell, the same fire serveing to heat this caldron that served to rost or boyle etc. any thing else.

Well   The way also of drawing water there with a double wheele, 2 buckets & 2 chaines, was not amisse, the water being drawn up with great ease. At each end of a chain that reachd as low as the water hung a bucket. This chaine went in a wheele of about 18 inches or 2 ft. diameter that hung perpendicular over the well a good heigth above the mouth. To the axis of the same wheele was fastend another, 2 or 3 times as big in diameter, in which also run an endlesse chaine, which hung downe by the side of the well which, when one puld, drew the great wheele which turnd with it the litle, & there with drew up the full bucket which, haveing a ring of Iron about the lip of it, was, when raisd above the mouth of the well, seised on by an iron hooke which, fastend in the midle of a cisterne that was placed on the side of the well, made it pour in its water, & then being let downe, the other was in like manner emptied into an other cisterne on the other side of the well.

Measures SUND. 28 AUG.   1 Bras contient   5 pieds.
                         1 Toise . . . . . .   6 pieds.

B. MOND. 29 AUG. Paid Mr. Banks £330 – o. Paid him also at Bloys, 6 Aug. £330 – o.

Angiers   This day we left Angiers, a towne built on the Men[2] about a league or some thing more before it falls into the Loire. The town

---

[1] The 'Ancienne Église Toussaint' is now in ruins.   [2] Maine.

is moderately built, but biger then Orleans by much. Both above & below it are large medows, but the town it self stands for the most part on a riseing ground on both sides the river, but the biger part by much is on the left side.

Hence we hired a litter for our selves, feareing the heat, & two horses for our servants, & there were with the litter 2 men on foot, al which at 1 Luisd'or per diem till their returne home.

All the way between Angers & Saumur the way (except the 1st league) by the Loir's side upon a banck to keepe out the inundations of this unruly river. The country all a long well planted with fruit trees & the trees of their hedgrows coverd with vines.

From Angers to Saumur 10 litle Leagues.

At Mme de La Riviere Huet's[1] 30s. per diem, excellently well.

TUESD. 30 AUG. This morning we left Saumur, a litle towne just under an high hill upon the edg of the Loire. All[2] streets narrow & crooked. Here we tooke 5 horses & a man for a guid[e] at £12 per diem, he to feed his horses. At the 3 Mores 40s. per diem, well enough. Saumur

From Saumur to Chinon 6 leagues. Chinon placed on the right side of the River Vienne, a long towne, strechd narrow between the river on one side & an high rocke on the other, upon which stands an old castle belonging to the Kings of France which hath great markes of antiquity & decay. Chinon

Chinon, if one consider either the number of houses in it whose dores are shut, or the ruine of those that are open, seems not to be over filld either with people or mony.

Here I saw them make wallnut oyle. The Kernels, cleansed from their shells, they first grinde in a mill like the oyle mils I saw at Montpellier, only much lighter. They being thus ground small, they heat them for about an hower togeather in fournace of cast Iron, continually turneing them with a shovell whilst they are over the fire, & when they are hot, they put them in the presse in a cloth Oyle of Wallnuts

---

[1] Huet de La Rivière was the name of a Protestant family of Angers. Its best known member at this period was Gabriel Huet, a convert to Catholicism, who brought over some of the other members of the family. The La Rivière Huet Locke lodged with is described as a banker in his second note-book (p. 38).

[2] MS. has (or appears to have) Ale.

& presse them with a scrue which runs into a square hole in a very thick beame, which is the place where the bag of ground & hot kernelles lie.

They use it to burne & poore people eat it in their soope. They aske for a pipe of it £80 this yeare that it is deare, nuts being scarce. Cheaper years they sell a pipe for £60. A pipe holds 200 pints. They were makeing now of old nuts, but that made of new[1] nuts when ripe is better.

Soe far we passed by the River Vienne (which was as far as from its falling into the Loire, 6 leagues above Saumur) to Chinon, & about ½ league above it are good meadows. From Chinon to Richelieu 4 leagues. At the Puis d'or 30s. pour couché, not very well.

Fountains At Chinon, though but a litle, durty, pore towne, yet, as in most of the walled towns in France, there was a conduit runing with fountain water.

Richleiu WED. 31 AUG. This morning we left Richlieu, the most compleat peice of building in France, where in the out side is an exact symetry, in the inside convenience & beauty, the richest guilding & best statues that are to be seen any where, the avenues on all sides exceeding handsome & magnificence on all sides. He that desires to be better informed may consult Vignier's Chasteau de Richlieu, printed at Saumur in 8° 1676, & the cuts that are to be sold of the house both in great & litle.[2]

The towne is built with the same exactness that the house, & though by it[s] natural situation it has not the convenience to be a towne of great trade, yet the great priviledges the Cardinal has got setled upon it, it being a free towne, exempt from Taile & salt, cheape liveing in it will always keep it full of people & the houses deare in it.

Milleray From Richleiue we went to Milleray,[3] 11 or 12 leagues crosse the country which the first part of the day was all corne feilds, set soe thick with wallnut & other trees that it looked like ploud lands in a wood. We passed through Dercy, Guenne, St. Jean de Sauve,

---

[1] MS. has *news*. [2] See entry for 24 Sept. 1678.
[3] La Meilleraye.

Cron, Tenze, Feriere, Soré¹ which they called bourghs, but,
considering the poornesse & fewnesse of the houses in most of
them, would in England but scarce amount to vilages. Their houses
generally were but one story; and though such low buildings, which
one can scarce see till one is amongst them, cost not much too keepe
them up, yet, like groveling bodys without soules, they also sinke
lower when they want inhabitants, of which sort of ruins we saw
great numbers in all these bourgs, whereby one would guesse that
the people of France doe not at present increase, at least in the
country. But yet the country is all tilled & well cultivated.

The bourg of Milleray is like the rest of it[s] neighbours. The
Chasteau belonging to a Duke of that name is litle &, I think, ill
seated, there being a great pond on each side just by the house.²
The country as we passed on both sides is all woodland about it.
Our Inne, the only one of the place, was just by the Chasteau,
which I shall remember for the ill supper & lodging we had there,
which was much more sensible to those that came from Richlieu.

THURSD. SEPT. 1. From Milleray to Niort 7 leagues, through an   Niort
inclosed country, mixed of woods, arable & pasture the first part,
the later part of the way, through an open champian country, all
corne.

Niort is a litle, walled towne on the   ,³ ill built, but of an
healthy situation. The most remarkeable things in it that I saw
was [sic] the Hale or market house, the longest & broadest I have
seen any where & very convenient, were it not soe darke, & the
steeple, a very handsome & high one, something like that of
Grantham, but comeing short of its heigth.

Here a poore bookseller's wife, which by the largenesse & furni-   Protestants
ture of her shop seemed not to have either much stock or trade,
told me that, there being last winter 1,200 soldiers quarterd in the   Quartering
towne, two were apointed for their share (for they were Protestants),
which, considering that they were to have 3 meales a day of flesh,
breakefast, dinner & supper, besides a collation in the afternoon, all

---

¹ Dercé, Guesnes, St Jean de Sauves, Craon, Thenezay, La Ferrière, Sauray.
² Built in 1635, the Château is now in ruins.
³ Left blank in MS. (The Sèvre Niortaise.)

which was better to give them, & a 5th meale too if they desired it, rather then displease them, these 2 soldiers, for the $3\frac{1}{2}$ months they were there, cost them at least 40 ecus.

Rochelle FRID. SEPT. 2. From Niort to Rochelle[1] 10 leagues through an open corne country, for between Richlieu & this we saw but few vineards.

Protestants SAT. SEPT. 3. Noe Protestants are sufferd to set up trades (c'est a dire estre metrisé)[2] in Rochell, nor noe Protestants to live there that were not borne in the town.[3]

Salt SUND. SEPT. 4. They make salt here all about the town & it is worth here about 5s. per boysseau. 'Tis observable that some pits cast whiter salt then others, though of the same water.

Measures MOND. SEPT. 5. Une Velthe conteines 4 pots measure of Paris, 2 Gallens English measure. The Barick,[4] i.e. Hoghead, conteines

at Rochelle	27 velthes.
at Nantes	29 velthes.
at Bourdeaux	32 velthes.

4 hogheads make a tun.

Brandy A hoghead of Brandy now at Rochelle is worth 40 ll. & a Tun of
Wine wine the same. It was formerly double or treble the rate. Mr. Lee.
Salt The pits where they make the salt (i.e. where the water is last let in for the salt to granulate, for it is much evaporated in other places before it comes thither) are about 10 steps quare[5] & the salt water in them about 4 or 5 inches deepe, the bottom very smooth. Out of one of these they in the heat of sommer draw out every day about a boisseau or $1\frac{1}{2}$ boisseau of salt. Some of the salt swims on

---

[1] Locke's correspondence gives his address here as 'chez M. Jean Raulté'. From his second note-book (p. 44) we learn that he was a banker. On the same page is another entry under the heading La Rochelle: 'Mᵉ Dalton, Irlandoise, the best inne. 60s. per diem. Mr. Quaile (?).'

[2] For *maîtrisé* (i.e. be admitted as a master to a guild). Furetière does not give an example of this use of the verb.

[3] In 1661 a decree was issued forbidding any Protestant to live at La Rochelle unless he could furnish proof of having lived there before 1627, the date of the rebellion and siege of the town. Those who could not do so were ordered to leave the town under penalty of a fine of 500 l. La Rochelle thus lost some 1,800 inhabitants. (J. Viénot, *Histoire de la Réforme Française*, vol. 1, Paris, 1926, pp. 408, 457.)

[4] *Barrique.*

[5] Perhaps merely a slip of the pen for *square*. O.E.D. gives this form of the verb, but not for the adjective.

top of the water like a thin ice & this is very white, but when the grains become big, they sinke to the bottom, from whence they rake all to one place by the side with a peice of wood, about 2000 long & about 250 broad, made of fir, at the end of a long pole. The skill is to draw this soe lightly & evenly as not to rake up any of the earth at the bottom with it. They that make it & looke after the pits have $\frac{1}{4}$ for their pains or $\frac{1}{3}$.

TUESD. SEPT. 6.[1] At Le Curieux, a kinde of Jack of all trades here, I saw the finest work in Ivory that can be imagind, a flower pot turned in ivory, a good deale biger then a goose egge, soe excessively thin that it yeilded to the least touch. Out of this came a plant, all whose foliage & branches & flowers were all very neat, thin & naturall. This, with the foot to it which was exceeding finely turnd, looked very neatly, & of this kinde were the most elaborate & accuratest peice of worke I had ever seen. There were a paire of these, an ornament for any lady's cabinet that would goe to the price of them.

Ivory worke

WED. SEPT. 7. The boisseau of salt they sell for 4 or 5s. The boisseau wherein I saw them measure, was a part of a cone, at the great end 1560 diameter in the cleare, at the litle end about 930 or 940, & the length of the axis 1010 or there abouts. They say it holds $32\frac{1}{2}$ pints of their measure de champ which they say is $\frac{1}{4}$ biger then the ordinary, & that a boisseau of salt weighs 90 lb. 24 boisseaus make a mui.

Boisseau Measures

Mui

The Cathedrall church at present at Rochelle was formerly the Protestants' temple,[2] built by the English & coverd with lead. It

Protestants

---

[1] Here is a medical note to which the names of Dr Richard and Dr Bouhereau, two well-known La Rochelle physicians, are appended. Élie Bouhereau (1643–?) took his M.D. at Orange in 1665. He emigrated after the Revocation and ended his career as pastor and librarian at Dublin. His cousin, Élie Richard (1645–1706), took his M.D. at Montpellier in 1666. He visited Oxford and was made an F.R.S., but remained in France after the Revocation. Locke concludes his note thus: 'This Dr. Richard is the author of the treatise at the end of Lortie in answer to Rohault.' This essay, entitled *Discours physique sur la Transsubstantiation, contre Monsieur Rohault* was published at Saumur in 1675 along with André Lortie's *Défense du sermon de Monsieur Hesper en* which Locke made notes from in the entry for 14 Nov. 1677.

[2] This was one of the conditions imposed by Louis XIII and Richelieu on the defeated rebels of La Rochelle in 1628. The present Cathedral, except for a fifteenth-century tower, dates from the eighteenth and nineteenth centuries.

is an oblong octogon. The roof of it is a good peice of architecture, for the breadth of the church being 44 steps & lenth being yet much more, there is noe pillar to susteine the roof.

Tide   Spring tides at Rochelle about 15 foot, sometimes 18, nepe tides 10. This is the first time I ever saw the Ocean.

Salt   Mr. Beaulot tells me that the salt of one range of pits is much better (the marke whereof is whitenesse) then that of an other; that here at Rochelle it is sold for 4 or 5s. the boyseau by the proprietors, but the marchant pays 44 or 45s., for out of every Boysseau the King has 40s. duty for all that is exported, but the inland vent pays yet a much higher tax, for the boisseau that by the proprietor is sold here at 4s., noe further off then Saumur is sold for 40 lb.[1]

Measurs   He says that the pint here is neare the pint of Paris, i.e. 2 lb.
Pint   i.e. 32 ozs., but the pinte de champs is 40 ozs., i.e. hath $\frac{1}{4}$ added to it.

He says there is a man here in town that makes rings of a mixture
Megrim   of silver & Iron togeather which people were for the Megrin & head ach. He sells many & therefor Mr. Beaulot thinks they may have some effect.[2]

Rochelle THURSD. SEPT. 8. This day we left Rochelle, a town on the north side of a narrow bay of the Ocean which makes a safe harbour, but I beleive it fills dayly with mud which is kept in by the banke of stones which Cardinall Richleiue made formerly at the seige of Rochelle crosse the mouth of the bay about $\frac{1}{2}$ mile below the towne, where in now there is now but a narrow gap for ships to passe.

The streets of this towne are the straitest & largest I have seen in any town in France, & though the houses are generally lowe because of the hard windes they have often there, yet there are many good houses in it. The houses are in most places set out into the street on both sides, with arches under which one walkes free from sun or rain, a convenient fashon, methinks, of building a great

---

[1] Hence the precautions against salt-smuggling taken at a town like Angers. (Cf. entry for 22 Aug.)

[2] Beaulot was presumably a doctor as his name is attached to various other medical notes which follow. Locke seems to have been impressed by this remedy for migraine as, two years later, he wrote to Thoynard to ask him to send one of these rings for a friend. (Ollion, p. 69.)

town either in a hot or cold country, haveing its convenience for walkers in both.

From Rochelle to Rochefort 5 leagues. Rochefort is a new town,[1] built upon the banke of Charante on the right side, 2 leagues from the sea, but 3 leagues from the mouth of the river which is lengthend by it[s] windeings. It is a convenient place for building of ships & to be a magazin maritime, both for the convenience of the river which is very deepe, though narrow, & the plenty of the country all about which supplys with all sort[s] of provisions at a cheape rate. The magazins here for all things are exceeding large & commodeous, placed all along the river side where there are stores of all sorts. In the yard which is of a large circuit, there is a generall store house for all things for ships, &, joyning to it, in a long range of building, particular stores for 60 ships, the names of each ship set over the dore. Besides this, a large building to keepe Masts in, another for planks, great forges for Ankers & other iron worke. In the yard there are now 5 vessells on the stocks, 2 large frigats of about 40 or 50 guns, 66 or 68, & 2 lesse, with a large vessell they call a flute.[2] There is also rideing in the river a very large ship which carrys 110 guns, called the Victorieuse,[3] built here, but not yet quite finishd. She is masted.

Up higher in the river, but within the walls of the towne, is the Corderie, a long building like a gallery, for makeing cables & cordage. It is 2 storys & the length is 200 brasses (1 Brasse is 5 foot 2 inches & the toise is 6 foot), & above that the Magazin of provisions & place for casting of Canons. These are all large, substantial, handsome buildings & at the Fondery there is this good invention that, a[4] vault being made all under the furnaces, there is a pent house on the outside of the building at each end which, being made with wooden shuts, they open them on the side which the winde blows & shut them on the other, which serves to blow the fire with great force.

Rochefort (margin)
Brasse (margin)

---

[1] The town and naval port were constructed by Colbert and his cousin, Colbert de Terron, the *Intendant* of Rochefort, between 1665 and 1668.

[2] A store-ship.

[3] The *Victorieux*. (See Le Conte, No. 105.)

[4] MS. has *an*, Locke having originally written 'an arch' and forgetting to correct *an* to *a*.

The towne, as those who are built at once, is laid most conveniently into strait streets, which cut one an other at right angles, soe that one sees from one end of the towne to the other. The streets that are broadest are 37 steps & soe there are of narower to 20, the distance between the streets about 100 steps. Mr. l'Intendant[1] thinks the streets too wide & intends, as he told me, to set them with trees, which will certainly make them very pleasant. The towne is not yet over well built, the houses being very low; but considering that 10 years since there were but 3 houses, if the maritime affaires & building continue here, it is like to be the prettyest towne in all France. All that is likely, in my opinion, to hinder it is the sicklynesse of the aire, for strangers that come here seldome scape a disease to season them, & at this time, we were told, $\frac{3}{4}$ were sick, the markes whereof we saw in the forgery where they were fain to give of workeing, not haveing people enough to continue it. They impute this to the overflow of the river, the spring tides, which rise here 20 ft., overflowing a great plain of meadows which lies on the other side. This morning we had here a very thick mist.

The Intendant, Mr. de Muin, is now incompasseing it with walls without bastions, but at certain distances angles for flankers,[2] for being noe frontier & the 3 leagues to the sea being difficult to passe in 2 or 3 tides by their owne vessells, they have no reason to apprehend any forraine attaque, & these walls are strong enough to keepe out any suddaine insurrection of the people, soe that if the building & peopleing the place mend the aire, a few years will probably make this one of the finest towns in France, for the imployment is here to be had & the freedome from impost on wine, salt & all other provisions cannot faile to people it & beautifie it with handsome buildings; for the narrownesse of the river (which

---

[1] Honoré Lucas de Muin, after serving as secretary to Colbert's brother, Colbert de Croissy, the French Ambassador in London, married a relative of the minister and was appointed in 1674 to succeed Colbert de Terron as *Intendant* of La Rochelle. Like his predecessor, he lived at Rochefort because of the importance of the port for the French Navy. He was dismissed from this post in 1684 and returned to Paris where he died shortly afterwards.

[2] *O.E.D.* 'A fortification projecting so as to flank or defend another part or to command the flank of an assailing enemy.'

some object) seems not to me to be any great inconvenience, the
water being deepe & the banks soft, soe that if a ship should chance
to run a ground, it can receive noe harme, for the rocks that are in
it are well known to their pilots, & I see noe great need there is to
turne a ship in the river. When it is once set right, it may goe soe.
And the very convenience of haveing provisions cheap here, espetially porke, which is found the properest to victuall with, will
always make this a place of stores to supply the King's fleet, both
here & at Brest too.

Mr. Marsiac[1] & Mr. de Touche,[2] at the recommendation of
Mr. Toinard, very civilly conducted us about to see all these fine
things which certainly cost a great deale of mony, & Mr. de Muin,
the Governor, a very civill & obleiging person,[3] made us dine with
him.

Mr. Marsiac hath lived long both at Angola & Bonos Aires. He   Bonos Aires
says Bonos Ayres which is 30 leagues up the River de la Plata, is
a very healthy country & plentifull in excellent fruit & abounding
in cattle. He has knowne a man there sell at one bargain 15,000 head
of cows & oxen. They furnish all Peru from whence there is
400 leagues by land.

SAT. SEPT. 10. From Rochefort to Xaintes 7 leagues, the country   Xaintes
most inclosed & full of walnut & other fruit trees. Xaintes is a litle
towne, seated on the left side of the Charante, which glides gently
through a fine vally of very rich meadows. The towne hath noe
thing in it very considerable that I saw. St. Peire, the Cathedrall,
is a pretty large church, neither beautifull nor beautified. From the
top of the steeple, which is handsome enough, one has a faire

---

[1] Massiac, a friend of Thoynard who had made his acquaintance at Lisbon.

[2] In a letter of 27 Aug. (MS. Locke, c. 21, ff. 5–6), enclosing letters of recommendation
to Massiac and De la Touche, Thoynard stated that the latter, a native of Toulon and
'le plus honeste provincial que je connoisse', was secretary to De Muin.

[3] He was very different in his treatment of the Protestants during his ten years as
Intendant of the province. Élie Benoît says that he was 'd'un caractère malin, envieux,
emporté, insultant, et il était tout cela dans un si haut degré qu'il n'y avoit pas lieu
d'espérer qu'il se corrigeât comme les autres; et en effet il porta la violence, l'injustice
et la cruauté aussi loin qu'on peut se l'imaginer' (IV, 302). On 1 September, just before
Locke's arrival at Rochefort, he had promulgated an edict which he had obtained from
Paris 'portant défenses à tous ceux de la religion P.R., de quelque qualité et condition
qu'ils soient, de suborner les catholiques, à peine de mille livres d'amende'. (*Ibid.* v, 97.)

prospect of the towne & of the country a great way about, espetially up the Charante. A litle without the towne are still the remaines of an Amphitheater which, haveing been built but of very small stones, hath not been able to preserve itself soe well as that of Nismes whose stones are to massive to be removd for other uses or devourd by time.

Petit Niort SUND. SEPT. 11. From Xantes to Petit Niort 8 leagues.

Blay MOND. SEPT. 12. From Petit Niort to Blay 6 [leagues]. The country between Xantes & Blay is a mixture of corne, wine, wood, meadow, champaine inclosure, wall nuts & chesnuts, but that which I ob-

Maiz servd particularly in it was plots of Maiz in severall parts, which the country people call bled d'Espagne, &, as they told me, serves poore people for bred. That which makes them sow it, is not only the great increase, but the convenience also which the blade & green about the stalke yeilds them, it being good nourishment for their cattle.

TUESD. SEPT. 13. From Blay to Bourdeaux by water 7 leagues. For a boat by ourselves with 5 rowers £5, but when you make a bargain with them for soe many rowers, you must have a care they put not boys instead of men. At Blaye at the Lyon d'Or 40 s. par jour, well enough.

Bourdeaux THURSD. SEPT. 15. We rode abroad a league or two into the country
Grave westward which they call Grave, from whence comes the Graves wine. The name, they say, comes from gravell, the soyle being indeed all sandy with small stones among & are full of vineards.

Paisants Talkeing in this country with a poore paisant's wife, she told us she had 3 children; that her husband got usually 7 s. per diem, findeing himself, which was to maintein their family, 5 in number. She indeed got 3 or 3½ s. per diem when she could get worke, which was but seldome. Other times she span hemp, which was for their clothes & yeilded noe mony. Out of this 7 s. per diem they 5 were to be mainteind, & house rent paid & their taile, & Sundays & holy days provided for.

For their house which, God wot, was a pore one roome & one story open to the tiles, without window, & a litle vineard which

was as bad as noe thing (for though they made out of it 4 or 5 tiers[1] Tiers
of wine—3 tiers make 2 hogheads—yet the labor & cost about the
vineard, makeing the wine & cask to put it in, being cast up, the
profit of it was very litle) they paid 12 ecus per annum rent & for
taile £4, for which, not long since, the collector had taken their
frying pan & dishes, mony not being ready.

Their ordinary food rie bread & water. Flesh is a thing seldome
seasons their pots &, as she said, they make noe destinction between
flesh & fasting days; but when their mony reaches to a more costly
meale, they buy the inwards of some beast in the market & then
they feast themselves. And yet they say that in Xantonge &
severall other parts of France the paisants are much more miserable
then these, for these they count the flourishing paisants which live
in Grave.

TUESD. SEPT. 20. We saw the Chasteau Trompet,[2] a very strong Chasteau
fort on the river's side, of 4 bastions, which, without shouting[3] off Trompet
one gun, has shooke down 4 churches & one side of the fairest &
best street of Bourdeaux in which one only house belonging to the
Abé   ,[4] that was yet pulling down when we were there, had cost
lately the building above 50,000 ecus. All this ruin has been made
to set this cittadell in a faire open space, free from incumbrance.[5]
There are in Garison in it about 500 French soldiers & 200 Swisse.
The French have 2 s. per diem & bred, which is worth about 1 s. Pay
more. The Swisse have 5 s. per diem & bred. The Governor of this
Cittadell, called Mr. le Comte de Montagu, is independent on the
Governor of the Province, called the Duke of Roclaure, resident
here in town.

They usually lade here in a year of the commoditys of this part Trade

---

[1] O.E.D. tierce: 'an old measure of capacity, equal to a third of a pipe (usually
42 gallons)'.
[2] The fortress of Château-Trompette dated back to 1454. It was demolished during
the Revolutionary period.
[3] O.E.D. gives this form of shooting.   [4] Left blank in MS.
[5] There was rather more to it than that. Bordeaux, perhaps because of its relations
with England, proved a thorn in the side of the Monarchy in the seventeenth century,
particularly during the Fronde. New taxes had led to serious riots in 1675, and to punish
the town and overawe it the fortress of Château-Trompette was enlarged, regardless of
the fine houses which had to be demolished.

Wine   of France 2,000 vessels. The present prohibition in England[1] much troubles them, which, joynd to the Dutch warre, makes the wine here now worth but about 25 ecus per tunneau, which formerly there sold for between 40 & 50, which was the price of the best sort of Graves wine, except Pontac which was sold for 80 or 100, & some others of a peculiar note.

Prunes   FRID. SEPT. 23. The best prunes grow about Montauban. They drye them as much as they can in the sun, & the difficiencys of that are supplyd by the heat of the oven. It is a great, black plumb, ripe in June, & they sel here now for 70 s. the Kentall.

Kerby   SAT. SEPT. 24. Left with Mr. Kerby[2] with some books of Mr. Banks's to be sent to England or Paris as he should receive order:

A Sea horse tooth.   Recd. Oct. 1679.
The cuts of Richleiue in litle, coverd with paper.
Hexameron rustique[3]
Methode pour commencer les humanites Greques et Latines
  p. Fevre[4]

Recd. of Mr. Daniel Oyens at Bourdeaux   650 – 0 – 0.
C.B.   Paid Mr. Banks   650 – 0 – 0.
Exchange   Taken up of Mr. Kerby £1,000 at 55¼ per crown.

Carthusians   We saw the Carthusians' convent,[5] about ¼ mile without the town, a large covent where is place for about 40, but there were not now above 25 moncks in it. The altar & all within the railes adornd with pillars of the finest marble that I have seen. The statues, painting & pillars with the other ornaments make it one of the finest peices I have seen. The marble there is of soe excellent a kinde (interlaced with veins, as it were, of gold) that the King hath been tempted to Wine   send for them away. There we saw great preparation for vintage which, had the weather been faire, they had began 23. They have grapes enough within the walls of the covent to make 150 or

---

[1] Parliament had prohibited all trade with France in March of this year, and for a few months the two countries were on the verge of war.
[2] There is a long medical note on Mrs Kerby's ailments on Thurs. Sept. 15.
[3] By La Mothe le Vayer.   [4] By Tanneguy Le Fèvre.
[5] *Colledg* is written above, but erased. The chapel of this monastery, founded in 1620, is now the Église Saint-Bruno. Needless to say, it is now well inside Bordeaux.

200 tun of wine, & with what they have in other places they make about 600 tun ordinarily.

1 Tun is 4 baricks.

1 Baric 110 pots.

1 Pot above 2 pints of Paris or 4 lb.

Measure
Baricks
Tun
Pot

I saw them make shot thus. The lead being melted & scumd, they Shot lade it with an iron spoon into an iron ladle peirced with holes (which is first well heated in the fire to neare the heat of the lead) which they hold over a bucket of water, & soe let it run into the cold water till the water be grown pretty warme, & then they change it into an other, for warme water does not soe well as cold. That which they let the warme lead thus strain into is not pure water, but there is about $\frac{1}{2}$ bucket of lees of wine mixed with an hoghead of water which makes the shot as bright as peauter[1] which in water would be black. They also, to polish it more, shake about 100 weight in a bag togeather. If the melted lead be too hot or too cold, it will not doe well. Each shot is at least twise as much in diameter as the hole the lead streams through. It is made of English lead which they buy now for 29 or 30 ecus per 1000 lb., & they sell the shot for $2\frac{1}{4}$ or $2\frac{1}{2}$s. per lb.[2]

SUND. 25 SEPT. To Begle to the Protestant church[3] about 2 English Begle mile out of Bourdeaux, a large church & congregation.

MOND. SEPT 26. From Bourdeaux to Cadiliac 6 leagues, through Cadiliac a sandy soile of wood land & vineards, & in many places the vine- Vineard ards set thus: 2 rows of vines & then between them 3 or 4 times that breadth of ploud land for corne. This way, I suppose, the grapes have more both direct & reflex sun & ripen better.

At Cadiliac upon a riseing ground, a flight shot or 2 from the Garon, on the right side, is a faire, large house,[4] built by the Duke of Espernon,[5] which, though not soe long since built as to feele the

[1] *O.E.D.* gives this form of *pewter*.

[2] From Bordeaux Locke appears to have written to Sir John Banks asking for his consent to his taking his son to Italy (see the latter's reply, dated 30 Sept. o.s.: MS. Locke, c. 3, ff. 114–15).

[3] The *Temple* at Bègles was demolished in 1685.

[4] Built between 1598 and 1615, the château is now in a ruined state.

[5] The first Duke, who built the château, died in 1642. His successor, the last male representative of the family, died in 1661.

decays of age, yet is like to perish with that family now at an end, whilst the contest between the pretenders to it, the Duke of Foix and le Comte   ,[1] exposes it to ruin.

The house is built as most of the great houses I have seen in France, a front & two wings, & has a graft[2] about it & a drawbridg. The front of the house is on the farther side the court opposite to the gate you come in at, which, with the wall that bounds the court where you enter, & the two wings on each side, makes the court neare about a square of 800[3] broad. On the out side the two wings on each side runs along a terras equall to the length of the building

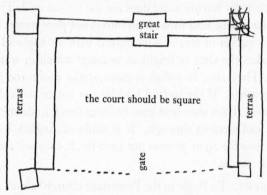

from outside to outside of 150 steps long. The offices are all underground & archd, & are suitable to the bignesse of the house, soe that the house is 4 storys high & much more capacious then the Chasteau of Richlieu within the moat.

They shew here a chimny peice in the King's Chamber which, they say, cost £50,000 & one great agat in it which they count worth £20,000, in all £70,000.

At the end of the wings stand out within the square of the building 4 pavilions which towards the entrance stand wholly without the line of the wall that bounds the court.

TUESD. SEPT. 27. At the 3 Kings at Cadiliac not over well. From Marmand Cadiliac to Marmand 7 leagues, long enough, most part vineards. At the Golden Lion 20s. per maister & 15s. per horse, well enough.

---

[1] Left blank in MS.   [2] O.E.D. 'moat'.   [3] Feet or paces?

WED. SEPT. 28. From Marmand to Agen 6 leagues. If I would buy   Marmand
land by the league, it should be in this country, for we were
10½ howers rideing those 6 leagues on good English horses. About
Tonnings,[1] 2 leagues from Marmand, we saw great quantities of   Tonnings
Tabaco planted.   Tobaco

At Agen at St. Jaques 30 s. per master & 15 s. horse, well. Agen
is a pretty large town.

THURSD. SEPT. 29. From Agen to Mosac.[2] From Cadiliac hither all   Mosa
along a rich valey & deep soile in which the Garonne runs. This
valey is in some places broad, in other more narrow. Mosac stands
on the right side the Tarre,[3] a league or more before it falls into the
Garonne. At Notre Dam 20 s. per Maistr, well.

FRID. SEPT. 30. From Mosac to Montaban   [4] leagues. Montaban   Montaban
is a litle towne, built of brick, well situated upon a risse [sic] on the
right side the Tar. The streets are[5] broad & handsome enough, &
I beleive the situation very healthy. At the Casque d'or 20 s. per
meale, not well.

SAT. OCT. 1. From Montaban to Tholose 7 leagues.

SUND. OCT. 2. In the Cathedrall church here, cald St. Estienne, one   Tolose
alter peice is the Virgin lifted up by angells, the Holy Gost over her   Virgin
head in the likenesse of a dove, & above God the Father represented
in an old man holding out a crown ready for her.

Rub your hand over with a pounded snaile & then pour on it   Scalding
boiling wax & it will not scald. Mr. Breteile.

Oyle or soape does the same for melted lead. ib.

If you have necessity to fasten any thing with melted lead under   Lead
water, doe but rub the place with grease & then let the lead melted
fall into the place. It will fasten without leapeing or sputtering in
the water. ib.

WED. OCT. 5. They wash very white in this towne as I saw by a laced
hankercheife about Our Lady's neck & a laced band & cuffs
about Our Saviour's in a church here.

---

[1] Tonneins.   [2] Moissac. For once Locke forgot to insert the distance·
[3] Tarn.   [4] Left blank in MS.   [5] MS. has '&'.

Chartereux THURSD. OCT. 6. The Chartereux[1] here very large and fine.

Reliques   We saw the reliques at St. Sernin[2] where there is the greatest store of them that I have met with any where. Besides others, there are 6 Apostles & the head of the 7th, viz. the two James's, Philip, Simon, Jude, Barnabas & the head of Barthelmey. We were told of the wonders these & the other reliques have donne, being caried in procession, & espetially the head of St. Edward, one of our Kings of England, which, caried in procession, deliverd the town from a plague some years since.

      At Tholose Chez Navarre 20 s. per repas, well, & 15 s. par jour for horse.

Castlenaudary SUND. 9 OCT. From Tolose to Castlenaudary 8 leagues. At the 3 Pigeons 30 s. pour homme et cheval a couché.

Carcassone MOND. 10 OCT. From Castelnaudary to Carcassone 6 leagues. A l'Ange 30 s. for horse & man for supper, lodging & breakfast.

Cavesac TUESD. 11 OCT. From Carcassone to Cavesac[3] 7 leagues. Not well.

Beziers WED. 12 OCT. From Cavesac to Beziers 4 leagues. A la Crox [sic] blanche 20 s. for horse & man for dinner, & 30 s. pour couché, horse & man, well.

Montpellier THURSD. 13 OCT. From Bezier to Montpellier 11 leagues.

Olive tree   Come from Tholose hither, one meets with noe olive trees till on this sid[e] Carcassone. They were this yeare very thick hung with olives al along the way we came.[4]

Botanica THURSD. OCT. 20.[5] Clusius[6] gives a good description of plants & speaks only of what he has seen, & soe also Lobelius[7] with Pena.[8]

---

[1] The chapel is now the Église Saint-Pierre (built between 1607 and 1612).
[2] Cf. Locke's earlier comments in the entry for 30 March 1677.
[3] Cabezac.
[4] In his second note-book (p. 194) Locke made the following entries in his accounts with Caleb Banks in Oct. 1678:

> 'Dr. 14. for given Dr. Barbyrac   03 – 0.
>   18. for pd. at Petit Paris   44 – 0.'

[5] The entry for 19 Oct., headed 'Veterinaria: Cough', is followed by the name of the Earl of Meath (William Brabazon, born c. 1635, who succeeded to the title in 1675 and died in 1685).
[6] Charles de L'Écluse (1526–1609).   [7] Mathias de Lobel (1538–1616).
[8] Pierre Pena and de Lobel published their *Stirpium Adversaria nova* in 1571.

Prosper Alpinus[1] also & Casalpinus[2] are both good botanists and describe the plants well & on their owne observation. Gaspar Bauhinus[3] a good botanist & his Pinax an admirable worke, but many faults in it. Matthiolus[4] has not very well describd the plants, but has set downe the vertues as he found account of them amongst the country people where they grew & who had had experience of them, & there are there many excellent remedies amongst them.

John Bauhinus[5] is but a compilator. Magnol.

SAT. OCT. 29.[6] A totall eclyps of the moone. It was sensible at 6.42 or 43 p.m., but Dr. Jolly who had calculated it & observed it, & those that were with him concluded it to begin at 6.40 p.m. *Eclypsis lunae*

The moon was totally eclypsed at 7.47 or 48, I thinke 47. J.L.

The observation following was made by Dr. Jolly at Montpellier of this same ecclips.

La Lune estant elevée de 18 d. peu moins a 6 heurs 45 minutes de nos montres a paru sensiblem[t] eclipsée de sorte qu'on peut conter le commencem[t] del'Eclypse depuis 6 h. 42 m.

A 7 h. 48 m. nous avons ete asseures que tout son disque etoit dans l'ombre, mais comme il y avoit des nuages qui la cachoient de tems en tems, il peut estre que tout son disque etoit dans l'ombre toute entiere quelques minutes plutot que nous l'avions estimé. La lune estoit pour lors ellevée de 27 d.

La Lune estant elevée de 44 d. et demy a 9 h. 29 m. de nos montres a commencé de sortir del'ombre.

---

[1] Superintendent of the Botanical Garden at Padua at the end of the sixteenth century.

[2] Andrea Cesalpino (1519–1603).

[3] Gaspard Bauhin (1560–1624). His *Pinax Theatri Botanici* appeared at Basle in 1596.

[4] Pietro Andrea Mattioli (1500–77).

[5] Jean Bauhin (1541–1613), brother of Gaspard.

[6] The entry for Oct. 24 contains notes on horse diseases followed by the name of Mr Cheny, and Oct. 27 has similar notes with the name of Mr Sydeny. The latter date also has some medical notes, associated with Dr Magnol: the first of these concludes 'v. *Botan: Monspeliens*'. Cheny (or rather Cheney) was an Irishman (see a letter from him, dated 1698, referring to his earlier acquaintance with Locke—MS. Locke, c. 5, ff. 83–4). A letter of Denis Grenville, of 24 Oct. 1678, is addressed to Locke 'Chez Mons[r] Cheny, Gentilhomme Anglois habitant proche l'Eglise de St. Pierre A Montpellier'. He seems to have acted as a tutor, since Charleton informed Locke in February 1679 that 'Mr. Cheney has order from Sir John Champante to conduct his son to Ireland towards Aprill' (MS. Locke, c. 5, ff. 29–30).

A 9 h. 58 m. avoit recouvré la lumiere dans toute la moitié de son disque.

A 10 h. 28 m. la lune estant elevée de 53 d. et demy, l'eclypse finit entierem^t.

Pont Lunel SUND. 30 OCT.¹ In the afternoon to Pont Lunell 4 leagues, 35 s. Master & horse, well, for couché.

Nismes MONDAY 31 OCT. To Nismes 4 leagues. 25 s. Master & horse, pour dinner, well, a la Luxembourg.

Ramoulin To Ramoulin² 3 leagues. At the Pont du Gard 30 s. Master & horse, ill. To this place the country by the way very full of olive trees.

Pont St. TUESD. NOV. 1. To Pont St. Esprit 6 leagues. At the Post 20 s.
Esprit Master & horse pour dinner, well.

Donzel To Donzel³ 3 leagues. At the Lyon d'or 30 s. pour couché for master & horse, very well.

From Ramoulin hither the country full of mulbery trees & in the great vally between this & St. Esprit store of almond trees & mulbery trees, all the rest corne, noe vineards to be seen nor olive trees all the plaine. On the rise of the hill where Donzel stands there are some, & as soon as one begins to rise above the levell of the vally, all the surface of the earth is coverd with pebles. Beyond
Olive trees this towards Lyons one findes noe olive trees.

Laureol WED. NOV. 2. To Laureole⁴ 6 leagues. At the Chariot d'or 25 s. dinner, horse & master, very well. The greatest part of this litle
Protestants place Protestants. Waterd meadows about the town. To Valence
Valence 3 great leagues. At the Grifon d'or. The country to-day corne, mulbery trees & wallnuts.

Taxes 5 millions abated in the taile,⁵ but ⅛ of the purchase to be paid of all Church or corporation Lands that have at any time been alienated. If they be decayd since the purchase, they pay ⅛ of the

---

¹ Before a list of books (reproduced in *The Library*) Locke wrote: 'Left with Mr. Charleton to be sent to Mr. Verchand at Paris for me in March next....'
² Remoulins.
³ Donzères.   ⁴ Loriol.
⁵ At the end of the war in 1678, various taxes were reduced. Clamageran gives the following figures for the *taille*: 1678, 40,480,000 l., 1679, 34,939,000 l.

purchase; if meliorated, they pay according to the improved value. He that refuses hath[1] a Garison of soldiers presently sent to his house.

THURSD. 3 NOV. From Valence to St. Valier 5 leagues. At the St. Valiere Lyon d'or not very well, 20s. horse & master for dinner. By the way hither at Thyn,[2] 3 leagues from Valence, we dranke excellent Hermitage wine which grows on a litle hill just by it, & a[t] 1½ leagues from Valence we ferried the rapid, untoward river called Lizar.[3]

From St. Valier to Piage[4] 4 leagues. At the Escu well enough. Piage

FRIDAY 4 NOV. To St. Florin[5] 5 leagues. At the Ecu well enough. St. Florin To Lyon 3 leagues.

The ordinary rates on all this road between this & Montpellier Rates is for horse & man for dinner 20s. & for couché 30s., but they will wrangle with strangers to get more. All along also from Montlimar, or rather Castelnau,[6] to Lyon the soile is in most places full with, & in many places quite coverd with, great peables in heigths much above the levell of the Rhosne.   Lyon

MOND. 7 NOV. We saw the Charitie, a very large & well regulated Charité hospital where young children, male & femal, not under 7 years old, are taken in & set to worke. Their great imployment is about Silke. They are taught alsoe to reade and some of the girles to sing, & thus they are bread up. When they are of age, they may goe out or marry if they will, & then they give the maide that is maried £100 to begin the world with, or they may stay in all their lives, & of these there are usually in the house about 1,500 poore & orphans, & if they have any thing, as it happens to some of the Orphans, the principall is restord to them when they goe out & the house has the use for their breeding. Some of the girles are taught to sing & sing well enough.

They rise at 5 & worke till darke in winter, & in sommer till

---

[1] In the MS. the words 'a garison presently' are twice inserted in this sentence.
[2] Tain.   [3] L'Isère.
[4] Le Péage.   [5] St Symphorien.
[6] Not to be found on the maps of the Rhône valley. Châteauneuf-sur-Rhône?

6 at night, but, counting their masse & breakfast in the morning, collation in the afternoon & time of dinner, their worke is not hard.

Their break fast & collation is bread & water. At dinner & supper they have a litle morsell of boiled flesh, each one about an ounce or two, & soope at dinner, but never roast meat, unlesse it be the singers who are treated better then the rest. They have all trades necessary for the house within them selves.

They bake, one week with an other, 100 asnes of wheat, partly for the use & consumption of the house, & partly to be distributed to the prisoners & poore of the towne. Though the portion of flesh be limited to every one, yet every one may have as much bread as he can eat.

They usually have in their granary a provision of 6 or 7,000 Asnes of wheat which 10 or 12 men are dayly imploid in turning. It lyes about a yard or more thick & the roome open to the aire without glasse or paper to the windows.

Measures
Asné

The Asné is two fold: 1. l'Asne de Boulanger, which conteines 6 Bichets or boisseau. 2. l'Asne de Bourgeois which conteines 7 Bichetts. The Asnes of the Charity is the Asné de Boulanger. The Bichet I saw there was about 1280 in diameter & about 706 high in the cleare, & a Bichett of wheat weighs about 60 or 62 lb.

Banks

Mr. Banks owes me now, upon ballanceing the whole account between us   £253 – 11.

Cookery

THURS. 10 NOV. Take fine wheat flower ¼ lb., water q.s. to make a liquid batter, the whites of 4 egs, sugar & rose water or any thing else to season it q.s. Take butter q.s., melt it in a skillet[1] & be soe hot that it smoakes, & into this butter over the fire let some of this batter, about 2 or 3 spoonfulls, run out of a tunnell[2] with 3 holes or litle pipes set at a distance one from an other, whose hollow is almost as big as that of a small goose quill. The tunnell must be let in to the end of a stick soe that when the batter is in & let run into the butter, it may be shaked up & downe soe that the streames of batter, falling crosse one an other, may make a kind of lace or net. When it is a litle boild in the butter, with an iron hooke turne

---

[1] *O.E.D. saucepan.*   [2] *O.E.D.* 'Obs. & Dial. funnel'.

it & soe let it boile on the other side, & then draw it out on a rolling pin & it will be something like a wafer, but it is presently boiled & has a very pleasant tast. My Lady Chichley[1] has one of the tunnells to make them.[2]

Lent Mr. Banks 14 half Luisd'or		£77 – 0.		Banks
which with our former account[3] makes him
deter to me					£330 – 11.

FRID. NOV. 11. In Switzerland a suit of Law costs noe thing, but is Law prosecuted at the publique charge by officers paid by the publique, which makes that suits are presently ended & as well for the pore as the rich.

TUESD. NOV. 15. From Lyons to Tarara[4] 6 leagues, the country Tarara all hilly, litle vineards, much pasture, most arable & almost all inclosure. Not much wood. At the Mutton well.

WED. NOV. 16. To Rouanne[5] 6 leagues over the Mountain Terrara, Rouanne a large towne on the left side the Loire. From a league above hence it is navigable to the sea. Rouanne is in Forez. At the Galere mediocrement for 40 s. couche, horse & man.

THURSD. 17 [NOV.]. To Palice[6] 8 leagues, a mixture of arable, Palice pasture, wood & heath, but of the two later not very much.

At Palice I saw a stone turnd by the water which, runing upon its Hemp circumference, like that which grindes olives in Languedoc or bark in England, prepared hemp, i.e. did the businesse of beating it, two or 3 people standing & turning it still as the stone passed, which

---

[1] Locke and his pupil were to have been accompanied to Italy by Thomas Tufton and probably Sir John Chicheley (see letter from Sir John Banks, MS. Locke, c. 3, ff. 116–17). Thomas Tufton fell ill at Lyons and was attended by Locke (see his letter of 17 Dec. from Montpellier: MS. Locke, c. 22, ff. 26–7).

[2] There are numerous medical notes in the entries for 10 and 12 Nov., followed by the name of 'Mr. Selapris'. The Lovelace Collection contains 13 letters addressed to Locke between 1677 and 1680 by 'Jacques Selapris l'aisné, marchand, rue de l'arbre secq, à Lyon'. Locke appears to have got to know him through Charleton who informed him in 1681 of Selapris's death from cholera. He sent on Locke's and Caleb Banks's luggage after their departure from Lyons, and was also responsible for dispatching by the *coche d'eau* a German called Sylvester Brownover whom Locke took on as a lackey on 14 November (see Second Note-book, p. 24) and who later became his *amanuensis*. On 14 November there are veterinary notes contributed by 'Mr. Bruning'.

[3] Locke gives a reference to the entry for 7 Nov.

[4] Tarare.			[5] Roanne.			[6] La Palisse.

made its rotation in a very litle time, being turnd by an horizontall water wheele something like that at Narouse.[1] The stone was about 4 foot broad as I guessed, & 1½ foot thick. As the Escu 25 s. man, 15 s. horse pour couché, very well.

Moulin FRID. 18 NOV. To Moulins 10 leagues. Much pasturage & inclosure & hedgrows of scrubbed[2] pollard oakes, not much vineards, the greatest part corne. Moulins is a pretty large town on the right side the Allier. The streets are large & the buildings pretty handsome, most of brick. Au Lion d'or 15 s. pour cheval et 25 s. pour homme pour couché, & if one stays longer then one night, 20 s. per repas, well enough.[3]

St. Peire SAT. 19 NOV. From Moulins to St. Peire[4] 7 leagues. At the Cheval blanc 40 s. horse & man pour couché et dejuner. The reasonablest people that I met with in France for they would not take mony for 3 picotins of oats we had extraordinary.

Nevers SUND. 20 NOV. To Nevers 5 leagues. It is pleasantly situated on the right side of the Loire on a riseing ground, the town not very big nor very well built. Moulins is famous for Cissars, razors & other litle works in Iron, as Nevers for all sorts of workes & trifles in glasse. Between Moulins & Nevers the country has much pasturage & inclosure &, here & there, wood.

Latch Memo. the Latch of the chamber dore where I lay at Nevers at the Fleur de Lys, which was raised by turning an iron botton[5] without, but was kept of by a spring within, soe that it tooke noe hold of the latch but when one puld as well as turnd the button. At the Fleur de Lys 20 s. per repas, very well, pour couche 25 s.

Cosne MOND. 21 NOV. To Cosne 10 leagues, the country less inclosed then yesterday. 4 leagues from hence towards Nevers we passed a litle place called Pouly[6] where the wine is excellent good, & the soyle where the vineards are, all full of litle stones soe as one would think it a very barren soyle.

---

[1] Naurouze (see entry for 5 March 1677). [2] *O.E.D.* 'stunted, dwarfed'.
[3] There follows an account of how the innkeeper was cured of dropsy 'by an empirik'.
[4] St Pierre-le-Moûtier.
[5] *O.E.D.* gives this spelling of *button*. [6] Pouilly-sur-Loire.

Here at Cosne the King has a forge for Ankers & an other for musquets & pistols, etc. 'Tis a convenient place for it, there being an Iron mine & worke at Donzy, 3 leagues up upon the litle river that falls here into the Loire, & colepits also from whence they have coles for their forge, though they are not very good.

A water mill boares their barrells. Each water wheele turns two boariers, which is done by two cords of sheep's guts, each as big as one's thumb, which, from a solid wooden wheele fixed on the axis of the water wheele, goes to two other solid wooden wheels, each not above half the diameter of that which turns them, soe that they turne very quick. In the center is a noch into which they put a borier as the wheele runs, & soe take it out & put in an other as they have occasion, & over against the end of the borier in the same line is fastend the barrell in a slideing peice of wood which a boy drives forward with his knees (for of that heigth it is above the ground) & thus one boy will boare 20 pistol barrells in a day. A litle spout from the water wheele conveys water upon the barrell to keep it from heating in boaring. *Boaring of guns*

At the Lyon d'or 40 s. pour couché, horse & man, well enough.

TUESD. 22 NOV. From Cosne to Gien 10 leagues. At the Escu at the same rate, mediocrement. There are 5 or 600 Protestants in this town & 2 ministers. *Gien*

Two leagues before we came to Gien we passed the Canale at Briare where by boats passe out of the Loire into the Sene, which communication betwixt these two rivers is of great convenience. The Canale cut is but 4 leagues longue & wants water in the summer. Cardinal Richleiue was the author of it[1] & under his care it came to be perfected, but being in the hands of private men (under grants & priviledges from Luis 13) who have both the management & profit of it. The King is going to make a communication of these 2 rivers Lower to passe by Montargis.[2] They pay here in the Canale of Briare 60 s. per foot for the length of the boat when *Briare*

---

[1] The Canal de Briare was begun in 1604, but work on it was held up by the death of Henry IV and was not resumed until 1638. It was completed in 1642, the year of Richelieu's death.

[2] The *Canal d'Orléans* (it runs from above Orleans to just below Montargis) was constructed between 1682 and 1692.

loaden with fish or such commoditys, when with heavier, v.g. wine, they pay more then a crown per foot.

Chasteau neuf WED. 23 NOV. To Chasteau neuf 9 leagues. What the country we passed in these 3 days is, I can not well say, there haveing been a continuall thick mist that one could scarce see a stone's cast before one.

Here at Chasteau neuf is a litle & not very fine house or chasteau belonging to Mr. de La Vriliere, Secretary of State for the clergy,[1] but the garden belonging to it recompences the largenesse of the house, being, I beleive, near 2 miles about & a making very fine, to which the Loire that washes the foot of a very long terras that bounds one side of it, addes a very great beauty, besides the walks, woods, basins & jet d'eaux which are already in it.

Orleans THURS. 24 NOV. To Orleans 6 leagues, mist still.

Microscope The Microscopes that soe magnifie are noe thing but litle lens of glasse, made of the smallest threads of glasse melted, which run of them selves into that figure, but in melting them in the flame of a candle there mixes some grease with them, which [is] to be avoided, either by the flame of well burnt charcoals as I imagin, or the flame of spirit of wine.[2] For Mr. Hautefeuille[3] who tells me this, says he has in vain tried to melt them with a burning glasse & Mr. Godfroy[4] says a burning glasse will not melt snow.

The manner of useing this litle microscope is to place it between a doubled plate of brasse or lead peirced with a very small hole & soe applying it to a thin peice of talke[5] which holds the object to a peice of 'cleare glasse, hold it as close as one can to the eye opposite to the light.

Wine A tun of wine holding two poinsons which contein 400 pints, is
Measures sold here now, vessell & all, for £7, the vessell itself being worth

---

[1] Louis Phélypeaux de La Vrillière (1599–1681). He succeeded his father as *Secrétaire d'État* in 1629.

[2] The old chemical symbol is used in the MS.

[3] Jean Hautefeuille (1647–1724), a well-known inventor of the time, with numerous publications to his name. There are references to him in a letter of Locke to Thoynard of 15 Aug. 1679 (Ollion, p. 32) and, indirectly, in a letter to Boyle of 27 July 1678.

[4] There are medical notes, followed by his name, in the entry for 25 Nov.

[5] *O.E.D. talc*: '1. Mica or Muscovy glass. 2. laminae or plates of hydrated silicate of magnesium.'

neare the mony, & this not bad or decayd wine, but that which is very good.

Eclypsis lunae 29 Oct. 1678 Parisiis.   *Eclypsis*

Hora

Initium	6 – 43′ – 40″
Immersio	7 – 41 – 0
Emersio	9 – 21 – 30
Finis	10 – 20 – 10

Est itaque

Medium Ecclypsis	8 – 31′ – 50″
Medium Immersionis	8 – 31 – 15.

SAT. NOV. 26. To Toury 10 leagues. At the 3 Kings 50s., horse & man, very ill.   *Toury*

SUND. NOV. 27. To Charter[1] 16 leagues. At the 3 Singes, very well. *Chartre* From Orleans to Estaps,[2] 20 leagues, is a plaine of noething but corne, thick set on both sides the road, with litle towns & parishes soe that in some places one may see in view 13 or 14 steeples from one standing.

MOND. NOV. 28. From Chartres to Paris 8 leagues.

WED. NOV. 30. Mr. Toynard shewd me a letter where in was re- *Flying* ported for certaine of a man here in France that flies with 4 winges laid over his shoulders, moveing those behinde with his feet as those before with his hands, & the motion of the wings is diagonal, the right wing before & the left wing behinde supporting & operateing at the same time, & thus he hath flown over his neigh- bours' houses, v. Journal des Scavants.[3]

THURSD. DEC. 1. The carrier pigeons flie from Alexandretta or *Pigeon* Scanderoon to Aleppo, which is 2 days' journey on horse back, in *carriers* 3 howers. Mr. Toynard.[4]

---

[1] Chartres.   [2] Étampes.

[3] The volume for 1678 contains (pp. 416–18) an article, with one illustration, entitled 'Extrait d'une lettre escrite à Monsieur Toynard sur une Machine d'une nouvelle invention pour voler en l'air'.

[4] For the same date there is an entry, also derived from Thoynard, on Old Testament terms. On 2 Dec. there is a note, derived from Selapris, on making horses' hoofs grow; and some notes on various measures, from Auzout.

Salt water | MOND. 5 DEC. Mr. Toynard told me of one that had found out the secret to sweeten salt water. Q. Dr. Wilkins?[1]

Possessed | WED. DEC. 14. The story of the Nuns of Lodun possessed was noe thing but a contrivance of Cardinall Richlieu to destroy a man Grandiere[2] he suspected to have writ a booke against him, who was condemnd for witchcraft in the case & burnt for it. The scene was

Capucins | managed by the Capucines, & the nuns plaid their tricks well, but all was a cheat.

Canon | I saw at Mr. Toynard's the modell of a Canon to be charged at the breetch, which was by a plug of Iron or brasse, made something bigger then the bore of the cannon, that reachd as far as the touch hole, just fited to the receptacle of it, & soe being thru[s]t into the breetch of the cannnon which is open behinde, is there fastend in with a key of steele, which peirces both it & both sides of the cannon, & there holds it tite. This is of great use, if practicable, as it seemes, & as he says it has been by the Hollanders in their late war.[3]

C.B. | Memo. that Mr. Banks tooke up about the begining of this month of Mme Herinx £1000.

King | WED. 28 DEC. At the King's Levé which I saw this morning at St. Germans, there is noe thing soe remarkable as his great devotion which is very exemplary, for as soon as ever he is dressed, he goes to his bed's side where he kneels downe to his prayers, severall preists kneeling by him, in which posture he continues for a pretty while, not being disturbd by the noise & buz of the rest of the chamber, which is full of people standing & talking one to an other.

FRID. 30 DEC. In the Library of the Abbé[4] of St. Germains Mr. Covell[5] & I saw two very old manuscripts of the New Testament,

[1] John Wilkins (1614–72), Bishop of Chester, the first secretary of the Royal Society? On the same date there is a medical note, followed by 'P. Ange, Orleans'.
[2] Urbain Grandier, Curé of Loudun, was burnt at the stake in 1634. Modern historians reject the theory that Richelieu had him put to death for publishing an attack on him.
[3] Here follows a note comparing English and French measures, and after it: 'Mr. Auzout'.
[4] Abbey.
[5] John Covell (1638–1722), was chaplain to the Levant Company in Constantinople from 1671 to 1676. He returned to England in January 1679 and settled down in Cambridge where he became Master of Christ's College. The British Museum possesses

the newest of which was, as appeard by the date of it, at least 800 years old, in each of which 1 John c. 5 v. 7 was quite wanting, & the end of the 8 verse ran thus, tres unum sunt. In an other old copy the 7 verse was, but with interlineing. In an other much more moderne copy verse 7 was also, butt differently from the old copy, & in two other old manuscripts also verse 7 was quite out, but, as I remember, in all of them the end of the 8th verse was tres unum sunt.[1]

1 John 5. 7

SAT. DEC. 31. La longueur du pendule de Paris contient 3 pieds 8½ lignes.

Pendule

1679[2]

SUND. 1 JAN. 1679. Amongst other things Mr. Covell told me how the Patriarchs of Constantinople are made at present by the Grand Signior, & how they buy out one an other, v. Patriarch. And how the Nonconformist Protestants were induced by him to take the Sacrament kneeleing, v. Conformity.[3]

Patriarch

Conformity

TUESD. JAN. 3. The Heraulds of France are but meane, petty trades men, commonly Chandelers.

Heralds[4]

---

parts of his correspondence (including some letters of Locke of a much later period) and the *Autograph Journals of Dr. John Covel during his travels in Asia Minor, Greece, Switzerland, Italy and France*: 16 Feb. 1676/7–12 Feb. 1679/80. Unfortunately reference to this latter manuscript (Add. MS. 22914) shows that, although he devotes a considerable number of pages to his journey from Geneva to Calais and mentions such common acquaintances as Justel, Thoynard, Auzout, Sir Thomas Lynch and Mr Monsteven, he did not think Locke worth a mention. Yet the Lovelace Collection contains a letter from him to Locke, dated 17 May 1679.

[1] A. Franklin, *Les Anciennes Bibliothèques de Paris* (Paris, 1867), 3 vols., I, 130, speaks of 'deux bibles latines du IXe siècle. La fameuse phrase *Et hi tres unum sunt*, se trouvait, paraît-il, dans l'une et n'existait pas dans l'autre'. The fire of 1794 presumably accounted for their disappearance (cf. entry for 23 July 1677).

[2] British Museum, Add. MS. 15642. In the same volume is bound an almanac, entitled: *Ephemeris ou Almanach Historial, pour l'an de grace, mil six cens septante-neuf* .... Par Me. L.C. Astrologue & Mathematicien, Disciple de M. Questier. Avec l'Almanach du Palais. A Troyes & se vendent a Paris Chez la V. Nicolas Oudot, rue veille [sic] Bouclerie.

[3] These cross-references are to a manuscript (MS. Locke. d. 1) which contains numerous entries arranged on Locke's system of 'commonplace books'. In this manuscript the two entries entitled 'Patriarch' and 'Conformity', the fruit of Covell's experiences as chaplain at Constantinople, are developed at greater length (pp. 5, 9, 53).

[4] MS. has *Helalds*.

Ausne WED. JAN. 4.[1] The Ausne of Paris is 3 foot 8 inches of the Paris foot.
Mr. Auzout.

Revieu THURS. JAN. 5.[2] This day was the review of the infantry of the
Maison du Roy, for soe the horse & foot guards are called. There
were 30 companys, if one may recon by their colours, of French
& 10 of Swisse, all new habited, both officers & soldiers. The
officers of the French gold or for the most part silver imbroidery or
lace in blew, & The Swisse officers all gold on red & much the
richer.

The French common soldiers all in new clothes, the coats &
breeches of cloth almost white, red vests laced with counter fait
silver, lace under or at least as much of it as was seen before was
red cloth, though if one looked farther, one should have found it
grafted to linin. Shoulder belt & bandeleirs of buffe leather laced
as their vests, red stocking & new shoes. A new hat laced, adorned
with a great white, woolen feather, though some were red. A new
paire of white gloves with woollen fringe, & a new sword, copper
gilt hilt. All which, I'm told, with a coat to were over it of a grey
stuff, cost but 44 livres, which is bated[3] out of their pay, out of
which, all defalcations being made, there remains for their maintenance 5 s. per diem. The soldiers, as I over tooke them comeing
home to Paris, had most of them oiled hat cases too, a part, I suppose, of their furniture,[4] & coorse, linin buskins after the fashon
of the country to save their red stockings.

The Swisse soldiers were habited in red coats & blew britches
cut after their fashon, with their points at the knees, & had noe
feathers. The pike men of both had back & breast, but the Swisse
had also head peices which the French had not. For the Swis[s]e
the King pays each captain for him self & all the men in his company 18 livre per mensem, which is all their pay, but the Captain's
profit lies in this, that he agrees with his officers as he can per
mensem & soe with the soldiers, who have some 9, some 14£ per
mensem & soe between as they can agree.

The French Colours were in a feild azure sprinkled with

---

[1] MS. has *Jan.* 3.   [2] MS. has *Jan.* 4.
[3] *O.E.D. deducted.*   [4] *O.E.D. equipment.*

flowerdelys or a crosse argent charged at every end with a crown
or. Thus they were all but one, which was azur 4 crowns or. The
Swisse colours were a crosse argent, the 4 cantons, filld with stripes
of yellow, azure & red,[1] wavy, all pointing to the center of the
crosse.

As the King passed at the hed of the line as they stood drawn up,
the officers at the heads of their companys & regiments in armer
with pikes in their hands saluted him with their pikes & then with
their hats, & he very courteously put of his hat to them again,
& soe he did again when, he takeing his stand, they marchd all
before him. He passed twise a long the whole front of them forwards & backwards, first by himself, the Dauphin etc., accompanying him, & then with the Queen, he rideing along by her coach
side.

The Serjeants complaining that their pay would not reach to
make them soe fine as was required, i.e. scarlet or red coats with
true gold galoon, to make them amends for it, they were alowed to
take more on their quarters.

The French for excuseing from quarters make them pay 24 ecus, Quartering
the Swisse but £18.

FRID. JAN. 6.[2] The observation of Lent at Paris is come almost to Lent
noe thing. Meat is openly to be had in the shambles & a dispensation commonly to be had from the Curat without any more
adoe, & people of sense laugh at it, & in Italy it self for 20s.
a dispensation is certainly to be had.

The best edition of the French Bible is that in folio of Elzevir in French
2 vols., but the notes are not very good.[3] The best notes are those Bible
of Diodati & his Italian Bible is very good.[4] Mr. Justel.

The best edition of Fra Paolo's History of the Council of Trent Paolo
is the Italian one printed at London.[5] This is the originall. ib.

MOND. JAN. 16.[6] A tun of gold is 40,000 crowns. Tun of gold
The 200th penny in Amsterdam in the year 1674 1,600 tuns of Amsterdam

---

[1] MS. appears to have *rend*.   [2] MS. has '*Jan*. 5'.
[3] Amsterdam, 1669.   [4] Geneva, 1607, 4°.
[5] In 1619.
[6] On 8 January, as on numerous other dates down to Locke's departure from Paris,
there are notes on the Gospels derived from Thoynard.

Taxes gold, but this sometimes they pay 5 or 6 times in a yeare, & during this last war with France they have sometimes paid in a yeare $\frac{1}{6}$ or $\frac{1}{7}$ of their estates, soe that since the yeare '74 their estates are lessend neare $\frac{1}{3}$.

Bills of At Paris the bills of Mortality usualy amount to 19 or 20,000 per
Mortality annum, & they count in the town about 500,000 souls, about 50,000 more then at London where the bills are less. Mr. Auzout. Q. whether the Quakers & Anabaptists & Jews that die in London are recond in the bills of Mortality? J.L.

Exchange MOND. JAN. 23.[1] Exchange 54$\frac{5}{8}$ pence d'Angleter for 1 Escu de France et $\frac{1}{200}$ pour commission, i.e. 55$\frac{1}{8}$ to be paid at deux usances, i.e. 2 Months from the date, At which Mr. Banks received £1306 – 2s. of Madame Herinx for 100l. sterling.

Taxes SAT. 28 [JAN].[2] The hackney coach men pay here £1 per diem & the chaire men £3 per weeke.

Sun WED. FEB. 1. Mr. Toinard shewd me a new systeme of our Tour-billion[3] wherein the center of the sun described a circle of the turbillion in which it made its periodical circuit in 6 months & Mercury moved about the sun as the moon doth about the earth.

Orange trees THURSD. FEB. 2. Mr. Toinard had orange trees sent him out of Portugal. They were great trees, as big as one's thigh, all the branches cut off close & soe put into boxes ramd full of good earth, & thus they remained three months before they were taken out to be set, & yet all grew at Orleance brave, flourishing trees.

Esteem FRID. FEB. 3. *That which the French* recommended, *people at court here were composing sonnets or* epigrams etc., *and at present a good quality in esteem is to sing.*

---

[1] Notes on the value of the *Patacon, Rixdollar* and *Ducaton* are to be found at this point in the MS.

[2] After a note on a cure for arthritis, dated Jan. 26, comes the sentence: 'This Mr. Claude who has had the gout this 7 or 8 years, findes to give him ease commonly at the first useing....' Was this Jean Claude (1619–87), pastor at Charenton and the adversary of Bossuet?

[3] The reference is to Descartes's system of *tourbillons* or *vortices*, replaced by Newton's theory of gravitation.

SAT. FEB. 11. In the Ile d'Elva in Italy there are toads above a foot   Toads
broad which the inhabitants will not suffer any one to kill, imagining
that they draw to them the venom of the Country.

The Marquis de Bordage[1] who maried Mr. Turenne's Niece,   Popery
being at Rome about the yeare '66 or '67 & being at a Masse where
the Pope was present, not being above a yard or two from him,
a very considerable cardinall who was just by him, asked him after
the Elevation: 'Che dice vostra signoria di tutta questa fanfanteria?'[2]

MOND. FEB. 13. P. Clerk,[3] procurator *of the Jesuits at Paris, cozened*   Jesuits
the Society of 100,000 *crowns or more, and having too much* familiarity
with an Abbess, was in the year '66 *sent to their convent at* Orleans,
kept there 2 *years a close* prisoner, *with bread and water* 2 *years, and*
died a prisoner in that convent. The King since gave them £100,000
to repair that and a trunk in their church in the Street *St Antoine yet*
stands as a mark of it.

P. Favarol *of the same convent was well whipped and then turned*
out for keeping a Mistress, *an other man's wife.*

The Abbesse answerd well to one who was commending to her   Nuns
the conveniencys of their retired life & the perplexitys of those who
were engaged in the world: 'Ay, but you are maried'.

At Angola when a woman has buried her husband, she retires   Angola
into a litle, obscure hut, where one can scarce enter but on all fours.
There her male relations & freinds goe to comfort her after the
fashon that her husband should, had he been alive, soe that as soon   Venus
as one has don & gon out, an other is ready at the dore to enter
& solace her in his turne. Mr. Massiac.

TUESD. FEB. 14. Yesterday morning at the Pallais[4] in the Grand   Vivonne
Chamber Mr. de Vivonne[5] was received & sworne Duke & Paire

---

[1] René de Montbourchier, Marquis de Bordage, was a wealthy Huguenot officer who
tried to flee abroad with his family in 1686. They were all arrested and imprisoned until
they were converted. He was killed at Philipsbourg in 1688.

[2] *Furfanteria* (trickery, knavery)?

[3] The scandal of Fathers Le Clerc and Faverolles is related in the letters of Condé
(ed. É. Magne, Paris, 1921, p. 251—28 Jan. 1666); the *Journal* of Olivier D'Ormesson
(ed. Chéruel, Paris, 1860, 2 vols., II, 447—Feb. 1666); and the *Letters of Guy Patin*
(Paris, 1846, 3 vols., III, 570-4—Dec. 1665).

[4] Palais de Justice.

[5] Louis Victor de Rochechouart (1636–88), the brother of Mme de Montespan. He
was made a *Maréchal de France* in 1675 and four years later *Duc et pair.*

de France & to day his son maried to Mr. Colbert's daughter.[1] Mr. Colbert gave with his daughter £600,000 & the King gave them, to cleare the estate of debts, £900,000.[2]

Childbeareing In Canada a French woman has been maried at 11 years old & had children before 12, & soe in Spain & Portugal; and in the Indies they mary them at 8.

Sexus In Portugal there are usually 9 girles borne for one boy. They impute it to this that the men marry not till they are pretty old & wasted with debauchery & the pox, & then they mary the women very young.

Eels FRID. FEB. 17. In Canada in the River St. Laurence about Kebec the[y] ketch vast quantities of eels that in the Spring time come from the Lakes above. They are some of them as big as a man's thigh & excellent good meat. They salt them thus. They put them alive into an hogshead with salt, SSS, without skining, guting or anything; theyr stiring makes a skum worke off, but they dye & will keep soe excellent good a long time. Mr. Toinard.

Puerperium The French borne at Canada are very handsome people, but the women have hard & dangerous labour. Their peas[3] are excellent, & the men, which in a colony of 2 or 3,000 people must be a pretty good number, are all very good marksmen, being all Chasseurs.

Sodomy SAT. FEB. 18. Pomey & Chauson[4] were burnt at Paris about the yeare '64 for keepeing a baudyhouse of Catamites. Mr. Toinard.

Bishopricks SAT. FEB. 25. The Bishoprick of Cahors is worth 12,000 ecus per annum, & there is on it a pension of £10,000. The Bishoprick of Lavor[5] worth £2,500 & a pension on it of £1,700.[6]

---

[1] Louis de Rochechouart, Duc de Mortemart, was the third ducal son-in-law of Colbert. His bride, Marie Anne de Colbert, was fourteen at the time of the marriage.

[2] According to Clément (II, 471) the King gave the Duke 1,000,000 *livres*.

[3] *Peaux* (furs)?

[4] Jacques Chausson and Jacques Paulmier, burnt at the stake in December 1661 (see F. Lachèvre, *Le Libertinage au XVIIe Siècle*, vol. v, *Les œuvres libertines de Claude Le Petit*, Paris, 1918, pp. 202–9).

[5] Lavaur. The figure given here for Cahors agrees with that given by contemporary sources (i.e. 36,000 l.), but that for Lavaur is given by Basville as 28,000 l., not 2,500.

[6] In his second note-book (p. 189) Locke notes in his accounts with Caleb Banks: 'Feb. 26. 0 – 8 – 0 given at Charanton'.

TUESD. MAR. 7. *Viper leather ready cured* 22s. per Livre.   Leather

WED. MAR. 8.[1] Mr. Banks tooke up 400 ecus at 55 pence of Mme.   Exchange
Herinx.

THURSD. MAR. 9. Pie de Paris 1440. Foot of London 1350 or   Measures
1351. Universal est du pie de Paris 1 pied 3 lines moins ⅙. Le
pendule de France a 4405 dont le pie de Paris a 1440. The English
foot with the foot of Paris Mr. Auzout & I compared togeather at
his lodging.

MOND. 13 [MARCH].[2] To day I saw the library of Mr. de Thou,[3]   Thuana
a great collection of choice & well bound books which are now to   Bibliotheca
be sold. Amongst others I saw there a Greeke manuscript written
by one Angelot, by which Stephen's[4] Greeke characters were first
made. There was also a picture of a procession in the time of the
League[5] wherein the munks of the severall orders are there represented armed, as indeed they were. Here also I had the honour
to see the Prince of Conti,[6] now in his 17th yeare, a very comely   Conti
young gent., but the beautys of his minde far excell those of his
body, being for his age very learned. He speaks Italian & German
as a native, understands Latin well, & Spanish & Portuguese indifferently, & is, as I am told, going to learne English.[7] A great
lover of Justice & honour, very civil & obleigeing to all, & one that
desires the acquaintance of persons of merit of any kinde; & though
I can pretend to none that might recommend me to one of the first
Princes of the Blood of France, yet he did me the honour to aske me
severall questions there & to repeat his commands to me to wait
upon him at his house.

At Manteau rouge *great man* 40 *or* 44 *tournois.*[8]

---

[1] Medical notes are given here, communicated by 'Mr. St. Colombe'. Sainte Colombe
was a friend of Thoynard, and there are numerous references to him in the latter's
correspondence with Locke.
[2] This and the next two entries are dated 13, 14 and 15 February in the MS.
[3] Jacques Auguste de Thou (1609–77), son of the historian and brother of Richelieu's
victim. He was appointed Ambassador to Holland in 1657.
[4] Robert Estienne (1503–59), the famous printer and publisher.
[5] A Catholic Confederation which was founded in 1576 by the Duc de Guise, and
fought against Henry III and later Henry IV.
[6] Louis Armand de Bourbon, a nephew of Condé. He died in 1685.
[7] A knowledge of English was extremely rare in seventeenth-century France.
[8] *Livres tournois.* The meaning of the entry is scarcely clear.

Modena TUESD. 14 [MARCH]. In all the country of Modena they dig wells to
Fountains a certain depth, & then the workman perces the rock with a borier
or some such other thing, but stands all the while in a bucket ready
to be drawn up as soon as he has made the hole, for the water
enters with soe much force as it were through a jet d'eau, that if he
be not drawn up quickly, he is in danger of drowning, & once in
one of these wells the water enterd soe fast that they were faine to
fill it up, as fast as they could, with earth or stones, fearing it would
drown the whole country. Mr. Toynard.

WED. 15 [MARCH]. I went this morning with Mr. Toynard to wait
on the Prince of Conti, but he was hasted away yesterday to St.
Germans, the Daulphin being ill.

I saw the P. Cherubin,[1] the Capucin soe famous in opticks, at
Telescope least the practicall part, in telescopes. He there shewd me one made
to looke in with both eyes at once. It was 3 foot & something more
in length, & the glasses, both object & ocular glasses, soe placed at
each end that by turneing a litle key one approachd or separated
the two object- or eye-glasses to that distance as may fit the eyes of
the looker.

Cisterne In the Capucins'[2] convent in the Rue St. Honore where the
P. Cherubin is, they have a cisterne in a litle Court which serves
their whole covent & a great many others with water, which is the
best water in Paris, being noe thing but rain water brought into
that court by Gutters from the building, not only round the court,
but[3] others farther off, & there by gutters of free stone conveyd to
Water each corner of the said court, where it falls in to fower lesser cisterns
that are filled with sand a great part of them, which being round
& their bottoms a litle leaneing to bring the water all to one part,
there is at that part a pipe of tin or copper fastend, at the end of
which is an hollow globe peirce on all sides with holes & filld with
spunges, after this fashon ⌇⌇⌇ , by which meanes the water
that falls from the house & ⌇⌇⌇ the court into the free stone

---

[1] Described in the catalogue of the Bibliothèque Nationale as 'le Père Chérubin
d'Orléans'. He was the author of numerous works on optics, including *La Vision
Parfaite* (1677).
[2] They acted as volunteer firemen; hence the gifts made to them by Molière's company
of actors (see Lagrange's Register). [3] *But* occurs twice in MS.

gutters & from thence is conveyd into the fower corners' cisternes, is soe straind by the sand & spunges that it drops cleare into the great cisterne which is always cleare. There will be often filth gatherd & rust upon top of the sand, which is upon occasion to be taken away from the top of the sand, and[1] the globes that conteine the spunges are also made to unskrew, to change them also when there is occasion by their roting· or otherwise. The Cisterne holds perfectly by a sement, found out & used by the builder of it.[2]

FRID. MAR. 17. I examind my Universal foot on which is the compas   Measures
of proportion, at Mr. l'Abbé Picar's[3] & he found it just. He also told me that a Pendulum of seconds conteind of our English measure 39⅛ inches, of the Paris measure 36 pouces 8½ lines or $36\frac{708}{1000}$ pouces.

The foot of Paris being divided into 1440, i.e. tenths of a line, the English foot conteines of them 1351.[4]

The sun in its midle motion in 24 howers looses 3 minutes   Sun
56 seconds, by which any pendulum may be examind whether it goes well or noe, for 'tis but to observe any fixed star & the returne   Clock
of the same star to the same meridian the next night, & if your watch wants then 3′ 56″, it is exact. Pendulum to goe true must be fixed well to a firme wall, for set on the floore of a roome, it is shaken by treading & soe alters. Mr. l'Abbé Picar.

SAT. MAR. 18. All this weeke has been very cold, hard frost the 4 or 5 first days & snow the begining of the weeke.

---

[1] MS. has *at*.

[2] Locke's account of his stay in France down to 10 May (30 April, o.s.) when he arrived back in London, occupies pp. 1–94 of this volume of the manuscript. The entries for 15 and 17 March are separated by a long series of notes, entitled 'Evangeliorum Harmonia', which take up pp. 33–64 of this volume.

[3] Abbé Jean Picard (1620–82), one of the most famous astronomers of the age. His fame rests chiefly on his measurement of the arc of the meridian in 1669–70. He was also the first person to determine the length of a sideral pendulum of seconds by star observations. Though he was appointed to a Chair at the *Collège Royal* and was one o the foundation members of the *Académie des Sciences*, it was Cassini who was appointed Director of the Observatoire, and Picard obtained only a modest lodging in the new building.

[4] In the Lovelace Collection, under the heading 'Science', there is a list of measures endorsed by Locke 'Mensurae. Mr. l'Abbé Picar. Mar. 79'.

Jansenius Jansenius[1] in some of his books says that Bellarmin, Suarez & Vasquese, 3 Jesuits, were Pelagiani aut Semipelagiani. This soe much provoked that order that they were resolved to ruin Jansenius & all his adherents, & they got the Popes Alexander 7 & Innocent 10 to condemne 5 propositions in Jansenius, which the Jansenists say are noe where in his works, & there upon have undertaken to mainteine that the Pope is infallible, not only in matter of doctrine, but also in matter of fact; & the Pope & King of France ordeind here in France about the year '55 that all the ecclesiastiques of France, even to the nuns, should subscribe (je reconnois),[2] that those 5 propositions were in Jansenius in the sense condemned by the Pope, the execution whereof was rigorously observed for many years till the King some years since[3] mitigated it by an edict.

Gold Gold softend. Mr. St. Colombe saw & handled at Lysbon gold soe softend that one could mould & figure it in one's hands like paste. He that was master of this secret was a Portugall who had learned it in China where it is kept as a great secret.

Capucins SUND. MAR. 19. The Capucins are the strictest & severest order in France,[4] soe that to mortifie those of their order they often command them seeming unreasonable things which, if not considered as conduceing to mortification, would be very irrationall & ridiculous, as to plant cabbadge plants the roots upwards, & then reprehend the planter because they doe not grow. As soon as they finde any one to have any inclinations any way, as P. Cherubin in opticks & telescopes, to take from him all he has don or may be usefull to him in that Science, & imploy him in something quite contrary; but he has now a particular lock & key to his cell which the gardian's key opens not, *by order of the King. Sometimes also they order a brother to enter the* refectoir *on all fours with an ass's pad on his back and a bridle in his mouth for* humiliation, *which happening once when a stranger was there, was like to have cost the* Gardian *his life.* This severity makes them not compassionate one to an other, what ever they would be to others.

---

[1] Cornelius Jansen (1585–1638), Bishop of Ypres, the author of the *Augustinus* which was published posthumously in 1640.

[2] The last two words are added above in the MS.

[3] In 1668, by the so-called 'Paix de l'Église'.   [4] MS. has *Frances*.

MUND. MAR. 20. At Mr. Romer's[1] chamber in the Observatoire Jupiter
I saw his inclusum continet arcae Jovem.[2] He has also a most
admirable levell but, being not there, I saw it not.[3]

Jupiter volvitur super axem suum horis 9–56'.

Periodus revolutionum satellitum Jovis.

	dies.	horae.	minut.	The model will produce as follows:		
1.	0 – – – – – –	42 – – – – – – –	28½	0 – – – – –	42 – – – –	29
2.	3 – – – – –	13 – – – – – – –	18 fere	3 – – – – –	13 – – – –	20
3.	7 – – – – –	4 – – – – – – –	0	7 – – – – –	4 – – – –	0
4.	16 – – – – –	18 – – – – – – –	4	16 – – – – –	18 – – – –	0

Motoris.

1	– – – 87	1.	22
2	– – – 63	2.	32
3	– – – 42	3.	43
4	– – – 28	4.	67

---

[1] Olaf Römer (1644–1710), the Danish astronomer. He came to France in 1672, was made a member of the *Académie des Sciences*, and appointed to teach mathematics to the Dauphin. In 1675, as a result of his observations of the eclipses of Jupiter, he discovered the speed of light. He visited England in 1679 (travelling, as we shall see, with Locke), and returned to Denmark in 1682. He made many other discoveries in astronomy and also invented a variety of optical instruments.

[2] The explanation of this expression and of the Latin text and figures which follow is to be found in a document (MS. Locke, c. 31, fol. 24) in the Lovelace Collection, reproduced below. This document, endorsed by Locke 'Jupiter et Satellites, Mar. 79', is a rough sketch of a model of Jupiter and its satellites.

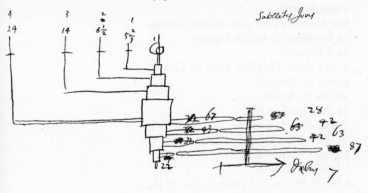

[3] See the entry for 28 March in Appendix B (p. 282).

263

TUESD. MAR. 21. Cardinal Richleieue haveing at last gaind the Jesuits, got one of their order to answer a booke then published called Optatus Gallus de cavendo schismate, writ by Mr. Hersen,[1] upon an apprehension that the Court of Rome had that they would set up a Patriarch here in France. The answer, called Optatus Gallus benignâ manu sectus, shews the King of France's power exempt from the Jurisdiction of the Pope. The author of it was le P. Rabardeau,[2] Jesuite, de la Ferté St. Aubin proche Orleans.

A bill of fare of those things that were deliverd to the 3 Holland Ambassadors by the King of France's officers for that day's provision, Monday 20 Mar. 1679, being one of the days they were enterteind at the King's Charge, being from Saturday 18 in the afternoon to Tuesday 21 in the afternoon, they haveing their Audience at St. Germains Monday morning:

Optatus Gallus

Bill of Fare
Ambassadours

3 Grands saumons
6 Grands carpes d'entre 20 & 24 pouces
6 Grands Brochets pres de 3 pies
36 moien brochets
50 moindres brochets
40 Moiens et moindres carps
12 Turbeaux
18 Barbeux
18 Soles
900 ecrevis
1.200 huistres
600 boutelles d'un pint du vin commun
12 boutelles du vin St. Lauren
12 d'Espagne
7 ou 8 petits boutelles d'eau de Cette
autant de Res solis
180 lb. de beurre
35 lb. d'huille a frire
3 pots d'huille á salade
68 douzen du pains d'environ 2s.
3 barills d'olives de Veron
2 barills d'anchois
6 lb. de beurre de Vembre á 40s. p. lb.

[1] Charles Hersent, whose *Optati Galli de cavendo schismata* was published in 1640.
[2] Michel Rabardeau (1593-1649). His *Optatus Gallus* was published in Paris in 1641.

12 Tortus
12 Macreuses
12 Fromage de brie
De petite patisserie de confiteur sech et fruit en proportion

THURSD. MAR. 23.

Sur la Troade de Pradon.

Quand jay veu de Pradon la piece miserable   Pradon
Admirant du destin le Caprice fatal,
Pour ta pert ay-je-dit Illion deplorable
Auras-tu toujours un Cheval?[1]

FRID. MAR. 24. Paid Mr. Daille[2] £110 which I received by Mr.   Rushout
Beaumont from Sir James Rushout.[3]

The Bishop of Belly[4] haveing writ against the Capucins & they   Belly
against him, Cardinal Richlieue undertooke their reconciliation &
they both promised peace; but the Capucins writeing again under
another name, the Bishop replyd, soe that the Cardinal seeing him
sometime after told him that, had he held his peace, he would have
cannonized him. That would doe well, replyd the Bishop, for then
we should each of us have what we desire, i.e. one should be Pope,
the other a saint. Cardinal Richlieue, having given him the Prince
of Balzac[5] & the Minister of Silhon[6] to read (which he had caused
to be writ, one as a Character of the King, & the other of him
self), demanded one day before the King his opinion of them, to
which the Bishop answerd: Le Prince n'est pas grand chose et le
minister ne vaut rien.

A devout Lady being sick & besiged by Carmes made her will

---

[1] Nicolas Pradon (1632–98), the rival of Racine. His *Troade* was first performed at
the Hôtel de Bourgogne on 17 January 1679. This epigram is given by the Frères Parfaict
in their *Histoire du Théâtre* (XII, 140).

[2] Jean Daillé (1628–90), son of the great Daillé and himself pastor at Charenton?

[3] Sir John Rushout (1644–98), son of a naturalized Flemish merchant, created a
Baronet in 1661 and an M.P. in numerous Parliaments. His widow is described as
a 'zealous Protestant'.

[4] Jean Pierre Camus (1582–1652), Bishop of Belley. He is chiefly known to-day for
his edifying novels, but among his two hundred works are various attacks on monks,
such as *Le Rabat-joie du triomphe monacal* and *La pauvreté évangélique et la désappro-
priation monacale*, both published in 1634.

[5] Guez de Balzac (1597–1654). *Le Prince* appeared in 1631.

[6] Jean de Silhon (d. 1667), one of Richelieu's secretaries and propagandists. *Le
Ministre d'État* appeared between 1631 and 1634.

& gave them all. The Bishop of Belly comeing to see her as soon as it was don, asked her whether she had made her will. She answerd yes & told him how. He convinced her 'twas not well &, she desireing to alter it, found it a difficulty how to doe it, being soe beset by the Friers. The Bishop bid her not truble her self for that, but presently tooke order that 2 Notarys, habited as Physitians, should come to her, who being by her bed's side, the Bishop told the company it was convenient all should with draw, & soe the former will was revoked & a new one made & put into the Bishop's hands. The Lady dies. The Carmes produce their will & for some time the Bishop lets them enjoy the pleasure of the inheritance, but at last, taking out the other, says to them: Mes freres, you are the sons of Eliah, children of the Old Testament, & have noe share in the New. This is that Bishop of Belly that hath writ soe much against munks & Munkery.

Confession   A preist confessing one that said but litle to him, began to ask him questions, as whether he had kept Lent, etc., to which he returnd still this answer: Je ne me vent[1] de rien.

Munsteevens SAT. MAR. 25. I was witnesse to a bill given Sir Thomas Lynch[2] by Mr. Munsteevens[3] to pay him 40 lb. either by Mr. James Vernon[4] or by himself or by his Executors.[5]

Oratoire TUESD. MAR. 28. Les peres del'Oratoire live togeather in society, but are under noe vow nor noe obedience to their superior but what respect & civility obleiges them to,[6] which gave just occasion to a Jacobin to demand of one of them if their superior had noe authority over them, who it was parted them when they went togeather by the ears.[7]

Exchange WED. MAR. 29. Exchange at Paris 54¾ pence of England for an ecu ffrancois to be paid at London a deux usance.

---

[1] *vante?*

[2] Sir Thomas Lynch (d. 1684?) was Governor of Jamaica.

[3] Covell mentions 'Mr. Monsteven' along with Sir Thomas Lynch among the people who saw him off from Paris in January 1679.

[4] James Vernon (1646–1727), Secretary of State?

[5] See Appendix B (pp. 282 f.) for entries which Locke omitted to insert in his Journal at this point.

[6] The *Oratoire* is a congregation of secular priests who do not take vows.

[7] Cf. Locke's account of the Jacobins' battle in the entry for 26 June 1677.

SAT. 1 APR. This weeke the 4 sols peices were abated in their value $\frac{1}{16}$.   Mony

THURSD. APR. 6. Very cold to day & 'twas said to be a frost in the morning.[1]

FRID. APR. 7.[2] £1,600 lent in the year 1596 produced £100 rent   Exchequer
to be paid forever. In the yeare 1662 there were 4 years' rent in
arreare which makes £2,000, for all which £325 is the purchase to be
paid, which is not yet paid neither. Mr. Sully was the first that
bated $\frac{1}{4}$ of the rent, since that $\frac{1}{4}$ being again bated by Colbert. The
vigil before Fouquet's Triall was the occasion of saveing him, some   Fouquet
of his judges haveing some of these rent charges.[3]

3 millions at 14 years' purchase amount to 42 millions which the   Revenue
King of France has now taken up.

TUESDAY 11 APR. Exchange 54⅝ payable at London a deux usance   Exchange
with ½ per cent a Mme Herinx pour provision, & thus Mr. Banks
received £1306 2s. for a bill on his father for 100 lb. sterling.

> L'Observatoire est à 48 d. 50. 10″.   Paris latitude
> Nostre dame a —— 48 – 51 – 0.
> La Porte de Montmartre 48 – 52 – 0.

Ainsi il y a dans Paris depuis lobservatoire a la Porte de Montmartre
Nord et Sud 2′.
Chaque minute fait 950 toises. Il y a de la Porte St. Jacques a la porte
St. Martin de dedans en dedans 1313 toises. Or la porte St. Jacques al
Observatoire 600 toises.

---

[1] Locke's second note-book (p. 78) has the following entry for 1679:
'6 Apr.   130 vieus of Paris et environ at 2 s. 6 d.
peice - - - - - - - - - - - - -   £16 – 5.
42 Vieus of Versailes - - - -   5 – 5.
61 Portraits - - - - - - - - -   3 – 0.'
[2] MS. has 'Apr. 17'.
[3] The reductions in the *Rentes* made by Colbert in 1662 and the following years were
extremely unpopular, and almost led to riots in Paris. This dissatisfaction with Colbert
undoubtedly helped to save Fouquet from the death penalty when his judges gave their
verdict in December 1664. The *rapporteur* of the case, Olivier D'Ormesson states in his
Journal (II, 271): 'Jamais il ne s'est fait tant de prières que pour cette affaire-là et la
conjoncture des rentes et autres où tout le monde se trouve blessé, fait qu'il n'est
personne qui ne souhaite le salut de M. Fouquet.'
O.E.D. does not cast any light on Locke's use of the word *vigil*.

St. Peter's in Rome   St. Piere's Church at Rome cost above 50 millions of £ Tournois & 'twill cost above 20 more to perfect the designe.

Lice
Bouillon   Within this year past were bills set up about Paris with a priviledg for a receit to kill lice where of the Duke of Bouillon[1] had the monopoly & the bills were in his name:[2]

Par permission   Ks   et privilege du roy
accordé a   arms   perpetuité a Mr le
Duc de Bouillion   grand Chamberlan de
France par lettres patentes du 17 Sept: 1677
Verifiées en Parlm^t par arest du 13
Dec. au dit Ann.
Le publique sera averti que lon vend
a Paris un petit Sachet de la grandure
d'une peice de 15 sols pour garantir
toute sorte de personnes de la vermin
et en retirer ceux qui en sont
incommodes sans mercure &c.
Il est fait deffenses a toutes personnes
de le faire ny contrefaire a peine de
trois mil livres d'amande.
Extrait del afiche.

Chariot   WED. 12 APR. I saw the Chariot now a makeing for the Duke of Vivonne which he designes a present to the King, which, they say, will cost 4 or 5 Luis d'or.[3] All the wooden work, even the spokes & vellys[4] of the wheels, are guilded &, except the vellys, carvd. Neptune siting with a trident behinde; a great part of the outside coverd with mother of perle, the inside lined with rich brochard.[5] The floor is silver inlaid with brasse guilt, & the outside of the roof coverd with blew velvet embroiderd with fleur de lys d'or. The coachman's footstoole a scolope shell guilt, etc.

Paveing   The stones they pave Paris with are brought from the Forest of Fountain bleau in peices about 9 or 12 inches square. These they

---

[1] The Duc de Bouillon (1639–1721) was appointed Grand Chamberlain in 1658.
[2] For some unaccountable reason, in the MS. this copy of the notice is detached from the preceding paragraph and placed at the end of the entry for 12 April.
[3] That is the sum given, no doubt erroneously, in the MS.
[4] *O.E.D. Felloe, felly*: 'In plural, the curved pieces of wood which, joined together, form the circular rim of a wheel.'
[5] *O.E.D.* gives only *brochad* as an alternative form of *brocade*.

split with a great heavy iron sledg,[1] made sharp at each end like a wedg, with which the labourer at one blow or 2 splits them, & when they are thus split, they are about 5 or 6 inches thick, & then with an other toole they square them. The toole is made of iron of this fashon, very ⟨drawing⟩ heavy of iron [sic], in which, puting an handle as into ⟨drawing⟩ a mason's hammer, they cut the stones with sidelong blows with one of the edges of this toole, & they say it does better then if it were made with a single edg. The stones thus prepared are set edgelong in the ground about 8 or 9 inches.

THURSD. APR. 13. A new map of Canada corrects the old ones thus. About the latitude 38 lies a range of mountains runing North & South out of which rises a river that falls into Chesapeack Bay. North of those hills runs from East to West a great river, called in the country Ohio for its beauty, which falls into the Gulf of Mexico. This river lies about 40. Something north of this is the great lake of Ery which extends its self from East to West & has communication with severall other great lakes which, taken togeather, make a vast sea of fresh water. This lake of Ery by a Cascade of 120 fathoms perpendicular[2] powers its water into the Lake Ontario, & from thence it runs into the sea by the great river St. Laurence. Bordering upon the East of the Lake Ery are the Iroquois. *{margin: Canada; Ery; Cascade}*

FRID. APR. 14. Mr. Toynard gave me a great peice of Angola wood with the pouder whereof the grandees of the country make a paste with which they cover them selves all over & then wash it off. This, they say, clenses & refreshes them very much. *{margin: Angola}*

This wood also, ground upon a stone with water, workes into a sort of past which, anoynted on the temples & forehead, is admirable for pains in the head or heat or want of sleep. The wood has a pretty sort of smell, is very hard & very heavy. *{margin: Cephalalgia; Agrypnia}*

He also gave me Tripoli de Venise, the Alchohol whereof upon a leather straind upon a peice of wood of the size of a hone whets razors as well as a hone.[3] *{margin: Tripoli}*

---

[1] O.E.D. 'sledge-hammer'.   [2] Niagara Falls.
[3] The entry for 17 April contains notes on Spanish sounds, and that for 22 April notes on the weight of various French coins.

St. Denise   MONDAY 24 APR. I saw upon the west dore of the Church of the Cordiliers, graved on[1] one of the valves, a litle statue in demi releive & under it St. Hanry, & on the other a woman with her head in her hand & under it St. Denise, which two saints are noe thing but a man & his wife of those names which were benefactors to this covent, & St. Denise has her head in her armes by conformity to St. Denis, her namesake.

Quebek   Quebek, the capital, lies upon the River St. Laurence 47 d. 20' northerne Latitude & 312 longitude.

Montreal   Montreal, an Island in the same River, 44½, 309½. Here R. des Hurons oú des Stasacs that comes from the Lac des Nipissiriniens falls into the R. St. Laurence that comes from the Lake Ontario.

Grand Saut   Le Grand Saut 42½, 297, in the midle of a canal of 12 leagues long by which the water runs out of the Lake Erie into that of Ontario. Here the water of that makes the great River St. Laurence. Falls neare 200 foot high perpendicular, & one may heare the noise

Ongiara   of this fall 10 or 12 leagues. This fall is called Ongiara.[2] Lac

Eriè   d'Erié: the southern side lies in 39, and perhaps farther south. In the Lake of Erié there is a great peninsula. The Isthmus where by

Hurons   it joyns to the continent of the Hurons lies in 41½, 293. Over against this Isthmus, northward & a litle to the East, is the country des Hurons. Mr. l'Abbé de Galinée observed the variation of the needle to be 11 d. 15', 21 Mar., about the year '68 or '69, equall to the Variation at Montreal.

Nipissiriniens   Lac de Nipissiriniens où Sorciers 46. 20', 297. This is a litle lake,
Sorciers   the highest of all those yet known in Canada, for out of it runs two great & rapid rivers full of falls, whereof one called the R. de Francois runs westward into the great Lake des Hurons or la mer douc, which great lake des Hurons empties it self into that of Erié & soe by the Grand Saut into the Lake Ontario, from whence it runs into the River St. Laurence. The other River is called des Stasacs ou des Hurons, which falls into that of St. Laurence above the Isle du Nom de Jesu, which Isle is parallel to that of Montreal.

---

[1] MS. has *one one.*
[2] Niagara.

Missimakina Ile 47. 20′, 286, respondant al emboucheur du lac Missimakina
des Ilinois.

St. Marie de Saut qui est au Saut du lac Superieur 48. 40′, 286. 10′.
The Jesuits have here an establishment & the country is very
pleasant. Here is plenty of Sturgeon taken. The Lake Superieur falls
into that of the Hurons by a chanell on which is the Saut St. Marie.

Le Lac Superieur a del West al est 200 lieux de long et 50 de
largeur, & is a pretty regular oval. The Lake des Hurons is much
biger, but the shore & figure very irregular. That of Erié biger then
the Lake Superieur, soe that here is a sea of fresh water. The
Jesuits have an establishment at the west end of the Lake Superior
amongst a warlike people called Nadoüessiou at a place called la   Nadoüessiou
point du St. Esprit.

This is an Extract taken out of a Map made by Mr. l'Abbé
Galinee upon the place, who lived in Canada 3 years, which map
was shewd Mr. Toinard & me in the Chambre de Mr. Tronson,[1]
superieur du Seminaire de St. Sulpice, Fauxbourg St. Germaine,
where it is kept.[2]

The Muscovites make the knot of their numeration at 9 v. Rerum   Numbers
Muscovitor. hist. p. Herbestin,[3] a thin book in fol. Mr. Toinard.

At the Seminary of St. Sulpice,[4] over the dore opposite to the   Virgin
gate, is the Virgin, a childe crowning her, & under her feet this
inscription: Interveni pro Clero.

Within in a great roome there was one singing their service, not   Service
as officiateing, but as practiseing the notes & way of singing &
outward, theatricall part, for here they learne & begin to practise
the mechanical part of their religion.

TUESD. 25 APR. The Protestants within these 20 years have had   Protestants
above 300 churches demolishd, & within these 2 months 15 more
condemned.[5]

---

[1] Louis Tronson (1622–1700), appointed Superior of St Sulpice in 1676.
[2] There follow entries on (1) a piece of wood given him by Thoynard, and (2) weights
of various gold coins, 'weighed on Mr. Romer's Statera' (=scales, balance).
[3] *Rerum Muscovitorum Commentarii* by Sigmund von Herberstein (Basle, 1551).
[4] The present building, which dates from 1820, replaced the original one, begun by
the founder, Olier, in 1642.
[5] The above figures agree roughly with those given for this period of twenty years by
Haag (x, 378–80), who lists twenty-five churches demolished in 1679.

Jews   The Jews in Holland would give half they are worth to have the liberty to live in Portugal.

Dominis   The letter of Ant. de Dominis[1] to Jos. Hall[2] about his returne to the Church of Rome was published by Mr. T.[3] who had the copy of it from Mr. Flavel, an English man who tooke the manuscript copy out of Mr. Hall, his friend's, study & copied it, but very ill.

Garden   THURSD. 27 APR. I saw Mr. St. Morin's garden at the Incurables,
Flowers   & amongst other things there Thlaspi semper virens semper florens which makes that plant extraordinary.

Limons   They have a sort of Limon at Florence which they call Cedrato, the pulpe where of has a most agreeable sharpenesse, the pill an admirable tast, but that which makes this sort very desirable, is that the leaves of the tree have a sweeter & more fragrant smell then the flowers them selves of most orange trees. Mr. Auzout.

                The Limoncino de Calabria is another species excelling in scent, and next to the Limoncino is the Spadafora. These two later are to be had at Genoa. ib.

Messire   Messire in French in giveing people their title answers to Sir in English.

Apples   There is lately brought into France an excellent sort of Apples out of Pomerany & are grafted in France. Mr. Toinard.

Exchange   TUESD. 2 MAY. The Exchange 54⅝. Mr. Banks received £1,200.
Revenue   74 enterd & went out 113,676,401. The true 90 m.[4]
                New Conquest offerd 88,000 by Farmers.[5]

---

[1] Marc Antonio de Dominis (1566–1624), Archbishop of Spalatro, took refuge in England in 1616 and abjured Catholicism. He left again six years later and returned to the Catholic fold. His *De Pace religionis...epistola ad...Josephum Hallum* was published at Besançon in 1666.

[2] Joseph Hall (1574–1656), Bishop of Norwich.

[3] Locke first wrote the name in full—or rather names, as *Toynard* and *Fromentin* are inextricably mingled in the MS. It is almost certain that 'Mr. T.' stands for Toynard, although it is often difficult to distinguish between capital T and capital F in the MS.

[4] Locke himself gives a cross-reference to p. 115 of the MS. At a later date, in the security of England, he wrote there: 'Revenue. The meaneing is that in the yeare 1674 the account in the Espargne du Roy was of 113,676,491 [sic] £ receits & soe disbursements; but the true state of the account was 90,000,000': i.e. that there was a deficit of over 23 million *livres*. Forbonnais (I, 488) gives a deficit of over 18 millions (109 against 81, in round figures) for 1674 and Clamageran (II, 672) one of 17 millions.

[5] The newly conquered provinces ('Les nouvelles conquêtes'). Forbonnais (I, 495) gives among the items of the revenue for 1679: 'Des nouvelles conquêtes: 1,800,880 l.'

Mr. Richaumont sur le quay des Morfondus has an excellent — Rarities
collection of stones, & amongst others the heads of all the Emperors — Stones
in seales antique.

Mr. Roussau, rue Calandrier, has an excellent collection of cuts. — Cuts
The King of France's collection of pictures is mighty well worth — Pictures
the seeing.

The pipinery from whence all the King's gardens are supplyd is — Nursery
worth seeing also. Mr. Justel.[1]

Pomade de Nerli one of the finest sweets to be bought at Rome. — Pomade de Nerli

Soape de Naples an excellent thing to wash the hands. To be — Soape de Naples
bought at the Orangery, Rue del arbre sec, £3 per 1 oz.

From Paris to Clermont 14 leagues. At the Ecu de France, well. — Clermont

WED. 3 MAY. From Clermont to Amiens 14 leagues post; we paid — Amiens
for 15. At St. Piere, well but deare. The country all champaine,
corne & some wood. In Nostre Dame, the great church, over the
holy water basen the left hand as one enters the west dore is this — Holy water
inscription:

Aqua benedicta sit nobis solus et vita
Hujus aquae factus propulset demonis actus.

Alhoneur de dieu et de la vierge mere NN. ont offert ce — Virgin
benistier 1656.

Just the same on the other side.

At the next pillar the Virgin treading on a serpent & death's head
with these words: Conteret caput tuum. A table hanging by with
this notice: Cest image de Nostre dame de victoire a été benite par
Monsr. levesque d Amiens 23 Sept. 1634 Lequel a concedé 40 jours
de pardon a ceux et celles qui diront trois fois ave Maria devant
cette image.

At the next pillar an image of the Virgin & God the Father
crowning her, with these words: Trahe nos post te...[2] suos, &
a table promise [sic] 40 days' indulgence to any one who shall say

---

[1] On leaving Paris, Locke had his leg pulled by his friends about the number of
interesting things he had not seen during his stay there; cf. his joking references to his
sins of omission in the letter which he wrote to Thoynard from Calais on 7 May
(Ollion, p. 21).

[2] One word illegible.

before this image on their knees thrice this prayer: Mater miseri-cordiae ora pro nobis.

Abbeville THURSD. 4 MAY. To Abbeville 10 leagues. All open corne country & some litle wood. At la teste de beufe, well.

Boisseau Le boisseau a cylinder 742 in diameter & 521 long.

Wheat The best wheat sold to day in the market per boisseau 15 s., almost double the price it was sold for at Christmas. 5 boisseau of Paris make 6 of these. 16 boisseaux here make one septier.

Jesuits There are in this towne of all the orders but Jesuits, whose establishment here the magistrates of the towne have always opposed & prevailed hitherto.

Montriel FRID. 5 MAY. To Montriel[1] 10 leagues & from thence to Boulogne
Boulogne 7 leagues.

Calais SAT. 6 MAY. To Calais 7 leagues.[2]

MOND. 8 MAY. Sailed at 11 a clocke in the Charlotte, Yacht, Captain Sanderson commander.

TUESD. 9 MAY. In the Thames over against Lee[3] where we lay for
Waves want of winde, we saw the waves roule along by us westward up the river when the winde & tide were both contrary & bent towards the sea. The seamen told us it was because the winde was east at sea.

Light The motion of light is soe swift that it moves 1 diameter of the earth in 3‴,[4] & the distance of the sun from the earth being of 12,000 semidiameters of the earth, Light moves one semidiameter of the orbis magni in 10 minutes.

---

[1] Montreuil.
[2] In a letter written to Thoynard on 7 and 8 May (Ollion, pp. 19f.) Locke gives us some information about his activities, and those of Römer and Caleb Banks, during their stay at Calais. On the 7th he writes: 'On verra icy aujourd'hui un revieu de 1600 Suisse qui vaudra bien votre revieu dans la plaine d'Ouille [cf. entry for 5 Jan.]. On bat au champ pendant que j'écris cela et ce n'est pas un spectacle ordinaire de voir 1.600 philosophes bien roges [sic], toutes grosses et grases.' On the following day he wrote: 'A cet heur je vous donneray les nouvelles de M. Romer, que je ne vis pas hier jusqu'au soir. Il s'estoit promené à cheval pour voir le pais et prier Dieu [three words missing in MS.] et aujourd'hui je crois qu'il sacrifiera au Neptune du fond de son coeur ou estomack.'
[3] Leigh. [4] I.e. three sixtieths of a second.

WED. {30 APR. ⎰ Mr. Romer's steele:
      {10 MAY. ⎱

The case or tinder box.
A the place for the steele.
B for the flints & tinder.
C for the matches which should

be made of the smallest wax candle is to be found, takeing away
the wax at both ends & diping them in melted brimstone.
　　Landed at the Temple.

APPENDIX A

DRAFT OF A LETTER OF LOCKE

3[1]

Montpellier, 1 Mar. 1675/6.

We left our two combatants with their hands lift up (as you know, Mr. Scudery[2] & other good authors, our predecessors, often doe) & holding each one the end of a sheet in them, & if the French fiercenesse carry it not sooner, yet at least the blaze of the faggot quickly goes out, their heat cooles & the English man at last is laid on his back, from which captiv[it]y he is releived early next morning at the command of Sultan Messenger[3] who is cheife commander in all these castles[4] where he comes, & sure is a very happy prince, for though his subjects goe through many hardships, yet they usually obey all his commands willingly. Are they summond before day to rise? Course & stinkeing lodging makes them forward. Are durty, heavy boots to be put on? Want of slippers takes away all reluctancy. Is leane, ill dressed meat to be eat? A good stomach bids it well come. Are you to be dismounted & thrust into a rascally Inne, 4 or 5 in a chamber? Ten or eleven leagues on a dull, hobling jade will make you glad of it.

But though I remember where we left our combatants, I have almost forgot where I left you. I think it was some where in the way between Bologne & Montriel. 'Tis all one where, for all the way is made up of plains, hills & dales, & these coverd all with corne or wood, unlesse it be some barren hills of sand that beare noe thing unlesse it be now & then a Mosse trooper. In a very convenient wood

---

[1] This fragment of a draft of a letter to an unknown friend is in the Lovelace Collection. It begins in the middle of Locke's journey from Calais to Paris, and breaks off shortly before his arrival there.

[2] Georges de Scudéry (1601–68), French poet and dramatist. His name appeared on the title-page of the novels of his sister, Madeleine.

[3] The *messager* who, in return for a fixed sum, provided travellers with horses and food between Calais and Paris (cf. Journal for 4 Dec. 1675).

[4] Inns.

2 or 3 leagues out of Boulong we lookd for our freinds of St. Omars,[1] but the Dons were affraid of the French, or us, or their trumpeter (for I dare not doe the gentlemen the injury to imagin they had any aversion to our mony) & soe we saw noe more whiskers. After we were passed this terrible place, those that had mony thought it their owne, & beleived their clothes might last them to Paris, where the Taylers lye in wait to strip you of your old clothes & pick your pockets, & I know not yet whether a taylor with his yard & sheirs, or a trooper with a sword & pistol in his hand, be the more dangerous creature. From this wood we marchd on merrily to Montriel, the remainder of this day's seven leagues, & arrived there Saturday, 30 Dec.,[2] in good time. Supper was ready before our boots were off &, being fish, almost as soon digested. Our lodging something better then Boulogne.

1 DEC., early in a frosty morning, we were with all the train on our march to Abevil, 10 leagues from Montriel. Abevil is a large towne, seated on the river of Amiens.[3] Here his Excellence dismissed his St. Omer's trumpeter.

2 DEC. The Ambasador[4] resolveing to goe by Amiens, our Governor, the messenger, was willing to goe the ordinary rode by Poy[5] which we, who went to seek adventures beyond Paris, easily consented to. We therefor plodded on the carriers' rode & pace[d] our 9 leagues to Poy, & though that way of travailing tires an Englishman sufficiently, yet we were noe sooner got into our chambers but we thought we were come there too soone, for the highway seemd the much sweater, cleaner & more desireable place. Had I not been of old acquainted with this memorable lodging,[6]

---

[1] St Omer, ceded to France in 1678 at the end of the war, was then in the Spanish Netherlands, and presumably there was some danger of raids from Spanish into French territory.

[2] Clearly a mistake for 30 November (see the Journal for that date).

[3] The Somme.

[4] John Berkeley (1607–78), a Royalist commander during the Civil War, was created Lord Berkeley of Stratton in 1658 while in exile. After the Restoration he was Lord Lieutenant of Ireland from 1670 to 1672, and was appointed Ambassador Extraordinary in July 1675 (Firth & Lomas, p. 23), but was compelled by illness to delay his departure for Paris until 14 November. (See Evelyn's *Diary* for that date.)

[5] Poix.

[6] Presumably on his journeys to and from Paris in 1672.

I should have suspected that General Messenger had been leading us against the Germans, & that now we had been just on those frontiers which both armys had pilaged at the end of the laste campagne & had left this castle garisond not with horse, but an other sort of 6 legd creature[1] to defend it against the next comers.

It being decreed we must stay there alnight, I cald, intreated & swaggerd a good while (for necessity multiplys one's ffrench mightily) for a pair of slippers. At last they were brought, & I sat me down on the only seat we had in our apartment, which at present was a forme, but, I beleive, had been heretofore a wooden horse, but, the legs being cut shorter & the ridg of the back taken down to the bredth of one's hand, it made a considerable part of the furniture of our chamber. My boots being off, I thought to ease my self of my soar by standing, but I assure you with noe very good successe, for the soles of my Pantofles, being sturdy timber, had very little compliance for my feet & soe made it somewhat uncomfortable for me to keep my self (as the French call standing) on one end.[2] This smal tast of Sabots gave me a surfet of them & left such an aversion to them in my stomach that I shall never make choise of a country to passe my pilgrimage in, where they are in fashion. 'Tis possible they may be very necessary to the aiery people of this country who, being able to run, skip & dance in these, would certainly mount into the aire & take most wonderfull frisks, were there not some such clogs at their heels; but I beleive a dul, heavy Englishman might be as soon brought to dance & jig with a pair of stocks about his ankles, as to walke the streets in such brogues as these, though they were never soe curiosly carved, as I have seen some of them.

Of these crabtree soled slippers we had two pair between three of us, & there could never happen a nicer case in breeding then there was then between us three, to know whether one were bound by the rules of civility to take one's self, or offer to an other, or refuse the offer of a pair of these slippers, it being still a doubt to this day, & like to remaine soe, whether barefoot in a ragged, brick floore or those slippers on were the better posture. However, to shew that we profited by our travails & were willing to improve our manners

---

[1] I.e. vermin.   [2] I.e. *debout.*

into the courtlynesse of the country, we made it a matter of complement. Many good things, I assure you, were spoke on this occasion.
We had shuffled favour, civility, obligacion, honour & many other
the like words (very usefull in travaild & well bred company) forwards & backwards in severall obleigeing repartees, & this fashionable conversacion had lasted longer, had not supper come in &
interrupted us.

Here the barefoot gent. thought to finde comfort in his humility
& the others in the stocks to divert their pain, but we quickly found
that a supper of ill meat & worse cookery was but an insignificant
sound, & served ill to fill one's belly. Soup & ragoo & such other
words of good savour lost here their relish quite, & out of 5 or 6 dishes
were served up to us, we patched up a very untoward supper; but be
it as rascally as it will & meane, it must not faill in the most material
part, to be fashionable. We had the ceremony of first & 2d course,
besides a disert in the close, for were your whole bill of fare noe
thing but some cabbage & a frog that was caught in it, & some haws
of the last season, you would have a treat in all its formalitys &
would not faile of three courses. The first would make a soope, the
2d a good fricasie (of which I have eaten), & 'twas not long since[1]
that preserved haws were served up for a disert to me & some others
of my country men, who could not tell what to make of this new
sort of fruit, they being something biger then ordinary & disguised
under the fine name of Pomet de Paradise, till on the next day our
Voiturin shewed us upon what sort of tree this that made so fine
a sweetmeat grew.

After supper we retreated to the place that usually gives redresse to
all sorts of moderate calamitys, but our beds served but to compleat
our vexacion, & seemd to be ordeind for antidotes against sleepe.
I will not complain of their hardnesse, because 'tis a quality I like,
but the thinnesse of what lay upon me & the tangible qualitys of
what was next me, & the savour of all about me made me quite
forget my slippers & supper, & 'twas impossible I should have lasted
in that strong perfume till morning, had not a large, convenient
hole in the wall at my bed's head powerd in plenty of fresh aire. As

---

[1] Cf. the entry in the Journal for 4 March 1676.

good luck would have it, we had a long journey of twelve leagues to goe next day, which made our stay here the shorter. We were rousd before day, & I heard nobody complain of it. We were glad to be released from this prison (for 'tis impossible to beleive freemen should stay themselves here) & willingly left it to those miserable soules were to succeed us. If Paris be heaven (for the French with their usuall justice extol it above althings on earth), Poy certainly is Purgatory in the way to it.

3 DEC. We dinde at Bauvais, 9 leagues from Poy, where I saw not any thing very remarkeable but the quire of a church,[1] very high & stately, built, as they say, by the English who, it seemes, had not time to compleat the whole church, nor have the French, it seems, thought fit ever since to finish it.[2] Were there a body of the church added to this peice, answerable to it, it would be a very magnificent structure, but as far as I have observd of the churches of both countrys, to make them every way exact, we ought to build, & they to adorne them. Hence we went three leagues to Tiliard[3] to bed. Good mutton & a good supper here, clean sheets of the country & a pretty girle to lay them on (who was an angell compard to the Feinds of Poy), made us some amends for the past night's sufferings. Doe not wonder that a man of my constitution & gravity mention to you a handsome face amongst his remarks, for I imagin that a travailer, though he carrys a cough with him, goes not yet out of his way when he takes notice of strange & extraordinary things.

4 DEC. We din'd or rather breakfasted at Beaumond, 5 leagues from Tiliard. This being the last assembly we were like to have of our company,[4] 'twas thought convenient here to even some small account had happend upon the road. One of the French men who had disbursd for our troope, was by the natural quicknesse of his temper carryed a good deale beyond the mark, & demanded for our shares more then we thought due, whereupon one of the English desird an account of particulars, not that the whole was so con-

---

[1] The Cathédrale Saint-Pierre.
[2] A transept was added in the sixteenth century, but the building still remains unfinished.
[3] Tillart.   [4] They arrived in Paris the same evening (see Journal).

siderable, but to keep a certain custome we had in England, not to pay mony without knowing for what. Monsieur answerd briskly he would give noe account, & the other as briskly that he would have it. This produced a reconing of the severall disbursements & an abatement of ¼ of the demands & a great demonstration of good nature, for Monsieur Steward shewd more civility & respect to the English gent. who had been warme with him after this litle contest then he had donn all the journey before.

APPENDIX B

A SUPPLEMENT TO THE JOURNAL FOR 1679

Oleum   25 MAR. 1679.[1] In some of the covents of France they lay up every yeare a pot of oyle which they keepe, soe that one may finde oyle in some Covents of 100 or 120 years old which is very good for achez & several other medicinall uses. Mr. Auzout.

Level   28 [MARCH]. I was shewd by Mr. Romer an instrument to levell with which was very simple & of exceeding quick dispatch, it being a telescope of 4 glasses about a foot long or something more which shewd the levell when two threads, one where of was fixd & the other moved by a plummet, came to hide one an other.

Septimana   Mr. Bernier told me that the Bramins Gentils, the old inhabitants of Indostan, count their time by weeks & give the days' denominations as we doe by the seven planets & in the same order, their day denominated from the sun being the same with our Sunday, & soe of the rest, & in numbering make their nodus as we doe at 10.

Rosecrucians   SAT. 1 APR. About the yeare 1618 or 20 Mr. Pallieure[2] who is mentiond in the preface of Mr. Pascal's Hydrostaticks, comeing to see one of his freinds at his lodging in Paris, found him & another of his acquaintance writeing, but soe as at his entrance they put aside the paper. But after a litle while one of them says: Why should he not make one? Agreed, says the other, & upon that they produce their paper which was the designe of a program to be posted up in severall parts of Paris to tell the people that there were certaine persons of a brotherhood come to town to cure all diseases & doe other rare things, amongst the rest, make them that desired it invisible, who were to be found such a day every weeke in such a place, nameing a street in the Fauxbourg St. Marceau which was

---

[1] A memoranda of books read (also in the Lovelace Collection), covering various years between 1676 and 1690 (44 ff.) contains on both sides of f. 11 a number of entries subsequently incorporated in the Journal, and, in addition, the notes reproduced in this Appendix which Locke omitted to insert in the text of his Journal.

[2] Le Pailleur, who died in 1651, was a mathematician of some repute among his contemporaries (see Pascal, *Œuvres complètes*, Paris, 1904–1914, 14 vols., I, 115–21, and Tallemant des Réaux, *Historiettes*, passim).

not to be found, &, there[1] lyeing on the table the Theatrum honoris of Rodulphus Conradus, they subscribed their bill R.C. These bills were posted up & downe Paris & had the effect they designed, which was to make them selves sport by seeing severall people &, amongst them, some of their acquaintance goe seeke these brothers R.C. in the Fauxbourg St. Marceau, their first designe being to play a trick to the Lullyists,[2] whereof there were many at that time at Paris.

But that which was a consequence of it which they did not designe nor foresee, was that there spread forthwith an opinion that there was a brotherhood or society of men that could be, when they pleased, invisible & had other great secrets & which they cald brothers of the Rosie Crosse. Who first gave it that name, Mr. Pallieur who counted this story to Mr. Toynard could not tell, but concluded it to have been an interpretation of the R.C. And thus began the invisible society of the Rosecruceans, which made such a noise at Paris & through all France that Naudaeus[3] a litle after writ a booke against them & the world have soe much talked of since without knowing any thing of them or their originall. And which is a pleasant instance[4] of the beleife of people when common fame has published any thing never soe false.[5] Mr. Pailleur, not long after goeing into Britanny, at Vannes meets with a young gent. of whom askeing what news, he told him that he had news from Paris of the Rosecruceans of whome all the world talked strange things, espetially of their being invisible, which the hostesse hearkening to as they were discoursing of it at table, told them that there had been two of them lately there who, haveing dined, vanishd, soe that she & her people could not perceive which way they were gon.[6]

---

[1] MS. has *thereing*.

[2] Followers of the mystical philosopher, Raymond Lully (1235–1315).

[3] Gabriel Naudé (1600–53). His *Instruction à la France sur la vérité de l'histoire des frères de la Rose-Croix*, appeared in 1623.

[4] MS. has *instances*.

[5] Amusingly enough, the latest work on the subject (F. Wittemans, *A New and Authentic History of the Rosicrucians*, London, 1937) includes Locke among the 'great figures' of the movement.

[6] The entries after this are numbered simply from 2 to 9, and the numbers do not correspond to the dates under which Locke inscribed in his Journal those which he took the trouble to copy out.

Sacerdotium 4. Is not only looked on, but in some places treated as a mariage, for at St. John de Luz the preist, the day he says his first masse, gives a ball & he himself leads up the first dance, & the preist who the last immediately before him had don this exercise, is invited as a principall guest & leads up the dances as King of the ball. Mr. *Thoynard* has been present at such a solemnity where the preist gets noe small credit if he can cut capers well.

Olea 6. The way of makeing sweet oyles is to wet a linin cloth in oyle of Been[1] & soe with the flowers of oranges etc. make stratum S.S. Repeat this till the clothes be well impregnated with the sent & then squeeze the oyle out of the clothes with a presse. Some times they use the oyle of sweet almonds for that of Been, but it turnes quickly rancid & soe is not soe good. Verchant.

Clemangis 7. Nic. Clemangis,[2] an author that has writ against the abuses of the Court of Rome. The impression was from a copy wherein there was a great deale wanting & soe there were many gaps in it. Mr. Toynard has a copy of it that is perfect & with notes almost as old as the author's time.

Consuetudo 9. Amongst a people about Buenos Ayres it is the custome that when any one looses a neare relation, he cuts of a joynt of one of his fingers & soe a 2d & a 3d, soe that some of them have a great many joynts cut away. Mr. Massiac.

Heralds (p. 9.) The Heraulds in France, even their King at armes, are but chandelers or some such ordinary tradesmen.[3]

Ferrum (p. 33.) Iron that when it is cast touches brick on any side, it is much harder in that part which touches the brick then in any other part. Mr. Toinard. The way to keepe it from rusting is to rub it with cat's grease. Mr. Covell.

Panis (p. 53.) The ammunition bread of the army, which is the allowance of a man for a day, weighs, being baked 22 ozs., in dow

---

[1] *O.E.D. Oil of Ben*: 'Oil obtained from the ben-nut'.

[2] Nicolas de Clamanges (*c*. 1360–*c*. 1434), a French theologian, the author of *De ruina et reparacione Ecclesie*, first printed in 1483 (see the edition published by A. Coville, Paris, 1936).

[3] Cf. the entry for 3 Jan. 1679 in the Journal. These last four notes are taken from MS. Locke, d. 1 (see note to entry for 1 Jan. 1679) and are given there under the date of 1679. They almost certainly belong to the period of Locke's last stay in Paris (the first certainly does).

unbaked 24 ozs., Paris weight, soe that, allowing $\frac{1}{12}$ of bran to be taken out, $1\frac{1}{2}$ lbs. of corne is a good allowance for a man per diem. (p. 101.) A Canon of 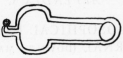 this fashon has been Bombarda invented by a goldsmith of Lyon & found of great force in com- parison of the weight & untactablenesse[1] of others. The touch hole is behinde the place to hold the charge of pouder, sphericall & biger then the bore. The length of the gun from thence forward only $1\frac{1}{2}$ diameter of the bore. All the inconveniencie of it on ship bord is that it recoiles much & therefor must have heavy & strong cariages. Mr. Toinard.

---

[1] *intractableness?*

APPENDIX C

LIST OF PHILOSOPHICAL PASSAGES IN THE JOURNAL (DOWN TO MAY 1679)[1]

1676

Pp. 123–6	25 Feb.	Obligation of Penal Laws	King, pp. 57–9
Pp. 173–4	27 March	Spacium	Aaron & Gibb, p. 77
P. 256	14 May	Extasy, Dreaming	... ...
Pp. 289–95	20 June	Extension	Aaron & Gibb, pp. 77–80
Pp. 313–14	9 July	Extension	Von Leyden
Pp. 317–19	13 July	Simple Ideas	Aaron & Gibb, pp. 80–1
P. 320	15 July	Mania	... ...
Pp. 320–5	15 July	Idolatry	Von Leyden
Pp. 325–47	16 July	Passions	Von Leyden
Pp. 354–5	20 July	Idolatry	Von Leyden
Pp. 358–9	22 July	Madnesse	... ...
Pp. 367–70	29 July	A Deity	Aaron & Gibb, pp. 81–2
P. 392	3 Aug.	Simple Ideas	Aaron & Gibb, p. 83
Pp. 412–15	23 Aug.	Toleration, Peace	Von Leyden
P. 416	24 Aug.	Faith & Reason	Von Leyden
Pp. 417–20	25 Aug.	Ignorance, Faith & Reason	Von Leyden
Pp. 420–4	26 Aug.	Faith & Reason (cont.)	Von Leyden
Pp. 424–8	27 Aug.	Faith & Reason (cont.)	Von Leyden
Pp. 428–9	28 Aug.	Faith & Reason (cont.)	Von Leyden
Pp. 430–2	1 Sept.	Knowledg	Von Leyden
Pp. 442–3	19 Sept.	Species	Aaron & Gibb, p. 83
Pp. 445–7	26 Sept.	Happynesse	... ...
P. 469	14 Oct.	Politica	... ...

1677

Pp. 42–55	8 Feb.	Understanding	Aaron & Gibb, pp. 84–90
Pp. 57–9	12 Feb.	Arguments positive & negative	Aaron & Gibb, pp. 90–1
Pp. 87–90, 91–3, 95–6, 97–100, 100–1, 114–17, 118–22, 124–40[2]		Study	King, pp. 90–108

[1] The reference to Von Leyden is to selections from unpublished philosophical material in the Lovelace Collection to be published by Dr W. von Leyden. Where passages are given in Aaron & Gibb as well as in King, references to the latter have been omitted, as the text he gives is never satisfactory.

[2] This essay begins on 26 March, but owing to the confusion in the Journal through Locke's illness at Bordeaux, it is impossible to assign precise dates to the later entries.

Pp. 226–7	8 Aug.	Cartesii Opera	Aaron & Gibb, p. 91
Pp. 247–52	4 Sept.	Adversaria	Aaron & Gibb, pp. 92–4
Pp. 265–9	16 Sept.	Space	Aaron & Gibb, pp. 94–6
Pp. 270–1	19 Sept.	Turks, Opinatrity	... ...
Pp. 280–2	1 Oct.	Sensation, Delight[1]	Aaron & Gibb, pp. 96–7
Pp. 319–20	5 Nov.	Madnesse	King, p. 328
Pp. 347–8	11 Nov.	Error	Aaron & Gibb, pp. 97–8
Pp. 356–8	19 Nov.	Species	Aaron & Gibb, pp. 98–9

1678

Pp. 5–16	20 Jan.	Relation, Space	Aaron & Gibb, pp. 99–103
Pp. 16–21	22 Jan.	Memory	Aaron & Gibb, pp. 103–5
Pp. 21–2	23 Jan.	Discourse	... ...
Pp. 24–5	24 Jan.	Space	Aaron & Gibb, p. 105
Pp. 49–60	7 March	Descartes	Aaron & Gibb, pp. 105–11
Pp. 69–79	20 March	Scrupulosity	King, pp. 109–13
P. 107	19 April	Toleration	... ...
Pp. 111–12	21 April	Law	King, p. 116
P. 193	12 July	Bruta sentiunt, Tradition	... ...
Pp. 201–2	15 July	Lex, Lex naturae	... ...
Pp. 205–6	16 July	Infinitum	Aaron & Gibb, pp. 111–12
P. 263	25 Aug.	Modes Complex	Aaron & Gibb, p. 112
Pp. 266–7	26 Aug.	Virtue, Atheists	... ...
Pp. 304–5	1 Oct.	Happynesse	King, p. 115
Pp. 351–7	2 Dec.	Recreation	King, pp. 323–5
Pp. 358–78	2 Dec.	Scrupulosity	King, pp. 113–15[2]
Pp. 381–2	12 Dec	Credit, Disgrace	King, pp. 108–9

1679

| P. 18 | 20 Feb. | Carolina | ... ... |

The following is a list of the passages bearing the title, *Atlantis*:

1676	pp. 280, 319.
1677	pp. 289, 296–8.
1678	pp. 92, 95, 142–3, 198–201.
1679	pp. 13–14, 18–22.

[1] Dr. von Leyden is publishing a lengthy shorthand passage which follows straight on from this entry.

[2] He obviously does not reproduce the whole of this passage.

INDEX

Gaillac, 53
Galinée, Abbé de, 270-1
Galleys
  punishment, 64, 222
  ships, 73-4, 79
Galls, 55, 92
Game laws, liii, 62
Gardening, xxx
  early flowers and vegetables, 12, 18, 20,
    23, 24, 73, 77, 92
  flowers, 67, 80, 106, 208-9, 272
  insecticide, 208
  royal nurseries, 273
  seeds, 44-5, 119-20
  trees and bushes, 17, 42, 59, 62, 80, 83,
    92, 100, 106, 144, 159-60, 162-3,
    164-5, 168
Gardens
  Angers, 226
  Avary, 209
  Beaugency, 80
  Blois, 210
  Castries, 65-6
  Champlâtreux, 169
  Chantilly, 168
  Chateauneuf-sur-Loire, 250
  Fontainebleau, 172-3
  Fontcaud, 106
  Hôtel de la Ferté, Paris, 201
  Incurables, Paris, 272
  Liancourt, 169
  Lusignan, 145
  Marseilles, 75-6
  Montpellier, 17, 20, 43, 44, 52, 59,
    67, 109
  Orleans, 208-9
  Pont Lunel, 62
  Rueil, 181
  St Cloud, 162-3
  Saumur, 219
  Toulon, 78
  Véretz, 216
  Versailles, 151-4
Gardes du Corps, 173-4, 185-7
Gardon, River, 15
Garigues, 125
Garonne, River, xvii, xxxiv, 139, 239,
  241
Gassendi, Pierre, xxiii
Gazette de France, 199
Gendron, Abbé François, 206
Générac, 86, 88
Geneva, 21, 121
Genoa, 42, 272

Germans, 278
Germany, 93, 177
Gévaudan, Jeanne de (Comtesse de
  Ganges), xliv, lvi, 30, 136
Gien, 249
Gigean, 124
Gill, Mr, 216
Gilminets, Mr, 104
Girald, Mr, 16
Gitto, Mr, 100
Glass, stoppers, 205
  ware, 248
Gloves, perfuming of, 163, 196
God the Father, pictures of, 19, 68, 72,
  172, 241
Godefroy, Dr, 206-8, 250
Gold softened, 262
Governors of Provinces, xliii, 19, 156
Grana Kermes, 43-4, 56, 94, 95, 99, 100,
  101
Grand Signior, 253
Grandier, Urbain, 252
Grantham, 112, 229
Graves, xx, lii, 236-7
Gravesend, xv, 1
Gravier, Mr, 198-9
Grenelle, Plaine de, 163
Grenoble, 22
Grenville, Denis, 118, 119, 243n.
Griffon, the, 73
Grigg, Mrs Anna, xvi, 204n.
Grimaldi, Cardinal, 82
Grotte de la Madeleine, 54
Grys, 161, 185
Guesnes, 228
Guilds
  admission to, 147
  and Protestants, 113
  taxes levied on, xlix, 146-7
Guis, Joseph, 71
Guise, Duc de, 197
Guise, Hôtel de, 200-1
Guise, House of, 163
Guise, Mlle de, 200
Guise, Mme de, 189
Guyenne, 142

Hackney coachmen, 256
Hainaut, 174
Hair, dyeing of, 189
Hall, Joseph, 272
Hand mill, 206
Handkerchiefs, xxxv, 204
Hangman, 157

Lucy-le-Bois, xxxiii, 2
Lullists, 283
Lully, Jean Baptiste, 170 n.
Lüneburg, 190
Lusansy, 66
Lusignan, 145
Luxembourg, Duc de, 187
Luxemburg, 174, 201
Lynch, Sir Thomas, 253 n., 266
Lyons, xv, xviii, xx, liv, lvi, 2, 3, 4–8, 12,
  13, 16, 18, 31, 59, 80, 244, 254–7,
  285

Mâcon, 3, 4, 112
Madame, 171, 173, 174, 179
Mademoiselle, la Grande, 4, 189
Mage, Father, 107
Magnol, Dr Pierre, xxxviii, 100, 112,
  242–3
Maine, River, 226–7
Maize, 236
Malauze, Marquis de, 113
Malebranche, Nicolas, xxxix
Mall, xxviii, 17, 18, 113
Mantell, Charles, 141
Manuscripts, ancient, 158, 160, 252–3, 259
Mapletoft, Dr John, xviii, 82 n., 178 n.,
  183 n., 188, 189, 195, 197
Maps, 174, 176, 202, 269, 270–1
Marie Thérèse, Queen of France, 156,
  170–1, 173, 186, 187, 190, 255
Marius, 11
Marmande, 240, 241
Marmoutier, 215–16
Marseilles, xv, 73–6, 77, 78, 83, 86, 136
  naval establishments, xxi, xlii, l, 73–4
Marshall, Mr, 204
Martha, St, lviii, 87
Martin, St, 223
Mary Magdalene, lvii, 81
Mascarades, 43
Masham, Lady, xxxi
Massiac, Mr, 235, 257, 284
Mathematics, 187
Mattioli, Pietro Andrea, 243
Meadows. See Agriculture
Meath, Earl of, 242 n.
Mechanical and other inventions, xxx–i,
  5–6, 78, 112, 113, 149, 173, 175–6,
  180, 194, 205, 206, 210–11, 213–14,
  226, 233, 248
Medicine
  Locke's notes on, xxiii, xxx; practises as
  doctor, xvii, 182, 183, 184 n., 188 n.

  cost of treatment, 158 n., 209 n.; doctor
    of, xxxvii, 57–8, 59
  surgery, 190 n.
  training, xxxvii, 50, 54
Mediterranean, xv, 16, 54, 55, 56, 61, 62,
  63, 70, 72, 118
Melons, 219, 221
Melun, 2
Menageries, xxxi, 153, 168–9
Ménars, 210, 211
Ménars, Marquis de, 210, 211
Mende, Bishop of, 38
Méounes, 80, 88
Mercœur, Louis de Bourbon, Duc de, 83,
  100
Mercury, 56, 184 n.
Mercury (planet), 256
Messager, 1, 276, 277, 278
Messina, 77
Messire, use of, 272
Metal industry, 74, 78, 189, 233, 239,
  249
Meudon, 163
Mexico, Gulf of, 269
Michard, Mr, 103, 104, 108, 109
Microscopes, 6, 99, 100, 250
Migraine, 232
Milles, Lady, 220
Millstones, 157
Mirepoix, 38
Mirrors, 180, 197
Missimakina Island, 271
Mistresses, xliv, 136
Modena, 260
Modena, Raimond de Mormoiron, Count
  of, 197
Mohammedans, 177
Moilives, Jacomo, 93
Moilives, Jovanni, 93
Moissac, 241
Molière, Jean Baptiste Poquelin, xxxviii
Molineaux, Father Thomas, 80
Monnier, Dr, 155 n.
Monsieur, xxxi, 162 n., 171, 172, 174, 179,
  190
Montagnac, 125
Montagu, Comte de, 237
Montagu, Ralph, xvii, xxxvi, 177 n.,
  183 n.
Montargis, 249
Montauban, 38, 238, 241
Montélimar, 9
Montespan, Mme de, xli, 257 n.
  poem to Louis XIV and his reply 122–3

Paulmier, Jacques, 258
Pavillon, Nicolas, 119
Peasants
 Locke's conversations with, 21, 56, 103, 105, 143
 diet, 111–12, 228, 236–7
 economic position, xx, l–liii, 88, 103, 105
 farming methods, 1, 103, 105
 housing, 229, 236–7
 pastimes, xxix, 109
 taxation, xlvi–viii, 103, 110, 147, 148, 207–8, 236–7
Peccais, 62–64, 73
Pelagians, 262
Pelletier, Mr, 149
Pembroke, Thomas Herbert, eighth earl of, xvii, xxxvi, 112, 151, 182, 188, 194
Pena, Pierre, 242
Pendulum, seconds', 160, 185, 253, 259, 261
 in watches, 167
Pénitents Blancs, 82, 99, 101
Pénitents Gris, 82
Pénitents Noirs, 82
Periwig, xxxv, 149
Perota, Mr, 116
Peru, 235
Petit Niort, 143, 236
Pézenas, 43, 124–5
Philosophical foot, 14, 161, 180, 185, 202, 214, 259, 261
Picansa, Carolus Anguisciola de, 13
Picard, Abbé Jean, xl, 261
Picardy, regiment of, 156
Pic St Loup, 89, 109
Pierpoynt, Mrs, xvii n.
Pierre-Scize, 7
Pigeons, 111
Pigs, 120
Pistole, value of, lxvi, 24
Ploughing, xxvii, 10, 45
Plutarch, 189, 197, 205
Poitiers, xvii, xxv, xlix, 145, 146, 149, 208
Poitou, lii, 144, 145
Poix, xxxiii 1, 277–80
Poland, 190, 202
Pomerania, 272
Pomade de Nerli, 273
Pommett de Paradise, 55, 279
Pons, 143–4, 145
Pont de Ruen, 146

Pont du Gard, xxviii, 13, 14, 15, 54, 66
Pont Lunel, 16, 61, 62, 64, 67, 86, 88, 244
Pont St Esprit, 9, 10, 11, 12, 13, 72, 244
Pont-sur-Yonne, 2
Pontac, Président, 142–3
Ponts-de-Cé, xxxiv, 221
Pontgibaud, 199
Popes
 Alexander VII, 262
 Innocent VI, lviii, 85
 Innocent X, 262
 abuses of court, 284
 and kings of France, 264
 at Avignon, 12
 infallibility, lvii, 85, 138, 262
 medals of, 178
Popular revolts, precautions against, 234
Population
 of countryside, lii, 229
 of Paris and London, 256
Portugal, 256, 258, 272
Potomac River, 269
Pouilly-sur-Loire, 248
Poulin, Mr, 202
Pouzols, 136
Pradon, Nicolas, xxxviii, 265
Pressburg, 190
Prévôts, 48
Price regulation, 171
Prices
 board and lodging, 1, 13, 16, 88, 95, 103, 108, 109, 136–40, 143–8, 150, 162, 179, 205, 219, 221, 227, 228, 236, 240–2, 244, 247–51
 clothing, 20, 42, 101, 104, 105, 107, 111, 131, 149, 179, 184
 fall in rents of land, li, 89; in prices of agricultural produce, l–lii
 food, xxix, 22, 39, 46, 58, 79, 105, 171
 fuel, 2, 18
 meals, 111, 148–51, 154–6, 158–60, 162, 164, 170, 178, 181, 184, 185, 189, 199
 transport, 56, 60, 130, 249–50
 travel, 1, 4, 16, 66, 130, 137–40, 143, 148, 153–4, 215, 219, 221, 227, 236
 wheat, 274
 wines and spirits, 50–51, 114, 142, 143, 214, 220, 225, 230, 238
Prideaux, Humphrey, 17 n.
Princes of the Blood, 156
Prints, xxxix n., 188, 228, 238, 267 n., 273

INDEX

Rochefort, xviii, 233–5
 naval establishments at, xlii, l, 233–5
Rohault, Jacques, 231n.
Roman antiquities, xxviii
 Arles, 69–71; Béziers, 125; Lyons, 5;
 Nîmes, 14–15, 71, 236; Orange, 11;
 Paris, 178; Pont du Gard, 13–15;
 Saintes, 236; Toulouse, 138; Vienne,
 8
Romans, King of the, 190
Rome, xviii, 38, 77, 93, 257, 273
 Court of, 264, 284
 St Peter's, 268
Römer, Olaf
 Locke's friendship with, xl, 177n.;
 accompanies him to London, xix:
 Römer prepares for Channel crossing,
 274n.
 speed of light, 274; tinder box, 275;
 levelling instrument, 263, 282; sketch
 of his model of Jupiter and satellites,
 263
Rooper, Sam, 142, 150
Roquelaure, Duc de, 142, 237
Rosicruceans, xxxi, 282–3
Rouen, 155
Roure, Comte du, 114–15
Rousseau, Mr, 273
Rueil, 181
Rushout, Sir James, 265
Rushworth, Sir J., 58
Russia, 271
Rust, prevention of, 194, 284

Sabots, 18, 278–9
Sagard, Gabriel, 209
St Amans, 126–7
St Chinian de la Corne, xxxiv, 125–6,
 133
St Clar, Mr, 112
St Cloud, 162–3, 196
St Denis, lviii, 270
St Étienne, 189
St Ferréol, basin of, 128–30
St Genest, 145
St Germain, 189, 252, 260
St Gilles, xxviii, xxix, 68
St Jean de Luz, 284
St Jean de Sauves, 228
St John's Day, 102, 200
St Lawrence, River, 201, 258, 269, 270
St Lazare, Knights of, 199
St Léger-lès-Melle, 144, 145
St Martin-de-Crau, 72

St Martin le Chastille sur Saône, 111–12
St Maximin, lvii, 80–1, 88
St Morin, Mr, 272
St Omer, 277
St Papoul, 38
St Pierre-le-Moûtier, 248
St Pons, 38, 126, 127
Saint-Simon, Duc de, lvi, 161n., 186n.
St Symphorien, 245
St Thibery, 133, 136
St Vallier, 9, 245
Ste Baume, lvii, 80, 81, 88
Sainte Colombe, Mr, 259, 262
Saintes, 144, 145, 235–6
Saintonges, liii, 144, 145, 237
Salads, 60, 135, 195
Sale of official posts, 48, 110
Salon, xxiii, 72–3
Salt, manufacture of, 63–4, 73, 230–1,
 232
 see also Gabelle
Sanderson, Captain, 274
Sandys, Mrs, 188
Saône, River, xv, xxvii, lvi, 2, 3, 7
Satellites, of Jupiter, 176, 263
 of Saturn, 176
Saturn, 176
Sault Ste Marie, 271
Saumur, xviii, li, 219–21, 227, 228,
 232
Sauray, 229
Sauvage, Mr, 141
Saxony, 190
Scalding, prevention of, 241
Scanderoon, 251
Scawen, Mr, 178
Sceaux, 149, 196
Science
 Locke's interest in, xxx
 Académie des Sciences, xlii
 Astronomy, xxx, xl; Comet, 202; eclipse
 of Moon, 243–4, 251, of Sun, 100–1;
 Jupiter and Satellites, 176, 202, 263;
 Mercury, 256; Moon, 176; Parhelia,
 127; Saturn and satellites, 176;
 seconds' pendulum, 160, 185, 253,
 259, 261; Sun, motion of, 261;
 theory of vortices, 256
 Ballistics, xxx, 9, 10, 191, 192–4,
 196–7, 200, 249, 252, 285; flying,
 251; light, speed of, 274
 Dyeing, 102, 106, 113, 189; fermentation, xxx, 192; galls, 55, 92; vacuum,
 water in, 187–8

LLJ   305   20